Introduction to Comparative Literature

Introduction to Comparative Literature

by

FRANÇOIS JOST

THE UNIVERSITY OF ILLINOIS

Pegasus: A Division of
The Bobbs-Merrill Company, Inc.
INDIANAPOLIS AND NEW YORK

Copyright © 1974 by The Bobbs-Merrill Company, Inc.
Printed in the United States of America
First Printing

Library of Congress Cataloging in Publication Data
Jost, François.
    Introduction to comparative literature.

    Bibliography: p.
    1. Literature, Comparative.   I.   Title.
PN871.J6   809   73–19849
ISBN 0–672–63657–3

Contents

Foreword

FOR almost all nations of the globe, the era of political and economic isolation belongs to the past. Western culture has been similarly internationalized, a phenomenon clearly mirrored in literature, although its territory will always somehow be held in shape by linguistic borders. For literary beauty is conditioned not only by themes, ideas, and structures, but also by elements particular to individual languages: sounds, rhythms, and verbal images. An exclusively nationalistic approach to literary history and criticism has become obsolete—as contemporary scholarship and the curricula of colleges and universities make evident. This modern intellectual orientation has given birth to a new academic discipline: whoever is concerned with the *international* rather than the *nationalistic* mode of the study of letters is practicing comparative literature.

All over the world today professors teach and students attend courses in comparative literature. In the United States and Canada every major institution of higher learning regularly offers undergraduate and graduate programs in the field, and in France comparative literature is even a compulsory part of the "agrégation"—the state examination that opens the way to a university career—for candidates in the humanities. Nearly all the other countries of the European continent recognize this new formula for literary inquiry, especially Germany and the Low Countries, Hungary and the Soviet

Union. Among other peoples, too, in China and Japan, in North Africa and Australia, an increasing number of scholars and writers are turning to comparatism for deeper literary insight and for original textual interpretations and conclusions in literary criticism and history.

This rapidly growing interest in comparative literature has not been accompanied, however, by sufficient understanding of its nature and objectives. Only a few publications adequately explain its essence or systematically present its subject matter. This book is intended to clarify concepts and illustrate procedures. It is concerned with theoretical and applied comparatistics, and it is written for the cultured public, including advanced undergraduates, graduate students, and their instructors.

The plan of the book is based on pragmatic thinking. All courses and publications in comparative literature can be grouped into four categories, with a special place reserved for the theory of the discipline. The first of these categories, the most heterogeneous, shows works in relation to others with which they have organic affinities. Specific links and ties are investigated in terms of the influence of one work upon another, with regard to the analogies between several works (whether or not they stand in a giver-receiver or cause-effect relationship to one another), and with respect to the translations of major books into different languages. Also considered in this category is the interdisciplinary aspect of comparative literature: numerous connections may be found between literature in its usual sense and other cultural domains, such as philosophy and psychology, sociology and linguistics, music and painting.

The second category of the four into which the field of comparative literature may be divided contains studies of movements and trends—like Renaissance, Baroque, Classicism, Romanticism, Realism —that characterize our Western civilization in its developmental phases. However dominant or striking a writer's talents may be, his work necessarily reflects a literary *Zeitgeist* because it was conceived and born at a specific stage of the culture that helped shape his intellectual and artistic personality. The third category comprises the analysis of literary works from the viewpoint of their inner and outer forms, their genre. This type of investigation, for years traditional on the national level, has become increasingly relevant on an international scale as well. The final category incorporates studies of themes and motifs—the more spectacular being those associated with types such as Ulysses and Prometheus, Don Juan and Faust. But themes and motifs may also be abstract and purely conceptual. They may be related to topics like patriotism, revolt, friendship, death.

These four categories can be aptly symbolized by the basic elements of ancient chemistry: air, water, earth, and fire. Air, which unifies the whole living world, suggests overall literary relations. Water represents literary movements. As streams of water are the classical image for the flux of time, studies in movements have to consider the chronological sequence of cultural events. Artistic moods and intellectual modes develop and progress as a river grows from a trickle at its source to a torrent at its mouth. Earth is the only solid element that assumes durable forms; it signifies, therefore, literary genres. And, to complete our analogy, fire illustrates the theme and the motif, the translucent soul of every literary product.

These metaphors are more than mnemonic devices for the various kinds of comparative studies: they should also remind us that literature is not a science like modern chemistry, but rather an art, because value judgments are called for in each of our four approaches. Beyond the critical tools and beyond the scholarly apparatus, beyond all dogmatic speculations exists the world of aesthetics, that world of literature proper. However, though literature itself elicits a contemplative response, its exegesis presupposes knowledge in the most diverse fields ranging from history to religion and to the fine arts. To various degrees, these aspects of comparative literature are considered throughout this volume.

The preliminary section of the book, Part I, deals with the rise and growth in western Europe of a literary community transcending linguistic frontiers, with the notion of *Weltliteratur*, and with the concept of comparative literature as it is understood by American, Canadian, French, and East European exponents of the discipline. Each of the following sections, Parts II, III, IV, and V, is preceded by an opening chapter, or prolegomenon, expounding theoretical questions. These four parts offer specific illustrations of the four comparative approaches to literature.

By itself, however, none of these approaches leads to a complete synthetic understanding of the literary phenomenon. To attain this goal or, at least, to come closer to it, literature should be contemplated from more than one of our four categorial vantage points. The four fundamental elements of our analogy are to be considered together, since they are not separated in nature either, where they unite equally in shaping the human environment. Not only one, but two, three, or all four basic methods of analysis and research may be used simultaneously. A study in genres may also reveal the interrelationships of all four; one in movements and trends may bring to light major themes and motifs. The critic proportions his four comparatistic ingredients, so to speak, according to the nature of his particular topic of study. Thus, comparative literature, to steal two of Thomson's lines, consists

> Of tempered sun, and water, earth, and air,
> In ever-changing composition mixed.*

* *The Complete Works of James Thomson*, ed. J. Logie Robertson (London, 1908), p. 155. *Seasons, Autumn*, lines 635–636.

Every literary problem of importance is virtually a tetrahedral problem.

※

Our *Introduction* is by no means a historical or critical outline of compartive literature. Its objective is to familiarize the reader with the categories of our four-dimensional discipline. Our illustrative topics, however, do not focus upon any special geographical region or upon any particular epoch. That Anglo-Saxon, Romance, and Germanic cultures are given greater emphasis than Slavic, African, and Oriental (even though these cultural areas of study are today attracting more scholars than they have in the past) bears out the principle that literatures that have been influential for centuries should have priority over those that have only recently entered the international orbit. This principle is particularly appropriate in a work intended essentially for readers with an occidental background.

No anthropologist has so far discovered the archetype of the *homo comparativus*. Small wonder; such an archetype does not exist. Whereas the scholars in Anglo-Saxon, Romance, and Germanic philology necessarily center their endeavors on one of these language groups, a comparatist, though taking as a point of departure one single cultural area or period, feels free to draw his principal nurture from varied combinations of elements in the whole realm of letters and its numerous, related fields.

This richness of choice may entail certain limitations in the contents of a book intended to be a sort of condensation or summary of the discipline. Because I am writing for readers with widely divergent cultural experiences and scholastic interests, I must perforce provide them with a large and diverse supply of examples. At the same time, the subjects chosen should have inherent significance within the entire tradition of the liberal arts. These two circumstances explain why none of our topics can be treated exhaustively. Such a task would require a long essay or monograph for each subject. I have, therefore, often had to content myself with mere allusions to works, though it should be understood that the proliferation of titles and proper names is not only inevitable but intentional: they are meant to suggest further research and parallel treatments, especially to those readers who do not conceive of comparative literature as simply a system of bilateral exchanges.

There is still another reason why our broad subjects have been preferred to neatly circumscribed inquiries: a series of restricted topics would give a distorted picture of comparative literature. The comparatist, it is true, is sometimes concerned with studies of detail, with concrete questions such as personal relations between writers or the role of cultural intermediaries. Yet in its very essence and end results, comparatism is a synopsis in the etymological sense of the word: the comparatist's effort and reward is to perceive the literary world in its fundamental unity. He shares the ideal of Faust to search for "whatever holds/The world together in its inmost folds." This primary *raison d'être* of the discipline has to be shown by examples of a synthetic and not an analytic nature, by examples leading to general and not particular conclusions.

Some of the problems concisely discussed in the following pages have been given more extensive treatment in a separate collection of essays that I wrote with this volume in mind, *Essais de littérature comparée.** Whether used with these supplements or as a single text, the present book is designed to introduce the cultured public, as well as students and future scholars, to comparative literature, one of the most difficult and most demanding of all humanistic disciplines.

F. J.

Urbana, Illinois

* 2 vols., vol. 1, *Helvetica* (Fribourg, 1964); vol. 2, *Europaeana* (Fribourg and Urbana, Ill., 1968).

Acknowledgments

I have written this book as Professor of Comparative Literature at the University of Illinois, where I have been able to discuss many aspects of the problems treated in the following pages with my students and my colleagues in the Comparative Literature Program—especially with Professor A. Owen Aldridge and Professor John R. Frey—as well as with many faculty members of the various literature departments. I am happy to have this occasion to express to all of them my deep gratitude. I am no less indebted to the University of Illinois, which, by its exceptional facilities of research in the humanities and by its sponsorship of the periodical *Comparative Literature Studies*, has substantially contributed to the promotion of the comparatist method not only among its own staff and students, but throughout America and the world.

F. J.

Introduction to Comparative Literature

PART I

The Discipline

1

The Historical Perspective

SINCE the Middle Ages, and more visibly since the seventeenth century, the political units and the linguistic areas of Europe have continuously tended to fuse their frontiers. A thousand-year-old linguistic map of the Continent does not remotely resemble the political map, while today, any geography student drawing the borderlines, for instance, of the Italian republic is perfectly aware that he is at the same time drawing rather truthfully those of the Italian language. In which European states are Spanish, Portuguese, Dutch, Danish, Swedish, Norwegian, Greek, Hungarian, and Polish spoken? The answer is self-evident. Each adjective designates both a nation and the language of its people.

In some countries, it is true, this rule does not apply. Belgium is bilingual: French and Flemish; Yugoslavia is trilingual: Serbo-Croatian, Slovenian, and Macedonian; Switzerland is quadrilingual: German, French, Italian, and Rhaeto-Romanic. There are other multilingual countries, too—the Soviet Union for example. There, however, Russian supersedes by far all other idioms and presumably is known to the educated person in the many regions of the Russian territory. On the other hand, not every state has within its boundaries all areas that speak its language—on which it claims, or seems to claim, a monopoly. Considerable parts of Belgium and of Switzerland use the language of France, and German is the tongue not only of the two

5

politically divided Germanys, but also of Vienna and Zurich. These exceptions, however, do not by any means reduce the validity of the general statement: historically, linguistic and political boundaries, at least during the last millennium, have tended to merge.

At the time of Henry II of England (1133–1189), it was impossible to define or identify one single European kingdom by naming the language of its population. Henry's territory, for instance, included Brittany and Normandy, Aquitaine and Gascony, while that of Louis VII (1121–1180) consisted of one-third of contemporary France and Flanders. The most polyglot country, however, was the Holy Roman Empire of the German Nation. Not only did its subjects speak Italian and German in the manifold dialects of the time, but French and even some Slavic languages as well. Members of the cultured class, the only one that "counted," could communicate in Latin, the universal language, which was also the language of administration and diplomacy. Often, though, monarchs knew the dialects of their peoples. Emperor Frederick II (1194–1250) had learned six of them and was fluent in all. Even treaties were sometimes formulated in vernacular idioms. The famous "Strasbourg oaths" taken in 842 by Charles the Bald and Louis the German were conserved in documents written in the native tongues of the two kings. And how proudly Roger Ascham, in the sixteenth century, reported to his correspondents the progress of his pupil Elizabeth, the future Queen of England (1533–1603), not only in the classical literatures but especially in those of more immediate use to her, French and Italian.

Imperceptibly, Latin became an artificial means of communication, although it remained until the end of the eighteenth century an absolutely indispensable tool in any liberal profession. Moreover, long after the fall of the Roman Empire it was still used by writers for its aesthetic value. During the Middle Ages, fine Latin poems were composed in all parts of Europe, and many prose texts did not lack elegance and beauty. The poet Hildebert of Lavardin can be cited, for instance, along with Peter Abelard, Adam of Saint Victor, and the anonymous author of the *Carmina Burana*. In the later Middle Ages, Poggio, Poliziano, and Enea Silvio Piccolomini (Pope Pius II) testify to the lasting values of the Roman literary tradition. During all this time the prestige of classical literature remained untarnished, and since the fifteenth century scores of talents have come on the list of neo-Latin contributors to European culture. Geniuses like Catullus and Tacitus, however, though rediscovered in the Renaissance, were never actually *reborn*, and the language that generated or fostered most others on the European continent was doomed to die, to become supplanted by the living ones. Petrarch and Boccaccio, it is true, completed great works in Latin; but neither Wolfram von Eschenbach nor Chaucer ever thought of writing masterpieces in any tongue other than their own.[1]

The rise and blossoming of various vernacular languages did not at the time engender or develop a sense of social or political unity in any specific area. Although the Augustan concept of *patria* persisted, especially in smaller autonomous communities, medieval patriotism often consisted mainly of a feeling of attachment to a tribe, to a family and friends, to a native city or village, a valley, a countryside; in brief, the homeland, simply a homestead, was the physical and moral environment in which old habits would continue to make life easy and pleasant. In Dante's (1265–1321) praise of Italy in all three parts of the *Divine Comedy*, sentiments are expressed other than those in Leopardi's (1798–1837) *All'Italia*, and, similarly, Walther von der Vogelweide's (ca. 1170–1230) poem *Ir sult sprechen willekomen*[2] reflects ideas different from those in Fichte's (1762–1814) manifesto *An die deutsche Nation*. The population, however, regardless of social class, also felt personal affection for the prince, or at least showed respect for the protector of the specific fatherlands or *patriae*. Joachim Du Bellay (1522–1560) was one of the first great writers to apply the word *patrie* to the whole of France. Interestingly enough, hc does it in a book in which the French language is proclaimed the national language of the kingdom of Henry II (1519–1559), whose lands at the end of his reign indeed hardly overlapped linguistic borders. He took Calais from the English and all the continental territory that they had been occupying for centuries, but he relinquished his possessions in Italy. This was a significant step toward national unity. Du Bellay, in his famous *Défense et illustration de la langue française* confcsses that "nothing but the natural love for his country made him write the work:"[3] *patrie* then meant the kingdom, the property, the estate of the king.

Languages became "naturalized" and so did literature; gradually, during the course of several centuries, dialects were absorbed by the major idioms and the concept of "national literature" was created, paralleling that of "national language."[4] As René Wellek points out, the motivation of most Renaissance scholars was patriotic: "Englishmen," he states, "compiled lists of writers in order to prove their glorious achievements in all subjects of learning; Frenchmen, Italians, and Germans did exactly the same."[5]

Historical and social phenomena are at the root of both these developments. From the second half of the Middle Ages, and most clearly during the declining years of the Renaissance, there appeared unmistakable signs that culture and education were becoming diffused into all layers of society. Culture, in its most apparent and refined expression, had been the privilege of the aristocracy and a privilege of the clergy. It was, in short, the property of a handful of the elect; later it came to be shared by the upper crust of the bourgeoisie, then by the middle class proper, and finally, to some degree, by the man on the street. At the same time, and for various reasons—the reorganization of political and economic patterns, the dispersion of the art of printing, the new means of communication, the creation of postal services,

and the invention of all sorts of new travel facilities—a steadily increasing portion of the population became keenly conscious of the
social homogeneousness deriving from a common language. Even today language retains its magic in the making of nations by establishing groups of interest. Thus authors found a collective reading public;
they felt they should write for their national community.

The development of national languages was most eloquently described, and also deplored, by d'Alembert (ca. 1717–1783). In the
Discours préliminaire that he wrote for the famous *Encyclopédie*, he
explains with misgivings the main cause of the decline of humanism
in the classical sense of the word: multilingualism combined with the
neglect of Latin. He noticed that French had widely replaced Latin,
the traditional vehicle of scholarly activity not only in France, but all
over Europe. From this fact there arose a difficulty, according to
d'Alembert, that the French should have foreseen: "The scholars of
other nations, for whom we had provided an example, believed
rightly that they could write still better in their own tongue than in
ours. England accordingly imitated us; Germany, where Latin seemed
to have found a refuge, is imperceptibly moving away from Latin: I
do not doubt that the Swedes, the Danes, and the Russians will
promptly follow. Thus, before the end of the eighteenth century, a
philosophe wishing to know the ideas and discoveries of his predecessors will be forced to tax his memory with seven or eight different
languages; and, after consuming the most precious time of his life in
learning them, he will die before commencing to instruct himself."
D'Alembert's prophecy has been largely fulfilled.[6]

The proliferation of works in the various vernacular languages
eventually generated a new sort of literary pride that has flourished
ever since the age of political absolutism, and even more so since the
rise of popular sovereignty. The poet, then, writing in the language
of his people, indirectly promoted the national consciousness and
came to assume a political role. In more recent times, problems of
culture and questions of language have sometimes been the pretext
for conquests and annexations, a cause of war just as religion was in
earlier periods. On the other hand, the history of European civilization principally since the eighteenth century—when the first national
anthems were composed—shows that literature may help in expand-
ing and strengthening political and economic influence, though this
was already Maecenas' intention or afterthought when he subsidized
Horace and Virgil. Today writers sustain the prestige of the state:
Parnassus has become the arena for stimulating competition among
peoples, as well as a vanity fair of the nations.[7]

⊷⊷

Many have deplored the dissection of the seamless robe of occidental culture. Often, however, great writers and critics have recog-

nized that diversity means wealth and that variety is the spice of intellectual life. It is necessary, they have concluded, to study several national literatures in order to become aware of the splendid multiformity of European and even universal letters, and, at the same time, to see their oneness and unity beyond all appearances. The discipline that today is called comparative literature is based on this reflection.

Clearly enough, the question of whether a critic would show a nationalistic or comparativistic approach to literature would depend to a certain degree on the political system of his country. Dryden's (1631–1700) work includes essays on genres like the satire, the drama, and philosophical and epic poems as well as essays on the parallels between poetry and painting. In these studies, models from several nations are examined. Boileau's (1636–1711) attitude is different. In his *Art poétique*, France alone, besides antiquity, furnishes the material for discussion. In the eighteenth century, however, cosmopolitanism increased on both sides of the English Channel. In 1755 Dr. Johnson planned to found a periodical that he wanted to name *Annals of Literature, Foreign as well as Domestick*. Many now forgotten comparative studies—in a rather loose sense of the term— were published in London, such as John Andrew's *Comparative View of the French and English Nations in Their Manners, Politics, and Literature* (1785), a title that evokes Shaftesbury's *Characteristics of Men, Manners, Opinions, Times* (1711). In England the tradition of international criticism—as object of research and interpretation— was established and practiced by men like Henry Hallam (1777–1859), author of an *Introduction to the Literature of Europe during the 15th, 16th and 17th Centuries* (1837–1839), Sir John Bowring (1792–1872), Carlyle (1795–1881), Macaulay (1800–1859), Matthew Arnold (1822– 1888), and Saintsbury (1845–1933).

France had, among other quite successful periodicals specializing in European letters, the *Journal étranger* (1754–1762) and the *Gazette littéraire de l'Europe* (1764–1766). As early as 1727 Voltaire had written an *Essai sur la poésie épique*, followed by his *Lettres anglaises* (1734). Jean-Baptiste-René Robinet's *Considérations sur l'état présent de la littérature en Europe* (1762) is more characteristic of the times, though the author's reputation does not compare with Voltaire's. At the beginning of the nineteenth century Madame de Staël (1766–1817), particularly in *De la littérature* and *De l'Allemagne*, and her most cosmopolitan circle of friends and admirers—such as August Wilhelm Schlegel, Simonde de Sismondi, Benjamin Constant, and Zacharias Werner—did not, in the Republic of Letters, represent their respective countries, France and Germany, but Europe. In Italy, Giovanni Mario Crescimbeni's *Storia della volgar poesia* (1698) was followed by Quadrio's *Della storia e ragione d'ogni poesia* (1736) and by Juan André's seven-volume compilation *Dell'origine, dei progressi e dello stato attuale d'ogni letteratura* (1782–1799).

German literature, while continuously influenced during the first three quarters of the eighteenth century by both French and English literatures, is characterized, since the period of *Sturm und Drang*, by its rising national consciousness. In German-speaking countries, the study of literary interchanges and interactions has always remained of great moment to theorists and critics. This concern can be traced from Bodmer's (1698–1783) and Breitinger's (1701–1776) numerous publications to Lessing's *Briefe die neueste Literatur betreffend* [Letters concerning the most recent literature] (1759–1765), and Herder's *Volkslieder* (1778–1779), entitled in the second edition *Stimmen der Völker in Liedern* [Voices of Peoples heard in their songs] (1807). Between 1801 and 1819 a comprehensive and at that time most celebrated twelve-volume history of poetry and eloquence appeared, which its author, Friedrich Bouterwek entitled *Geschichte der Poesie und Beredsamkeit seit dem Ende des 13. Jahrhunderts* [The history of poetry and rhetoric since the end of the thirteenth century]. Friedrich Schlegel called romantic poetry "progressive Universalpoesie," and his older brother August Wilhelm wrote—characteristically enough in French—a *Comparaison entre la Phèdre de Racine et celle d'Euripide* [Comparison between Racine's and Euripides' Phaedra] (1807). Up to World War I the number of comparatists increased to such an extent in most European countries that only a few names can be suggested: Brandes and Farinelli, Betz and Robertson, Hazard and Baldensperger.[8]

In countries that were only rather recently integrated into the Confederation of Occidental Literature, like Russia and the United States, the interests of critics, poets, and novelists have not necessarily been centered on national problems or themes. Pushkin's (1799–1837) intellectual kinship with Byron is well known. Alexander Veselovsky (1838–1906), one of the earliest Russian critics, is at the same time a protagonist of nineteenth-century comparatism. In the United States, even after the birth of American literature and its recognition as an autonomous field of inquiry, comparative literature has been practiced and promoted by men like Emerson (1803–1882), Longfellow (1807–1882), and Lowell (1819–1891); the "Editor's Study" (1886–1892) of *Harper's Magazine* by William Dean Howells (1837–1920) regularly called attention to publications from abroad.

⚶

In the course of the nineteenth century, comparative literature became both an academic discipline and a critical system, recognized as such, probably for the first time, by one of the founders of modern criticism: Sainte-Beuve (1804–1869). In his first article on Jean-Jacques Ampère (1800–1864), written in 1840 and published in *Portraits contemporains*, Sainte-Beuve uses the expression "histoire littéraire comparée"; in his second article of 1868, printed in *Nou-*

veaux lundis, he refers to "littérature comparée."[9] The latter essay appeared first in the well-known *Revue des Deux Mondes,* the name and content already announcing the new trends in literary studies.

As to the expression "littérature comparée," which gave birth to "comparative literature," it existed a half century before Sainte-Beuve employed it. The date of the birth of "comparative literature," however, can hardly be accurately established. It may not have been used long before 1886, when Hutcheson M. Posnett chose it as the title of a book forgotten by now . . . except in our bibliography. After 1800, converging tendencies may be noted not only in the various humanistic fields, such as philology and history, but in most areas of human knowledge, including law and religion. In France the word *comparé* was most fashionable at that time and much used in the world of letters and of science as well. The founder of comparative anatomy, Georges Cuvier (1769–1832) published his famous *Leçons d'anatomie comparée* in 1800. Madame de Staël's *De la littérature*—a simultaneous view of most European literatures—appeared in that same year; here the magic word, however, is not pronounced. A friend of hers, Charles de Villers (1765–1815), who was in correspondence with Cuvier, put it in the title of a work that obtained some celebrity: *Erotique comparée, ou essai sur la manière essentiellement différente dont les poètes français et allemands traitent l'amour* (1807); Villers' *Comparative Erotics* is one of the first comprehensive studies on troubadours and minnesingers.

As early as 1816, Jean-François-Michel Noël uses the phrase "littérature comparée" in the title of a series of textbooks that he published with two collaborators: *Cours de littérature comparée.*[10] However, Noël's anthology was compiled from several single literatures and does not in the slightest foreshadow comparative techniques as they developed later in the century; in the title we may see the origin of the term, but by no means the origin of the discipline within the work itself. The reader of Noël's collection, it is true, enjoying the convenience of finding in this literary supermarket a great variety of goods from diverse countries, was somehow directly encouraged to compare them and to draw some comprehensive conclusions on literary phenomena in Europe. Obviously, he could have done so as well by selecting several single volumes. Quite a few works similar to Noël's, though without the term "vergleichende Literatur" or "vergleichende Literaturgeschichte," had been printed earlier in Germany, following the example of Bouterwek.[11]

Such studies, varying only in length and quality, were available in most countries throughout the century. Abel-François Villemain (1790–1870) and Ampère, however, compiled not only anthologies but extensive studies on various European literatures, which appeared between 1828 and 1841. Both critics occasionally use the expression "littérature comparée."[12] From 1841 to 1845, Amédée Duquesnel published in Paris the eight volumes of his *Histoire des lettres; cours des littératures comparées;* and when nominated in 1849 to the University of Dijon, Louis Benloew entitled his inaugural address "Introduction à l'histoire comparée des littératures." Similar examples can be found in England and Germany, and in Italy too, where the discipline, however, did not appear until several decades later than in France.

Often the founding of scholarly journals and associations, and especially the creation of university chairs, reflect changes in cultural approaches, interests, or needs. The first comparative periodical was the *Acta Comparationis Litterarum Universarum* (1877–1888), edited in Klausenburg, now Cluj, Romania, by Hugo von Meltzl, of Lomnitz. The quarterly *Zeitschrift für vergleichende Literaturgeschichte* ran from 1887 to 1910. Within this span of time its principal editor, Max Koch, of Leipzig, also published a scholarly series called *Studien zur vergleichenden Literaturgeschichte* (1901–1909). In the United States Columbia University's short-lived *Journal of Comparative Literature* appeared in 1903. For at least two decades, comparative literature has been present in all sectors of the study of letters; at the present time many specialized periodicals on the subject are published throughout the world, such as the *Revue de littérature comparée*, Paris, since 1921; *Orbis Litterarum*, Odense, Denmark, since 1943; *Rivista di letterature moderne e comparate*, Florence, since 1948; *Comparative Literature*, University of Oregon, since 1949; *Yearbook of Comparative and General Literature*, Indiana University, since 1952; *Zagadnienia Rodjazów Literachick*, Lódź, Poland, since 1958; *Comparative Literature Studies*, University of Illinois, since 1964; *Arcadia*, Berlin, since 1966, *Neohelicon*, Budapest, since 1973.[13]

As early as the 1860s, some scholarly journals in fields other than literature proper promoted the idea of literary comparatism, such as the *Zeitschrift für Völkerpsychologie* (Berlin, 1864). And some still do, such as *Ethno-psychologie, Revue de psychologie des peuples*, which has appeared in Le Havre since 1945, and *Europa Ethnica*, published in Vienna, which is now in its thirtieth year.[14] Similar examples can be given in other spheres of study like folklore and the fine arts. Today literary periodicals often contain more than their titles promise; although specializing in a particular national literature, many of them regularly include articles of a clearly comparative nature.

Parallel developments can be seen in the domain of higher education. The first chair of comparative literature was formally established in 1861 at the University of Naples, where Francesco De Sanctis started teaching "letteratura comparata" in 1871. Literature, he suggested, constitutes a whole. If for practical reasons the field has to be divided into several areas, the divisions should be made according to criteria less artificial than linguistic and political frontiers. Literary works should be studied together, whatever their national origins, as soon as they are ideationally or factually related, as soon as they belong to the same current or period of time, the same aesthetic category or genre, or as soon as they illustrate the same themes or motifs. By the time of De Sanctis' teaching, these new principles of literary and cultural studies were already being applied by many other professors of international reputation at universities that even today still insist on officially maintaining artificial partitions within humanistic learning. Little by little, however, chairs or lectureships in comparative literature were created in various parts of the Western world: in 1891 at Harvard, in 1896 at Zurich, in 1897 at Lyon, in 1899 at Columbia, in 1910 at the Sorbonne.

Today, in numerous centers of higher learning within Europe and the United States, as well as within other areas, comparative literature is taught as a regular field of academic inquiry. They tend to forsake systems and methods based on the belief in intellectual national autarkies and recognize the necessity of studying the natural ties among individual cultures. The increasing development and steady expansion of the discipline suggest optimistic conclusions in regard to its future as a most valid approach to literary history and criticism.[15]

2

The Meaning of World Literature

THE evolution of cultural and intellectual attitudes and proclivities in Western countries was greatly furthered by outstanding writers and thinkers. In modern times, Johann Wolfgang von Goethe was one of the most prominent and influential. Not only was this giant of German letters familiar with other European literatures, especially French, English, and Italian, but he had expanded his knowledge to oriental cultures. His *West-Östlicher Divan* (1819, *Divan of West and East*) and his *Chinesisch-Deutsche Jahres und Tageszeiten* (1830, *Chinese-German Hours and Seasons*) are brilliant attempts to join together civilizations that, at first glance, seem to have little in common. In his opinion "the East and the West can no longer be separated": "Orient and Occident sind nicht mehr zu trennen."[1] It is by no means a simple coincidence that Goethe was the one who coined the word *Weltliteratur*.[2]

Goethe's originality consisted in emphatically stressing "world literature" as a concept of literary knowledge. Meanwhile, his generation launched the notion of "European literature"—one that became a sort of commonplace among the critics of the early nineteenth century. There was, for example, more fervor than newness in the statement of young Giuseppe Mazzini (1805–1872), when he wrote about the solidarity of all European letters in his incisive essay *Di una letteratura europea* (1829). In keeping with the spirit of the time, he ex-

14

pands his conception of this study from literature to politics: "The individual history of nations is about to come to an end, and European history is about to arise."[3] Mazzini's statement confirms that historiography underwent an evolution similar to that of literature: *Weltliteratur* and *Weltgeschichte* in the modern senses of the words are parallel concepts. Hallam, who wrote on the literature of Europe, not only published his well-known *Constitutional History of England* (1827), but also—to provide a comparative background—*The View of the State of Europe during the Middle Ages* (1818). The historian and the comparatist have this in common: in the course of the last one hundred and fifty years, both have transformed their respective fields into humane disciplines. Cases in point include Jacob Burckhardt's *Weltgeschichtliche Betrachtungen* (1905, *Considerations on Universal History*), Oswald Spengler's *Der Untergang des Abendlandes* (1918–1922, *The Decline of the West*), Arnold J. Toynbee's *A Study of History* (1934–1954), and Gonzague de Reynold's *La Formation de l'Europe* (1944–1954).

This solidarity among the European peoples was strongly felt all over the Continent. When the guns of Waterloo fell silent, the great chessboard on which scores of battles had just taken place came to symbolize a moral unity among nations. Under the leadership of Russian Emperor Alexander I and the patronage of the Holy Alliance, Europe was about to become the United States of the Old World, a new unity that, despite many striking diversities, had a common literary tradition. Not only was it true that all national literatures of the West, to various degrees, rooted in antiquity, but during the course of their development continual interchanges had occurred among them. Such works as *Fiammetta* and *Lazarillo de Tormes*, authors of the stature of Petrarch and Cervantes, Tasso and Lope de Vega, Ariosto and Calderon had succeeded very quickly in finding a reading public beyond the Pyrenees and the Alps. Since the Renaissance a host of Spanish and Italian books were available in central and northern Europe in translations or adaptations, and were—in addition to classical literature—included in the corpus of recommended works for the cultivated man. During the seventeenth century, more French books than ever before crossed the North Sea and the Rhine; in the eighteenth century, great English works swept the Continent; and in the last quarter of that century a number of first-rate German writers had a European audience. At the end of the Napoleonic wars, Russian literary productions came west for the first time, while creations of Scandinavia found their way south.

It was at this juncture that Goethe, in a conversation of January 31, 1827, with his friend and secretary, Eckermann, instead of speaking of *Europaliteratur* uttered the magic word *Weltliteratur*. What he meant is clear from the context. He is censuring the literary provincialism of the poet Friedrich Matthisson (1761–1831), who thought of himself as the sole or special favorite of the Muses. After all, Goethe remarks, the Chinese were writing novels at a time when the Germans were still living in their forests. He feels that one should not confine oneself to the narrow circle of a single linguistic domain or any isolated part of the globe. "For this reason," he says, "I like to look at other nations and I advise everyone to do the same. National literature has little meaning today; the time has come for the epoch of world literature to begin, and everyone must now do his share to hasten its realization."[4] Goethe goes on to describe literature as a universal rather than a national phenomenon. Why, then, should Germans interested in literature read exclusively German works, or British, British works? A certain eclectism, it is true, would be the rule. It would be the choice of each individual to acquire his literary education from the best works available, which would not necessarily be those of his countrymen. The selection of his readings would be made according to aesthetic criteria, not patriotic considerations. Weltliteratur is first of all the total of *valuable works*, the library of masterpieces: it is the universal *Wertliteratur*.[5]

Another meaning is suggested when Goethe, six months later, again used the term. This time the topic of conversation is Thomas Carlyle, who had not only published a remarkable biography of Schiller in 1825, but also, one year previously, *Wilhelm Meister's Apprenticeship*, a translation of Goethe's novel, *Wilhelm Meisters Lehrjahre* (1795–1796). Goethe's comment to Eckermann is: "It is splendid that we now, because of the lively interchange among the French, English, and Germans, have come to a point where we can correct each other. This is the great benefit which results and will continue to result from a world literature."[6] As a further consequence of literary intercourse, criticism had become international, too, and Goethe went so far as to maintain that foreign critics were the best. Carlyle, he boldly thought, was able to judge Schiller more correctly than the Germans themselves, and the Germans were deemed to be in a better position than the English to interpret Shakespeare and Byron.

Neither of Goethe's two pronouncements presages comparative literature as a field of literary study and research. In the first, the necessity of a rapprochement or of a comparison among the various individual works is not directly suggested, and with the second statement he hardly initiates new critical techniques.[7] Because foreign criticism is not immediately "involved," "committed," or "engaged," it can sometimes reach more valid verdicts than indigenous criticism, but this is not to be construed as an absolute rule in spite of many examples. Abbé Desfontaines, in his translation of *Joseph Andrews*, wrote much better criticism on Fielding than anyone in London, Gray and Richardson included. Swinburne gave some of the finest analyses of Victor Hugo's work. It does not follow, however, that the English are the sovereign judges of Baudelaire, the French of Thomas Mann, or the Germans of Bernard Shaw. These writers have been best understood in their own countries. Chauvinism, on the other hand, may lead to shortsighted or one-sided judgments or engender indifference for foreign works, an attitude that deprives the judge of indispensable perspective. When the French novelist and playwright Jules Renard (1864–1910) was urged to read *Anna Karenina*, he refused, as Gide reports, on the ground that "nothing that was not of French origin could interest him."[8] Of course, biased verdicts on specific literatures have been rendered by foreigners as well as by nationals. Madame de Staël's *De l'Allemagne* is in many ways an encomium of Germany, and Heine's *Romantische Schule* an attack against German romanticism. Both books are equally tendentious. Only a neutral jury, autochthonous or foreign, would be in a position to render a generally and internationally accepted judgment.

Goethe's ideal had already been partly realized by Shaftesbury, Voltaire, and Lessing, who constantly included works of different languages in their critical discussions, thereby laying the foundation for the message of world literature that was later to be formulated. In this context, Goethe appears to be the catalyst rather than the inventor of the concept. However, he certainly was one of the earliest, if not the first, to expand it to virtually all literatures of the globe and to use the very adequate term Weltliteratur. No one thinks of disputing this honorable paternity.

⊰✦⊱

Under such illustrious a patronage, the propaganda for Weltliteratur was most efficient. Nonetheless, this general interest in literary interchange was in odd contrast to the desire for fragmentation—in a sense, a narrowing of culture—that arose at the same time. The abundance of works that in the course of the nineteenth century had become accessible to all *amateurs* of literature produced an unforeseen reaction among the learned. Because the mass of publications defied any attempt to explicate all parts of the literary body, scholars devoted their energies to exhaustive exegeses of a few books. Their attitude was a side effect of the individualistic romantic ideal. Shortly after Goethe pointed to the universal character of belles lettres, modern criticism—which not only concentrates on interrelations between national literatures, but on the genesis, the sources, and the intrinsic value of the works as well—was born.[9] Almost immediately this criticism became rather highly specialized. Yet excessive specialization is precisely what Weltliteratur seeks to counteract. Civilization and nature seem to produce at once their poisons and their antidotes.

How deeply true culture suffers from overspecialization has already been stated by Dostoevski: "The majority of our specialists are profoundly ill-instructed people. . . . What good can they accomplish for humanity?"[10] The situation thus lamented has improved in the course of the last hundred years, though it is still reflected in research and in the general structure of many universities, where it is often felt that one century of one national literature and its history will fully tax the intellectual capacities of a contemporary professor and scholar. To be a specialist in Dante or Shakespeare, Cervantes or Rousseau is still the rule, though often these writers are studied within a broad cultural context.

Those exclusively dedicated to specialization clearly have an excuse, however fallacious: today no single mind can absorb the gigantic mass of works stored in thousands of libraries all over the world, of data and findings, of conjectures and inventions provided by an army of scholars. A general practitioner in literature, a comparatist, is supposed to know why English ladies swooned from reading late eighteenth-century novels. A general practitioner in medicine may today comfort some of his patients with occasional paraprofessional remarks on the progressive wasting away, in older times, of these sentimental readers of the fair sex, implying that there is no risk, in the twentieth century, of dying from the same sort of "consumption." An abyss separates the natural sciences from the field of letters. The physician will always *venerate* Hippocrates; the literary man will forever *study* Homer. For Homer is a master whose work will retain its validity as long as our culture lasts; Hippocrates' genius destined him for his role as a pioneer—in the history of mankind, this is the role of every scientist—and hence he merely represents a stage of medical knowledge long ago surpassed. Homer has not only inspired generations of poets and libraries of critical studies, but he is still an active cultural leaven; of Hippocrates we have primarily a pious memory, possibly symbolized by a bust at the hospital entrance. What has survived of the Greek physician's work does not so much relate to medicine proper as to the general history of civilization. On the contrary, what survives of Homer *is* literature.

The question arises whether it is still possible under the circumstances to acquire general culture. A hundred and fifty years ago the "reading list" for a "cultured" person was incomparably shorter than it is today. In his essay "On the Multiplicity of Books" (1811), the French historian and politician Louis de Bonald (1754–1840) suggests that the "grand siècle" had not left posterity more than two hundred works of literature worthy of being remembered.[11] In 1966 René Etiemble presented quite another viewpoint:

> Suppose our span of conscious life is fifty years; you will have 18,262 days. After taking account of sleep, meals, the obligations and pleasures of life, and your career, estimate the time that remains to you for the reading of masterpieces, with

a view merely to understanding what literature really is. I generously grant you the capability of reading on the average one great book every day, from among those accessible to you in your own language and also in the foreign languages at your command. Further, you may read these works either in translation or in the original. You know that you will not read *The Magic Mountain* in one day, nor, for that matter, *The Arabian Nights;* however, I take into account the fact that, with just the right amount of luck and zeal, you can sample in one day *Hojoki,* the *Romancero gitano, Menexenus,* and *On the Spirit of Conquest* by Benjamin Constant. All of this will give you the few days you will need for *Quiet Flows the Don* of Sholokhov. What are 18,262 titles in relation to the number of fine books that exist? Nothing—une misère.[12]

In the perspective of a French comparatist, at least two thousand works out of almost twenty thousand should belong to the seventeenth-century classical period. Bonald is ten times less exacting than Etiemble, who, however, very well realizes that his proposal is not only unrealistic, but ignores the fact that a *monstrum eruditionis* is not necessarily a paragon of wisdom. The books in the library of a literary man, or even a scholarly one, share the fate of the pieces of furniture in his mansion, where old chairs first are moved out from the salon to the entrance hall, and then from there to the attic. The cathartic virtue of time saves the comparatist from intellectual indigestion. Hobbes was most skeptical about omnivorous readers. "Had I read as many books as they have," he once said, "I would be as ignorant as they are." The sally is a modern translation of an old maxim: *eruditio ancilla sapientiae.* Erudition and wisdom are not synonymous.[13]

Etiemble's ironic statement does remind us that a certain encyclopedism has become a necessity; Weltliteratur is more than an adventure to be approached with zest and enthusiasm. To cover the entire literary spectrum of the world is indeed a doughty task. It requires knowledge, *Belesenheit*—derived from *belesen,* "well read" —and judgment. The accuracy of the final synthesis depends on the choice and the amount of details taken into account. Full information obviously is essential in the formulation of such syntheses, which are the very purpose of all inquiry in world literature. Yet to understand the whole rather than to know everything is the ultimate goal. "The scholar," says Emerson, "is that man who must take up into himself all the ability of the time, all the contributions of the past, all the hopes of the future. He must be a university of knowledges."[14] The method for achieving this ideal has to be heuristic, leading students and teachers who already possess some of this knowledge to investigate further by themselves and thus to furnish their own contributions to the understanding of the common cultural patrimony.

⊱⊰

"World literature" helps man to come to terms with an apparently insoluble dilemma: should he be the victim of an exclusive, devitalizing specialization leading to the antipodes of true culture, or ought he surmount specialization; must the literary universe grow more narrow for him, or is he called upon to enlarge it? The solution may be found in the conciliation between the extremes. The true understanding of Dante or Shakespeare, Cervantes or Rousseau supposes that they are viewed in both their national perspectives and in their international contexts, and their best specialists are men of general education. Similar remarks can be made about Latin American literatures. The dichotomy exists only for the scholar who would think that works of minor writers deserve an exclusive lifetime effort, whereas they are at best worthwhile as pretexts for scholastic exercises, topics for articles in professional journals, or as prey for doctoral candidates. They are transitory specialties; they play the role of witnesses in literary history, but they do not help to stamp or to shape literary history. A great genius, on the contrary, may remain the permanent preoccupation of several "specialists," for, to understand him, they all have to know the intellectual geography of the globe, the cultural substratum common to all literatures. The great genius becomes an organizing and crystallizing principle. Here, however, we are no longer in the domain of Weltliteratur. We are on the threshold of *comparative literature*.

A Philosophy of Letters

"WORLD LITERATURE" and "comparative literature" are not identical notions. The former is a prerequisite for the latter, and it provides the scholar with raw materials and information, which he groups according to critical and historical principles. Comparative literature, therefore, may be defined as an organic Weltliteratur; it is an articulated account, historical and critical, of the literary phenomenon considered as a whole. The comparatist does not merely incorporate great works from all nations into his list of books to be read and analyzed; rather, he sees the concatenation of significant literary events, and he endeavors to assign writers a place in the general history of ideas and aesthetics. Not only does he juxtapose, he coordinates. To him literature is an amalgam, a compound, not a series of individual works. It is a cycle and a sum. A cultural reality is at the origin of the discipline: factually or idealistically interconnected conditions link one literature to others. The scholar, bearing in mind this fundamental truth, conceives of comparatism as the *novum organum* of literary criticism.

The very expression "comparative literature" is a source of confusion, an illustration of the perils and pitfalls of critical terminology.[1] It affirms the idea that literature is to be compared, but does not

21

indicate the terms of the comparison. Thus Harry Levin could ironically entitle his presidential address delivered in 1968 to the American Comparative Literature Association "Comparing the Literature."[2] Usually, however, the term is understood to mean what it suggests: a mutual, even a systematic, comparison of national literatures.

There are two definitions of the concept "national literature," one popular, the other scholarly. The first is tautological: English literature is the literature of England, and Portuguese, of Portugal. The adjective refers to the country. As to the second, two combined criteria in literary scholarship adequately circumscribe a national literature: on the one hand, it consists of works that adhere to identical codes of aesthetics and that are consequently written in the same language. On the other hand, their authors have the same cultural background. It is that body of books generally considered to be the expression of one specific culture, by means of a common vocabulary and a common syntax. American literature is created in the American language, which is rather distinct from the British, and in the mold of American civilization; however, no critic would banish Irishmen such as Yeats and Joyce, Shaw and Synge from the handbooks of English literature. Many more names could indeed be added to the list of Irish-born writers: Farquhar, Sterne, Goldsmith, Sheridan, Swift, Parnell, Wilde. The Germans take delight in reading Austrian and Swiss authors, whom they rightly consider their literary countrymen: Stifter and Grillparzer, Keller and Dürrenmatt. Similarly, a history of French literature should include Verhaeren, de Coster, and Maeterlinck, as well as Ramuz, Blaise Cendras, and Denis de Rougemont. On the contrary, Joseph Roumanille and Frédéric Mistral, writing in the Provençal language, are French nationals only, but not French poets. It is the cultural and linguistic community—inside of which endemic and independent regionalisms may develop at will—that characterizes individual literatures. Ideas and political ideals alone do not constitute literary borderlines. "East German Literature" or "West German Literature," for instance, are not critical concepts, only journalistic verbal commodities. The comparison of individual literatures or parts of them was the goal of the first comparatists in the technical sense of the word, those who, at the beginning of the twentieth century, launched this new critical mode, like the French critics Paul Hazard and Fernand Baldensperger, Paul Van Tieghem and Jean-Marie Carré.

The confrontation of single literatures, of course, is not a recent development. Upon closer analysis, one sees that literatures have always been set side by side with the implicit purpose of viewing them simultaneously and synthetically. In this sense, comparatism is almost as old as literature itself. It came into being on that certain day when a writer discovered he had a colleague beyond the frontiers of his linguistic and cultural sphere. From the moment the two established vital relations with each other through their works, and realized that their basic concerns and problems were identical or different, that is, comparable, comparative literature, though not yet a critical system, may properly be said to have come into existence as a reference point for insight and knowledge. Such intellectual communion existed, to be sure, before Charlemagne and the Moorish influence on both sides of the Pyrenees; before Apuleius, who was educated in Carthage and Athens prior to teaching rhetoric in Rome; before Heliodorus, whose *Aethiopica* initiated the cultural entrance of Ethiopia into Mediterranean literatures; indeed, before Alexander, whom legend reports to have been in correspondence with the Brahmins of India; and even before the Jews in exile in Egypt and Babylonia. As to specifics, it is possible to date comparative literature from Dante, as Werner P. Friederich wisely hints, although any precise statement necessarily remains arbitrary.[3] The *Divina commedia*, in its inspiration both Italian and European, is the very symbol of comparative literature. The comparative idea, which can be claimed to be as old as the Tower of Babel, or as Prometheus, whom Settembrini in *Der Zauberberg* calls "den ersten Humanisten," is revealed with particular brilliance in the later Middle Ages. Petrarch writes that he considers all the books of the world his faithful companions with whom he likes to converse by turns.[4] In the Renaissance period literary cosmopolitanism was more than ever flourishing. The most important literary wars that broke out during the course of the seventeenth century were in reality caused by comparatists. A major example is the "Quarrel of the Ancients and the Moderns," the phases of which are witnessed and described by scores of works such as Jonathan Swift's *Battle of the Books* (written in 1697) and Charles Perrault's series *Parallèles des Anciens et des Modernes* (first volume, 1688). However, we are in the technical sense still much more in the domain of Weltliteratur than of comparative literature, which presupposes the existence of modern concepts of criticism.

It is often claimed that comparative literature has its specific critical methods. This is not quite true: the procedure of investigation is basically the same whether the subject matter belongs to one single literature or to several literatures. We can read the *Volksbuch vom Doktor Faust* [Chapbook of Doctor Faust] printed by Johannes Spiess (1587) and discover in it elements comparable with those in Klinger's (1791) and in Goethe's (1808) *Faust*. We might find similar analogies between Christopher Marlowe's *Tragical History of Doctor Faustus* (first performed in 1594) and William Mountfort's farce *Life and Death of Doctor Faustus* (1684). In both cases we would be pursuing a literary study on the national level. However, should we fancy to include in this Faust study the German as well as the English works, or should we dare to consider also works like Imre Madách's *Tragedy of Man* (1862), we would be infringing upon the territory of comparatism, although the same amount of "comparison" may be involved when examining the German Fausts and the English Fausts separately, and by-passing the Hungarian. The materials and some tools —be they linguistic and bibliographical—rather than the general procedures are different. It becomes obvious that the name of the discipline can itself be misleading. Rather than *comparative* literature, it should be called *comprehensive* literature, since its differentia specifica lies in its encompassing nature.

These remarks do not only apply to studies in thematics, as in the case of Faust. It is commonly agreed, for instance, that the examination of Shakespeare's influence on Ben Jonson belongs to English scholarship, but the examination of Shakespeare's influence on Schiller to comparative scholarship. It is possible and valid to investigate the rise of the epistolary novel in eighteenth-century England, but possible and valid, too, to expand the field of inquiry to France, Germany, and other nations as well. In brief, all the ways that lead to general literary understanding—studies in relations and analogies, movements and trends, genres and forms, themes and motifs—are those also known and chosen by scholars in any national literature, or in fragments of national literatures. It is impossible to find in any library of the world one single book or one single essay on "applied comparatistics" that would substantiate the assertion made in many articles and treatises on "theoretical comparatistics"—namely, that not only the *matter* but also the *method* is significantly different in studies of comparative and of national literatures. In both types of studies one may use, for instance, the synchronic and the diachronic methods.[5] One may proceed by deduction or induction, rely on documents or detect analogies. The facts and factors, the means and techniques may vary, but no specific and autonomous comparative methodology exists. A. Owen Aldridge states that "the study of comparative literature is fundamentally not any different from the study of national literatures except that its subject matter is much vaster, taken as it is from more than one literature."[6] The methodological similarity or identity between both literary disciplines is implied in Victor M. Zhirmunsky's statement: "Comparative study, either within or beyond the limits of a national literature must be regarded as a fundamental principle of literary research."[7] In other words, since every literary study, whatever its subject, has to be "comparative" and, therefore, necessarily has to be treated with the comparative method, comparative literature, according to the Soviet scholar, is identical with literary criticism or literature itself. In his *Theory of Literature*, René Wellek had reached the same conclusion some twenty-five years earlier, though after a different argumentation.[8] While Wellek suggests that comparative literature is just literature, Zhirmunsky asserts that all literature is nothing but comparative literature.

꙳

The three major "schools" of comparatists—the French, the American, and the Russian—have concentrated their efforts on three different approaches to the discipline. Today these "schools" represent scarcely more than three general aspects of literary criticism as applied in particular to comparative literature. Thus the French comparatists, at the time their specialty was integrated into the academic life, merely followed the trend common among the scholars in their country: they combined historicism and positivism with strong national feelings. France indeed had a great literature, but the French thought it was the greatest. In their opinion it formed the backbone of the universal literary system, and the task of the comparatist consisted in examining how and why the English, German, Spanish, Italian, and Russian ribs were attached to it. This literary anatomy is reflected in the works of eminent masters in the field until the middle of the present century; they were mostly concerned with externals, with sources and influences, chronological developments and evolutions. In the "French school," comparative literature has been mainly an ancillary discipline within the field of French literary history; instead of being international, it has heretofore been only transnational in its approach. Less than twenty years ago, Jean-Marie Carré maintained: "Comparative literature is a branch of literary history,"[9] and twenty years earlier, Paul Van Tieghem had declared: "A clear and distinct idea of comparative literature supposes first of all a clear and distinct idea of literary history, of which it is a branch."[10] These statements contrast sharply with those made in other countries. In 1878 Heinrich and Julius Hart declared in their *Deutsche Monatshefte:* "Even though our periodical is to devote itself first of all to the interests of German literature, we shall not forget that every national literature is only a branch in the tree of *Weltliteratur,* and can be grasped in its true significance only in relation to the latter."[11] More recently in France nationalistic and factographic principles have given way to broader views and even to a generous cosmopolitanism. The distance covered during the last three or four decades can be measured by two books, both of which bear the title *La Littérature comparée:* that of Paul Van Tieghem (1931), a historical document, and that of Claude Pichois and André-M. Rousseau (1967), a contemporary textbook written in the new mode.

To focus comparatism on American literature and its history would be a preposterous idea: one century and a half is not enough to build up a literary tradition in the sense in which it is usually understood, and American literature must continue to be studied against its Anglo-Saxon background. The American comparatists, however, have other reasons for not adopting patriotic prepossession like the French. The United States is a nation of immigrants, "a race of races," to quote Walt Whitman. The majority of American critics —and this applies also to the Canadians—still recognize their old cultural homeland on other continents, mostly in Europe, even if they have never lived there themselves. Many of them, consequently, possess an "anima naturaliter comparatistica." Furthermore, while professors in French universities are, as a rule, required to be French nationals, in the United States American citizenship is not necessary for nomination to a chair, and thus faculties may show a most cosmopolitan stamp. Trends like "new criticism" have affected comparative literature more deeply in the United States than in France,[12] where the theory is applied to French literature rather than to world literature. As a result comparative literature as a university discipline and a field of scholarly research in North America is characterized, on the one hand, by the multiplicity of literary theories arising from an almost absolute freedom in academic teaching and, on the other hand, by a nearly complete absence of national concerns. These are the only two common denominators to be discovered among American comparatists. The two principles allow an infinite variety of tendencies in literary inquiry and interpretation, and there is hardly more cohesion in the "American school" than there was, for instance, in the "Lake school" in which Coleridge, Wordsworth, and Southey, far from working for common objectives, individually realized their romantic ideal. The American school of comparative literature does not proclaim a precise doctrine or program, but practices tolerance and eclecticism. It is the school in which, to repeat Wellek's phrase, it is "best to speak simply of literature."[13]

In so-called bourgeois and capitalistic countries, it is not generally known or recognized that Marx and Engels were among the first and most eloquent promoters of comparative literature. In their *Manifesto of the Communist Party* (1848) they spoke of the universal interdependence of nations in the material and in the spiritual sphere as well. "The intellectual creations of individual nations become common property," they say, ". . . and from the numerous national and local literatures there arises a world literature."[14] Here, however, world literature is not any more, as Goethe saw it, a library of works chosen according to aesthetic rather than nationalistic standards; it is the epitome of the universal literary phenomenon considered as a whole. In other words, it is comparative literature. Similarily, the A. M. Gorki Institute for World Literature in Moscow is actually an Institute of Comparative Literature.

In the Soviet Union, however, literature, according to government decisions, has to serve the interests of the state, which is, as the first paragraph of the Constitution defines it "a socialist state of workers and peasants." Literary utilitarianism is always dry and dull, be it racial or confessional, philosophical or theological, economical or political. More than other schools, *socialist* realism emphasizes *social* realism. In that respect, Victor Zhirmunsky may be considered the spokesman of the Soviet comparatists. The principle that dominates and pervades all Soviet criticism is that literature in all its parts is essentially a product of society.[15] "Literary movements in general," he writes, "and literary facts in particular, considered as international phenomena, are partly based on similar historical developments in the social life of the respective peoples, and partly on the reciprocal cultural and literary intercourse between them. When considering international trends in the evolution of literature we must therefore distinguish between typological[16] analogies and cultural importations or 'influences' which are themselves based on similarities of social evolution."[17] This concept of the relationship between literature and society is a corollary of the Russian theory of socialist realism adopted by the first congress of Soviet writers held in 1934.[18] Socialist realism became the official literary doctrine in Communist countries, putting an end to tendencies like formalism,[19] which was based on symbolism and the analysis of styles and genres, and which was most energetically promoted by scholars like Victor Shklovsky, Roman Jacobson, Boris Eichenbaum, Yury Tynyanov, and the young Zhirmunsky. Although in Russia social and socialist criticism may be traced back at least to Belinski (1811–1848), it was not integrated into a cohesive method of literary interpretation until thirty or forty years ago.

The traditional objection to Soviet literary ideals is that it neglects the aesthetic aspect of culture, seems to ignore the spontaneity of the human mind, and hesitates or refuses to pay credit to the merit of the individual. No collective intelligence, it is argued, ever engendered beauty, and every work of art bears a highly personal character. If society creates a novel, the inmates of Newgate are the authors of *Moll Flanders*, the Harlow clan of *Clarissa*, the Spanish caballeros of *Don Quixote*, the Russian people of *Evgény Onégin*. Proper names, however, are attached to these works. Somebody had to arrange the fifty thousand or five hundred thousand words in a certain way. And while these works were in the making, no vote was ever taken: Defoe and Richardson alone, Cervantes and Pushkin alone assumed the responsibility for these masterpieces, each of which retains its own unique beauty and mystery through and beyond all analysis. Moreover, certain literary habits and certain literary forms were clearly imposed upon the people by one specific writer, or a group of writers. Individual writers, not society at large—not even the exclusive courtly society of the thirteenth century—were the creators of the sonnet, although the sonnet obviously had to appeal to a certain social class.

Socialist realists would not disagree with this reasoning. They would, nonetheless, rightly observe that historical circumstances, cultural situations, and institutional conditions form the necessary infrastructure of any piece of literature. These conditions are the primary and, so to speak, the geological, data. Each work is embedded in a particular human soil and has become possible thanks mainly to a specific human milieu. Adolphe, the hero of Constant's novel, and Oblomov, that of Goncharov's both illustrate a similar aspect of human nature: a certain state of indecision and inertia, the incapacity to act. They are pictures and symbols of a passive life: one is obviously French, the other unmistakably Russian. And the language, too, is a product of society, which decides on some of the basic aesthetic rules. In political terms, society is the legislature; the artist retains the executive power, although he may not always, to begin with, govern with a majority. Most of the time, however, his personal merit is measured according to standards that he himself did not establish.

The theories and doctrines, the opinions and convictions that seem to characterize the specific "schools" are far from monopolized by any one of the countries designated by the adjectives "American," "Russian," and "French." Etiemble[20] may be called an "American," Robert Escarpit[21] a "Russian," while a few other Frenchmen remain . . . "French." It should be recognized that these "schools" represent specific attitudes of comparatists and major aspects of comparative criticism. Literary history shows that great art has in turns been thought personal, impersonal, or collective. Romanticism, formalism, and socialist realism are only three recent expressions of the trichotomy. Each of the "schools" mentioned teases or assails the other two for overemphasizing those aspects of the discipline that its own pupils do not sufficiently take into account. A satirical tone can often be detected in this rather circular criticism. The French are blamed for playing the role of intellectual customs officers checking on cultural importations and exportations, and for being eager to state that their nation still holds the hardest literary currency. These Greeks of our times often seem to look with condescension, even with contempt, upon the barbarian world surrounding them. The Americans are rebuked on the ground that they do not penetrate "le fond des choses," practice a vague aestheticism, and, as a nation still in search of a tradition, delight in the dehypostatization of national literatures. The Soviets incur reprobation for their dogmatism; whatever truth may be contained in the Russians' creed, it is received with skepticism because it has the taste of an ideology: socialist realism has been declared true by a majority vote and serves the interests of the party. In fact, the three theories complement each other, and no prophetic gift is needed to foresee that within the next decades the comparativistic crucible will harmoniously melt them together into the fundamental substance of the discipline.

⚓︎

Today the general and generating principles of comparative literature are widely accepted in the entire scholarly world, at least in theory. That European culture—which includes all national cultures expressing themselves in European languages—forms an indivisible whole, has been recognized for a long time. Western criticism, however, is still reluctant to integrate into the *corpus litterarum* the literatures of so-called exotic continents, for no reason, however, other than ignorance of exotic civilizations and languages.[22] China, Japan, India, the Near East, the West Indies and Africa may as well as any European region contribute to the understanding of the essence of literary creation, to defining its characteristics, and to fixing criteria for value judgments. The times of national hermeneutics are over, even in the Far East. In the West it is generally thought that James and Proust cannot be adequately studied and understood independently of each other, nor Poe and Baudelaire, Scott and Manzoni, Alfieri and Schiller, Hauptmann and Miller. There is hardly an inquiring mind that does not refer to Milton or to Aesop while studying Klopstock's *Messias* or La Fontaine's *Fables*. In universities where the administrators know literature, Tolstoy and Stendhal, Shaw and Strindberg, O'Neill and Pirandello are not always interpreted in different departments and different lecture halls. Much effort has been spent in checking scars on the literary body; often, however, the marks one may notice, on closer analysis, turn out to be mere "maquillage."

Comparative literature represents a philosophy of letters, a new humanism. Its fundamental principle consists of the belief in the wholeness of the literary phenomenon, in the negation of national autarkies in cultural economics, and, as a consequence, in the necessity of a new axiology. "National literature" cannot constitute an intelligible field of study[23] because of its arbitrarily limited perspective: international contextualism in literary history and criticism has become a law. Comparative literature represents more than an academic discipline. It is an overall view of literature, of the world of letters, a humanistic ecology, a literary *Weltanschauung*, a vision of the cultural universe, inclusive and comprehensive. Since antiquity, the ideal education has been a *studium generale;* the appropriate school founded in the Middle Ages, was called *Universitas*. The university of the twentieth century has been transformed into a *Diversitas*. Comparatism is destined to restore and renew, in the realm of letters, the ancient spirit, and to reconvert diversities into universities. Indeed, it is much more than a reconversion, because comparatism means the abolition of any *barbaricum*, ancient or modern. In the section "Happiness of the Age" of *Human, All-Too-Human,* Nietzsche describes the new intellectual horizon that man is now able to contemplate. Not only does he enjoy all past cultures and their productions, but he stands sufficiently near the magic forces that are giving birth to what might be called universalism. Whereas earlier civilizations could delight only in self-contemplation, at the present time. The entire globe shares identical literary interests and pursues similar literary goals.[24] The cultural history of mankind presents the classical image of concentric circles. The first ones are those of the family and the tribe; that of the nations follows, and that of humanity necessarily has to include all others. Comparative literature is the ineluctable result of general historical developments.

PART II

Relations: Analogies and Influences

4

Prolegomenon A

COMPARATISTIC inquiry, as stated in the foreword of this book, is divided into four basic fields: influences and analogies; movements and trends; genres and forms; and motifs, types, and themes. The first of these categories has produced by far the greatest number of comparative studies; influences and analogies have often been considered the two sole objectives of the discipline. In fact, any study in any area of human knowledge could, in a sense, be reduced to a study of relationships in terms of influence or analogy. Also, the literary scholar may analyze a movement, a genre, or a motif in order to understand interrelationships among national literatures. And the reciprocal is true: a study of relationships may at the same time lead to the understanding of movements, genres, or motifs, or of all three simultaneously, since the scholar is confronted with specific works, all of which obviously contain themes and motifs and belong to a genre and movement. Clearly, no sharp distinction can be made among the four categories.

Generally speaking, a study in influences or analogies is a species of literary research that focuses upon the interactions and resemblances between two or more national literatures, works, or authors, or upon the particular function of certain personalities in the transmission of various literary doctrines or techniques. Furthermore, this area of research may be subdivided into many more segments, such as *source* (the inspiration or information supplied or nourished by foreign authors or books), *fortune* (the response or the success or the impact that the literature of one country attains in the literature of another), and *image* or *mirage* (the true or false idea that one nation has of the literature of another). The affinities between literature and other arts or disciplines also fall within the scope of studies of influences and analogies.

There are many kinds of literary interrelations. Whole literatures are sometimes involved. Laurence M. Price studied *English Literature in Germany* (Berkeley, 1953), Laurie Magnus *English Literature and Its Foreign Relations, 1300–1800* (New York, 1927), Henry A. Pochmann *German Culture in America: Philosophical and Literary Influences 1600–1900* (Madison, 1957), Philippe Van Tieghem *Les Influences étrangères sur la littérature française, 1550–1800* (Paris, 1961), Louis Reynaud *L'Influence allemande en France au XVIIIᵉ et au XIXᵉ siècle* (Paris, 1922). In a collection of essays, *Letterature comparate* (Milan, 1942), editor Attilo Momigliano furnishes a reasonably complete survey of Italian intellectual imports and exports.

There are numerous studies of a less comprehensive scope. A single author may have exercised an influence on one or more authors of a literature foreign to his own, or upon the totality of that literature. Thus, we can trace Richardson's influence on Rousseau, Walter Scott's on both Dumas and Hugo, Shakespeare's on French literature as a whole. Yet instead of giving most of our attention to the emitting source, to Pirandello, for example, as influencing contemporary drama, we can also focus on the situation of the receiver; in other words, we can concentrate our efforts on the world of contemporary drama as it reflects Pirandello's thought and manner. In the first case, we analyze the "how" of transmission, although certainly without neglecting its effects. In the second case, we are more concerned with the result or degree of absorption.

For all these inquiries about literary relations, the scholar may adopt different points of view. Rather than discuss the influence exerted by a single writer, he can analyze that of a whole group or school of several authors: for example, Tolstoy, Dostoevski and Turgenev's joint influence on Thomas Mann, or on a whole generation of German authors. And here still the two methods of treating influence studies remain valid; the comparatist may treat the question from the viewpoint of the writer who influences or from the viewpoint of the writer who is influenced. In addition, whatever stand he adopts, he may still stress, or at least take into account, specific aspects of the problem: one critic examines the relations between styles or themes, genres or ideas, while another specializes in resemblances in language or structure.

The choice of any particular approach obviously depends on the position that the authors and works so treated occupy in literary criticism. For the history of Western culture, it is important to know that the *Roman de Troie* by the Franco-Norman Benoit de Sainte-Maure and Boccaccio's *Il Filostrato* lead to all three of these works: to Chaucer's *Troilus and Criseyde* and Shakespeare's and Dryden's *Troilus and Cressida*. It is likewise a rewarding task for the critic to try to decide from which man of letters Shakespeare drew materials for his *Hamlet:* Saxo Grammaticus, Thomas Kyd, or François de Belleforest.

The study of "sources," however—plausible and abundant as the sources may be—would remain of little value if it were not, at the same time to lead to conclusions about the intellectual quality, the emotional content, and the aesthetic nature of a work. It is questionable whether the mere knowledge of external stimuli, even literary ones, automatically improves the understanding of a masterpiece or the appreciation of artistic excellence. The recognition of sources is a pleasure, if perceived spontaneously or, after examining the source problem, on rereading. This deeper comprehension becomes possible if the reader immediately recognizes basic relations between works, passages, or images used by different writers. Novelists and poets write for such readers. Parallel passages revealed only in the footnotes of an erudite editor do little more than satisfy curiosity—though they might be momentous for the history of civilization.

Influences are exercised indirectly as well as directly. The media of transmission, however, are not always obvious, and the scholar's task is to identify the intermediaries. Those who remain nothing but intermediaries and do not become distinctive literary personalities rarely deserve our sustained attention; their names can be replaced in literary criticism by impersonal pronouns. It is the work transmitted and not the transmitter that interests us, for one should not attach more importance to the middlemen than to the authors, to the mailmen than to the persons who wrote the letters. In one sense, of course, the great geniuses are the true intermediaries; they are themselves the authentic links in the long chain of civilization. They have all received and given not only on the national but on the intercultural level as well. Milton with his *Paradise Lost* is an intermediary; he took from the Italians and he gave to Klopstock. Most intermediaries, however, are not geniuses; these minor figures, owing to some particular circumstance or to their personal merit, have played a rather considerable role in the transfer of literary assets. For example, the very goal of the authors of the famous *Correspondance littéraire*, Melchior Grimm and Jacques-Henri Meister, was to provide links between Paris and the rest of continental Europe. Intermediaries—which all writers are to varying degrees—if they are great, are named: Milton, Rousseau, Goethe; if they are minor, and if their role has been merely instrumental, they are simply styled intermediaries. In literary criticism the word "intermediary" has come to designate a rank, whereas it should only define a function.

Translators, whom Pushkin calls "the workhorses of our civilization," have played a crucial role in the diffusion of new thoughts and techniques. Changes of direction that have occurred in themes and styles, and literary fashions that have arisen in the course of the ages have often developed after the intrusion, and sometimes the invasion, of foreign works, both famous and scarcely known in their original languages. We can hardly overrate the importance of the translations that were made, for example, in the Renaissance. Under the Tudors and James I, England appropriated for itself the ancient Greek and Latin authors. Chapman made an admirable version of Homer, and Dryden translated Virgil. During this period, and in the eighteenth century as well, antiquity was part of English literature as it was part of all other European literatures, especially the Romance and the Germanic. In this connection, one may think of Amyot's Plutarch or later translations such as Hölderlin's Sophocles. There are many examples of most artistically translated modern works: Poe was translated by Baudelaire, Baudelaire by Stefan George. Both Coleridge and Benjamin Constant published a translation of Schiller's *Wallenstein*. Most great writers, from Chaucer to Kazantzakis, have translated one or more works of Weltliteratur.

At all times linguistic frontiers have been no more than thin, permeable membranes, and cultural osmosis is one of the most significant phenomena in this history of mankind. Today thousands of translations of the most diverse literary works are readily available at an increasing rate, and books on methods and techniques of translation are multiplying. UNESCO has published an *Index translationum* every year since 1949, and the *Yearbook of Comparative and General Literature* regularly includes a list of translations, although it is limited to English translations published in the United States. The international journal on translations, *Babel*, which appears in Paris, is now in its fifteenth year. In the United States the first issue of *Delos, a Journal on and of Translation*, sponsored by the National Translation Center, appeared in the spring of 1969.[1] The interpenetration of different literatures is a continuous process, and partly explains why the knowledge of only a single national literature gives a most incomplete and even erroneous idea of literature itself. Literary criticism is often not conscious enough of the cultural consequences that translations have had in all stages of any specific civilization of the West.

One may certainly speak of a certain mechanism of translation that can be studied within the framework of comparative literature. However, a literary translation also poses the question of creation or imitation, or even the question of influence, since the translator places himself under the strongest possible intellectual dependence. "The Muses Bound" could be the title of a study examining this problem, which obviously is primarily one of literary theory, while the study of the role of translations as media clearly belongs to "applied comparatistics."

Research in literary relations need not be wholly concerned with facts, for its subject is the interplay of ideas as well as the recording of data. The traditional study of national literature has accustomed us to see culture as a rather strictly chronological development and sometimes to identify succession with necessary filiation. Although the majority of critics are no longer under the naturalistic spell, many of them continue to judge literature almost exclusively in terms of the genetic process. One literary movement, they believe, engenders another, a work stems from another, a writer gives birth to another. Sometimes historians of literature even consider the existence of personal connections between authors or direct links between specific literary phenomena a necessary condition to undertake any study of relations; here is positivism at its worst.

Comparatists also like to contemplate analogies and resemblances as the basis of their analyses. They attach as much importance to confluences as to direct influences, to simple convergencies as to established ancestries, to ideational relationships as to factual associations. Indeed, they believe that affinities are better than direct influences for proving the fundamental homogeneity of a particular civilization and the literary intelligence common to all national elites. To ascertain that a Chinese novelist, independent of all immediate contact, built his work according to principles similar to those followed by an American novelist should be at least as valuable to us as listing the elements relating, for example, Velez de Guevara's *El diablo cojuelo* (1641) to Lesage's *Le Diable boiteux* (1707)—the latter being simply an adaptation, though not without personal merit, of the former. For anyone understanding English and French, *Rasselas* and *Candide*, both of the same year, belong somehow to the same literature. Since the comparatist is concerned with the comparable elements—whether the authors he studies view and treat these elements in a parallel or contrasting manner—he demands no material justification of his synthetic vision. If a critic sights a horse and a bull grazing together in his pasture and supposes that both, rather than either one alone, can help him to understand *his* literary quadrupeds, *his* mammals, and *his* herbivores, he may certainly compare them intellectually without having to prove beforehand that the bull descended from the horse. Relational studies for the comparatist can proceed from an agenetic or polygenetic method, from one that does or does not refer to cause and effect.

The comparatist not only concerns himself with the internal relations of the Republic of Letters, but also with the connections of literature with other disciplines, notably with the fine arts. Men like Diderot and Lessing, remembering Horace's *ut pictura poesis*, had a strong sense of the harmony between the arts of poetry, painting, and —in Lessing's case—sculpture. The comparatist's field, furthermore, touches upon philosophy, religion, psychology, sociology, history, and political science, though his efforts are centered on literary works. The widening of his horizon illustrates the evolution that comparative literature has undergone during these last decades. Often even in the post-World War II period, the discipline still restricted itself to the study of the foreign relations developed and maintained by a particular national literature that, paradoxically, somehow remained nationalistic. In the past twenty years, comparatism has acquired other dimensions: "foreign," for the comparatist, does not mean foreign to a country; it signifies foreign to the proper domain of literature.

Despite the usefulness of studies in influence, they seldom adequately explain the appearance and migration of specific techniques, attitudes, or ideas, for a people must be receptive to the new modes before it can accept them. To complement their studies in influence, therefore, scholars have turned to the second category in the entire field of cultural relations, namely, to that of literary analogies. They have analyzed parallel situations and developments, that is, they have examined literary similarities and identities in different ethnic and cultural settings. In a sense, such studies yield richer, more substantial results than influence studies, for the latter can at best reveal particular relations between specific works, whereas the former more frequently suggests conclusions regarding aesthetic or philosophical attitudes in general. Influence studies can explain the Byronic elements in Pushkin's poetry; but studies in parallel situations and developments can reveal the reason why nineteenth-century Russian culture could absorb or integrate Byron's esprit. In other words, it is quite possible that the same mood would have infected Russia had Byron never lived. Structural and thematic analogies, which exist between various cultural spheres, have been studied in all countries—in Spain by Eugenio d'Ors, in Germany by Max Scheler, in Sweden by Oscar Levertin.

In a recent article, Mikail Borisovic Chrapcenko says that "works of art, and so literature, are social in all their parts."[2] One recognizes here the prime methodological axiom adopted by the Soviet writers at their first Congress in 1934. Usually the so-called bourgeois critic sees here only a rule: literary works are *somehow* social in *most* of their parts. This statement, however, is nearly a truism inasmuch as language—the raw material of literature—is obviously a social phenomenon in both its origin and its evolution. Such socio-literary influences within single nations do not imply literary cross-influences among several nations. For different peoples may, under comparable social circumstances, develop comparable literary moods, types, or genres. Calvin S. Brown recalls the natural evolution of the drama from religious ritual in ancient Greece and India and in medieval Japan and Europe: there is no question of influence. Nor is there any in numerous other instances. "Between the eighth and the thirteenth centuries," Brown says, "the Vikings ranged in long voyages over the North Atlantic, making various settlements (notably in Iceland, Greenland, and North America).... They preserved the history of these heroic days in a series of sagas carefully memorized and handed down by oral tradition. These sagas are works of art, told in a clipped, forceful, colloquial prose, metaphorical, but not ornamented. It is not so well known that during these same centuries, on the opposite side of the world, the Polynesians spread out in even longer voyages from Hawaii to New Zealand, from the Solomons to Easter Island, that they also preserved the memory of these adventures in a series of sagas handed down by oral tradition, and that these sagas are told in prose which, in both style and effect, strongly resemble that of the Icelandic sagas. There is not even a remote possibility of any exchange of influence between the Vikings and the South-Sea Islanders."[3] The *Heike Monogatari* [The story of the house of Heike] of the twelfth century has in turn been compared with the *Iliad* and the *Chanson de Roland*. A direct influence of these two works on the Japanese epic poem is excluded. Similar social conditions produced similar cultural effects.

Comparable views with individual nuances are expressed in the writings of Zhirmunsky and Wellek. "When considering international trends in the evolution of literature," Zhirmunsky says, "we must . . . distinguish between typological analogies and cultural importations or 'influences' which are themselves based on similarities of social evolution."[4] And he provides an illustration: "Wordsworth in his pantheistic sense of nature (e.g. in 'Tintern Abbey') was akin to his German contemporaries Tieck and Novalis, though he had never studied German philosophy as his friend Coleridge had done. But, on the other hand, there is no doubt that the development of the historical novel and of the lyrical poem in Europe during the age of romanticism is traceable in its concrete forms to international literary intercourse: to the influence of such individual literary models as the novels of Walter Scott and the poetry of Byron, just as romantic historical drama drew on the literary heritage of Shakespeare's tragedies and historical plays. Without these models romantic literature in Europe would have developed similar *general* tendencies, but they would have taken other *individual* forms."[5] Wellek's comments on the subject seem to complement rather than to contradict Zhirmunsky's. "Among the English *Romantics*," he states, "only Coleridge and De Quincey show the influence of German Romantic ideas; among the Germans, English Romantic influences from Byron and Scott come later. The two movements existed at the same time, but they ran parallel without making deeper contacts, if we except Coleridge, whose very isolation points to the gulf between the two movements. But lack of historical contacts does not, of course, preclude similarities and even deep affinities. . . . As partial explanation one can point to common antecedents in history, e.g. the very general similarity between the thought of Wordsworth and Coleridge and that of Schelling and thus generally of the German Romantics is marked even before Coleridge has read Schelling. It is due to the common background in the tradition of Neo-Platonism, in mysticism such as Böhme's, and in varieties of pietism."[6] Diverse factors—individual and social—account for differences and analogies. At any rate, "we must leave something to chance," Wellek concludes, "to that obscure force, national character. Why not agree that we are faced here with some ultimate *data?*"[7]

The study of direct contacts seldom results in final explanations for similarities. In *Fearful Symmetry* Northrop Frye noticed that Nerval, who never read Blake, happens to be closer to him than Yeats, who edited him. Relation studies, whether concerned with influences or analogies, should take into account the social climate of cultural groups, the direct contacts between men and books, and, finally, the individualities of the writers themselves, which bestow a character of uniqueness on each work of art.

≫≪

Two types of literary relations are to be illustrated here. The first study "Jean-Jacques Rousseau and American Thought," traces analogies rather than influences, while the second study, of the reception of Russian letters in France in the course of the nineteenth century, reflects a more firmly established academic method, since it is concerned with problems of fortune, mirage, reception, and transmission.[8]

5

Immanence or Influence? Jean-Jacques Rousseau and North American Thought

THE history of civilization teaches us that epoch-making doctrines rarely stem from one genius alone. They usually appear simultaneously in more than one cultural area—though often disguised in varying intellectual garb—and their complex growth furnishes fascinating material for literary inquiry. The vast diffusion of the philosophy akin to that which Rousseau represents, and which often bears his name, exemplifies such polygenesis. There is, in other words, a Rousseauism without Rousseau, just as there is Cartesianism without Descartes.

Our question concerns Rousseau's contribution to American Rousseauism. Whether Rousseauistic ideas sprang up independently of his work (this can be illustrated by many examples), or whether they were generated by his direct influence (as a few other instances seem to show), his doctrine is clearly reflected in a number of concepts basic to North American pedagogical, philosophical, and political thinking. But there is yet another possible course to follow in the study of Rousseau and the American tradition; a general history of ideas could well examine whether or not Rousseau received as much from America as he gave to it, whether or not his own thought was modified in important ways by opinions and notions that were commonplace on the new continent. In some respects, North American thought serves as a valuable mirror to view Jean-Jacques Rousseau's doctrine, as the following example illustrates.

Until 1749, Rousseau had composed only rather mediocre poems and a few opéra ballets. In that year he began to write the series of works on which he intended to build his fame. In his first discourse, his *Discours sur les sciences et les arts*, which was to be published in 1750, he replied to a question posed by the Academy of Dijon: did the arts and sciences contribute to the spiritual prosperity of human society? We know his answer: civilization, in the form that it had assumed during the eighteenth century, was corrupting mankind. It represented an obstacle to happiness, at least to happiness as conceived by Rousseau. To support his theory that man's welfare was possible only in the "state of nature," he proposed for the readers' attention the example of the Indian tribes, "these happy nations who are ignorant even of the name of those vices which we have so much difficulty in repressing—of those savages of America, whose simple scheme of social life Montaigne did not hesitate to prefer not only to the *Laws* of Plato, but even to any conceivable system that philosophy might ever imagine for the governance of peoples."[1] These principles expressed in the *Premier discours*, which led directly to the pedagogical system as illustrated in *Emile*, were already well known in the New World.

In that same year, 1749, Benjamin Franklin (1706–1790), geographically somewhat closer to the "savages" of whom Rousseau (1712–1778) spoke, drafted his *Proposals Relating to the Education of Youth in Pennsylvania*. Rousseau, who claimed that the arts and sciences corrupted morals, and his American contemporary Franklin, who suggested plans for an academy, express fundamentally similar attitudes that might be summarized by their rejection of luxury, wealth, and cultural progress as the source of man's prosperity and happiness. Franklin, like Rousseau, wanted young people to acquire knowledge for practical ends, and he showed hardly any concern for the development of a social or intellectual elite. In brief, erudition was excluded from Franklin's school, where the American pupil could learn precisely that which Emile was to learn with his mentor— what is "most useful."[2]

The two primary rules of the proposed Pennsylvania institution were, first, "that the boarding scholars diet together, plainly, temperately, and frugally," and, second, "that to keep them in health, and to strengthen and render active their bodies, they be frequently exercised in running, leaping, wrestling, and swimming etc."[3] Additional remarks further illustrate that Franklin had in mind an education that would prepare the student for a useful social and professional life, the sole education that was to meet an immediate need in America. The student must, for example, learn botany—Rousseau worked for years on a *Dictionnaire de botanique*—a discipline that would be profitable to the whole nation. All abstract knowledge should be related to a concrete problem: "Might not a little gardening," Franklin asks, "planting, grafting, inoculating etc., be taught and practiced?" Interestingly enough, Franklin himself, as is well known, was one of the most famous early American experimenters; and Rousseau, too, did research not only in botany, but in chemistry and musicology. Independently of one another, Rousseau and Franklin came to nearly perfect agreement. Rousseau, however, shocked his reading public; he provoked a reaction, because he had to combat excesses. Franklin desired an evolution; he wanted to create, to mold a continent.

In the case of Rousseau and Franklin, then, we see that identical ideals arose simultaneously on both sides of the Atlantic Ocean. When the political works of Rousseau crossed this body of water, the colonists or the first citizens of the United States could recognize in them maxims with which they were already familiar. A basic, immanent solidarity seemed to unite the two worlds, at least on a philosophical plane. Essential parts of Rousseau's doctrine were the same as those in the system of ideas that Franklin acquired from his own social and intellectual milieu. Franklin's country was still quite colored with primitivism and still bathed in a puritan morality, circumstances that help explain Rousseau's reception in the New World.

The role Rousseau played in American thought and cultural life has not yet been fully examined.[4] The partial studies that have appeared show that questions of origin and influence may sometimes be puzzling and subject to quibbles.[5] Such studies are complicated by the fact that American thinking was confronted with Montesquieu and Voltaire at about the same time that it was confronted with Rousseau, and the traces of these three writers are often mingled and confused. Then, too, Rousseau had carefully studied English political thinkers like Hobbes and Locke, whose works had also been absorbed in North America.[6] Furthermore, quite a few of Rousseau's disciples were not only well known, but sometimes very influential in the United States, like Johann Georg Zimmermann and his book On Solitude, or, much more important, Heinrich Pestalozzi and his epoch-making pedagogical work. The question of direct and indirect influence can hardly be separated.

For those who suspect that Rousseau really did influence America's leaders by his writings, one of the first problems to be solved would concern the availability of his works in English and American editions.[7] In the main, scholars have examined Rousseau's philosophy as reflected in the doctrines of Adams, Paine, Franklin, and Thoreau. Certain aspects of these relations have been the subject matter of useful works. In L'Esprit révolutionnaire en France et aux Etats-Unis, Bernard Faÿ interprets Rousseau's thought as a kind of ferment in the political realm; in Nature in American Literature, Norman Foerster furnishes valuable evidence that American lyricism could have been derived from that of the "promeneur solitaire"[8]; and Gilbert Chinard, the great specialist of Franco-American relations, has given all possible literary and historical explanations for Rousseauean concepts common to both countries, concepts such as the original "bonté ou méchanceté," the goodness or the wickedness of man.[9] Some hundred books and articles could be included in a bibliography of works dealing at least partly with Rousseau in America. Most of them try to trace some influence where primarily immanence or simultaneous independent developments can be seen. This approach is understandable, for such cause-effect relations between several cultures have so far been most frequently the principal object of comparatistic inquiry. However, since comparative literature is essentially the *Literaturanschauung* that consists in viewing literature as a whole instead of studying its history and critical problems along national and linguistic lines, the analysis of similarities and correspondences should be practiced as well as the analysis of factual dependency and interchange.

What follows belongs to some extent to both types of studies. It is an examination of the interplay between influence and immanence, that is, between the possibility that Rousseau exerted a direct influence on the historical evolution of American thought, and the possibility that despite some striking resemblances, American thought developed independently of Rousseau's doctrines. The problem does not assume, however, the form of a dilemma: immanence does not preclude influence any more than influence precludes immanence.

I

Early in its history, America was receptive to the kind of primitive simplicity later espoused by Rousseau. Indeed, the impact a doctrine may exercise on a land and its people does not depend solely on a printing press. A certain composition of the soil permits a particular plant to take root more easily, just as a nation may accept or reject a thought according to its traditions, its ethnopsychological disposition, and its pre-existing propensities and preconceived aversions.

During the period of discovery, the term "New World" suggested its literal meaning: a new continent, a place to create a purer race of men untouched by the decadence of Western civilization. The first colonists, however, driven by the search for wealth or religious freedom, maintained their hostility towards the Indians until later travelers and pioneers—those, perhaps, with a more idealistic bent— "discovered" that the plumed heads of the Iroquois were as capable of intelligent thought as the bald heads of European academicians. This observation, which summarizes one of the major issues of Rousseau's second discourse, challenged the widely held belief in the absolute superiority of European culture. The new land furnished Rousseau with arguments as well as illustrations.

Intelligence, the Indians helped to prove, was the most justly apportioned and equally shared of all human resources. The so-called civilized man possessed it, but so did the man "in the state of nature"—an idea popularized, but not invented, by Rousseau. The American Indian forced the European to confront the notion of the relativity of cultures. Soon after Columbus' exploit, the "noble savage," the "bon sauvage," assumed in the minds of the explorers a shape well defined by Hoxie N. Fairchild: the aborigine was a "free and wild being who draws directly from nature virtues which raise doubts as to the value of civilization."[10] As Tacitus had contrasted the male vigor and nobility of the Germans with the effeminate mores of a Rome foundering under the weight of luxury and corruption, authors and readers of accounts of expeditions compared the Sioux and the Apaches with the Spanish and the Portuguese, and contrasted redskins in general with whiteskins. The remarks and conclusions repeated in thousands of travel and adventure reports suggested a challenge to the old Continent, a challenge that was finally forged into a coherent doctrine in the work of Jean-Jacques Rousseau.

On the new continent free men lived, at least theoretically, in a free nature. While the colonists had landed with the tastes and prejudices of their distant native land, they were quick to forget some of them, not the least important of which was the belief in the advantages of their homeland's aristocratic social structure. All men are equal in law; such was soon to be the maxim of the new elite.[11] Thus one of the first liberal political thinkers of New England, Roger Williams (1604–1683), a minister of Salem, friend of Milton, and great defender of the Indians, demanded for the natives the same privilege to purchase land as was enjoyed by the English. He contested the right of civil government to punish citizens for religious beliefs, set himself up as the champion of liberty of conscience, and extolled the separation of church and state.

To some extent liberalism, known but repressed in England, flowered in America before its independence. In North America the struggle for tolerance started in the seventeenth century, but there was still a long way to go for the decisive victory. Among the first apostles of this gospel were Richard Mather, a New England Congregational clergyman who most actively advocated the "Half-Way Covenant" (1643), a document that indirectly promoted a spirit of toleration. Similar feelings were already expressed, though timidly, in Nathaniel Ward's "Body of Liberties" (1641) (Massachusetts' first legal code), and John Wise shows the same intellectual attitude in his *Vindication of the Government of New England Churches* (1717), a work that contains remarks foreshadowing Rousseau's *Contrat social*. In the state of nature, says Wise, men are free and equal; in forming political societies they renounce certain natural rights for the commonweal.

Various Christian faiths soon flourished on the new continent, and in the religious sphere, too, tolerance gained ground, though self-enclosed sectarianism continued its development. Calvinism, Rousseau's religious background, was particularly well represented, not only by theologians such as Jonathan Edwards, but by literary figures such as the great John Milton and the French Calvinist poet Du Bartas, whose *Divine Weekes and Workes* was known in Sylvestre's mediocre translation of 1608. The children, often educated by severe and intransigent parents, learned early that they were but miserable "sinners in the hands of an angry God." Huguenots and Lutherans, persecuted in their native countries, crossed the ocean in great numbers to institute in small American cities a morality as austere as that of Geneva. A striking similarity exists between the main ideas of Rousseau's diatribe against the theater, his *Lettre à D'Alembert sur les spectacles*, and some of the decisions taken in 1774 by the Continental Congress that classed theatrical representations among the causes of public evil, along with horse racing, cock fighting, and gambling.

Like the government of Geneva, but even more generously, the Protestants of America, by and large, extended their tolerance to all faiths save one, the Catholic. The followers of the Roman creed were especially numerous in Maryland, where their colony had been founded by George Calvert, Lord Baltimore, to serve as a refuge for Catholics who had been victims of persecution during the Gunpowder Plot and the decades of harassment that followed. But it was precisely in Maryland that they experienced the worst persecutions. The colonial authorities, forgetful of the Toleration Act of 1649, passed a repressive law in 1691 that forbade the "Papists" from celebrating their religious offices, save in particular houses, and deprived them of all political rights. It was the Geneva of Rousseau: "Whoever dares to say: *outside of the Church, there is no salvation*, must be driven out of the state,"[12] a sentence that appears in the last chapter of the *Contrat social*. Other parallels have to be noticed. Locke wrote his *Letter on Toleration* and Voltaire his *Traité sur la tolérance* at a time when North America was almost exclusively under English and French influence.

The education of the colonists' children was based on some of the principles that would later be claimed by Rousseau. A single book sufficed for elementary education, not the *Robinson Crusoe* recommended by the Genevan pedagogue, but the Bible, from which the child learned to read. Above all, the inhabitant of the New World possessed, in Rousseau's words, the "great book of nature" itself, indispensable to Rousseau's pupil. By the age of twelve, the Emiles of both shores of the Atlantic scarcely knew how to distinguish intellectually their left hands from their right, but they were surpassingly agile at the use of either. It was often in the middle of the woods and prairies that the education begun on school benches was really completed.[13] In theory the young colonists learned a trade; but in actuality they learned a great variety of trades. Further, they were expert in the culture of the fields—self-made agriculturalists. It would have been quite strange if such a country had remained impervious to Rousseau's works, since it could recognize in them many principles that it already practiced.

The predilection shown by eighteenth-century America for ideas that often bear remarkable similarity to those of Rousseau renders difficult the task of distinguishing influence from pure coincidence. Contradictions abound in American criticism when it sets about the study of sources supposedly used by certain writers. A hundred years ago, for example, Thoreau was proclaimed "an American Rousseau,"[14] so evident did the affinities seem to be between the anchorite of Walden Pond and the "solitary stroller" of the Ermitage. A more recent book insists on the contrary: "There is nothing in the fifteen volumes of Thoreau that authorizes saying he had any interest in the philosopher of Geneva."[15] If Thoreau did not in fact learn his attitudes and theories from Rousseau, then how can the affinities between them be accounted for? In this respect, analogous disagreements divide the critics of Emerson, Whitman, Hawthorne, and even Margaret Fuller. What seems evident is that for many American writers the reading of Rousseau did not mean the discovery of a new doctrine. Often it was only a revelation to them of their own sentiments, an explication, or an expression in well-turned phrases, of what they had been feeling for many years. So far as North American thought and Rousseau are concerned, distinctions between an autochthonous tradition and a foreign influence are seldom clear-cut. American writers recognized their own *Weltanschauung* in the works of the citizen of Geneva.

II

Several English translations of Rousseau's books came from Great Britain to the colonies. It seems impossible, however, to find a clear answer to the question of their direct influence on American life. Paul M. Spurlin, after investigating the subject for twenty years, came to a most discouraging conclusion: "The two *Discourses* obviously made little, if any impact on eighteenth-century America."[16] And furthermore, he writes: "The *Social Contract* exerted no palpable influence on political thought in the United States in the eighteenth century."[17] Only *La Nouvelle Héloïse* and *Emile* found a large reading public. It is true that Rousseau's writings were widely advertised, but it is impossible to know the number of actual buyers. Quite a

few influential persons kept his books in their libraries, but to conclude that they read them is an unsupportable assumption. On John
Adams' bookshelves were the nine volumes of the handsome 1764
edition of Rousseau's work; but this did not prevent their owner from
calling Rousseau a "coxcomb" and a "fool." However Adams regarded
the Genevan, it is safe to conclude that Rousseau's presence in America should be the object of a study in analogies or parallel intellectual
development, rather than one in direct influence. Such a study belongs
to comparative criticism and history, since it involves an international approach to literature.

Rousseau's readers or admirers may be divided into several categories. The first of them arose among a group of literate men, émigrés
or their sons. The Catholic Crèvecœur and the Huguenot Freneau
were younger than Rousseau, the first by twenty-three years, the other
by forty. Crèvecœur expressed his physiocrat and primitivist views in
his twelve *Letters from an American Farmer* published in 1782. Freneau, a man of the sea transformed into a man of letters, began his
career as a writer with some articles that the *Contrat social* could
have inspired. A small number of Jacobin sympathizers later proclaimed him the American poet of the French Revolution. In 1795
Freneau published *Republican Genius of Europe*, and during the same
year, *God Save the Rights of Man.* He also left a series of portraits in
which he presents himself as "the Philosopher of the Forest," a sage
who believes in the same doctrine as enunciated by Rousseau's
"Vicaire savoyard," a moralist filled with unction, preaching to his
audience an unsophisticated existence at the bosom of nature.

The work of Michel-Guillaume Jean de Crèvecœur, also known
as J. Hector St. John de Crèvecœur, presents a vision of colonial
America practicing and preaching an ideal almost identical with
Rousseau's. His work exalts the rustic, simple life, celebrates the
kind of communion with nature Rousseau ceaselessly recommended,
and upholds the notion that between persons of differing national
backgrounds there may be perfect understanding. "We have no
princes, for whom we toil, starve, and bleed," he declares in the third
letter of the *American Farmer*. He adds: "We are the most perfect
society now existing in the world," and: "Here man is free, as he
ought to be."[18] These solemn declarations echo the passages of
Rousseau's writings referring to the Swiss cantons.

The domestic economy of the free man described by Crèvecœur
recalls the practice of Rousseau's heroine, Julie, in her home at
Clarens. "The philosopher's stone of an American farmer is to do
everything within his own family; to trouble his neighbors by borrowing as little as possible; and to abstain from buying European commodities. He that follows the golden rule and has a good wife is
almost sure of succeeding."[19] Besides his politics of autarky, Crèvecœur shares with Rousseau a penchant for botany and a delight in

solitary promenades. There are even similarities in their techniques as writers. The two famous letters (1763) in which Rousseau creates for the Maréchal de Luxembourg a living picture of Switzerland, especially in the Môtiers region, near Neuchâtel, resemble in tone and structure those written by the American planter. As a bilingual author, Crèvecœur managed to transpose descriptive features typical for French writers into his English style.

One aspect of the question of influence—the matter of personal contact—arises quite naturally. The *Letters from an American Farmer* are dedicated to Abbé Guillaume-Thomas Raynal, author of the famous *Histoire philosophique et politique des établissements et du commerce des Européens dans les deux Indes*,[20] which a French critic considered "the incoherent and undigested summation of the ideas of Voltaire, Rousseau, and Diderot."[21] The writings of Crèvecœur illustrate to what extent source research can sometimes be misleading. Did the rural philosopher take from Raynal what Raynal took from Rousseau? The question cannot be resolved; yet various speculations remain possible. The fact is that Crèvecœur left France in 1754 when he was nineteen, the year of the *Deuxième discours*, and he did not see his native land again until 1781. This practically eliminates the possibility of Rousseau's personal contact with him, because Rousseau died in 1778, but he may, of course, have become acquainted with Rousseau's work in America. Crèvecœur's book was first printed in 1782 and went through eight editions in two years. When Crèvecœur returned to Paris, it is possible that rather than reading Rousseau's works he limited himself to conversations with Rousseau's lady friends and female admirers. He is known to have visited Madame d'Houdetot, one of the inspirers of the *Nouvelle Héloïse;* Madame Necker, the mother of Madame de Staël; and also Madame Cottin, a novelist as sentimental as she was popular during that period. The harmony of ideas and sentiments between the citizen of Geneva and the Frenchman-turned-American is seen again in the three-volume work *Voyage dans la haute Pennsylvanie et dans l'Etat de New York*, the definitive edition of which was published in 1801. Finally, after serving several years as a French diplomat in New York, the cosmopolitan agronomist returned to his Norman compatriots, among whom he tried to promote a taste for potatoes, his way, at the end of his days, of cultivating his garden.[22] In brief, despite the strong resemblance between Crèvecœur's thinking and Rousseau's, the question of direct influence must remain open. The example of Crèvecœur is typical: the study of other cases—especially of French émigrés—would end on a similarly inconclusive note.

❧❦

Besides the French émigrés, another set of writers who put themselves in contact with Rousseau's doctrines was a group of old-stock

Anglo-Saxons. James Otis (1725–1783) quotes Rousseau in his famous brochure *The Rights of the British Colonists Asserted and Proved* (1764), and the writings and speeches of Thomas Paine, Thomas Jefferson, and Alexander Hamilton also seem to indicate familiarity with Rousseau's works.[23] Moreover, the special approach Rousseau shows in studying the relations between government and society is reflected in many American publications. Several passages from Paine's *Common Sense*, for example, repeat lines of reasoning developed in the *Contrat social*. The influence seems obvious when Paine declares: "Some writers have so confounded society with government, as to leave little or no distinction between them; whereas they are not only different, but have different origins. Society is produced by our wants and government by our wickedness; the former promotes our happiness positively by uniting our affections, the latter negatively by restraining our vices. The one encourages intercourse, the other creates distinctions. The first is a patron, the last a punisher."[24] Paine, in the manner of Rousseau, advocates a frequent interchange between the sovereign—that is, the people—and its officers; or, as Paine says, between the body of electors and the elected. It should be noted at this point that *Common Sense* appeared six months before the Declaration of Independence. In his *Rights of Man*, Paine not only illustrates that he knows Rousseau's writings, but openly professes his appreciation for them. He finds in them "a loveliness of sentiments in favor of liberty, that excites respect, and elevates the human faculties."[25] The "Profession of Faith" Paine placed at the beginning of his *Age of Reason* resembles the last chapter of the *Social Contract*, entitled "De la religion civile," which repeats the key ideas of Rousseau's "Profession de foi du Vicaire savoyard."

But there is still another question: were the men responsible for the Constitution of 1787 inspired, consciously or not, by Rousseau? Certain phrases in their works seem to hint at direct influence, but such influence cannot be proved. A similar question arises in regard to the Declaration of Independence. Here again, appearances immediately suggest that Rousseau acted as a partial source of inspiration. It would seem improbable that all this republican enthusiasm, this passion for personal and national liberty that characterized the birth of the United States did not owe something to the work considered by the old continent as the great charter of modern democracies. But the lack of data concerning the route this supposed influence traveled continues to embarrass the modern scholar.

Was Rousseau's thought present in America at the time of the founding of the United States, and did it have any effect on the attitudes of the statesmen responsible for the great events leading to the creation of the new republic? To make a judgment necessitates ascertaining whether they had read Rousseau, or at least his political works, and, more importantly, whether they had integrated this message with their actions. At first view, the answer seems deceptive, for there is no evidence that the principal drafter of the Declaration of Independence, Jefferson, although a collector of fine books, ever read the *Contrat social*,[26] and it is doubtful that anyone will ever tell us anything definitive about the reactions of Franklin and George Washington, who both owned copies of the work. The same puzzling question arises in connection with Hamilton, who seemed to be familiar with authors that Rousseau himself had pondered: Montesquieu, Grotius, Pufendorf. Many aspects of Hamilton's thought are related to the doctrine of Rousseau, though in none of his articles published in *The Federalist* does Hamilton actually refer to it. In Jefferson, Hamilton, and Rousseau's view, federalism unites the advantages of big and small states; and it guarantees most efficaciously minority liberties and personal freedom.[27]

Today's reader of the Declaration is most impressed by its dearth of new ideas. It summarizes the old aspirations of those Americans desirous of separating themselves from the English crown. Only one passage—the last grievance—would have astonished the eulogist of the noble savage: the complaint of the colonists that the king of Great Britain has neglected to protect them against the "merciless Indian savages, whose known rule of warfare is an undistinguished destruction of all ages, sexes, and conditions." That the first task of the government is to protect the life, liberty, and property of citizens was an assumption on which Locke, before Rousseau, had based much of his political doctrine. Rousseau, a thorough reader of Locke, took up these ideas and humanized them. What are life, liberty, and property except means for attaining the supreme good, happiness? Rousseau's presence is felt, too, in the first sections of the Declaration, those that deal with general principles governing men and society.

At the end of the eighteenth century, these trends are illustrated not only by the statesmen already named, but also by Madison and Barlow, poets like Freneau, educators like Dwight, and novelists like Brown—the latter mixing the elements taken from Rousseau with some borrowings from Richardson. This was also the time when Orestes A. Brownson discussed the political writings of Rousseau at length; he refused to accept some of their conclusions, although he subscribed to the essentials of the works. The politico-social literature idealistically associated with Rousseau, which then developed mainly in the gazettes, was to be reflected also in pamphlets and in books, such as the anonymous volume published at Albany in 1797, *A Dissertation on Political Economy to Which Is Added a Treatise on the Social Compact; or, the Principles of Political Law*. Analogies abound, influences are impossible to prove.

Thus far we have hardly dealt with literature in its narrower sense, but with philosophy and politics. Indeed, as late as the end of the eighteenth century, no one spoke of American literature. American letters were connected to and dependent on those of the mother country, although in 1775 the *Pennsylvania Magazine*, edited by Robert Aitken and Thomas Paine, had postulated the literary independence of the colonies. In the minds of the promulgators of this concept, artistic independence would promote a national consciousness. The *United States Magazine* of 1779 followed this example, as did the *Columbian Magazine* of 1786 and the *American Museum* of 1787, each printed in Philadelphia.[28] Their claims, however, remained mere expressions of wishful thinking for another half century. England continued in these years to be the great center of intellectual resources for the new world, and the diffusion of Rousseau's work on American soil, therefore, paralleled its diffusion in England.[29] An English edition of the *Nouvelle Héloïse* appeared in London the same year as its original publication in French, and it was bought in the bookstores of Boston, Philadelphia, and Annapolis as early as 1761. *Emile* and the *Contrat social* followed closely and were available in all North American cities of any importance. Shortly after Rousseau's *Miscellaneous Works* in five volumes[30] were put on sale in the British capital in May, 1767, they also became available to the North American colonists. The *Confessions* crossed the Atlantic in English dress only two years after the Parisians had first read the work. Obviously, England was the great intermediary.

The dissemination of Rousseau's writings in America was, nevertheless, rather sluggish. Some of the reasons for this may be readily detected. Criticism sometimes forgets that at the beginning of the French Revolution, the United States counted fewer than four million inhabitants. Its intellectual elite consisted of rather small groups to be found in settlements spread throughout the vast country. The economic crisis set loose in Europe and on the international market by the wars of the Convention, the Directory, and the Consulship of Bonaparte, and finally those of the French Empire, had an adverse effect on the commerce of books. The sale of Rousseau's works in the United States also ran into other difficulties. Puritan America was going to recoil for some time before wholly accepting any work stained with notorious immorality. The *Confessions* were thought to be preposterous, as was the *Nouvelle Héloïse*. Many Americans considered these books of Rousseau insidious, often not aware that they subsumed some of their dearest ideas. In fact, in the opinion of some of the more stiff-necked pastors, Rousseau was not only a vile seducer deprived of all moral sense, but a dangerous philosopher, a troublemaker, and a fomenter of revolutions.

Because England, as we have just observed, often played an eminent role in the spreading of European culture in America, it should be noted that a similar unfavorable opinion of Rousseau was expressed in one of the most widely distributed periodicals in the Anglo-Saxon world, the *Quarterly Review*. In its view, Rousseau "has done more harm to the world than almost any other that can be named."[31] The *Edinburgh Review*, too, emerged hostile to the citizen of Geneva. Burke launched vehement attacks on Rousseau as a symbol of the French Revolution, and Burke's authority was more harmful to Rousseau than any of the arguments which Rousseau had himself proposed. Later, similar attitudes also found expression in France. Toward the end of Napoleon's reign and under the French Restoration, the *Correspondance littéraire* of Grimm and Meister as well as the *Mémoires* of Madame d'Epinay were printed; these contained partially unjust, even calumnious appraisals of Rousseau. America, in other words, participated in the general current of opinion of the time. The reputation of the philosopher was hardly rehabilitated in the eyes of the world before the rise of a new literary epoch.

With the onset of English and French romanticism at the turn of the century, the reconsideration of Rousseau began. James Mackintosh, Godwin, Shelley, Hazlitt, Keats, Byron, and especially Coleridge[32] all confessed their spiritual affinity with him, and two works —the *Essais sur Rousseau* (1818) of Bernardin de Saint-Pierre and Musset-Pathay's biography of Rousseau (1821)—were influential in promoting this reevaluation, which had repercussions even in the United States. Margaret Fuller, William Ellery Channing, and Brownson became Rousseau's disciples and enthusiasts in their generation of Americans. The increasing interest in Rousseau's work, then, noticeable toward the end of the eighteenth century, developed further in the nineteenth century.

III

In Rousseau's view, the concept of property is foreign to that of the "state of nature." It is only when man, losing his nomadic instincts, begins to cultivate land and to feel he should pay his neighbors for their services, that property, and with it civil society, is born. Nevertheless, the ideal remains of the family sufficient unto itself, and living without commerce, mass production, or machines. In accordance with this view, economic independence is considered the best guarantee of personal liberty, the supreme good that must be protected above all things.

Although the experiments in communal living that arose in the mid-nineteenth century—especially those of Brook Farm (1841–1847) and Fruitlands (1844–1845)—seem to echo these precepts of Rousseau, the question remains whether we can accurately speak of direct influences. We are probably confronted with one more case of coincidental, or parallel, intellectual development. Furthermore, these concerns for reforming social and economic laws may have been partly inspired by English philosophers and poets. In 1794 Coleridge, who was well acquainted with Rousseau's work, dreamed of a modern utopia he called pantisocracy. He planned, with Southey, to found a small rural community in America liberated from the tyranny of prejudice and convention, in which individual property would cease to exist. But, instead of embarking for the United States, Coleridge wrote pleasant sonnets on his "pantisocratic" system and delegated, so to speak, the Brookfarmers and the Fruitlanders to execute his project half a century later—and to suffer the odium of its failure as well. Or was it "la faute à Rousseau," to quote Gavroche's song of Hugo's *Misérables?*

Brook Farm was one of the most famous attempts at remodeling society, and the most characteristic, although in reality very modest and quite limited in scope. The transcendentalists, who assumed the spiritual sponsorship of this experiment, shared with the Brook-farmers many of their views on religion and philosophy, and on the organization of social life as well. The questions they asked were Rousseau's. Do modern institutions guarantee the free development of the individual? Do they not in fact tend to advance the interests of a class at the expense of the majority? Would it not be just to say, as did the Genevan economist and man of letters Simonde de Sismondi (a correspondent of Channing's from 1831), that because some labor and toil others are able to enjoy repose? Walt Whitman remarked, not without bitterness, that the laws always were disposed to favor the haves against the have-nots. It follows that society cannot be useful to all men unless a certain economic equality goes hand in hand with political equality. All these thoughts underlie Rousseau's *Contrat social*, and more particularly his *Considérations sur le gouvernement de Pologne* and his *Projet de constitution pour la Corse.* The principles of democracy should not be anchored solely in the Declaration of Independence, but in economic laws as well.

In 1842 George Ripley, a paterfamilias of the old tradition, moved himself and his family to a farm about ten miles from Boston. Known as Brook Farm, his community attracted many socially minded writers including Emerson, Margaret Fuller, and Hawthorne. "The most ancient of all societies is that of the family," Rousseau had said in his *Contrat social*. Ripley, unconsciously emulating Rousseau, established a regenerated family, a community in which each member could enjoy the fruit of his toil. His objective is thus defined by John Thomas Codman in his memoirs of Brook Farm: "The imperative duty of this time and country, nay, more its only salvation and the salvation of civilized countries, lies in the reorganization of society according to the unchanging laws of human nature, and of universal harmony."[33] Although enthusiasm sustained the efforts of these improvised farmers, they were at best amateurs at their new work, philosophers engaged in agriculture. The enterprise was destined for failure. When Rousseau's ideal was replaced, after a few years, by Fourier's doctrine—the theory of personal freedom through the practice of collective labor—financial breakdown threatened the communal society of Brook Farm, and when the main building, the Phalanstery, caught fire on the eve of the inauguration ceremony, nothing remained but despair. The modest fortune of Nathaniel Hawthorne was consumed with the Phalanstery.

Not only did Hawthorne nostalgically evoke his sojourn at Brook Farm in *The Blithedale Romance,* he also touched on the question of personal property. Those who desired to settle on uncultivated and fertile lands, he maintained, were to be its actual possessors. When Hawthorne had to deal with the allocation of property to prospective purchasers in Waldo County in Maine, he acted according to the principles expounded in the *Contrat social:* the possession of the land is effected "not by a vain ceremony but by labor and culture, the only tokens of property."[34] Hawthorne's principles correspond to Rousseau's: when the claimant settles down, the land should not yet be occupied by anyone; more important, no one has the right to possess a tract larger than necessary to satisfy his needs; finally, the possession of land should not be achieved by vain signatures and seals, but by force of labor. Drag the plow across a field and it is yours.

The Fruitlands experiment of 1844 also brought Rousseauean theory into contact with reality. A dozen persons formed the nucleus of this community, some twenty-five miles west of Boston, which was from time to time favored by the visit of such eminent men as Emerson, Thoreau, and Channing, and other members of the Concord Club. It was in Fruitlands village that Amos Bronson Alcott founded his agricultural seminary before transferring it to Harvard. Here poets did not tend cows, nor did philosophers feed pigs. In fact, animal husbandry was forbidden in the institute; the workers specialized in the art of sowing wheat and gathering apples. Alcott justified his attitude with many reasons, some religious, others philosophic and economic. As his wife, Anna, explained in her *Journal:* "Life was given to the animals not to be destroyed by men, but to make them happy, and that they might enjoy life." The Alcotts believed that the consumption of meat tends to corrupt the body, and, by extension, the soul. The Fruitlands kitchen, therefore, never knew the odor of beefsteak or roast lamb. There was to be no fish, no eggs or milk, no butter or cheese, no tea or coffee, no spices or luxury goods of any kind on the table of these new Fathers of the Desert. Fruits, grains, herbs, and roots were the stuff to make men. Similarly, alcoholic beverages were forbidden; spring water only could quench the thirst of these idealists longing for social reforms.

By depriving themselves of all animal substance, the Fruitlanders intended to symbolize their doctrine of a rural economy. Consumption of meat presupposes animal breeding which, in turn, makes man base; he becomes the slave of his beasts. The care they demand devours his own time, and to the Fruitlanders, the ability to use one's hours according to one's own will is the quintessence of true liberty. In Thoreau's *Walden*, too, leisure, not wealth, was the root of happiness.[35] These transcendentalists, however, who fancied themselves endowed with practical aptitudes, threw themselves into some mathematical calculations of a rather fantastic nature: they concluded that if one renounced the eating of beef, one could be nourished from a quarter of the land previously necessary for the subsistence of one individual. They predicted the closing of the "maisons de carnage" (Voltaire's term), the slaughterhouses, "in which so many corpses are sold in order to nourish our own." These calculations, however, did not convince very many other Americans.

The Fruitlands experiment was really an attempt to return to the state of nature. The experimenters tried to realize on earth what Rousseau himself had never considered to be anything more than a theory. If the state of nature ever had existed on earth, he thought, we were too far from those happy days to be able to return to them. Man cannot swim against the current of time, a principle that the enlightened dreamers of Fruitlands did not recognize. Their efforts were as futile as they were heroic. One of them even went so far as to regard clothing as an obstacle to the "return" to the earlier state; it supposedly hampered the movements of the body as well as the soul. The only concession he made to modesty consisted of a light morning jacket. His was not the dogma of Alcott and the majority of their companions, who planted mulberry trees in front of their houses and, thanks to the silkworm, fabricated part of their own garments. It was an essential tenet of their economy that the farm maintain its self-sufficiency, a law also applied at Brook Farm. The experiment of little Sparta, Fruitlands, lasted seven months only. In "Transcendental Wild Oats" Louisa Alcott, Bronson's daughter, describes the rise and fall of the enterprise. Further attempts and failures to establish communities similar to those of Brook Farm and Fruitlands were made in other areas of America. In 1842 the Frenchman Etienne Cabet published his utopian novel *Voyage en Icarie*, the economic principles of which he tried to put into practice in Texas and Illinois. Comparisons could be made with the Anglo-German socialistic Harmony Society communities at Economy, Pennsylvania, and New Harmony, Indiana.

We have seen that complete autarky claimed by most of these innovators in the United States was also a postulate that Rousseau formulated in several works. Such was the rule, especially at the Clarens estate of Julie in the *Nouvelle Héloïse*, where money was scarce but goods plentiful. Rousseau had wished to restrict commerce, at the most, to exchanges of products between neighbors and friends.

He felt that commerce needlessly complicated the economic process, brought about the rule of the machine, and popularized luxury, that is to say, unhappiness. Thoreau's was the most eloquent American voice for these Rousseauean principles.[36] To Thoreau, the farmer who cannot produce all that he requires to assure his subsistance does not organize his existence according to the norms of common sense. "To get his shoestrings he speculates in herds of cattle. With consummate skill he has set his trap with a hair spring to catch comfort and independence, and then, as he turned, got his own leg into it. This is the reason he is poor; and for a similar reason we are all poor in respect to a thousand savage comforts, though surrounded by luxuries."[37] Self-sufficiency was indeed the ideal by which Brook Farm and Fruitlands strove to live. They preferred the theory of the physiocrats to that of the mercantilists; hence, their final goal was to restore to the degenerated *homo economicus* his personal liberty, the inalienable right of man. It was perhaps not necessary that Rousseau advise Americans in this matter, but his doctrine made them conscious of their own, and reminded them of man's essential attributes.

⚜

To trace possible influences of Rousseau's political thought on the American Constitution and on the political ideas of some American writers and philosophers, it is necessary to define some of the key terms of the *Social Contract*. The words *souverain, république, démocratie,* for example, have quite a different meaning in Rousseau's writings from the words "sovereign," "republic," "democracy" in most other eighteenth-century works—as well as in common twentieth-century usage within the sphere of Western civilization. The souverain, for Rousseau, is the people. The people, as far as they incarnate the legislative power of the state, are the only qualified lawmakers. It is the people's inalienable privilege to be the only souverain of their country; should they lose this privilege, they cease to exist as people and become a mere conglomerate of humans.

For practical reasons, however, delegates elected and controlled by the people may, in their behalf, exercise *souveraineté.* A state built upon such a principle Rousseau calls "une république." It follows that "tout gouvernement légitime est républicain," and, clearly enough, Rousseau implies that the king of France, because he and not the people of France was the lawmaker, was usurping the most sacred right of his subjects. They, therefore, did not constitute a people in the political sense of the word: they were nothing more than the inhabitants of France. The French people would be born on the day they assumed their souveraineté, which, symbolically, occurred on the fourteenth of July, 1789.

The executive power, according to Rousseau, may be in the hands of one person, or one group, chosen, in either case, by the citizens—

or the entire people. In other words, a république could be a monarchy, an aristocracy, or a democracy. According to this rather unusual terminology, the United States is a monarchy, the executive power being held by one president elected and controlled by the souverain—the people or their delegates. A démocratie, on the other hand, could not today be found anywhere on this earth because no nation exists in which every member of the souverain—that is, the citizenry—is at the same time minister or secretary of state. Such an ideal government exists only in Utopia. If there were "a people of gods," Rousseau suggests, "it would be democratically ruled."[38] Obviously, the author of the *Social Contract* gives the terms république and démocratie a meaning quite different from that we find in our contemporary lexicons, where republic and democracy are practically synonymous. The following paragraphs, however, must be read with Rousseau's definitions in mind.

To Rousseau, the republican form of state represents the offspring of personal liberty for a man on the verge of becoming a victim of society. Only that form of state can guarantee an individual's independence. A republican constitution, to be sure, may imply submission to a force as subjugating as the arbitrary will of an absolute ruler, since any majority—if one is not part of it—may seem as tyrannical and cruel as the order of a dictator. Quite so. But to advance this argument seriously would be to ignore the importance of the psychological element in the functioning of the state. What is most intolerable to a so-called free man is the power that another individual can exercise over him. The action of a collective of which a man feels himself a part proves to be infinitely more bearable. A republic alone excludes the obedience of one man to another since it places the law equally above all citizens who, by virtue of their general will, created that law.

Rousseau's political doctrine is based on the supremacy of each individual over society, although some concessions to society have to be made. This fundamental principle, which is expounded in works other than the *Social Contract*, is in many ways illustrated by several major American authors, among them Hawthorne. We may recall similarities in plot between *La Nouvelle Héloïse* and the *Scarlet Letter;* in his great novel, the American writer also expresses several aspects of Rousseau's political and social doctrine. Chillingworth is presented as the worst of criminals: his crime is that he is a man without a heart, guided by cold reason, who seeks to exercise a personal and absolute power over his entourage. True republicanism for Hawthorne and Rousseau is derived from an interior attitude: a man who loves his own liberty will respect that of his neighbor's. This personal liberty presupposes a personal responsibility with regard to the community as a whole. The seat of this responsibility is in the conscience of the citizen. And this leads to another postulate of the transcendentalists: the individual's conscience is the most solid foundation for the state.

The idea of slavery is obviously not reconcilable with such points of view. "All men are created free and equal," cried Thoreau, who remains one of the major figures in American anti-slavery thought. He had simply quoted the Bill of Rights. This cry, though, was but an echo of Rousseau, who had insisted, "Man is born free."[39] Thoreau's opposition to the government of Massachusetts for tolerating and protecting slavery clearly demonstrates the analogy of thought between the emancipationists of New England and the philosopher of Geneva. Thoreau's other complaint against his state's government arose from a different matter. For six years the sage of Walden Pond did not pay his taxes. The repeated summons of the law fell upon deaf ears, for the stubborn citizen refused to do his civic duty. The police finally did theirs: Thoreau was arrested. It is hard to decide which to admire more in this tragicomic adventure, the patience of the authorities or the generosity of an aunt with moderate means who paid the bill. Thoreau was not alone in choosing this form of rebellion; Alcott had undergone a similar adventure two years earlier, in 1843.

In his *Resistance to Civil Government* (later entitled *Civil Disobedience*), Thoreau specifies the reasons why he felt compelled to oppose the magistrates of Massachusetts. Rhetoric has its part here just as it does in the *Contrat social*. The vigor of Thoreau's pamphlet later struck Mahatma Gandhi, who read it while in Africa in 1907 and had it printed in *Indian Opinion*, an avant-garde periodical that he edited.[40] Similarities of style aside, Thoreau's text relates to Rousseau's work in many ways. The depositories of executive power, according to the *Contrat*, are not at all the masters of the people, but their officers. The people—and the term here means the nation, the citizens as constituting one people—can at their own will, therefore, establish their officers in their responsibility or deprive them of it. Not only Thoreau, but Walt Whitman has well expressed this opinion. In *Democratic Vistas* (Rousseau, obviously, would say "Republican Vistas") Whitman points out that the President is in the White House only for the citizens.[41] As his biographers have noticed, Whitman had copied whole pages verbatim from the *Contrat*,[42] though nobody has ever demonstrated that Rousseau played a major role in his intellectual evolution. "An American poet," Whitman wrote, "may read Rousseau, but shall never imitate him."[43] F. B. Gummere has, nevertheless, indicated similarities between the social and political theories of both writers.[44]

On the question of civil liberties, the resemblance between Rousseau's and Thoreau's reasoning is most striking. Thoreau writes: "The government itself, which is only the mode which the people have chosen to execute their will, is equally liable to be abused and perverted before the people can act through it." Since the government

of his state was corrupt, Thoreau thought himself justified in taking
the initiative: "I ask for, not at once no government, but *at once* a better government. Let every man make known what kind of government
would command his respect, and that will be one step toward obtaining it."[45] And if his petition had to encounter the resistance of political authorities, he would not recoil even from using force. "All men,"
Thoreau states, "recognize the right of revolution: that is, the right
to refuse allegiance to and resist the government, when its tyranny
or its inefficiency are great and unendurable."[46] These are certainly
opinions that could emanate from the *Contrat social*. Citizens, according to Rousseau, are to be convoked in an assembly periodically. They
are to be invited first to answer questions that are not merely formal:
"If it please the sovereign—i.e. the people—to conserve the present
form of government. . . . If it please the people to leave its administration to those who are currently charged with it."[47] Thoreau is clearly
in agreement with Rousseau, although he does not formally recognize
him as the source of his own beliefs.[48]

These considerations show that in most cases the problem of
Rousseau's actual influence on American social, political, and intellectual life cannot be satisfactorily solved. Major links will always be
missing in the demonstration. When the problem is restricted to that
of cultural similarities, however, the study of Rousseau and American
thought yields overwhelming proofs of close analogies and strong
affinities.

≫≪

A long series of monographs could be written to trace Rousseau's
doctrine in American works. But to give them substance, one would
have to assume that all "Rousseauean" ideas in America were
engendered by Rousseau rather than by his favorite English authors,
especially Locke. "Rousseau in North American Thought" remains
somehow a puzzling subject. Hawthorne's *The Scarlet Letter* presents
a plot, as we have seen, and Thoreau's *Walden* reveals a mood, recall-
ing specific works of Rousseau's. James Fenimore Cooper, Washington Irving, William Cullen Bryant share beliefs or attitudes with
Rousseau. These resemblances, however, cannot be based on direct
influences. American criticism, too, was concerned with Rousseau's
doctrine. Scores of American scholars have written articles and
books on his life and thought, from James Russell Lowell's essay
"Rousseau and the Sentimentalists" to Irving Babbitt's *Rousseau and
Romanticism*.

Rousseau found a spiritual home in America. He knew how to crystallize more convincingly and surely than anyone else the profound
tendencies of primitivism and democracy on both sides of the Atlantic. If we consider him the representative of a particular set of
ideas, it is not because he invented them, but because he expressed

them in the most effective manner. He was the putative father of certain political, pedagogical, and religious theories, and in this role he became a symbol. Even before Rousseau was born, the ideas he is still said to have invented—or at least a large number of them—were widely dispersed over two continents, as an immanent philosophy. Rousseau's optimisitc confidence in man, as exemplified in his republican conception of the state, and his cult of childhood and nature, were all the more easily integrated into the spiritual heritage of the newborn nation, as the seeds of such ideas were already planted in the American soil. The works of Rousseau came to America at an optimum time for figuring strongly in the particular direction of the nation's growth.

If the first category of comparatistic inquiry, that of literary relations, consisted only of the study of neatly traceable influences without comprising also questions of cultural immanence, most of the facts expounded in this chapter would seem irrelevant to the discipline and most of the thoughts vain and futile. At the risk of sounding repetitious, we should here, once more, be reminded of one of the major objectives of comparative literature: the analysis of affinities and resemblances, common sources, and similar repercussions throughout territories broken up into linguistic segments. Such analyses reveal the artificiality of literary studies pursued exclusively with one particular national tradition in mind.

It is impossible, of course, for questions of analogy to receive scientifically accurate answers. Only a few problems of cultural relations—as we have suggested—can be solved with certitude, and what is then most frequently demonstrated is that real influence was improbable or unlikely. The question, for example, of whether Rousseau's thought directly influenced the Declaration of Independence, the Articles of Confederation, or the Constitution can be rather safely answered in the negative. If Rousseau, instead of taking the trouble to write the two *Discours* and the *Contrat social,* had spent an uneventful, quiet life in his hometown, a life of which he so often dreamed—repairing watches and clocks in his father's shop—probably not one single iota would be missing from the *American State Papers* today. But if he had ever drafted a constitution for the settlers of America, drawing on the ideas in his published works—as he had actually done for his Corsican and Polish friends—an unknowing reader of such a draft would be inclined to believe its author an intellectual ancestor of the United States, if not one of its Founding Fathers. The comparative study of literature and of civilization in general leads to conclusions concerning the basic cultural unity of vast areas of our globe.

Russia in French Letters: Milestones of a Discovery

THE complete history of the cultural relations between France and Russia has not yet been written, probably because such an extraordinarily complex enterprise intimidates modern scholars. Even if a courageous author tried to tackle part of the project by limiting himself solely to literary phenomena, he would be forced to touch upon such diverse domains as the fine arts, philosophy, and politics as well as history and diplomacy, sociology, economy, and ethnology. He would suddenly discover that he was confronted not merely with two states but with two worlds, two universes.

In many respects, the problem posed by international cultural exchanges among European nations other than the Slavic countries is simpler: a sort of intellectual kinship ties them together. Constant interchanges between the literature of France and Italy, France and Spain, France and England, and later—since about 1760—between France and Germany have taken place for centuries. In fact, a cultural community, though temporarily disturbed by the rise of absolutism and nationalism, has existed in western Europe since the Middle Ages. The situation, however, is quite different in some areas of the Continent that never belonged to the Holy Roman Empire, and until very recently the peoples of eastern Europe have been almost totally excluded from the general confederation of occidental letters. Traditionally, these peoples constituted a Pan-Slavic system of cultural relations in which Church Slavonic served as catalyst. When Parisian interest in works emanating from beyond the Channel or the Rhine was at its peak, there were still no Russian authors capable of appealing to even the most modest reading public in the West. Until 1750 or 1775, the period in which Anglomania was attaining its apogee in France, no significant Russian work had been translated into any language of western Europe. By contrast, translations of major English books had already entered the French metropolis by 1600, or shortly thereafter. In the course of the seventeenth century, Paris became acquainted with Sidney's *Arcadia* (1624), More's *Utopia* (1643), Hobbes' *De Cive* (1649), Locke's *Thoughts concerning Education* (1695), his *Reasonableness of Christianity* (1696), and his *Essay Concerning Human Understanding* (1700). Though few besides those in the court circle and some philosophers took any great interest in what happened on the British political scene, at least names pertaining to the sphere of general culture were familiar even to Frenchmen who did not belong to the upper crust of society.

During the eighteenth century the writings of Shaftesbury, Addison, Pope, Swift, Milton, and Collins were eagerly read in the French capital. Whole libraries of books dealing with the English streamed from the presses, books such as Béat de Muralt's *Les Lettres sur les Anglais et les Français* and Voltaire's *Les Lettres philosophiques*, while *Clarissa* was being devoured by avid readers in the adaptation of Abbé Prévost.

It was also during the eighteenth century that the French made their first acquaintance with Russian writings. One of the earliest French translations from the Russian was the *Satyres du Prince Cantemir*, made in 1749 by the Abbé Octavien Guasco. A few studies on Russian works also appeared in several eighteenth-century French periodicals. Thus Karamzin, in November, 1797, published in the *Spectateur du Nord* an article entitled "Un mot sur la littérature russe" [A word on Russian literature]. Although it is chiefly devoted to a summary of his own *Letters of a Russian Traveler*, Karamzin's essay also discusses the epic tradition of his homeland and describes, among other medievel poems, *The Lay of the Host of Igor*. All these efforts were, however, but feeble beginnings of the Russian impact on French literature.

Little by little, more Russian publications trickled into France and, on occasion, made some reputation. Vladimir Boutchik has listed fifteen Russian works that appeared in France up to the eve of the French Revolution.[1] Though his list is admittedly incomplete, it is minuscule compared with the hundreds of English works published in translation in Paris. The quality of the Russian works, moreover, whether they amounted to fifteen or fifty volumes, could not possibly, on the whole, be ranked—according to French criteria—with the translated English masterpieces.[2]

France, of course, was not the only Western nation to experience the spread, however slow, of Russian culture. England[3] and also Germany, which was geographically closer to the Slavic world, felt its influence in many ways. Halle—not to speak of Dorpat—was one of the capitals of German Slavophiles, while in Leipzig Gottsched and his friends eagerly studied Lomonosov and Cantemir.[4] Klinger published widely on educational problems as seen by the Moscovites, and Lenz, with his *Der falsche Dimitri*, was a forerunner of Schiller, who was also tempted by the Dimitri story and treated it in an unfinished play. Russian themes abound in the works of Kotzebue and August Lafontaine. Such is the critical and historical context in which Franco-Russian literary relations should be analyzed.

While the preceding chapter was mainly concerned with literary and philosophical analogies and affinities, with a common historical and ethnical background explaining, partly at least, cultural similarities, the present pages belong to another kind of relation studies. They will treat problems of reception, mediation, and influence in an almost positivistic sense. An extended series of narrowly circumscribed topics could, of course, be developed within the overall area of Franco-Russian relations, topics such as Mérimée's, Flaubert's and Gide's reaction to or borrowings from specific Russian works, or Turgenev's, Dostoevski's, and Tolstoy's understanding of French literature. It is more useful, more to our purpose here, however, to discuss a broader problem and to undertake a study of two French intermediaries and interpreters of Russian culture and of Russian literature, Madame de Staël and the Vicomte de Vogüé. This necessarily rather short analysis will be preceded by a loosely chronological survey of earlier intellectual encounters between the two nations.

I

It is well known that the curiosity of the Parisian is inevitably thrilled by the novel. Montesquieu perfectly illustrated the average Frenchman's eagerness to be astonished when Rica, a character of the *Lettres persanes*, comes to Paris and hears a murmur of surprise in the crowd: "Comment peut-on être Persan?" Similarly, when Count Peter Orlov ate eggs, shells and all, in the best salons of Paris —a feat that won him many invitations—the hostesses of the soirées at which he performed had good reason to wonder, or perhaps to exclaim in comparable bewilderment: "How can one be Russian!" In the eighteenth century, French curiosity about the Slavic world belonged to the history of exoticism: cultivated Parisians considered Muscovite or Siamese, Chinese or Peruvian, Ukrainian or Indian, each as quaint and foreign as the other. In the minds of most Frenchmen of that period, all these races were mingled; they existed merely as the subject matters of picturesque tales passed on by travelers, sometimes with a basis in fact, sometimes without. They were the gossamer creatures of distant and, thereby, unreal countries, furnishing incomplete and contradictory data upon which the restless and lively spirits of the Parisians might embroider their own fancy and illusions.

Sometimes, in the realm of literature, nothing more than this embroidery remained. Many Frenchmen who referred to Russia did so in a manner hardly more clear, detailed, and convincing than that adopted by theologians in discussions of Limbo. Their ignorance joined company with the traditional fear of the East, of the Turks and Mongols, and of the awful and foreboding shadow of some Genghis Khan. From time to time a historian would become fascinated by Peter the Great or Ivan the Terrible.

The reality of Russia was revealed to the majority of the French nation only by the flames of Moscow, the ice of the Berezina, the defeat of Napoleon. The *grande armée* retreating over the Rhine after Leipzig shocked the First Empire out of its misconceptions, and the French peasant lad, taking off his threadbare uniform in order to take up his plow again, looked back in horror to the strange blackness of the Russian soil, the famous *chernozem*, an earth he was only too glad not to have enriched further with his own body. It was inevitable that with the clash of French and Russian armies, mutual influences were bound to develop; yet it was only later in the nineteenth and in the twentieth century that Russian literature was truly revealed to French authors. Even today there are occasions in which French writers treat Russia in a manner best described as dreamlike and faraway. In the eighteenth century, only a few serious and intuitive minds foresaw the existence of the great cultural, political, economic, and military force that was to come from beyond the Vistula, the Dvina, and the Dniester.

The first concern of the historian of literary interchange between France and Russia should be the study of diplomatic relations, since in both countries culture most of the time has depended strongly on political developments. In the early Middle Ages, all of eastern Europe remained *terra incognita* for France in every sense. In 1051, however, Henry the First married the fair Anna, daughter of Yaroslav, Grand Duke of Kiev; this event marked the modest beginning of the friendship between the two nations, which, it should be noted, was never completely broken for any significant length of time, except under Napoleon I and Napoleon III.

Early French visitors to Russia gave absolutely no thought to its language. An adventurer named Margeret, who lived at the end of the fifteenth century, is said to have been the first Frenchman to learn the Russian tongue. Later, especially from the second half of the eighteenth century, quite a few travelers, gifted reporters, and talented historians like Masson, Levesques, Leclerc, and Lescallier, evidently understood the idiom of the land that they saw and described. Their example, however, is not characteristic. A profound indifference toward the Russian language can be noticed not only among the high society of Paris, but also in the small group of Frenchmen who crossed the Niemen and the Dniester, including the diplomatic representatives to Saint Petersburg. This indifference is perfectly understandable, since it was well known in Paris that many upper-class Russians did not speak the language of their own country and that every Frenchman is, of course, of the upper class by birth. Count Andrault de Langeron spent thirty years in Russia, and although he learned some rudiments of Russian, he did not speak it except with his dog, French being the language of the noblesse, whether Russian or French. The general ascendancy of the French language and the non-existence, in the mind of the French, of a Russian cultural world are illustrated in Comte de Rivarol's celebrated *Discours sur l'universalité de la langue française* [Discourse on the universality of the French language] (1784) which includes remarks on each European culture, with the exception of the Slavic.

Authors more famous than Rivarol, however, spoke to the French people about the country of the czars. As early as 1731 Voltaire's *Histoire de Charles XII* attracted European attention to the empire of Peter the Great, against which the heroic career of Charles XII, King of Sweden, had come to an end. Later, Catherine II encouraged Voltaire to write a historical work on her country. His *Histoire de Russie sous Pierre le Grand* [History of Russia under Peter the Great] was published in 1759. From that point on, interest in anything Russian grew significantly in France—an interest that was to be transformed into empirical knowledge only after Madame de Staël's journey to Russia after 1813.

The list of noted Frenchmen of the ancien régime who visited Saint Petersburg (few among them saw more of Russia than the capital) is relatively short, though impressive: among them were writers and philosophes, like Diderot and Grimm, Bernardin de Saint-Pierre, the Prince de Ligne, and Sénac de Meilhan; painters and sculptors, Le Lorrain and Madame Vigée-Lebrun, Gillet and Falconet. Some less distinguished personalities accompanied these notables, and posts as preceptors and secretaries were given to scores of Frenchmen at the Russian court and in noble families.[5] As a result, numbers of French nationals contributed most efficaciously to the penetration of French culture into Slavic territories. Upon their return, these visitors popularized Slavic culture in France.

The attitude of the Frenchmen who managed to make their way into Russia was too often one of disappointment. They seemed to be unhappy at not finding their own beloved France in this foreign country; they felt tricked and deceived. For centuries they had strolled across Europe with the nostalgia, the "mal du pays" of a

Comte d'Erfeuil, a character in Madame de Staël's *Corinne*, totally infatuated with *patrie*. Sometimes they not only lost their Parisian polish, but forgot all their education. Bernardin de Saint-Pierre exemplifies this occasional lack of politeness toward his hosts. In 1762, as a man of twenty-five, he dreamed of establishing a society of ideologues on the shores of the Aral Sea, a society of idealists who might have been the predecessors of the "Fruitlanders" and "Brookfarmers" of a later epoch and from another continent.[6] After his departure, he composed some *Observations on Russia*, which reveal his most unflattering opinions of the Slavs.[7] They were "inconstant, jealous, deceitful, and gross, respecting only what they feared"—a far from exhaustive catalog of insults which the ungrateful guest invented. For this utopian, the Russians epitomized all the wickedness of the human race. The views of the author of *Paul et Virginie* and those of the author of the *Discourse on Inequality* are strangely complementary. To the west of France, Rousseau finds the *noble savage*, his friend Bernardin de Saint-Pierre encounters, to the east, the *ignoble savage*.

One personage, however, inspired general enthusiasm in France: Catherine the Great. She represented more than a royal figure; she incarnated Russia for a large number of visitors to her realm, notably for Diderot. "I saw scarcely anything but the sovereign," he declared to Madame Necker, the mother of little Germaine—later Madame de Staël—who was not yet dreaming of the grand sight-seeing tour she would undertake forty years later across the immense Russian plains.

II

It would be wrong to bestow upon Madame de Staël the honor of having been the first to formulate a valid judgment on Russia, to have *discovered* it. Some excellent travel reports and stories as well as many essays existed before her famous account, *Dix années d'exil* (*Ten Years of Exile*).[8] However, she occupies a unique position as an intermediary between the Russian world and France, first because of her personality; secondly, because of the quality of her observations; and finally because of the boundless though not blind sympathy —noticed by Pushkin—that she brought to her study of the Slavic people.[9] Many Russians knew her either personally or through correspondence.[10]

The various travel books just alluded to were not in any sense the major sources upon which Madame de Staël drew for her own work: she studied Russia *in vivo*, not *ex libris*. She took notes along the way just as the foreign correspondents of newspapers in our own day. Her remarks were written on the spot in a notebook, a *Carnet de route*,[11] which she later had at her disposal while composing the first draft of *Dix années d'exil*. The book was first printed in 1821, four

years after her death. She never considered her remarks on Russia
to have any definitive character, based as they were on records and
sketches, which she never re-examined, and not on secondary materials, which she hardly ever consulted. She wrote from experience
and intuition. The stylistic gaps, errors of composition, and even
weaknesses of interpretation make evident the author's spontaneity
and sincerity.

In all of her literary output, Madame de Staël had been inclined
to describe her characters in terms of their typical national temper:
in *Delphine*, the French, in *Corinne; ou, l'Italie* the English and the
Italian, and in *De l'Allemagne*, the German. Now she turned her attention to the Slavic realm. As one of the first champions of sociology
and ethnic psychology in literature, she attempted to reveal the
Russian soul in the second part of *Dix années d'exil*—the first part
recounting the trials she had to undergo by order of the emperor of
the French.

It was difficult for Madame de Staël to maintain scientific objec-
tivity in the face of a despotic ruler. She had incurred the displeasure
of Napoleon when he was still only Bonaparte; he had no reason to
forgive her cosmopolitan—ergo anti-French—attitudes when he became emperor. Besides, Napoleon had always considered the empire
of the czars a menace to his regime, a danger vague and imminent
by turns. Many of the judgments displayed in *Dix années d'exil* reveal
the hatred the author felt for the usurper of the throne of France. It
was for having dealt objectively with Germany in *De l'Allemagne*, at
least as objectively as a woman of the early nineteenth century
could, that she was driven into exile. She avenged herself by rendering justice to Russia, just as she had already done, in *Corinne*, to Italy.
The same attitude inspired her to praise the English in eulogies that
energetically contrasted the deceit of the dictatorial Corsican with
the admirable uprightness and inviolable fidelity manifested by the
English. Yet the attacks of the exiled author were never aimed at
the nation to which she remained unshakably attached. This outcry
comes directly from her heart: "Can a foreign tyrant reduce me to
hoping for the defeat of the French?" But only the defeat of the
French could bring about Napoleon's. She remained in Russia, as she
had been in England, Italy, Germany, Austria, and Switzerland, the
ambassadress of French culture, and everywhere she was known as
the enemy of the man who lorded over France; she attested to the
idea that authentic patriotism ought to be enlightened by cosmopolitanism.

In the second section of *Dix années d'exil*, the section dealing with
her Russian experience, Madame de Staël first speaks of the different
aspects of the country she saw: of the Russian landscape, which impressed her by its monotony; of the Russian people, who depressed
her by their melancholy. But these people, though primitive, or be-

cause they are primitive, are good, hospitable, and masters of their own future. However, when she comes to allude to the cultural life of Russia, she can hardly express an optimistic opinion, even in Saint Petersburg: the frozen Neva does not bring back memories of Paris to her mind.

Not only did Madame de Staël ever read a Russian work in the original, but she probably did not even know any such work through the intermediary of a translation. Very few translations would at any rate have been available before her journey in 1812. Russia, she felt, was a new country; neither France nor the nine Muses had so far discovered it. A certain instability, the heritage of a nomadic past, she suggests, has prevented the Russians from fully participating in Western culture, which in 1812 was still the only true culture for almost every European. A certain disorder of the imagination kept the Slav from finding "happiness in duration," as she puts it. Led more by impulses and excesses of feeling than reflection, not really suited to meditation, the *homo slavicus* had produced hardly any literary works worthy of comparison with those of the other great European countries. He had not been made famous by "the fine arts or poetry." And if he had any intention of gaining celebrity in these fields, he was frustrated in his efforts because he had begun "to imitate French literature" rather than to rely upon the genius of his people and upon his own language.[12]

On many occasions Madame de Staël praised the Russian language that she regretted not to have had an opportunity to learn: "It is uniquely resounding," she writes. "I would say that it possesses a quality almost metallic in nature; one hears brass striking brass when the Russians pronounce certain letters."[13] Elsewhere she insisted on the sweetness and the brilliance of the sound of their language, qualities noted by precisely those who do not understand it; she considered it very suitable for music and poetry.[14]

Sometimes Madame de Staël was tempted to conclude from the Russian's noble physical appearance that he was predestined to become a promoter of the arts. She also suggested that his beard added to the religious expression of his facial features and created an impression of venerability.[15] But it was in vain, it seemed to her, that the Russian language was harmonious and the Russian beard most respectable: "Poetry, eloquence, and literature," she insists, "are not to be found in Russia." And again, in her *Carnet de route*, she notices that ". . . obligingness characterizes the Russians, but not sensibility or profundity,"[16] while in the account of her exile she writes: "They are more capable of superstition than of emotion."[17] The Russians did not seem prepared for aesthetics as understood by the French.

Several decades later, the historian Charles-François Masson goes so far as to maintain: "It is not in Russia that one must seek out *Julies* in love with *Saint-Preux*, and still less Julies who have married

Wolmar. . . . The country of slavery is certainly not that of fine passions; one would have difficulty in finding matter for a novel there."[18]
Masson condemned, while Madame de Staël arose as an advocate for a
client who was certainly not without fault, but who had only committed and still was committing the sins of youth. She reminded the
French that they had sinned as much in earlier periods of their history. In *Dix années d'exil* she testified to having seen in Russia men
who were extremely advanced in the sciences as well as belles lettres,
even though she admitted that they were still few in number. According to her, the character of the Russians was too violent, too passionate (and she opposed passion to sentiment) to prize thoughts that
were at all abstract; this people had not yet had the time to develop
the taste for converting particulars to general ideas.

Madame de Staël seems to have happened on the Russians during
a period of growing pains. Her observations made her think the
Russians would produce geniuses in fine arts and literature at some
future date when they would be able to bring their true talents to
bear upon these pursuits. She was firmly convinced that the *nation*
must make literature, and that the *soul* of the people must be expressed in this literature: "It is always among the people that we
must search for the sap of the national genius."[19] Even before visiting
Russia, Madame de Staël proved herself an apologist for the Russian
people; while traveling in Germany she observed: "The civilization
of the Slavs [she uses the word *Esclavons*] has been more modern
and more hurried than that of other nations; we see in them till now
imitation rather than originality: what there is of the European in
them is French; what they possess of the Asiatic is too little developed
for their writers to be able to manifest the true character which
would be natural to them."[20] After seeing Russia at firsthand, she
predicted that it would produce a great literature as soon as its
writers drew their inspiration from what was "most intimate at
the bottom of their souls," when they grew accustomed to speaking
from the depths of *their heart* and *their spirit*. These sentiments are
only variations on one of her major themes: "Be Russian in your
souls"; and, in fact, the success of Pushkin, Gogol, Tolstoy, Dostoevski, Turgenev is based on this principle.[21]

For Madame de Staël, the immense Russian Empire was marked
by the most violent contrasts, both of peoples and of landscape. To
her, its regions resembled the plays of Shakespeare as seen by Voltaire: "All that is not a fault is sublime and all that is not sublime is
a fault."[22] "Gigantesque" was the term she used in her notebook.[23]
And she employed the word again in *Dix années d'exil:* "What characterizes this people is something *gigantesque* in every respect:
ordinary dimensions are not applicable to it at all. I do not mean that
true greatness and stability are not to be encountered there, but
boldness and imagination among the Russians know no limits; with

them everything is colossal rather than proportioned, audacious rather than cerebral, and if the goal is not attained, it is because it is surpassed."[24] She believed that after a few more years the hubris of the Russian nation would be mastered by a sense of harmony; exaggeration would tend toward a certain equilibrium, and exuberance would become a kind of symmetry. Madame de Staël traveled to Russia too early to witness these new developments. She died (in 1817) twenty years before Pushkin, and fifty years before the publication of *War and Peace* and *Crime and Punishment*. Russian artistic achievements, therefore, could not be among her major concerns.

III

The discovery of Russia by western Europe is one of the last chapters in the history of international cultural relations. Some of the reasons that help explain this long delay have already been mentioned: Russia was not thought of as really picturesque in its totality, nor was its climate considered hospitable. Further, it had no tradition represented by a so-called high society, either wealthy or cultivated. And if Russia had a culture, it was expressed in a language that, it was generally believed, could not be put in direct relationship with any language spoken in the occidental part of Europe. The Russian alphabet alone created an obstacle to communication. It is true that many western men of letters knew Greek—all of them knew Latin and some Hebrew as well—and theoretically they should have been able to master the Russian as speedily as any other European idiom. But he who has the gift of tongues does not necessarily have the taste for travel. The curiosity of the seventeenth century was directed toward classical antiquity rather than barbaric mystery. In the eighteenth century, attitudes slowly started to change, and the nineteenth saw the ultimate triumph of the northern and eastern countries. After England and Scotland, after Germany and Scandinavia, Russia and the other Slavic nations sooner or later had to join in the general market of literary exchange.

In the post-Napoleonic era of the Holy Alliance (1815–1854), the number of descriptions of voyages to Russia and critical studies on Russian matters increased significantly. It was then that Russian letters found their first admirers in western Europe, among them many Frenchmen: Dupré de Saint-Maur, Ancelot, Custine, Dumas, Gautier, Prosper Mérimée and his brother Henri. Russia also made its entry into fiction. The characters of *Adolphe* (1806), it is true, do not cross the Russian border; the final scenes take place in a Polish mansion. But works other than Constant's hinted more clearly at the fashion to come, such as Madame Cottin's *Elisabeth ou les exilés de Sibérie* (1802), and Xavier de Maistre's *Les Prisonniers du Caucase*, as well as his *La Jeune Sibérienne* (both in 1825). His elder brother, Joseph, wrote *Les Soirées de Saint-Pétersbourg,* which was philosophical in nature; it appeared posthumously in 1821. Many examples followed, and were quite frequent by the time Comte de Gobineau, in 1876, tried to recreate a Slavic climate in his *Danseuse de Chamaka,* an episode of his *Nouvelles asiatiques.* Jules Verne wrote *Michel Strogoff* (1880) and Georges Ohnet *Serge Panina* (1881).

None of these authors, however, sought any inspiration from Russian writers, whose techniques, themes, and literary ideals could not retain their attention. The host of French romanticists and realists took little or no interest in what was happening in the European Far East. Neither Hugo nor Stendhal wished to stage their creative dreams with a Russian background. In the works just cited the Slavic framework furnished only a little local color or atmosphere. They do not reflect any serious concern with the Russian people or with their literary life. Nor does the creation of a chair of Slavic literatures in the Collège de France in 1840 correspond to a general interest; the chair was evidently designed only to encourage philological specialists, and the innovation by no means met an intellectual need on the part of the cultural and critical elite. Even Balzac could not see any literary promises in the Russian world. The author of the *Comédie humaine* used to profess a sovereign scorn for literatures other than French. In *Le Cousin Pons,* published in 1847, he even suggested that in higher education the occult sciences should take preference over Slavic studies. "It is singular," he complains, "that at the moment when there are created at Paris chairs in Slavic, in Manchu, and in literatures so little *teachable* as the literatures of the North, which instead of furnishing us with lessons should receive them . . . that there should not be reinstituted under the name of anthropology, instruction of occult philosophy, one of the glories of the University in the past."[25] Nowadays the reader cannot consider these remarks without smiling, especially if he remembers that the first professor holding that chair was the great Polish poet Adam Mickiewicz, a fellow citizen of Balzac's future wife, Madame Hanska. In Germany, interestingly enough, the tradition of university chairs in Slavic languages (Dorpat, Halle) goes back to the last quarter of the eighteenth century.

The degree to which literature transcends national concerns depends on several variables, including the military and diplomatic. Bismarck, especially at the time of the *Dreikaiserbund* (League of the Three Emperors, 1873–1878), efficiently promoted the penetration of the works of Pushkin, Gogol, Turgenev, Dostoevski, and Tolstoy into western Europe. The French Republic, not being a member of the league, actively sought a rapprochement with Russia—which culminated in the Franco–Russian alliance of 1893. As the nineteenth century progressed, interest in Russian literature spread more and more rapidly throughout western Europe. France's interest is verified in many ways. Among the first popular French translations of Russian works are Gogol's *Taras Bulba* and Pushkin's *The Captain's Daughter*, published in 1835 and 1836 respectively. Some sixty years later, Tolstoy's *Kreutzer Sonata* was read in almost every country of occidental tradition.[26] By then Turgenev and Dostoevski had begun to reach the French elite as well. Russian works became international by diffusion, but also by means of the direct, personal relationships that their authors cultivated beyond the border of their homeland. Their names appeared more frequently in the press, and journals published many articles on the characteristics of their literary output. These trends may be observed in such French periodicals as the *Revue des Deux Mondes*, the *Mercure de France*, the *Nouvelle revue française*, the *Revue bleue*, the *Revue encyclopédique*, and even the *Revue britannique*. Germany illustrates the same process with *Das Magazin, Unsere Zeit, Die deutsche Rundschau*, and *Die Gegenwart*, while in England this critical Russophilia found famous vehicles to continue a tradition already established in the *Foreign Review Quarterly, Edinburgh Review, Quarterly Review*, and *Blackwood's Magazine*.

Anthologies of Russian authors were also offered to the attention of the public. The first famous example in France was the *Anthologie russe* of Dupré de Saint-Maur, published in 1823. The best-known German anthology was edited in 1820 by Karl Friedrich von der Borg: *Poetische Erzeugnisse der Russen*. Significantly, the volumes of the well-known English publication *Russian Anthology*, by Sir John Bowring, were published from 1820 to 1823. These dates illustrate a unity of literary concerns and tastes in at least three major West European countries at a specific period of time. Similar books continued to prosper, especially during the last quarter of the nineteenth century, years in which an intelligent criticism of Russian works finally arose.

IV

Some critics select Prosper Mérimée as the first Frenchman to understand Russia correctly; he spoke the tongue of the country, translated quite a few works, and, therefore, seemed best prepared to fathom the spirit of the people. Those who place Mérimée in this role consider Eugène Melchior Vicomte de Vogüé,[27] whose creative works hardly survive, a follower, or perhaps an imitator, of his more famous compatriot. The true French discoverer of Russian literature, nonetheless, was Vogüé, rather than Mérimée. Though Mérimée has unquestionable distinction, it was not possible for him to have made the discovery he is sometimes credited with, and this for a sound reason: at the time Russia captivated his interests, Russian literature, if we understand by literature poetry and prose fiction of standards comparable with those of western Europe, did not yet exist. Certainly, poets, novelists, and even critics had appeared, but the combined total of their books did not form a whole, did not constitute a literary corpus. A tradition had begun, but it was not yet felt as such. There had been, to begin with, Cantemir, Karamzin, Trediakovsky, Lomonosov, Derzhavin, and Sumarokov. In spite of the amiable letters that this last author sent to Voltaire,[28] and the sole reply that has been preserved, and in spite of certain salon relationships cultivated by the first two, these men were puppet figures. They left no durable work in their lifetime that was valued on the international plane. Lomonsov himself, rightly considered great within the borders of his own country, did not transcend them, although he did not remain completely unknown outside of the Russian cultural sphere. While Mérimée also knew writers like Gogol and Pushkin, and, perhaps best of all, Turgenev, he could not recognize their merit. Vogüé, on the contrary, fully realized their importance for the development of European literature.

One further difference exists between Mérimée's and Vogüé's criticism. Mérimée did not leave a systematic work dealing with Russian letters in any appreciable degree of breadth and depth; his preoccupations and methods were rather those of a historian or of a philosopher. Vogüé, however, was primarily concerned with presenting a survey of Franco-Russian literary affinities. He drew the first literary map of Russia, which was obviously a major contribution to the general knowledge of European culture. Understandably, of course, this first map does not offer absolute completeness and accuracy.

Vogüé was ambassador to Saint Petersburg, where he learned Russian and married Alexandra Annenkova, a lady in waiting to the Czarina. His volume Le Roman russe (1886), the result of careful and constant readings and reflections, had first appeared in the form of six articles in the Revue des Deux Mondes.[29] After transforming them and after maturely reconsidering his interpretations, he published them as chapters of his book—which is much more than a composite juxtaposition of fragments or an output of bits and pieces. Le Roman russe is an organic creation, a work structured with a solid architectural conception. Vogüé attempts to embrace the nature of Russian literature in its totality and to explain and evaluate it.[30] Here we are no longer concerned with a sort of historical patchwork touching upon a cultural territory that had scarcely been explored and in no way exploited. Vogüé deals with fundamental questions. Is there a Russian literature? If so, is this literature essentially different from other national literatures? In what particular ways may it be distinguished from these literatures? What are its peculiar excellences? What is the Russian contribution to the patrimony of the Occident, or, quite simply, of our globe? Both by his manner of posing the problems and of treating them, Vogüé is a comparatist in the contemporary sense of the term.

Vogüé's criticism would furnish ample matter for a monograph of its own, and there can be no question of undertaking here a detailed

analysis of the book, or of pronouncing a verdict on particular problems dealt with in it. Posterity has not failed to point at misinterpre-
tations and, in some instances, to a narrowness of judgment. Gide,
for example, has sufficiently indicated Vogüé's transient failure to
comprehend Dostoevski; the two critics were the least made to
understand one another. Ironically, posterity has not been any more
tolerant of Gide's own weak sides in the treatment of the Russian
master in *Dostoïevsky d'après sa Correspondance* (1908) and *Dostoïevsky* (1923).[31]

It is difficult to object to Gide's denunciation of certain short-
comings in *Le Roman russe*, although it is tempting to add that the
twenty years that intervened between Vogüé and Gide offered the
latter a patently superior perspective on the Russian scene. What
strikes today's reader is the surprising validity of many of Vogüé's
judgments, surprising in that his admittedly personal tone and his
nearness in time to the writers treated hardly vitiate his insight, as
might be expected. The transitory and superficial aspects of his
criticism have been noted, scored, and then forgotten; the permanent
elements capture our attention all the more.

A great number of Vogüé's observations stem from ethnopsychol-
ogy as revealed by the most authentic interpreters of a people's
thoughts and feelings: the novelists themselves. He is one of the first
Frenchmen to create a psychological portrait of the Russians, of this
people whose genius consists in contemplating the invisible and
attempting to express the ineffable. *Le Roman russe* conveyed to the
French the religion of suffering, universal compassion, theoretical
and practical pessimism, philosophic nihilism, and the sense of the
mystique of a whole nation. Vogüé could grasp the feeling of Russian
poetry; he could understand the novels, which appeared to be the
first epics of a people. For years he had devoted himself to studying
books—celebrated in Saint Petersburg, and unknown in Paris—
which throbbed with an exceptionally intense interior life. His predecessors observed customs and mores, institutions and life habits.
Whereas they saw mainly decor and local color, Vogüé detected the
psyche of the Slavs hidden under bright or dull exteriors. With his
criticism, the annals of Russian letters cease to be merely a chapter
in the history of exoticism in France.

Quite another chapter of the history of Russian influence had already begun when the great Russian novelists started traveling in
Western Europe. While Vogüé wrote not only under new factual but
under new psychological conditions, since literary contacts were
already established between the two countries, Turgenev occupied a
regular seat in the meetings at the Goncourt brothers. He was acquainted with Flaubert and George Sand; he knew Mérimée, Zola,
Bourget, Maupassant, and Huysmans personally. Tolstoy also left
Russia, first in 1857, then in 1860 and again in 1861; Dostoevski lived

abroad from 1867 to 1871. Both returned to Russia more Russian than ever, as did many of their compatriots at the termination of their *Wanderjahre*. The true influence of the Russian triumvirs upon West European literature was only to be felt after years of waiting, while their direct connections with French authors partly explain why Vogüé's criticism of their work enjoyed an immediate success in Paris.

⤲⤳

Vogüé's main ideas about Russian literature are not difficult to define. First he confirms Madame de Staël's predictions; Russian literature was great the very instant it took root in the Russian soil, when it ceased to be a literature of borrowings. If Western works circulated freely in the territory of an intellectual common market, it was because they were the crop of a common literary ground. Linguistic differences did not outweigh the cultural congeniality among most Western nations. Russia, conversely, was either held apart, or held itself apart from the rest of Europe. The reasons for this segregation were not purely political, geographical, or historical. More fundamental factors, of an aesthetic and philosophic order, were involved; they were related to a *Weltanschauung* and a *Weltinterpretation*.

This world was expressed in a language unique in sound and structure. "The Russian poets," Vogüé concludes, "are not, and never will be translated. A lyric poem is a living being, living a furtive life which resides in the arrangement of words; we cannot transport this life into a foreign body. Some time ago, I read a Russian translation of Musset's *Nuits*, which was extremely exact and suitable; this gave the same pleasure as the cadaver of a lovely woman; the soul has flown, the aroma which is the essence of the quality of these divine syllables. The problem is even more insoluble when the exchange is carried out from the most poetic language of Europe to the least poetic of continental idioms. Certain verses of Pushkin and Lermontov are among the most beautiful poetry in the world; there remains of them only a pale scrap of prose containing a banal thought after the negative alchemy of translation goes to work on them. People have tried it, people will persist in trying to translate the untranslatable; the result is not worth the effort it costs."[32] In poetry every translation is necessarily an adaptation, since not only words, but a specific aesthetic code has to be translated, Vogüé said. Congeniality is the rule. In the domain of the novel, therefore, Flaubert would have to translate Tolstoy, Balzac, and Dostoevski. Then, one would not know which to admire more, the original or the translation. In that case, the words *translation* and *original* would lose their meaning: there would have been creation on both sides. France needed considerable time to divine, to hear, and to understand the "vague, musical language, and the supple raiment of ideas"[33] expressed in Russian literature.

Fidelity to the soil: this is the mark of Russian realism.[34] In his *Histoire de la littérature contemporaine de Russie*, which appeared ten years before Vogüé's work, Céleste Courrière had already recognized in realism the fundamental trait of the very character of the people, a character that must perforce be reflected in its literature. Especially with Tolstoy we come to the theory of detail for detail's sake, at a period when in Paris, to consider the question of realism again from a French point of view, the school of art for art's sake was taking flight. Vogüé himself had nothing but scorn for Gautier and his disciples who boasted of having nothing to say, instead of trying to excuse themselves for this defect. Yet both Tolstoy and Gautier took pride in a total indifference with regard to the moral scope of a scene, a portrait, or a description. In perfecting the art of observation, the Russian novelists have contributed more than Balzac, Flaubert, or Zola to shifting the axis of the literary world. Vogüé sees the explanation of this fact in a radical, indeed an ethnological difference between the French and the Russians: "We and all our racial brothers have inherited the genius for the *absolute* from our Latin masters; the races of the North, whether Slavs or Anglo-Germans, have the genius of the *relative;* this is true whether it is a question of religious beliefs, legal principles, or literary procedures. The statements hold good across all that long history of Europe in which this fundamental difference has manifested itself."[35] Vogüé's declaration suggests that the French are realists only by accident, while the Russians are so by essence, by their nature. He also noted the close relationship between Russian and English realism. Dickens, Thackeray, and George Eliot enjoy the full admiration of the author of *Le Roman russe*.

From the absence of precise purpose or utilitarian design, one might infer an absence of logic. As Vogüé pointed out, logic fails to explain the actions of Tolstoy's characters, and a contemporary critic could reasonably try to defend the hypothesis that the literature of the absurd is essentially Slavic in origin with a dramatist like the Romanian Ionesco serving as an intermediary. The Russians had still other lessons to give: Camus, Sartre, and Malraux imply and, on occasion, affirm that no genius has more profoundly marked their generation than that of Dostoevski—this subtle and simple Dostoevski, choked by universal pity from his infant days at the Poor Hospital,[36] then, by virtue of his birth, seized with commiseration for "the humiliated and the offended," drunk with occultism and with illuminism, author of novels that are at once psychological and terrifying, tortured by his tragic vision of man. Vogüé interprets these various, even opposing, qualities in the Russian character as a type of hesitation or suspense: "The irresolute soul of the Russians evolves across all philosophies and all errors; it performs its stations of the cross in nihilism and pessimism; a superficial reader could sometimes confound Tolstoy and Flaubert." Similar traditional comparisons connect Dostoevski with Zola. "But this nihilism," he continues, "is never accepted without revolt, this soul is never impenitent, we hear it moaning and seeking; finally it gets hold of itself once more and redeems itself through charity; a charity which is more or less active in Turgenev and Tolstoy, and becomes a dolorous passion in the work of Dostoevski."[37] The word *nihilisme* was imported to France from Russia. In *Fathers and Sons* several characters try to define this emptiest of all philosophical "isms."

Nineteenth-century French critics other than Vogüé remained somewhat undecided as to the order of preference to be accorded the major Russian writers. For Ernest Depuy the immortal names are Gogol, Turgenev, and Tolstoy, rather than Pushkin or Dostoevski, and Francisque Sarcey expresses a similar opinion in a series of articles published in the *Nouvelle Revue* (1885–1886). As far as Vogüé is concerned, Pushkin definitely does not incarnate the Russian national character, at least not in the most decisive manner. Here the most accurate scale of values, however, may be irrelevant: a precise hierarchy might even make us forget, or at any rate might lead to the obscuring of the primary message of *Le Roman russe:* that the French could revive their exhausted literature by the reading of imported books, that is, works conceived in social milieus far removed from Paris.

✺

The essential question of influence studies in comparative literature concerns the degree to which influence becomes assimilation, that is, the degree to which one nation absorbs, transforms, or re-creates the literature of another. Vogüé himself suggests that France must, and would, absorb, transform, and re-create the literature of Russia. He may have read the comment of the Duke of Rovigo, Napoleon's minister of police, whom Madame de Staël quotes in her *Ten Years of Exile:* "We are not yet reduced to seeking models in countries that you admire." Vogüé takes up the challenge: "Just as everything that exists, literature is an organism which lives by nutrition; it must ceaselessly assimilate elements which are foreign to it so as to transform them into its own substance. If its stomach is good, this assimilation involves no dangers; if it is worn out, there only remains the choice of perishing by starvation or by indigestion. If such was our position, a dish of Russian gruel more or less would not change our death sentence one bit."[38]

Vogüé draws still other consequences. He is one of the first Frenchmen to have had enough intellectual honesty to say aloud what many of his contemporaries must have felt. "The general ideas which are transforming Europe no longer issue from the French soul."[39] He had studied and even witnessed the decline of that intellectual authority that had been for ages the "uncontested patrimony" of France. Henceforth, it was to be in Russia that French writers would find the sense of the real, or of the beautiful in the real, and thus they would renew their art. Russia would bestow new capacities upon them; it would unmask the most delicate emotions together with the most brutal passions. After being for centuries the schoolmistress of Europe, France would be called upon to find the courage to enroll in her turn in the school of her former disciples: she would be faced with a necessity of the hour.

PART III

Movements and Trends

7

Prolegomenon B

WORDS like *movement, current, trend,* and *school* belong to the daily vocabulary of literary criticism. In practice, such terms are often employed synonymously, and like other concepts in the critical field, they lack firm boundaries. Nevertheless, a rather clear distinction can be made between a movement and a trend insofar as movement refers to the characteristics of a much wider and varied group of works than a trend, which denotes a more particular phenomenon and often represents a temporary literary fashion. A movement expresses cultural conditions in a majority of literary products in a given period of time. A movement, therefore, is a general, widespread phenomenon, like the baroque or the enlightenment. Trends, on the other hand, may be observed within a movement; neo-hellenism, for example, is a trend within romanticism.[1] Moreover, the characteristics of a movement are more consistent and have a more lasting effect, though they are not always more striking than those of a trend.

Discussions about literary movements or currents—and the words are commonly used interchangeably—are sometimes fruitless because of underlying misconceptions. It is readily understood that movements or currents represent the historical dimension of literature. They are most meaningful categories in which to classify literary periods or epochs, and especially the phases of their evolution. Thus, movement and current suggest a sort of Heraclitean view of culture: everything in the universe of letters is in a state of flux. And the same observation could be made about German and French equivalents like *Strömung* and *courant*. Regardless of the language, these terms mean development or growth. In reality, however, critical studies in literary movements are more often centered on situations than on the rise and gradual unfolding of new cultural idiosyncrasies—with the result that an exclusively *dynamic* term is used for a *static* fact. Instead of speaking uniquely about literary *movements,* the critic must also consider literary *moments,* assuming, of course, that some moments can be protracted to a period of a century or more. In other words, since no language is more illogical—or more ironical—than that of literary criticism, both movement and current actually designate not only an evolution but also a fixed state, an era rather than a process of change. A study of naturalism, for example, not only would consist of an examination of its genesis, an analysis of the manner in which it was born from realism, it would attempt also to understand the intrinsic qualities of naturalism and to relate them to specific works. It practically stands for epoch or period.

We begin to speak of a movement as soon as we notice *differentiae specificae* significant enough to provide common ground for literary studies on a wide scale. Significance is determined by the degree to which similar traits penetrate various literary genres in a single epoch on both a national and international level. Movements, however, are not necessarily international, although parallel developments may often be noticed in different countries. *Junges Deutschland* or *Young Germany*, for instance, concerns only the German *Sprachraum*—the German linguistic area, or space—but comparable currents existed simultaneously in many other areas: in Italy (*La giovina Italia*), in France (*La jeune France*), and in Poland (*Mloda Polska*). *Young Europe* would be considered a "movement," while its individual national expressions should rather be termed "schools." Normally, a school identifies a group of writers who self-consciously give allegiance to a certain style. European romanticism is a movement, but on a national level, Heine speaks of "Romantische Schule" and Hugo of "Ecole romantique," a phrase more frequently used in painting, however, than in literature. This synonymy—or confusion—is most eloquently illustrated in international criticism; the Anglo-Saxons would find "Romantic school" rather an eccentric expression. A literary school, furthermore, incarnates the doctrines underlying either a movement or a trend. It is usually formed by a group of critics, who may or may not be in personal contact with each other, who expound new conceptions about literature. As critics Heine and Hugo belong to their respective national romantic schools, but as writers they belong to the romantic movement. It should be added that throughout the Western world only a few important movements have failed to generate echoes or reflections in several different literatures.[2] It should also be noticed that national movements may have an influence on parallel movements in other countries. Thus, in comparative literature certain studies are both studies in movements and relations concerned with literary phenomena occurring in the same span of time.[3]

From time to time, voices are heard proclaiming that the concept of literary movements is misleading or illusory. It is argued that a masterpiece—and, after all, masterpieces do make up the literary corpus—exists only insofar as it reflects a writer's personality. Dante may be of interest because he is Dante, and not primarily because he is part of the cultural world of the early fourteenth century. The study of literary movements, therefore, can at times take the critic away from the work itself. Instead of recognizing its ingenious and exceptional character, he sometimes insists unduly on connecting it to the aesthetics, morals, or philosophies of the time; he strives to detect either the influence exerted on it by a multitude of inferior authors or to measure its impact on other writers of lesser genius.

It does not follow from this observation, however, that we can afford to neglect the study of literary movements. Each masterpiece is surrounded by a series of good, average, and mediocre works, all of them, at least in principle, its rivals. Through an abuse of language, it is claimed that the *Decameron, Pantagruel, Don Quixote, Paradise Lost, Faust,* and *Anna Karenina* are unique in their genres. Actually they are unique only in the sense that each of these works is superior to most other examples of its particular species. All the works just cited can and ought to be studied in a very extended context; then it becomes immediately clear that it is not genre but rank within the genre that distinguishes a masterpiece from other, inferior works.

Consequently, we are justified in basing the general history of literature not only on accurate chronology, but also on the study of international currents, the manifestations of which may or may not appear at the same time in all countries. Such a perspective resembles that which Arnold Toynbee developed in his celebrated comparative book on the evolutionary forces of mankind, *A Study of History.* Historic movements, like cultural movements, cannot be enclosed within the extremes of two limiting dates. Not nations, nor even periods, but civilizations—Toynbee distinguishes twenty-six of them, past and present—form the intelligible units of history. One may believe that the same situation exists in the history of letters. From this perspective, movements and trends would be part of the general framework of literary history; natural groupings of literary facts would constitute intelligible units similar to those described by Toynbee.

Unfortunately, the problem of breaking down the whole literary substance into organic chapters is a great deal more complex than appearances suggest. A movement may not manifest itself in all nations. Moreover, they are not all of the same nature, and their importance varies considerably from one literature to another. Classicism, for example, and modernism as well, affect everything that involves intellectual activity, and even to a certain extent the exact sciences. But formalism[4] and even symbolism, though important for the morphology of culture, scarcely represent a significant step in the history of ideas. Some currents shape thought more than language, while others relate to form almost to the exclusion of contextual matters. Certain movements reputed to be literary are only partially so; indeed, their influence is felt only in limited areas of literature, and, for this reason, we would more properly speak of trends than of movements. Thus mannerism and more obviously *Jugendstil* belong above all to the province of *Stilforschung*—style research. Similar stylistic trends may also be noticed in various literatures: euphuism, gongorism, marinism, *préciosité, marivaudage*. The baroque, on the other hand, although first recognized in architecture where it refers to style, extends also to the structural elements of literary works. Expressionism and impressionism, surrealism and dadaism succeed more in plastic art than in literature. Finally, the picaresque and costumbrismo, which are sometimes treated as literary movements, in reality only define genres or species: costumbristic novels and picaresque novels exist, but they were never important enough to color an entire epoch or literature.

It is thus difficult, sometimes impossible, to find a simple common denominator for the many works thought of as belonging to a specific movement or current, trend or school. Movements and trends, however, represent one of the least artificial means of portraying literary history. Judiciously and systematically carried out, such studies represent much more than the chronology of the literary process. They help to solve the problem of periodization. One may, of course, take the reign of a single monarch as a rubric for a period, at least on the national level. But to speak of the Elizabethan Age, the Stuart Restoration, or the Victorian Period is to impute tacitly to some monarchs a role in letters that they never possessed. Literary movements are not primarily determined by the contingencies of a throne or the vagaries of the calendar. A monarch can be a Maecenas or an iconoclast; ministers can decisively aid or hinder the spread of literature. In some instances, political authority may give letters a new direction. But the importance of this kind of influence has, nevertheless, generally been exaggerated. Literatures are faithful expressions of societies, not necessarily governments.

In designating literary periods, the Germans replace the aristocracy of blood by one of genius, and speak, for example, of a *Goethezeit*, assuming that Goethe had indeed represented the epitome of German literature for over two generations. Such denominations are meaningful only within a national literature. As for the French and the Italians, they rejoice in the centennial view of history, chopping it up neatly into centuries. But this system, once again, cannot convey the least intellectual unity, on either the national or the international plane. The "century" of classicism is far from being the same in all national literatures. In some countries, the flowering of classicism lasted but a few decades, while in others it persisted well beyond one hundred years. It might obviously have happened that here and there a new spirit was born in 1600, possibly in 1700 or 1800. In his *Essai sur les éléments de philosophie*, d'Alembert proposed reckoning the hundred years from the middle of centuries: "It seems that for three hundred years nature has destined the middle of each century as the period of a revolution in the human mind. . . ." We could as well maintain that the tenth or twentieth year of the century was the crucial one, at least in France: 1610, the year of the assassination of Henri IV; 1715, the death of Louis XIV; 1815, the end of Napoleon's imperium; and 1918, the armistice. It would perhaps be more prudent to organize the study of a national literature in the manner suggested by Henri Peyre, that is, around succeeding generations. But the method could only rarely be applied in comparative literature, and, after all, a new generation is born each second.

Periods, however, are seldom if ever characterized by one single cultural current. A scholar studying seventeenth-century French literature would be greatly misled in his research if he were to assume the existence of unified aesthetic principles among all writers in that epoch. Corneille belongs to the baroque as well as to classicism, and the theories of the enlightenment are already clearly visible from Henri II to Louis XIV. Similarly, Wordsworth's and Keats's contemporaries cannot all be called romantic on merely historical grounds, nor can Tieck's or Eichendorff's. Moreover, the romantic phenomenon obviously differs not only from one country to another, but even in the same linguistic area; the writers are not necessarily romantic to the same degree or in the same way.[5]

The first of the following two essays provides an explanation of some of the variations encountered in European romanticism. It is a study of a literary movement in its gestation, of a word not only prefiguring but defining the movement to come. The second essay explains the main characteristics of exoticism and its significance for Western letters. The purpose of juxtaposing these two essays, however, is not so much to analyze or to stress the difference between a movement and a trend as it is to point up, from a study of each, that works belonging to different national literatures are parts of similar movements or trends in Weltliteratur. In both chapters, common elements of the two literary phenomena are detected in heterogeneous groups of works. Both studies, consequently, should be understood as illustrations of one of the four categories in our system of comparatistic inquiry. The analysis of movements and trends, like that of relations, genres, and motifs, reveals the international character of culture; to identify and ascertain that character is one of the chief aims of comparative literature.[6]

8

A Lesson in a Word: "Romantic" and European Romanticism

FOR some decades, literary criticism has been debating certain identical questions with an astonishing regularity. One question, for example, is whether creative works can be classified according to specific categories. Another is whether cultural trends like the baroque, neoclassicism, and naturalism are anything more than convenient words to allow editors of literary encyclopedias to organize their material properly. This very problem has often arisen with regard to romanticism. Does the word romanticism designate a reality? Has such a movement ever existed in Europe, that is, one that is distinct from all others, a movement with its own idiosyncracies and worthy of being studied as a cultural phenomenon endowed with its own aesthetic system and stemming from some recognizable internal impulse?

Fifty years ago, an article "On the Discrimination of Romanticisms"[1] put the literary world into a state of doubt concerning the nature and quality of romanticism as a homogeneous literary current. Its author, Arthur O. Lovejoy, insisted emphatically on the problematical character of a European romantic movement. Three decades later René Wellek, in "The Concept of Romanticism in Literary History" and "Romanticism Re-examined,"[2] suggested that a truce be signed inviting criticism to prepare the ground for a peaceful settlement on suitable definitions and descriptions of romanticism.

The majority of critics have readily accepted the new definitions and descriptions emphasizing the international elements of romanticism and not those pertaining to single peoples, and the goal of the present chapter is certainly not to reopen the debate and thus endanger a peace so brilliantly negotiated.

One problem related to that of romanticism proper is to be treated here: the term *romantic,* and its origin and evolution in various parts of Europe. The lack of such a comparative analysis of the term has caused part of the uncertainty and confusion among scholars who deal with romanticism as a literary movement. Since Wellek notes in the first of the two articles cited that he is not concerned "with the early history of *romantic,*"[3] readers may consider what follows a kind of preamble to his publications on European romanticism: it is a study of romanticism in the making.

Before we proceed further, one question needs to be answered. Because we are mainly concerned with a word and its change of meanings, are we not dealing with a problem of semantics rather than one of literature? In most university curricula today, the field unanimously called philology half a century ago has now been divided into several subdisciplines: languages; linguistics; semantics; literature proper, its theory and its history. The comparatist, who is naturally inclined to detect the basic unity of the entire humanistic territory, is keenly aware of the artificiality of such a fragmentation imposed upon philology. A language is more than a mere vehicle of literature: it is part of it. The semantic evolution of terms like reason, heart, sentiment, harmony, for example, and their equivalents among different peoples, is directly related to an evolution in philosophical ideas and literary tastes in Europe. In studying the semantic change of romantic, we are, at each stage, implicitly detecting symptoms of a literary mood, of a literary movement that began if not at the first appearance of "romantic" at least with the general use of the word that came to designate the movement itself. The word *romantic* witnesses to the rise and growth of European romanticism. This should be the meaning of the following pages.

At somewhat widely separated points in time, the term *romantic* appeared in different languages on the Continent after being in use in the British Kingdom for many decades. Variants should be noted. In seventeenth-century England, both *romance* (as an adjective) and *romantic* were common; France, before adopting *romantique,* had *pittoresque* and *romanesque* (while the English *romanesque* referred to the style of architecture popular in the early Middle Ages); Germany, besides *romantisch,* used *romanhaft* and *abenteuerlich;* in Italy we notice *patetico, romanzesco* and *romantico;* in Poland there was *romantyczny;* and in Russia *romantichesky.* Quite a few other synonyms cropped up all over Europe, from Scandinavia to the Bay of Biscay and the Aegean Sea. This migration of an important critical term and its synonyms urges the historian of letters to examine its birth and life, its semantic ramifications and literary implications in all relevant linguistic areas, and, finally, its functions and true meaning in specific works. While a considerable array of scholars have studied the appearance of the word romantic in one specific culture, independently from the corresponding literary current, none of them has tried to relate these diverse inquiries and draw some general conclusion from the whole series of parallel phenomena.[4] In the present analysis, the evolution of the term romantic, and its metamorphoses on European soil, will be examined with particular emphasis on the nations that played the most significant role in the flowering and the dissemination of romanticism: England, Germany, France, and, in some respects, Italy and Russia.

I

England can lay claim to having been the first country in Europe to accredit the word romantic. True, the word goes back to an old French noun, romaunt and romaunce[5] that the elegant classes of the seventeenth century still sometimes used to designate a romance. In his celebrated Wörterbuch Jacob Grimm mentioned a manuscript from the fifteenth century in which a particular book is described as romanticus, that is, pertaining to the genre of the romance, a work of the imagination. The Swiss Pastor Gotthard Heidegger (1666–1711) used the Latin epithet in the same sense in the title of a pamphlet published in 1689: Mythoscopia romantica oder Discours von den so benannten Romans. English writers, in the seventeenth century, had a selection of synonyms, including romance, romanticall, romancial, romancy, romantic, most of the time capitalized. Their final choice fell on romantic, until around 1750 frequently spelled romantick, and rather rarely romantique.[6] Romantic and romantick became quite common from the beginning of the eighteenth century.

Words do not arise without cause. When a new term appears, it displays its raison d'être; it represents an object or fact, an emotion or an idea. A profound change in English sensibility was announced with the very advent of the word romantic, a change that was to gain momentum during the Restoration and to reach its peak in the time of Defoe, Richardson, and Fielding. Earlier, the authors of narrative works and fictional histories had found the principal source of their inspiration in the realm of fantasy. Now, more and more, they sought it in daily experience, in reality. They needed a term with which to establish the new tendencies against the old. Originally, romantic referred to the manner of the old romances (again a word with multiple meanings), epics, and pastorals, more generally, in other words, to the manner of the past. Applied to a group of writers, the term would have designated the reactionary ones. The common use of the word in English letters since 1650 proves to be one of the first symptoms of a sort of cold war between the ancients and the moderns.

Romantic and romance show a parallel semantic evolution. This latter adjective, referring to the languages developed from Vulgar Latin, means, as a noun, either a species of tales in Romance dialects, or a specific genre; it may translate the Spanish *romanz*. Romance, therefore, also signifies an imaginative, and even a dreamy habit of the mind (a person full of romance), and the corresponding adjective is romantic. The meaning of "romantic: medieval," relating to the kind of literary imagination peculiar to the Middle Ages, is substantiated in numerous texts. Henry More, in *The Immortality of the Soul* (1659) speaks of "that imagination which is most free, such as we use in Romantick inventions."[7] In a 1662 English version of the *Berger extravagant* by Charles Sorel, the translator comments in his preface: "Lysy's [a character] contempt of good books shews he esteems all pedantry that is not Romantick."[8] The translation of Huet's *Essai sur l'origine des romans* in 1672 contains several examples of the term or related forms. Speaking of the art of the narrative in antiquity, Huet reaches the conclusion that "the Romancing science made no considerable progress among the Greeks before their Conquest over the Persians, from whom they received it."[9] John Evelyn, ten years later, complains to one of his correspondents: "The story of King Edgar is monstrously romantic and the pretended deed I doubt will appear but spurious."[10]

Here a critical tone can already be discerned. Romantic no longer refers to the purely imaginary, but alludes to, and insists on the absence of logic, consistency, and substance. That which is derived not only from fancy, but from an eccentric world is romantic. Now this notion, however, of the "romantic: marvelous" superseding the original meaning of "romantic: medieval" has a pejorative tinge. It implies disordered transport of the imagination, exaltation of the senses. The new attitude is detectable in these frivolous lines that a certain Mrs. S. F. Egerton published in 1705:

> Curse on the whimsical Romantick fool,
> That yielded first to that Phantastick rule.[11]

The word is similarly found in contexts such as the following: "After he has turned this as Romantically as he could"; "He tells us Romantickally in the same argument"; "A mere Romantick fancy of such who would be thought to be much wiser."[12] The term clearly signifies the unreal and the extraordinary, and often even the extravagant is implied, a meaning that creeps in also in the nineteenth century.

During the second quarter of the eighteenth century, romantic started to assume new tasks: it served to describe a type of landscape, the landscape as it was currently illustrated in romances and pastorals, where the action usually unfurled in quiet, pleasant sites.

"Romantic: picturesque" was one of these new nuances assumed by the adjective. George Lyttleton, speaking of the "river Dee winding in so romantic and charming a manner," may represent an entire school of landscapists.[13] When English writers painted the countryside, they thought they were being precise by applying the epithet romantic to it; in truth they were merely attempting to suggest a certain atmosphere.

Another semantic change should be noted. The old romances, often marked by bizarre and improbable plots, had to create their own type of scenery, a background of distant, isolated, mysterious, foreign regions that the authors described without reluctance: the romantic scenery. Romantic was used as a kind of literary *topos* to characterize a locale that was as yet uncultivated by man. "It is so romantic a scene that it has always probably given occasion to . . . chimerical relations." That is the perspective in which Addison depicts the desert near Cassis in his *Remarks on Several Parts of Italy*.[14] The landscape is now more than a background for human situations.

The term subsequently took on the meaning of *unpeopled*. It referred to specific geographic regions, not as much to accidentally uncultivated, unsettled areas as to vast uncultivable, uninhabitable ones: bogs, swamps, prairies, mountains. It is at this time—in the first half of the eighteenth century—that the mountain makes its triumphal entry into European letters. Romantic assumes the meaning of "romantic: rugged," and Scotland provides one of the early examples. "The country of Scotch warriors described [in the song *Chevy Chase*] has a fine Romantick situation and affords a couple of smooth words for verse," comments Addison in his *Spectator*.[15] In his *Seasons*, James Thomson also points out the "romantic: rugged" character of the northern part of Britain:

> . . . And here a while the muse,
> High hovering o'er the broad cerulean scene,
> Sees Caledonia in romantic view. . . .[16]

The physical roughness of the landscape that the writers of this period loved presages the ideal of asymmetry and apparent disorder that the romantic schools of many countries later preach: "A certain savage, irregular beauty."[17] For the classical mind the very terms *asymmetry* and *beauty* resound with contradiction, and irregularity means deformity. Pope, it is true, dares to depict in *Windsor Forest* (1713) a world "harmoniously confused." But long after Pope, the mountains were still considered ulcers on the globe. The aesthetic theory of that ugliness was developed later, by romantic sentimentality, when voyagers and even geographers came to use romantic in their descriptions of landscapes, just as novelists did in their characterizations of heroes and psychologists of the Richardsonian school did in their analyses of the human soul. *The New and Complete*

Dictionary of the English Language, edited by J. Ash and published in 1775, gave these synonyms for romantic: "Wild, improbable, resembling romance; false, fictitious." Thomas Sheridan, in his dictionary printed in 1780 added, "full of wild scenery," which epitomizes the meanings of the passages cited in this paragraph. Romantic is thus suited to characterize in literature a landscape as well as a state of mind.

Mountains especially seem to lend themselves to being considered romantic. When Evelyn, in his *Diary* on June 17, 1654, refers to a country property as "very *romantic*," he specifies that it is situated on the slopes of a mountain, "a horrid Alp." The hour of the real Alps did not come, however, until the middle or end of the eighteenth century, when in descriptions of vast mountain ranges romantic became a favorite recurring adjective. Evelyn remains a forerunner of these later writers, for he injects into the word certain nuances that it will officially contain only several decades later. On July 23, 1679, he wrote: "I went to Clifden, that stupendous natural rock, . . . The grotts in the chalky rock are pretty: 'tis a Romantic object, and the place altogether answers the most poetical description that can be made of a solitude, precipice, prospect, or whatever can contribute to a thing so very like their imaginations."[18]

The British Pennine Chain does not have the ruggedness of the Alps and there are no sharp peaks comparable with the Matterhorn in the mountains surrounding Matlock. However, Matlock and its environs, at the time of William Whitehead's following verses, contributed toward an evolution in the meaning of romantic. In *An Hymn to the Nymph of Bristol* we read:

> Enchanting Matlock, from whose rocks like thine
> Romantic foliage hangs and rills descend
> And echoes murmur.[19]

The last generation of the century nourished its romanticism with the same geographic images:

> Romantick Matlock: are thy tufted rocks
> Thy fring'd declivities, the dim retreat . . .[20]

These verses from the *Ode for His Majesty's Birthday* by Thomas Warton, the Younger, corroborated the idea that romanticism does not make its first appearance in the highest summits. Initially it climbed more accessible mountains, which were sometimes mere hills. Then, in their turn, mountains famous since the dawn of Western history, volcanoes crowned by smoke and glory became romantic. We read in this same *Ode* of Warton's:

> The cliffs that wav'd with oak and pine
> And Etna's hoar romantic pile.[21]

For sensitive souls landscapes have always symbolized and often created a spiritual reaction. Irregular contours become movements of the heart, the chiaroscuro in which nature reposes, in which a picture bathes, feeds emotions, or harmonizes with them. Even Richardson, the worst English landscapist of the eighteenth century, speaks in *Clarissa* of the "romanticness of the place,"[22] probably seeking to arouse sensibilities nourished by the sight of brooks and lakes, of forests and meadows. Two different landscapes—the rough mountains and the solitary plains—both called romantic, correspond to two variations of hypersensitivity: tumult and languor. Since the middle third of the eighteenth century, romantic very frequently has the sense of "romantic: sentimental: unbalanced."

Toward the halfway mark of the century, certain descriptive motifs return with the insistence of a recurring theme. Ruins and castles are especially suitable for the purpose of reviving and diffusing an atmosphere of medieval tradition. Lyttleton, in 1759, describes with relish "the ruins of an old castle situated upon the top of a conical hill, the foot of which is washed by the sea, and which has every feature that can give a romantic appearance."[23] Twenty years later the Countess of Carlisle wrote to George Selwyn: "There are two castles of the oldest and most romantic description: one belonging to Tarascon, and the other situated on a high rock near the town of Beaucaire."[24] Soon after, the Gothic novel as well as occultism appeared in English letters, both occupied with similar motifs.

Diverse significations of the descriptive term romantic succeed each other in the course of history. But often they overlap. Writers found themselves wavering between several attitudes, all of which could be expressed by the term romantic. Frequently, however, they gave their preferences to one specific meaning, according to their own temperaments. Authors as far from each other as Henry Fielding and Samuel Johnson, for example, use the very same word romantic, but obviously in different ways and contexts. Fielding, it is true, avails himself of all the meanings of romantic: "Romantic whining coxcombs" is encountered in *The Jesuit Caught in His Own Trap;* "romantic" adventures are narrated in *Don Quixote in England,* and expressions like "the most romantic generosity" or "the most romantic notion of honor," appear to describe the heroine's sentiments in *Amelia.* In *The History of Tom Jones* (1749), however, romantic is employed primarily to defend a conception of love, or to characterize ironically those who fail to honor this conception. This conception of love is precisely the romantic one: spontaneous love, love without calculations, love holding primary rights over those of reason. In almost all eight instances in which romantic occurs in *Tom Jones,* Fielding uses it in the sense "romantic: spontaneous, natural," as the following passages indicate:

1. "He [Blifil] was indeed perfectly well satisfied with his prospect of

success; for as to that entire and absolute possession of the heart of his mistress which romantic lovers require, the very idea of it never entered his head."

2. [Mrs. Western speaking to her brother] "It is by living at home with you that she [Sophia] hath learned romantic notions of love and nonsense."

3. ". . . she [Mrs. Western] proceeded to read her [Sophia] a long lecture on the subject of matrimony which she treated not as a romantic scheme of happiness arising from love, as it hath been described by the poets. . . . She considered it rather as a fund in which prudent women deposit their fortunes to the best advantage in order to receive a larger interest for them than they could have elsewhere."

4. "Believe me, child [Sophia] I [Mrs. Western] know these things better than you. You will allow me, I think, to have seen the world, in which I have not an acquaintance who would not rather be thought to dislike her husband than to like him. The contrary is such out of fashion romantic nonsense that the very imagination of it is shocking."

5. "Jones had some heroic ingredients in his composition, and was a hearty well-wisher to the glorious causes of liberty and the Protestant religion. It is no wonder therefore that in circumstances which would have warranted a much more romantic and wild undertaking, it should occur to him to serve as a volunteer in this expedition."

6. "For she [Mrs. Fitzpatrick] did not in the least doubt but that the prudent lady [Lady Bellaston], who had often ridiculed romantic love and indiscreet marriages in her conversation, would very readily concur in her sentiments concerning this match [Jones-Sophia], and would lend her utmost assistance to prevent it."   ,

7. "The discourses turned at present, as before, on love, and Mrs. Nightingale again expressed many of those warm, generous, and disinterested sentiments upon this subject, which wise and sober men call romantic, but which wise and sober women generally regard in a better light."

8. "The bane of all young women is the country. There they learn a set of romantic notions of love."[25]

These examples tell us that although in Fielding's time romantic often denoted a negative quality, in *Tom Jones* the pejorative aspect is not accepted. The whole novel extols the "romantic love" that its protagonists have for each other. It is precisely this phenomenon that permits us to infer the semantic value the word had taken over about 1750.[26]

The semantic change—or rather expansion—most relevant to literary history and theory can be observed in works published during the last third of the eighteenth century. Then, romantic was more and more frequently used in England to designate a new manner of writing, of expressing new forms and new aesthetical notions as well. The term began to assume the meaning of "literarily romantic," even though schools to define and represent such a concept were not foreseen as yet. Their hour came finally in the early nineteenth century. While campaigning for a tolerance of their own principles, these schools showed themselves in many respects intolerant of other attitudes and of other principles, as Heine's *Romantische Schule* most convincingly illustrates. The sentimental affectation, which Senancour called *sentimanie*, was to become in Europe, and especially in Great Britain, a particular affectation of style as well as of behavior.

By the end of the eighteenth century, English writers were using the word romantic in the perspective of a long tradition, while in many other important regions of Europe the notion romantic was first beginning to make its appearance. In England it was even a word "à la mode": Walter Scott was confident of winning his case with his readers when in 1808 he published, as he expressed it to Robert Surtees, "three quarto volumes of romantic poetry."[27] Romantic also became more and more the opposite of classic: "Contrasting instead of representing the classic or romantic characters," as Charles-Robert Maturin has one of his heroes say.[28] At the beginning of the nineteenth century the word also appeared in literary criticism. In his *History of Modern Criticism*, Wellek says: "The terms *a romantic, a romanticist* were used in England for the first time by Carlyle in reference to the Germans, but an English romantic school did not become established in textbooks of literary history until the 50's, obviously under Continental influence."[29] Poets love to enroll in such schools, to swear allegiance to them, but they are apt thereby to become the targets for later satire, like T.S. Eliot's. Eliot observes: "From time to time writers have labelled themselves romanticists or classicists, just as they have from time to time banded themselves together under other names. These names which groups of writers and artists give themselves are the delight of professors and historians of literature, but should not be taken very seriously; their chief value is temporary and political—that, simply, of helping to make the authors known to a contemporary public; and I doubt whether any poet has ever done himself anything but harm by attempting to write as a *romantic* or as a *classicist*. No sensible author, in the midst of something that he is trying to write, can stop to consider whether it is going to be romantic or the opposite."[30] Eliot's sentiment, although true, cannot alter the reality of a romanticism defined by characteristics distinct from those of any other literary movement, as the evidence can show.

⚝

Germany was the first continental country to introduce the word romantic. Soon afterward other Germanic regions followed, then France and, sometime later, Italy. The term gradually began to figure actively in all provinces of Western thought, literature and philosophy, painting and psychology; and it was equated variously with a wide range of attributes: medieval, marvelous, rugged, extravagant, sensitive, unbalanced, and anticlassical. The evolution of the word exemplifies a phenomenon that is well known to linguists: like a torrent, a word is more apt to gather and drag along new meanings than to lose them. Thus it is less a question of the word romantic undergoing changes of meanings than of accumulating new ones; the word assumes a separate and suitable meaning for each context. In spite of some hesitations, resistance, and setbacks, *romantisch, romantique, romantico* eventually achieved positive acceptance.

Germany received *romantisch* into her tongue toward the end of the seventeenth century. In a German-French-Latin dictionary published in Geneva in 1695, the anonymous author translates *romanesque* by "fabelhaft, romantisch."[31] But the term had not, at this point, gained recognition through literary usage. Before the final triumph of the form romantisch, synonyms were fairly numerous: *romanisch, romanzisch, romanhaft, romanenhaft, romanenmässig.* These adjectives are clearly derivations of *die Romanze* and *der Roman.* They refer to fictitious narrative works that were not inspired by ordinary, everyday events. In the romance, the extraordinary, which need not be fantastic, is the contrary of common experience. Romantisch was then contrasted with *alltäglich*, "daily" or "ordinary." Soon thereafter this opposition applied not only to action and events but also to emotions. Herder remembers the *romantische Zeit* ("romantic time") he spent at Darmstadt (1771) with his future wife Caroline Flachsland. Expressions like *romantisches Mädchen* ("romantic girl") and *romantische Liebe* ("romantic love") became frequent after 1775. Five years earlier, Kant had written: "Cervantes hätte besser getan, wenn er anstatt die phantastische und romantische Leidenschaft lächerlich zu machen, sie besser dirigiert hätte" ("Cervantes would have done better, if instead of making fantastic and romantic passion ridiculous, he had directed it better").[32] But in 1776, Johann Georg Jacobi speaks of a story "voll einfältiger Sitte, voll ungekünstelter Lieb' und Treue, dabei romantisch genug, um auch unsren artigsten Fräulein gefallen zu dürfen" ("full of human innocence and simplicity, full of unaffected love and faithfulness, but at the same time romantic enough to please even our loveliest young ladies").[33]

Goethe suggested quite a different idea concerning romantisch when in 1827 he reviewed Carlyle's famous anthology, *German Romance.* He explains the title by saying that the collection includes "Musterstücke romantischer, auch märchenhafter Art, ausgewählt aus den Werken deutscher Autoren, welche sich in diesem Fache hervorgetan haben; sie enthalten kleinere und grössere Erzählungen von Musäus, Tieck, Hoffmann, Jean Paul Richter und Goethe [the progression is interesting] in freier, anmutiger Sprache" ("exemplary specimens of the romantic genre and also fairy tales, selected from the works of German authors who have distinguished themselves in this category; they contain smaller or larger narrations by Musäus, Tieck, Hoffmann, Jean Paul Richter, and Goethe in a natural and charming language").[34] Here the word refers to *Roman*, a word—like *roman* in French—to be found in German earlier than *novel* in English. In terms of value judgment, the word romantisch carries with it all the various shades of blame and approbation of romantic.

By the last quarter of the eighteenth century, romantisch was quite readily used by the public,[35] but its acceptation remained varied and often vague. Thanks to Wieland and Herder, the word became part of the jargon of every man of letters, and the Schlegel brothers, their friends and disciples were able to diffuse its meaning even further. They introduced it into another context: it designated the program of a literary school.

✤

In their continual battle against any contamination of their language, the French resisted more valiantly against romantic than they have recently been able to do against drugstore, playboy and striptease. It took the little word romantic some one hundred and fifty years to cross the Channel. France, however, had *romanesque*, which appeared at least as early as 1661 and was often capitalized like its English equivalent. In his *Grand Dictionnaire historique des précieuses*, published the same year, Saumaise speaks of "amours Romanesques" ; the term thus suggests a comparison with novels and romances. Molière uses the word after 1663. In *L'Etourdi* [The blunderer] Mascarille utters this line: "Vous êtes romanesque avecque vos chimères." The English version of 1732 reads: "You are extremely Romantic, Sir, with your fine chimeras." *The Romantic Ladies* translates *Les Précieuses ridicules*. On the other hand, romanesque was a favorite word of Madame de Sévigné, to whom it signified a character resembling a hero like Honoré d'Urfé's and his rivals'; she used it to express certain nuances that adjectives such as marvelous and fabulous lacked.

The first major transformation of romanesque occurred in 1722, the year the French read Addison's *Remarks on Several Parts of Italy* in their own language. This work pictures mountains "qui forment une scène si romanesque qu'elle a probablement donné lieu à de semblables fables."[36] Instead of a romance creating the landscape, it is the landscape that suggests the romance. The French realized that the term could describe a countryside of mountains and valleys as well as specific kinds of parks and gardens. In 1745 the Abbé Jean-Bernard Leblanc made this clear in his celebrated *Lettres d'un Français*. Of English gardens he writes: "Plusieurs Anglais essaient de donner aux leurs un air qu'ils appellent en leur langue *Romantic*, c'est-à-dire à peu près *pittoresque* et le manquent, faute de goût" ("Some Englishmen try to give to their gardens an air that they call *Romantic* in their language, that is to say, almost *picturesque*, and they fail because of their lack of taste").[37] And in 1769, rendering into French *An Account of a Tour in Corsica* by Boswell, the anonymous translator explains in a note the exact meaning of a passage describing a particular aspect of the island: "Les Anglais ont pour l'exprimer le terme énergique de *Romantick*, comme on dirait qui n'existe que dans les romans" ("The English have the energetic term *Romantick* to express it, as one might say, existing only in novels").[38] This was the period in which pittoresque became almost synonymous with romanesque. Diderot, on the twentieth of October, 1759, spoke to Sophie Volland of "un coup d'oeil tout à fait sauvage et pittoresque" ("a completely wild and *picturesque* view"). Ten days later, talking about the tortuous course of the river Marne, he added: "C'est un aspect vraiment romanesque" ("it is a truly romanesque [romantic] prospect").[39]

Sauvage ("wild") also became appended to romantique at the beginning of Rousseau's *Cinquième Rêverie* (written in 1777 and published in 1782), the very first instance of the epithet being used in a significant French literary work. Henceforth wild was to supplant, or at least duplicate, both romanesque and picturesque. On the first of August, 1765, Jean-Baptiste-Antoine Suard, in the *Gazette Littéraire de l'Europe*, also tried to render into French the word romantic, used by Blair to describe Ossianic scenes. While Suard chose to say "sauvage et romanesque," Rousseau twelve years after him wrote "sauvage et romantique." Both writers, however, in combining these words, were verging slightly upon the sin of pleonasm. The two sets of adjectives formed a sort of topos. In any case, toward 1775 romanesque enjoyed the same popularity in France as romantisch did in Germany.[40] In the sixty-third letter of Laclos' *Liaisons dangereuses* (1782), for example, the Marquise de Merteuil chides Valmont for having been detained in a village "par un amour romanesque et malheureux" ("by a romantic and unhappy love"); the French are still hesitant about using the word romantique. It would be regarded as an anglicism for some more years, until 1800, or 1810, although the *Dictionnaire de l'Académie française* had endorsed it in 1798.

In the last quarter of the eighteenth century, France slowly grew familiar with *âme romantique* and the notion of *paysage romantique*. The important dates in this process are 1776 and 1777, when the term appeared in the preliminary discourse Pierre Le Tourneur wrote to his Shakespeare translation, and then in a small but influential essay by the Marquis Louis-René de Girardin, *De la composition des paysages*. One finds in them the first two known instances of the use of the word in print. But both works belong to the history of culture rather than to creative literature and Rousseau's example is much more significant for literary criticism. There are even some generally forgotten instances of a much earlier use of the term. In a pamphlet anonymously published in 1675, *Réponse aux faussetés et invectives qui se lisent dans la relation du voyage de Sorbière en Angleterre*, romantique designates the manner in which the landscape of Kent is described in Samuel Sorbière's book ("termes romantiques"). In 1699 the numismatist and scholar Claude Nicaise used it in a letter to a friend, Jean-Alphonse Turrettini. Commenting on the behavior of some members of the Arcadia Academy in Rome he asks: "Que dites-vous de ces pastoureaux [shepherds, i.e. academicians], ne sont-ils pas bien romantiques?"[41] Here the adjective means strange, eccentric. This was, then, one of the most current meanings romantic had in England. Nicaise must have known that Jean-Alphonse and the entire Turrettini family of Geneva, a city perhaps more than any other on the Continent under the influence of English culture, had many friends in England and would understand this anglicism.

The final victory of romantique may be ascribed to Etienne Pivert de Senancour's epistolary novel *Obermann*. The work was written in Switzerland in 1802 and 1803 and features Alpine scenery. If Rousseau introduced the term into French literature, Senancour definitely consecrated its usage; and if Chateaubriand, with his *Génie du Christianisme* of 1802, was one of the most powerful writers to launch romanticism in France, Senancour deserves credit for having launched the word romantique. The "Fragment" inserted between Letter 38 and 39 of *Obermann* is entitled "De l'expression romantique, et du ranz des vaches" [On romantic expression and the Ranz des Vaches].[42] In referring to the Ranz des Vaches, song of the Swiss cowherds, Senancour points out the romantic quality of certain music: "C'est dans les sons que la nature a placé la plus forte expression du caractère romantique: et c'est surtout au sens de l'ouïe que l'on peut rendre sensibles, en peu de traits et d'une manière énergique, les lieux et les choses extraordinaires" ("It is in sounds that nature has placed the strongest expression of the romantic quality: and it is above all through our sense of hearing that we can, in a few strokes and in an energetic manner, give the feeling of extraordinary places and things").[43] Letter 56 similarly emphasizes these virtues of music: "Je ne sens plus que ce qui est extraordinaire. Il me faut des sons romantiques pour que je commence à entendre, et des lieux sublimes pour que je me rappelle ce que j'aimais dans un autre âge" ("I no longer feel anything except the extraordinary. I need romantic sounds in order to really hear, and sublime places in order to remember what I loved in another age").[44] Senancour, in his *Rêveries sur la nature primitive de l'homme*, published five years before *Obermann*, had already announced these ideas; he had connected "repos sauvage" and "sons romantiques."[45]

It should be recalled that *La Vallée d'Obermann*—followed by

Improvisata sur le Ranz des Vaches de Ferdinand Huber—is one of the finest piano compositions of young Franz Liszt. Not only music but every sound that the human ear perceives may confer upon the receptive soul that emotion Senancour wanted to illustrate throughout his novel. He writes of the forest of Fontainebleau: "Il faut des bêtes fauves errantes dans ces solitudes: elles sont intéressantes et pittoresques, quand on entend des cerfs bramer la nuit à des distances inégales, quand l'écureuil saute de branches en branches dans les beaux bois de Tillas avec son petit cri d'alarme. Sons isolés de l'être vivant: vous ne peuplez point les solitudes . . . vous les rendez plus profondes, plus mystérieuses; c'est par vous qu'elles sont romantiques" ("We need deer wandering in these solitudes: solitudes are interesting and picturesque, when we hear stags bellowing in the night from various distances, and when the squirrel jumps from branch to branch in the fair wood of Tillas, giving its small cry of alarm. Isolated sounds of living beings, you do not people the solitudes . . . you render them more profound, more mysterious; it is through you that they are romantic".)[46] Thus Senancour is one of the first modern advocates of musical tableaux, an old idea he incorporated into the new cultural trends. This does not mean that the old idea was not also expressed in other literatures. James Thomson, for example, in his poem *Liberty* spoke of an "artless voice" that "Untaught and wild, yet marbled thro the woods/Romantic lays."[47] Senancour, however, was the first writer to systematically include sound effects in his work as part of his romantic conception of the world. As the first Frenchman to use romantique extensively, Senancour plays a significant role in the history of the word. Moreover, he introduced the term romantisme into the French language at a date rather close to that of the appearance of Romantik in German literature. However, both Senancour and Novalis (about 1800) used the neologism in a sense different from its later meaning. In German it was at first simply a synonym of *Romankunst*, the art or craft of story-telling or story-writing, while Senancour employed romantisme to designate a quality of scenic sublimity. In Letter 87 of *Obermann*, he explains that feelings may increase the *romantisme* (italics in the text) of Alpine sites.[48] He inaugurated the brand of romanticism that was to be Lamartine's, a prose inauguration, of course, since the era of French romantic poetry was not to open until after the fall of the First Empire. But Napoleon, whose infatuation with *Werther* is well known, could not favor preromanticism or romanticism, for they were movements that included too many foreign elements.

In brief, indigenous forces on both sides of the Rhine and the Channel led to a new interpretation of a word, and to a new conception of literature. In 1813, at the moment Madame de Staël published her great work *De l'Allemagne*—a work obviously inspired by the preceptor of her children, August Wilhelm Schlegel—which may be considered the first general study of German romanticism, the adjectives romantic, romantisch, and romantique synonymously expressed the sensibility of at least three peoples.

If need creates words, taste sanctions them. *Romantico* took a long time becoming acceptable to the country of classicism. In Italy, the word was not known before 1810. Here again, Madame de Staël's influence becomes apparent. Her affinity for the country in which she had many friends, like Monti, and which she had celebrated in *Corinne* (1807), greatly contributed to the introduction of the new vocabulary into the peninsula. It is true that in 1814 the eleventh and twelfth issues of the *Spettatore italiano,* the avant-guarde journal of the time, still refused to assume responsibility for the usage of romantico. It described the new literary trends as fitting "questo moderno gusto che Mme de Staël e i tedeschi chiaman romantico" ("this modern taste that Mme de Staël and the Germans call romantic").[49] The text also shows that Italian romanticism regarded German romanticism as its authority rather than the English, even though the Settecento had been strongly inspired by Great Britain; one of the most romantic Italian works is perhaps *Le ultime lettere di Jacopo Ortis* [The last letters of Jacopo Ortis] (1798), the Italian *Werther,* by Ugo Foscolo.

The London correspondent of the *Spettatore* addressed his countrymen in these words: "I teatri danno ora ben rare volte le produzioni immortali di Shakespeare, ma in vece loro, molte operette corniche nel genere sentimentale e romantico" ("Nowadays theatres offer the immortal productions of Shakespeare only quite rarely; in their stead, they put on minor works in the sentimental and romantic vein").[50] The publishers of the journal apparently felt that the word romantico would not be understood, for they explain it in a note: "Un po' più stravagante e capriccioso che *romanzesco*" ("a little more extravagant and capricious than *romanzesco*"), romanzesco being the equivalent of the French romanesque. Later the *Spettatore* printed a lecture by a certain Le Jai that deals with the "genere romantico" and concludes that plays like Shakespeare's *The Tempest* belong to that genre.[51] Silvio Pellico, the author of one of the most romantic love stories *Le mie prigioni* (1832, *My Prisons*) combined with political issues, was the first Italian writer to use romantico unreservedly by according it a literary meaning. In a letter to his brother Luigi on December 11, 1815, he writes: "Non è l'osservanza o la violazione dell'unità di tempo e di luogo che constituisce i generi chiamati classico e romantico" ("It is not the faithful observing or the violating of the unity of time and of place that determines whether a genre is called classical or romantic"). To use the word in a personal letter is to use it unofficially and privately; we must wait some years yet before romantico becomes as common in Italy as romantique in France, romantic in England, and romantisch in Germany.

Interestingly, in Italy romantico was applied to a literary school before it was to the landscape. It is possible, indeed probable, that the prize for having employed it for the first time in a pastoral sense goes to Giovanni Agrati who, in 1819, translated Girardin's essay on landscapes. In chapter 15 we read: "La situazione pittoresca [the French original has pittoresque] incanta gli occhi, se la situazione poetica interessa lo spirito e la memoria, tracciandoci le scene arcadiche; se l'una e l'altra composizione può essere formata dal depintore e dal poeta, v'ha un'altra situazione che dalla sola natura offerire si può, ed è la romantica [romantique]" ("The picturesque scene gives pleasure to the eyes while the poetical scene, by bringing before us the happy pictures of Arcadia, interests our mind and memory; and if it is in the power of painter or poet to produce both sorts of scenes, there is still another that only nature may produce, and this is the romantic").[52]

From the second quarter of the eighteenth century, the Italians had had at their disposal a word for a certain type of narrative: romanzesco; it corresponded to the noun romanzo and was usually defined as "belonging to romances." During the first half of the eighteenth century romanzo was sometimes an adjective. In his book Della ragione poetica (1718), Giovanni Vincenzo Gravina, the master of the poet Metastasio, speaks of "poemi romanzi, ovvero romanensi," and he specifies that both terms are adjectives;[53] in 1731 Giovanni Mario Crescimbeni is found to use romanzi, romanzesco, romanzare, romanzatori,[54] and G. C. Gecelli, in the following year, has the expression "cronaca romanzesca."[55] The adjective plainly did not yet possess a figurative sense. Gradually, however, it came to be applied vaguely to heroes of romances and their deeds, and eventually served to describe landscapes. Melchiorre Cesarotti comments in 1772 on a poem of Ossian, in a note referring to a brook: "Questo è forse quel piccolo ruscello che ritiene ancora il nome di Balva e scorre per la romanzesca valle di Glentivar nella contea di Stirling. Belva significa un ruscello taciturno e Glentivar la valle romita" ("This is perhaps that small brook that still retains the name of Balva and runs through the romantic valley of Glentivar in the county of Stirling. Balva means a quiet brook and Glentivar, the lonely valley").[56] It is solitude, it is nature untransformed by the hand of man that is suggested by romanzesco. But it can insinuate more, namely, the romanticism consisting of melancholy solitude that will be preached by Chateaubriand as found in his Atala and René. Cesarotti, in a comment on his translation, the Compendio della dissertazione sopra i poemi di Ossian del Dottor Ugo Blair, writes: "Gli eventi rammemorati sono tutti seri e gravi e lo ascenaggiamento è per ogni lato selvaggio e romanzesco. Le deserte piagge stese sulla riva del mare, le montagne ombreggiate di nebbi, i torrenti che si precipitano per le solitarie valli, le sparse quercie, le tombe dei guerrieri ricoperte di musco, tutto sveglia une solenna attenzione nello spirito e lo prepara ad eventi grandi e straordinari" ("The remembered events are all serious and grave, and the staging is wild and romantic everywhere. The deserted beaches stretched out on the shores of the sea, the mountains shaded with fog, the torrents rushed through solitary valleys, the scattered oaks, the tombs of heroes covered with moss, everything arouses solemn attention in the spirit and prepares it for great and extraordinary events").[57] Again the same adjectives appear together: "wild and romantic," "selvaggio e romanzesco." It is a European topos.

The Italian language had two other suggestive words, in addition to romanzesco, that meant almost the same thing as romantic: *patetico* and *pittoresco.* The first is encountered in a poem, *La notte,* by a rather little-known author, Angelo Mazza (1747–1817), where he mentions an *usignol patetico* ["romantic nightingale"], and in one of Monti's letters to Madame de Staël, in which he speaks of the *patetico silenzio della natura* [romantic silence of nature]. The second, pittoresco, which is not met with as frequently as is *pittoresque* in France, had the same meaning as its homologues, at that time, in the rest of Europe.

Italy was not the last country to accept the term romantic, which was destined for international usage. It is true that we find it earlier in Scandinavia and in the Netherlands, where it came into use shortly after its introduction in Germany. The term was used in Poland long before 1822, the nominal date for the inception of Polish romanticism. In Russia Zhukovsky, the celebrated precursor of Pushkin and translator of Gray's *Elegy* and of Bürger's *Lenore,* was one of the first champions of the romantic movement in that nation, where *romanichesky* (romanesque, *Romanhaft*) seems to have appeared during the second half of the eighteenth century, but already had the meaning of *romantichesky* (romantic). In the first quarter of the nineteenth century, Spain and the Balkan countries also became familiar with the term. Everywhere, although with differences and numerous interferences, the history of the word shows the same ultimate result: in all European nations it finally became established with several of the acceptations it had in English, sometimes even with all of them.

The various meanings of the term romantic were mentioned in the first parts of this study. When summarizing them here it is important to remember that in the beginning romantic was related to a literary genre or subspecies, the romance, which had its roots in the Middle Ages. Accordingly, deeds and feelings similar to those of heroes of romances came to be designated as *romantic;* hence the first two meanings:

1. romantic: medieval, romance-like
2. romantic: marvelous, fanciful

Next the adjective reflected the scenic background against which characters of romances evolved. The plots were acted out far from cities, in some rustic or seignorial retreat. The notion of solitude is almost always implied, but two essentially different landscapes can be distinguished:

   3. romantic: picturesque (lakes, hills, gardens, parks)
   4. romantic: rugged (sea, mountains, deserts, forests)

These landscapes sometimes created or reflected two different states of mind, and *romantic* may be applied to either one:

   5. romantic: spontaneous, natural (as opposed to artificial, fictitious)
   6. romantic: oversentimental, eccentric (as opposed to sensitive, simple)

Finally, there is a seventh meaning, designating a specific theory of criticism and even a Weltanschauung. Not only do late eighteenth-century and early nineteenth-century writers create romantic characters and evoke romantic sceneries, they become romantic themselves, possibly in their personal lives, but chiefly in their activity as writers. They develop a definite taste for the Middle Ages that replaces the one for classical antiquity, a taste for the description of landscapes either harmoniously idyllic or disorderly wild, for hybridized literary genres that allow them to express more easily their own personality, forgetting the old rules and ignoring much of the cultural past. In many ways they incarnated as writers the *personae* they had created, an identification that may best be rendered tautologically: "romantic: romantic." The adjectives describing countries and places, feelings and attitudes, came to designate a literary school. The last acceptation, then, of romantic is artistic and ideational.

The multiple meanings of the word romantic are one of the main sources of difficulty in defining the romantic movement. Romanticism encompasses seemingly opposite and irreconcilable notions. Common denominators exist, however, for most romanticisms: individualism, egocentricity, types of lyricism, formal elements and ideas, themes, preferences, and aversions.

≫≪

The semantic variations of the words romantic and romantisch, romantique and romantico in successive periods permit us to speculate about the nature and development of the romantic movement. The study of these adjectives in the history of European literature by no means accurately explains the complex romantic phenomenon; however, it provides a feeling for its many elements and a recognition of its roots. Furthermore, it yields a strikingly adequate sketch of all major characteristics of the literary landscape one may call *Euro-*

manticum; in fact, *romantic* and its equivalents are the embryo of *romanticism.* Lexical studies are often most useful for literary ones.

The study of romantic does shed some light on new attitudes toward life, on new ways of envisaging and interpreting human existence. Just as the main acceptations of the word are alike from one literature to another, some fundamental traits of romanticism remain identical everywhere, even though they are not always readily apparent, and even though their expressions vary. Among these basic characteristics are tendencies toward social alienation, toward metaphysical isolation, and toward the displacement of cultural and aesthetic values. Generally, romantic writers share a propensity for the mystical and the transcendental; yet romanticism is characterized by the affirmation of the ego coupled with the integration of the self into nature or into another world, and by the artist's detachment from rationalism together with the assertion of the rights of the imagination and the heart.

On another level, however, the meaning of romantic often appears contradictory: it refers to the old and to the new, to the tender and to the rough, to nature and to the human mind. The variations and evolutions of the term prefigure or echo the alleged inconsistency of the literary current to which it gave its name. Thus the romantic writers should be expected to resemble one another only in their fundamental attitudes, which they betray in a hundred different and sometimes divergent ways. There is no reason to require, in order to justify romanticism as a uniform or as a coherent literary movement, that *all* those who profess allegiance to it center their lives and writings on dreams and aspirations. Nor should they *all* turn into Catholics like many German romantics did, or defend free love and feminism, or convert themselves into passionate protectors of childhood. Neither should *all* of them decide in unison to forget their classics to admire more efficaciously *Mahâbhâratas, Eddas,* and the troubadours. These are not the fundamental traits of European romanticism, but merely some of the external manifestations for deeper realities. Neither a doctor nor a critic should take the symptom for the illness.

It can readily be seen what a delicate task falls upon those who seek to formulate the statutes of the romantic school. Perhaps it would be better to rest content with explaining and describing them. Indeed, all attempts at a proper definition have proved vain, or at best unsatisfactory. They have been deficient on account of their varying degrees of vagueness, partiality, or extremity, and they astonish or amuse more than they instruct. Musset felt romanticism was an inexhaustible source of poetic inspiration. For him romanticism was "a cistern under the palm trees" in the literary desert left after the Enlightenment. Victor Hugo asserts that "romanticism, so many times defined, has perhaps as its real definition nothing else but liberalism in literature." The same opinion is expressed in George Sand's *Lettre à Monsieur Nisard*. Sainte-Beuve appears to have subscribed to this view without reserve; for him, "the qualification of romantique extends to all those among us who, whether by doctrine or practice, have attempted to renew art and to free it from certain conventional rules." This is less a definition, however, than a pragmatic declaration, similar in intent to that which Baudelaire had in mind when he declared romanticism to be "the most recent expression of the beautiful." This concept was rooted in Stendhal's famous passage from *Racine et Shakespeare:* "Romanticism is the art of presenting to the people literary works, which, in the current state of their habits and beliefs, are capable of giving them the most pleasure possible. Classicism, on the contrary, presents to them the literature which gave the greatest pleasure possible to their great-grandfathers." It was Mark Twain who, speaking of "The Disappearance of Literature," invented the most piquant variant of this last conception: "A classic is something that everybody wants to have read and nobody wants to read." To Giraudoux, romanticism is "the pantheism of civilized periods." Ironically enough, the etymology of the word romantic leads back to Rome, one of the hometowns of classicism.

In Germany Schelling suggested that the classical temperament is inclined toward the study of the past and the romantic temper looks to the future. Friedrich Schlegel already had defined *die Romantik* as "progressive Universalpoesie." But Heine, for his part, looked searchingly into the past and affirmed that romanticism was essentially a resurrection of the Middle Ages. As to Goethe, he gave his friend Eckermann a well-known distinction between classicism and romanticism: "A new expression has come to me, which does not define the relation badly. I call classical that which is healthy, and romantic, that which is sick and unsound. According to this view, the *Nibelungenlied* is as classic as Homer, for both are healthy and fit. The newest thing is not romantic because it is new, but rather because it is weak, sickly, and ill; and the old is not classic, because it is old, but rather because it is strong, fresh, joyful, and healthy. If we distinguish classic and romantic in accordance with such qualities, we shall quickly reach an understanding of the matter."

The Anglo-Saxon world has been no less inventive with incidental phrases that could well serve as epigraphs to books on romanticism. For Walter Pater it consists in "the addition of strangeness to beauty," and for Hoxie N. Fairchild it remains "a desire to find the infinite within the finite, to effect a synthesis of the real and the unreal." With these and some other definitions in mind, Musset could be a companion of Shelley, and Lamartine might rub elbows with the Schlegel brothers, Wordsworth with Chateaubriand, Keats with Eichendorff, Vigny with Foscolo, Byron with Hoffmann. It is only by reviewing a mosaic composed of thousands of romantic tesserae from a remote vantage point that we can distinguish its design and grasp the essential unity that pervaded Western civilization. If the study of the word alone cannot lead to a full understanding of romantic literature, it furnishes essential materials that the scholar may apply to his analysis of romanticism as a pan-European cultural movement.

9

Literary Exoticism

A literary trend, such as exoticism, differs from a literary movement or current, such as the baroque, romanticism, or naturalism, because it is not restricted to either a particular period or a specific geographic area. It follows neither a homogeneous pattern of development nor a logical sequence, and its history is characterized by irregularity and discontinuity. Unlike a movement, a trend can be illustrated in a series of manifestations that wax and wane sporadically, although not always unpredictably, in various countries and periods. On the national level it can sometimes take on the semblance, or even more, the importance, of a current, as in France, England, and Germany during the eighteenth and nineteenth centuries. Let it be noted, however, that no sharp borderline exists between the two notions of trend and movement. Rather than emphasizing the nuances or differences between them, we wish to show in this chapter that a study in a literary trend, just as our study in a literary movement, fulfills the general purpose of comparatistic inquiry. They both lead, as do studies in the three other categories of our discipline—those in relations, genres, and motifs—to conclusions concerning not only one single literature, but a cross section of the international literary life.

Exoticism, in its broadest sense, originates from a variety of psychological attitudes. It often expresses man's wish to escape the artifice of civilization and to find another natural and social environment, foreign and strange; it helps to nourish one of man's fondest dreams, the dream of the faraway, the unknown, the mysterious. Another kind of exoticism, which stems from a need for action, is concretized in the propensity for exploration, adventure, and discovery. In literature exoticism often arises from particular historical occurrences that have resulted from the attempt to realize certain ideals. Thus a religious ideal motivated the armies of Mohammed, the Crusaders, and the missionaries; and a cultural ideal—economically and politically based—drove the nations of western Europe to adopt colonial and imperialist policies.[1] As a consequence of so much religious, military, commercial, and diplomatic activity, civilizations clashed and intermingled, and this phenomenon was necessarily reflected in national and international letters.

I

The term *exotic* originated in Greece, where the adjective *eksotikos* generally meant "foreign" and was applied to what was outside the limits of the state—a meaning close to that of *barbaros* or *barbarikos*—or simply beyond the family threshold. When the Athenian wished to praise a meal he had enjoyed at a neighbor's house, he could resort to the expression *eksotike estiasis:* he had had an "exotic dinner."[2] The epithet obviously designated something outside the pale of the home and its customary experiences. But the word often assumed a much more exclusive sense: only that which pertained to *faraway* places could properly be called exotic. Thus Plautus uses the phrase *exotica unguenta* and speaks of *exoticum* with reference, among other things, to clothing worn in foreign nations.[3]

In all periods of time exotic was often reserved, and still is, for discussions of natural history or intercontinental commerce; a plant, an animal, or a spice might be exotic. In *Pantagruel*, Rabelais alludes to "exotic and peregrine goods which were to be found in the markets of the port,"[4] and in the *Nouvelle Héloïse*, Saint-Preux describes Julie's garden in these words: "If I did not find any exotic plants or products of the Indies here, I saw the indigenous ones arranged in such a way as to produce a more agreeable and pleasant effect."[5] This is also the meaning that the term customarily carries in England, where it was common at the end of the sixteenth century, and in Germany, although, it seems, it was not in use there before the first quarter of the eighteenth century.

Derivatives of the adjective are found in various tongues: *exoticism* (more current in English than *exotism*), the French *exotisme*, and the German *Exotismus* are internationally well-known terms. The word *exoticness* of eighteenth-century England never crossed the Channel; *exotical* and *exoticalness* have been lost, while the substantive *exotics*, which can designate plants and objects, has survived. The Germans have *Der Exote* (the title of a novel by Ernst Wiechert) and *der Exotist* (a person living in an exotic country), a term that does have an equivalent in English: *exoticist*. In contemporary Greek the noun *eksotike* belongs to the fairy tale; it refers to a nixie or undine—an instance of exoticism of the imagination.

The contemporary connotation of exotic is much more than just a synonymity with foreign. We may say that literary exoticism is the integration or intrusion into the literary world of unusual geographical and ethnological features; it expresses the writer's taste for countries that seem excitingly strange and charmingly new, and betrays his enchantment with the diversity, with the vagary even of climate and custom. If he is a moralist or a philosopher, these materials capture his interest because of the lessons they may furnish; if he is a novelist or poet, he is fascinated by the mirage they are likely to produce. Whether natural historian, folklorist, botanist, or simple globe-trotter, an "exotic writer" always takes delight in recounting, in informing and in amazing others. They all adopt similar techniques: they transpose certain scenes or places familiar to the reader into a new setting under distant skies, into a realm that boasts the charm of the unknown and the unexpected, into alluringly beautiful and mysterious parts of the world. Exotic decor satisfies our taste for the picturesque and the eccentric, and it thereby imparts an increased intensity to certain types of narrative and poetry.

Works classed as exotic automatically transport the reader into far-off regions, to peoples or tribes, the names of which are often barely known. The countryside, the fauna and flora, the appearance and the mores of the natives, their traditions and institutions, their castes and governments—all these factors may form the center of the writer's and the reader's interests. Besides enlivening the action, these elements may be used to explain or justify the singularity of events and certain psychological reactions. Exoticism, furthermore, may fulfill other purposes: it can be utilized for social criticism or edification, in which case one could refer to satirical or didactic exoticism. We may also speak of an imported exoticism: the Chinese in Oliver Goldsmith's *Citizen of the World* and the Persians in Montesquieu's *Lettres persanes* came to Europe in order to teach moral lessons to the English and the French.[6]

❧

It is not possible to examine here the impact of exoticism on every single culture. A few remarks on the relations between Europe and the Far East may shed light on some general aspects of this literary trend.

The culture of China is one of the most venerable in the world, and is also one of the most opaque and impermeable. Marco Polo illustrates the cleft between Asiatic and European attitudes. When, at the end of the thirteenth century, he returned from Peking to Venice after seventeen years at the imperial court, the account of his experiences and discoveries transformed not only the map of the earth, but also the philosophical systems of the Western world. A new conception of the cosmos came into being. The reaction of the Chinese, however, was different. Their silk had found its way to Athens and Rome during antiquity, and they had seen Arabs establish themselves on the southern shores of their empire in the eighth century. But they scarcely noticed the arrival and sojourn of that Western intruder, Marco Polo. Virtually no trace of his adventures is to be found in Chinese letters. Yet what an impetus this could have been for exoticism in Far Eastern literatures.

Commercial and bellicose motives occasionally took the Asians to Europe in the course of the centuries. But it was the Europeans who left their land with a firm determination to discover a route to China, not the Chinese who showed such instincts.[7] There are no place names outside China that recall a Chinese conqueror. The sea expeditions to Aden and the Somali coast undertaken by Yung Lo (1360–1424), the third emperor of the Ming dynasty, remained rather unique adventures with hardly any permanent international repercussions; they were not part of any national tradition or instinct. Nor can the idioms of Japan, the Philippines, Africa, or India be found in the toponymy beyond their own territories. And a name, in such an instance, not only marks the high deed of a great adventure, but the character of an exploring and pioneering people. All the wisdom of Confucius did not enable the Chinese to discover the pineapple of the Caribbees or the girls of Baghdad.

China by tradition has been isolated from the rest of the world; her wall is a symbol. Conscious of possessing a civilization, the value of which has been essentially moral, the Chinese did not allow themselves to be unsaddled from their feeling of superiority, and until recently remained indifferent to the technical supremacy of the Western barbarians. Many European explorers, missionaries, and merchants were successful in finding protectors among the men of Han; but among the Chinese elite there was never a movement comparable to the French anglomania, nothing to rival the francomania of Germany, or, indeed, the sinomania of all Europe. Only since the last century has China allowed herself to be seriously influenced by occidental art and letters.[8] Now for the first time she has begun to borrow literary themes, genres, and techniques. The Chinese writer, however, creates his exotic atmosphere without the use of African, Indian, or European landscapes. Unlike scores of French and English heroes who have indulged in reverie on the immense plains of the Iroquois or under the palm trees of unknown islands, characters in Chinese works do not like to daydream in the shade of faraway Alpine spruces or in the sun of Mediterranean beaches. In Asia, exoticism affected literature only to a very limited extent, for it did not correspond to an inner need either on the part of the public or of the poet—one further proof of the basically introverted character of Eastern peoples.

Exoticism ordinarily does not flourish in autarkic and self-enclosed nations. In this respect, the Japanese were not much different from their continental neighbors. For long periods of time they manifested no serious urge to know the Western world, although they knew all about China. In the seventeenth century, however, they translated Aesop; and in 1774 they could read *Gulliver's Travels* in their own tongue. Yet it was only during the reign of Emperor Mutsuhito (1867–1912) that occidental culture started to invade their country and provide the Japanese with ideas and customs markedly different from their own.

If the Chinese and Japanese were not concerned with Western culture until recent decades, the West had long been receptive to the Orient. Chinese art began to spread decidedly over Europe as early as the sixteenth century. French, Dutch, and Spanish merchants started to handle Chinese silk, fans, and parasols. Porcelain—which became china just as japan came to mean lacquerware—and tea contributed to building up China's reputation in matters of luxury. At the same time, Matteo Ricci (1552–1610) and Juan Gonzales de Mendoza (1540–1617) popularized exotic cultures in their travel accounts, reports, and tales. Chinoiseries—that could not be distinguished from Japonaiseries any better than some sedentary Europeans today can distinguish a Chinese face from a Japanese—were displayed in the best salons of Rome, Paris, and London. Chinese culture can be clearly recognized in baroque architecture, but especially in the rococo that followed. British sinomania was promoted by writers and painters as well as by landscape gardeners and architects like Sir William Chambers who, upon his return from Canton, published his famous *Designs of Chinese Buildings* (1757) and included a well-known pagoda among the ornamental constructions at Kew Palace, Surrey. The traditional Chinese art of arranging plants and laying parks was well remembered during the conflict waged between those who preferred the French garden according to the model of André Le Nôtre to the English garden of William Kent and their "romantic" antagonists. Even Chinese baths became fashionable; Paris had such an establishment on the Boulevard des Italiens between 1792 and 1856. During the romantic age, Chinese birds and flowers were as stylish on wallpaper in Paris as Swiss lakes and mountains. French fad for things Chinese is most richly illustrated in Flaubert's *Education sentimentale;* Chinese bibelots decorate the apartments of all the principal characters.[9]

≫≪

The perfumes of exoticism that inundated Europe at irregular intervals did not all come from far distant lands. Even for Europeans, the eastern and southern shores of the Mediterranean have to this day retained the charm and magic they possessed in the centuries of the Caesars' glory. Among the Roman elite, it was ancient Egypt especially that exercised an unchallenged power. Mark Antony illustrates the spell that exoticism could cast on a triumvir's destiny. One day Scipio Africanus went to Carthage; Hannibal's elephants, another day, threatened the gates of the Urbs. Black slaves toiled their lives away in the villas of the aristocrats, and in the circus Numidian wild beasts died to satisfy the appetite of the crowd. Long before Daudet's Tartarin—and with better results than he had—people went to the dark continent to hunt lions; and in Juvenal's time, bread and games— *panem et circenses*—was the slogan for a happy life: daily subsistence and dreamworlds of exoticism. Not only ancient history, but literature and mainly mythology is filled with exotic elements. Traditionally the Amazons' homeland, for instance, was either Phrygia or Lycia, or other areas of Asia Minor—except for Homer, who has a contingent of them come from Thrace to rescue King Priam.

The West has always been interested in Turkey, Syria, and Armenia.[10] In the fourth century B.C., Alexander's soldiers went as far as the Ganges, after ten thousand Greeks, as Xenophon relates, had explored Babylonia a hundred years before. But it was Islam and the Arabian culture that really penetrated into many parts of Europe, initiating significant transformations. Abd-er-Rahman's army had already reached the plain of Poitiers before he was stopped by Charles Martel, and Spain was profoundly influenced by the Mohammedan invasion.[11] The Moorish impact was far more powerful in Spain than anywhere else in Christendom, and it can be observed both in Spanish literature and architecture. At the time of Charlemagne and his paladins, the Saracens entered the civilization of many other Western countries. Philosophers of Persia and Arabia, among them Avicenna and Averroes, played a major role in the development of medieval thought. The Koran was known not only by the elite; its doctrine circulated with the general currents of ideas. The Arabs and the Turks were the only highly cultured peoples who subjugated great parts of Europe by force, and in so doing presented them with all the riches of their arts, their sciences, and their philosophy. The arabesque was brought to the Europeans—while the Europeans had to go to China to find the chinoiseries. Also, though it is often forgotten, Judeo-Christian culture has presented strikingly exotic elements. Moreover, the Crusades fill an important chapter in the history of exoticism. Along with the memory of their defeats, the Crusaders brought back new criteria by which to appreciate the countries through which they had traveled and in which a great number of them had spent many years of their lives. Hence the Near East continued to fascinate Europe.

It was not until the beginning of the eighteenth century, however, that a French text of *Mille et une nuits* appeared in a work soon to be translated into many other European languages, and it was through *The Arabian Nights* that new themes were introduced into Western letters. Oriental scholar Antoine Galland familiarized the West with this collection of tales, which were supposedly gathered in Cairo in the midst of the fifteenth century; its origins are shrouded in mystery.[12] In the early nineteenth century some European countries, especially Germany, borrowed from the Arabs—as the Hindus, the Persians, and the Turks had done hundreds of years before—a lyrical genre, the ghasel or ghazal, successfully illustrated by Rückert and Platen. The most sumptuous incarnation of oriental splendors in the nineteenth century is surely Flaubert's *Salammbô* (1862), and the equivalent for our times is Lawrence Durrell's *The Alexandria Quartet* (1957–1960).

II

From the fifteenth century on, travel accounts played a significant part in the rise of literary exoticism. It was the time when famous explorers of the globe returned from their voyages, and when the newly established knowledge of the roundness of the earth rendered anachronous the terms *occident* and *orient*. The successors of Marco Polo—the Portuguese Álvaro Fernandes and Ferdinand Magellan, the Italian Christopher Columbus, the French Jacques Cartier, and the Spanish Juan Fernández—contributed decisively to the launching of a new literary genre, the travel account, which naturally assigned a generous amount of space to exoticism. These are only some of the best-known names, for attention could also be called to the large assembly of less glorious conquerors who penetrated beyond the equator, and who, according to the famous verse of José María de Heredia, stood on the bridge of their ships, and watched new stars rising from the depths of the ocean.

A general history of travel literature could be inserted here, one in which Spain, Portugal, and Italy would take an important place. It would also include French works like Abbé Prévost's *Histoire générale des voyages*, published from 1746 to 1789, and Boucher de la Richarderie's *Bibliothèque générale des voyages*, which appeared in 1808. In Germany Johann Beckmann wrote a *Literatur der älteren Reisen* (1807–1810), and one of the first British works of this kind was Richard Hakluyt's *The Principall Navigations, Voiages and Discoveries of the English Nation* (1589), which was preceded and followed by numerous monographs written by travelers and merchants. Those of Samuel Purchas (1626) and Sir John Chardin (1686), and James Cook's *Account of a Voyage Round the World in the Years 1768–1771*, were among the most popular.

Academic scholarship has traced this chronicle of voyages in the vast perspective of universal history. It has tried to explain the origins and developments of this aspect of human endeavor in terms of the spiritual fever that affected Western man with a kind of physical malady and anxiety, causing him to start the process—now at its height—of melding the peoples of the world. "De la stabilité au mouvement," such is the title given by Paul Hazard to the first chapter of his *Crise de la conscience européenne*.[13] A complete history of travel would narrate the gests of the great captains as well as the pirates, whether occasional or professional, and also the deeds, impossible to remember in their details, of the anonymous adventurers and the simple sailors who contributed to creating this state of mind.

By the eighteenth century the reports of voyages were clearly being transformed into a literary genre—one that is specifically European.[14] It was the West, as has been noted, that took the initiative in the exploration of the earth. While all the exotic, alien characters of English, French, and German novels, who supposedly explore London or Paris, or espy the court of Potsdam, or Vienna, are products of the creative mind, the Europeans—materialists as well as idealists, merchants as well as missionaries[15]—really made the arduous voyages to the home countries of these imaginary guests and established themselves there in settlements. After the age of exploration came that of the fusion of reality and fancy. Documents became novels, exotic ones. Thousands of travel books printed in every country of the old continent excited and exalted the fervent attention of the reading public. In their pages the luxurious nature of the distant tropics glittered, as did the sensual charm of lonely beaches and the impenetrable mystery of crowded, burning, and shining cities. People found in them the memories of fairy tales that suddenly ceased to be fairy tales. A whole world, which had been unreal up to that time, suddenly took shape and breathed. The history of the discovery of the different continents is a great adventure, even greater than that of an astronaut's return from the moon with a few dusty pebbles and some photographs of a crater, although space expeditions and science fiction may well renew the sources—and the formula—of exoticism.

※

As opposed to utopian or imaginary exoticism, sixteenth- and seventeenth-century western Europe developed and popularized realistic exoticism in travel literature. An army of navigators and pioneers allied themselves to write this formidable epic of a Ulysses going beyond the Pillars of Hercules into the unknown Western Sea—an epic whose last song was to be the general inventory of our planet. The gradual intrusion of the Middle East, and especially of the Far East and the Americas, into the West greatly contributed to furthering historical, cultural, and religious relativism. In the eighteenth century, exoticism developed other results. It was exploited for philosophical,

moral, and political purposes. The opposition, however, between the
two exoticisms, that of the writer and poet and that of the thinker
and ruler, was far from being absolute, although sharp enough to deserve notice. Travel accounts of the two centuries preceding that of
the Enlightenment generally bore witness to the writer's passionate
concern with geographical accuracy, and the conclusions drawn were
promptly surpassed by subsequent discoveries. The philosophes, on
the contrary, liked to show a certain idealism or ideology in these
stories, which often included few exact sociological observations and
little well-documented ethnographical material. Diderot's *Supplément
au Voyage de M. Bougainville* does not add one geographical or ethnological detail to Bougainville's travel account: it is its philosophical
epilogue. Rousseau alluded to that development when he complained:
"Of all the countries of Europe, there is none where so many travel
tales and accounts are printed as in France, and none where the
genius and mores of other nations is less understood."[16] These remarks apply also to natural history. The sort of fauna and flora found
in *Robinson Crusoe* does not testify to the scientific interests of the
author: Alexander Selkirk's description of the Juan Fernández Island
in the South Pacific inspired Defoe's description of the Tobago Island
in the equatorial Atlantic, where the action of the novel is supposed
to take place.

In the literature of travel, the Age of Enlightenment discovered
practical examples to support the arguments for its favorite doctrines
and theses. Travel accounts, real or imaginary, illustrated man's original goodness, his natural intelligence and wisdom. Both physiocrats
and philosophes delighted in turning their gaze westward, to the New
World, where Indian tribes, so they thought, were living out their
golden age. Physiocrats, however, and philosophes were also inspired
by the rising sun, the Levant, the Near East, Cipango and Cathay, by
the regions in which Mongolian khans ruled and by those in which
Buddhas offered up their oracles to the questing people. Thus, from
the Far West came the myth of the noble savage, and from the Far
East the myth of the Chinese sage whose wisdom rivaled that of the
Egyptian and the Brahman.[17]

How deeply Europe was impressed by both things Indian and
things Hindu is most strikingly illustrated by German poets. A man
like Gellert so equitably shares his love between the East and West
Indies that for him these regions come to form together one single
country. In his *Inkle and Yariko*, inspired by Steele, who first treated
the theme, he has the hero going to "Amerika" in the first part of the
poem, and in the last he has him returning from "Indien."[18] The
majority of German writers, however, indicated more geographical
accurateness. The Indian inspired Schiller for his lament of the
Dakota Sioux, expressed in *Nadowessiers Totenlied*,[19] constituted
the subject of Adelbert von Chamisso's *Rede des alten Kriegers*

Bunte-Schlange, of Lenau's *Die drei Indianer*, of Freiligrath's *Tod des Führers*. The Hindi occupies an important role in Goethe's *West-Östlicher Divan*, and is the subject of works such as Friedrich Schlegel's *Über die Sprache und Weisheit der Inder* and Rückert's *Weisheit der Brahmanen*. Ninteenth-century German literature was strongly influenced by the Indies[20] and the impact of oriental thought on American transcendentalism is well known.[21] Exotic elements penetrated not only works of fiction, but philosophic systems and doctrines as well.

III

In western Europe the eighteenth century is also the age of literary exoticism proper, the age of the rise of the exotic novel and of philosophical exoticism. The nineteenth century is the age of the rise of exotic poetry. If we wished to determine the most fertile terrain in the Enlightenment for the exotic novel, we would have to turn to England, and if we wanted to discover, during the same period, the most hospitable habitat of philosophical exoticism, our choice would have to be France. Still, these are debatable choices because the two genres abound in both countries as they do indeed in European letters at large.

Perhaps more than the writers of other countries, British novelists have displayed a spirit of adventure in their books and in their lives. They belong to a seafaring race. The Abbé Prevost characterizes the English most aptly when he notes: "Half their nation is ceaselessly in motion toward the most remote corners of the Earth. England has almost as many vessels as houses, and one can say of the entire island what the historians of China say of Nanking: that a great part of the large population lives habitually on water."[22] In the eighteenth century, a large number of British writers departed from their native island at some time or other. A few months before his death, Sterne came back to England in order to publish his *Sentimental Journey through France and Italy* (1768); Fielding and Smollett, worn out by work and agitations of all kinds and bent by fevers and impatience, went to dream their last dreams in seaports of the Midi: one at Lisbon, the other at Leghorn, where they died within seventeen years of each other.

Both Fielding and Smollett show their predisposition to exoticism in their restless heroes. Fielding's are always traveling when not eating or sleeping, which they frequently forget to do. The outdoors is the natural arena for their actions. What a contrast with Richardson—Great Britain, too, has had her sedentary people—whose characters habitually keep to their homes and huddle in their sitting rooms, unless some Lovelace happens to conceive the idea of arranging an abduction; but even then the action merely moves from one chamber to the other. For full-blown exoticism in literature we must go to other writers, to Smollett, for example. As a surgeon's mate aboard the *Cumberland*, he witnessed all the horrors of the siege of Cartagena. In Jamaica he fell in love with a colonist's daughter who was to become his wife—a living memory, in his creative years, of his restless youth. *Roderick Random* should appeal to anyone who likes sea adventures. And if *Peregrine Pickle, Ferdinand Count Fathom*, and *The Expedition of Humphry Clinker* merely repeat in a few spots the echo of distant lands, one feels that these are the novels of a great voyager.

The Expedition of Humphry Clinker shows with admirable eloquence that the English do not scorn travel in Britain. It was Defoe, it seems, who revived the fashion of the zigzag trip through one's own country well before the time of Rodolphe Töpffer. In 1724 the first volume of *A Tour thro' the Whole Island of Great Britain* appeared, a work not entirely novel in its goal and scope. Its tradition goes back to the *Magnae Britanniae Deliciae*, published in 1613, an account, moreover, that was followed by a series of other *délices*—travel books on Italy, Holland, and Switzerland. Not only were all the corners of the old continent explored, but they were meticulously described in travel guides, just as travel agencies and tourist organizations publish such matter today. Consequently, distant lands gradually experienced an upswing in popularity. "Europe, in fact," wrote Gérard de Nerval, "is perfectly known to everyone; a traveler can therefore do nothing more than relate the itinerary of his trip, the chronicle of his adventures, and, if necessary, the varieties of his menus."[23] This passage does not so much indict Nerval's sterile imagination as it contributes to an explanation of the increasing success of exoticism. This upswing in popularity started with Defoe's work. Yet, his *Robinson Crusoe* (1719), most important for the history of exoticism, was preceded by the novels of Aphra Behn, the first Englishwoman who succeeded in living—not very luxuriously—by her pen. She went to the northern coast of South America, to Surinam, probably as the mistress of William Scott, son of the regicide Thomas Scott. There she met the slave-prince Oroonoko who inspired the title of her celebrated book *Oroonoko, or the Royal Slave* (1678), in which was recounted the touching and tragic love between the noble Negro and fair Imoinda, whose heirs we later find installed in *Uncle Tom's Cabin* (1852). *Robinson Crusoe* was also preceded by Steele's *Inkle and Yarico*, published in the eleventh issue of the *Spectator* (1711). Both Defoe's narrative and Steele's tragic story demonstrate most vividly the ascendancy in England of travel accounts and tales of adventure about unknown lands including moralizing plots.

Countless "robinsonades" appeared in the eighteenth century and later, as did many imitations of Steele's little work, the best one being perhaps George Colman's romantic comedy, which kept the name of its model. As for Defoe, one is inclined to regard him as either a highwayman fond of literature or some kind of literate sea pirate,[24] although he never followed such a calling. His biographers, besides an engraving, have found only one description of his physical appearance, his police record. When he was wanted by the authorities for sporting too much irony in a pamphlet against the government, a reward was issued for his capture and arrest. The delinquent was described as "a middle-sized spare man, about forty years old, of a brown complexion, and dark-brown coloured hair, but wears a wig, a hooked nose, a sharp chin, grey eyes and a large mole near his mouth." At any rate, Defoe's information for *Robinson Crusoe* was bookish, and his settings were plagiarisms or clichés. Nevertheless, his heroes, the immortal islander and his friend Friday, certainly have a secure place in the history of the rise of realism. But the history of exoticism—not descriptive or lyrical exoticism, but the geographical kind—would also include *The Life, Adventures, and Piracies of the Famous Captain Singleton,* the bold mariner who sailed round the then-navigable world. Nor could it ignore the curious *History and Remarkable Life of the Truly Honorable Colonel Jacque,* the action of which takes the reader to Newgate Prison, the plantations of Virginia, France, Germany, Italy, and Hungary. For *Moll Flanders,* the superb *picara,* Newgate *was* a new gate, the portal opening the way to a life of adventures. She is consumed with travel fever, journeys to the American colonies, and finally and wisely returns to London at seventy—an age at which one can gracefully and without loss repent one's sins.

The works of many English writers may be approached on the level of exoticism: Swift injected exoticism into *Gulliver's Travels* (1726), Goldsmith into *The Citizen of the World* (1762). Among the promoters of English orientalism, Sir William Jones, the British champion of comparative philology, holds one of the first ranks. Orientalism found its literary expression in works as far apart from each other as Doctor Johnson's *History of Rasselas, Prince of Abyssinia* (1759) and William Beckford's *Vathek* (French 1782, English 1786). In addition, it was expressed in *An Arabian Tale* (1786), which like *Vathek* was first written in French, and in Robert Bage's *The Fair Syrian* (1787). The oriental tale was not less authentically emulated by numerous minor authors: in 1761, John Hawkesworth published *Almoran and Hamet,* and Charles Johnstone, in 1774, *Alsaces.*[25] In the nineteenth century, English literature could boast of exoticists like Walter Pater, James Thomson, Swinburne, and Oscar Wilde.

Exoticism also invaded British theater and poetry. With *The West Indian* (1771) Richard Cumberland illustrates the former, with *Kubla Khan* Coleridge, before the close of the eighteenth century, exemplifies the latter. Coleridge considered exoticism, which he liked to cultivate with the aid of opium, as "a source of luxurious sensations."[26] We cannot include here a systematic study of the exotic trend in English literature, of course, but the titles of a few other significant works may be quoted to illustrate the point. Southey, for instance, wrote *Thalaba the Destroyer*, *The Curse of Kehama*, and *A Tale of Paraguay*, while Landor published *Gebir* and *Gebirus*, and *Imaginary Conversations*—comparative in nature—eight with an oriental and three with an American setting. During the eighteenth century, as we have indicated, descriptions of far-off countries, foreign customs, and habits often served as pretexts for social and political criticism. Now most of the romantic writers were definitely moving away from this philosophical and satirical exoticism.[27] Not only in England, but also in the literatures of the European continent exoticism began pervading poetry; and the poets wrote their exotic poems with nothing but poetic effects in mind.

✄

This development can be clearly traced in French literature. Striking resemblances exist between *Candide* and *Rasselas*, both published in 1759, though not between the authors themselves or their theses. Both writers, however, prove that on either side of the Channel some people thought an exotic atmosphere would enhance, for the public, the plausibility of a plot, and, by extension, the truth of its inherent doctrine. In *Candide, ou l'optimisme*, the exotic charm begins to assert itself in the second chapter, when the scene of action shifts from Germany to Bulgaria. It becomes especially effective in the adventure scenes that take place in Paraguay, Buenos Aires, the Peruvian Eldorado, Surinam, and the land of the Oreillons. The garden that the older and wiser Candide cultivates is quite different from the orchard of the family chateau of Thunder-ten-tronckh in Westphalia; it is on Turkish ground, at Constantinople.

Should we review all the *contes* of Voltaire, all his dramatic pieces, his treatises, essays, histories, and dictionaries, we would see exoticism almost everywhere, and almost everywhere we would find it connected with satire. Its role is not to suggest or create or re-create a world, but to emphasize contrasts, to confront two ways of life, two attitudes, two religions, two doctrines. The kind of irony and satire that Voltaire develops, however, has a rather long tradition in French literature. It characterizes particularly a certain chapter of Montaigne's *Essais*, where the most salient difference between Frenchmen and Brazilians is bared by the exclamation that terminates the description of the cannibals: "Good Lord! They don't wear any breeches!" Speaking of the Indians of Brazil, Montaigne observes: "There is nothing barbarous and savage in this nation, by anything that I can gather, excepting, that every one gives the title of barbarism to everything that is not in use in his own country. . . . They are savages at the same rate that we say fruits are wild, which nature produces of herself and by her own ordinary progress."[28] Analogous authorial intentions may be seen in innumerable eighteenth-century works.

French preromanticism launched the idea of exoticism at the service of sentiment. Manon Lescaut, in Abbé Prévost's 1731 novel, declares to Des Grieux: "It is to New Orleans that one must go to taste the true delights of love." And Paul and Virginie, in Bernardin de Saint-Pierre's 1787 romance, could not have loved each other anywhere as much as they did in the shade of the grapefruit tree on a lost island of the Indian Ocean. And a few years later, at the very beginning of the nineteenth century, Chateaubriand's *René*, his *Atala, Les Natchez*, and *Les Aventures du dernier des Abencérages* make distinctly exotic impressions. Thanks to literary individualism, exemplified by Chateaubriand's heroes, exotic types began to be endowed with specific characteristics, while Voltaire's Hurons had not differed essentially from his Peruvians, Arabs, or Turks, just as in many books of the time Indians and Negroes did not have their proper racial status. In the early nineteenth century, owing to their predilection for the picturesque, writers began to observe even the nuances that separate the Japanese from the Chinese. Similar observations can be made in their descriptions of countrysides. Moreover, French exoticism, like the English, no longer aimed primarily at delivering lessons of wisdom or at recounting tales of adventure. It became poetry; it was to the imagination and to the senses, not to reason, that the writer addressed himself.

Most significant illustrations may be shown one or two generations later, in Charles Baudelaire, for example, who was sensitive to the influence of Edgar Allen Poe and Thomas De Quincey. Baudelaire paid tribute to exoticism by means of a number of poems that are among the best of the *Fleurs du mal: La Chevelure, Du Vin et du haschisch, Sed non satiata, Parfum exotique, A une dame créole*. In France a whole literary school could be identified as exotic and could be regrouped around its master, Baudelaire. Its doctrine could be summed up with the motto: *erotica per exotica*.[29] These trends may be traced in the works of Leconte de Lisle, Heredia, Gautier, Mérimée, Nerval, Flaubert, Rimbaud, Huysmans, as well as many less illustrious talents, notably Le Poittevin, Soulary, and Bouilhet. But the French did not have a monopoly on sensual exoticism—that refined carnality that both purified and intensified the exotic strand of literature. We recognize this quality in Heinse's *Ardinghello*, though exoticism here does not go farther than Greece, and we find it again in numerous works of Gabriele D'Annunzio, and in the verses of Russia's symbolists, especially in those of Konstantin Dmitrievich Balmont.

The great French poets discovered exoticism by personal experience: they were all energetic voyagers. Baudelaire went to the Isle of Maurice, east of Madagascar; Leconte de Lisle was born and spent his youth on Bourbon Island, then wandered over the Indies and the Indonesian archipelago; Heredia was a native of Cuba, where he returned for a time after his studies in Paris; Jules Supervielle's birthplace was Montevideo in Uruguay, a country he never renounced; Gautier visited Algeria and Turkey; Mérimée went to Asia Minor; Nerval saw, among other countries, Egypt and Syria; and Flaubert explored the Near East, while Rimbaud pushed on to Ethiopia, Arabia, Sumatra, and Java. The French of the nineteenth century had a vagabond spirit that has been analyzed in a series of monographs. The titles of two Parisian periodicals—the first still published—assume a symbolic value: *La Revue des Deux Mondes* (1829) and *Le Globe* (1824). The same phenomenon is observed in England, where *The Globe* and *The Traveller* were most popular journals. It was the age when comparatism as a literary discipline was born.

⁂

Although universal in character, exoticism varies in externals according to the nations and continents in which it is found. These differences are determined by certain qualities of each people, their nomadic or sedentary traditions, their xenophobic or hospitable attitudes, their philosophic and religious guidance. Exoticism also depends on more concrete factors, such as social, political, and economic conditions of a particular country, the state of its communications, its fleet, or the transportation facilities it can provide for the traveler to its interior. It was inevitable that exoticism in various literatures should exhibit virtually no regularity or uniformity.

Regions regarded as exotic in one period, moreover, may cease to merit the epithet during another. In antiquity, for example, all of *barbaricum* was exotic. In Tacitus' *Germania* the Germanic tribes and their lands were looked upon as exotic by the Romans of the first century after Christ, while to a Roman of the twentieth century there is hardly anything exotic about either of the two German republics.[30] With the progressive internationalization of man's way of life, exoticism in the traditional sense of the word seems condemned to fade, or, at best, to be preserved and cultivated artificially in a hothouse atmosphere, thanks to patriotic and folkloristic organizations. It will find a refuge in reservations not unlike those in which the American government places its Indians. There, exoticism will eke out a meager existence fabricating beads, blankets, and tapestries, seeking to recall the exciting and colorful days of yore.

Modern man is assaulted by so many impressions, whether simultaneous or successive, that he does not always distinguish the autochthonous from the exotic. If he is in the habit of taking long trips, he is immunized against most surprises that distant lands hold in store for novices. If he prefers to stay at home, he is overwhelmed by the energy of the press, television, radio, books, and travel brochures. The effect is the same. He becomes an expert in exoticism through the enthusiasm that travel-bureau advertisements exude. If an American, this modern man also experiences exoticism in a military uniform, or domestically in Alaska and Hawaii. Western man in the big city, especially, becomes more and more impermeable to exoticism; some metropolises reserve entire neighborhoods for specific races. Europeans no longer have to await the arrival of a circus to see various specimens of the human family. One restaurant serves Chinese meals, another Mexican delicacies. Vast crowds pour into museums of natural history and ethnography. In the present day everything may be *foreign*, but nothing is necessarily *strange*. For centuries the Arabic numbers have not been Arabic any more, and how often does a Berliner or a Londoner, when eating a banana, think of the Indies or Senegal? The day is coming when the urchin of New York or Paris will adjudge a goat more exotic than a tiger, an oak stranger than a gingko.

Exoticism in the West has also invaded the auditory as well as the visual arts. Jazz, for instance, provides ample evidence of African influence, and the history of music abounds with examples of composers' interest in orientalism: Rameau's *Indes Galantes*, Gluck's *Die Pilgrime von Mekka*, Mozart's *Die Entführung aus dem Serail*, and Boieldieu's *Le Calife de Bagdad*. It is true, of course, that there is more exoticism in the title and costumes than in the musical content of these works. The nineteenth-century Italian opera is most typical in this respect. Rossini's North Africa (*L'Italiana in Algeri*) and his Babylonia (*Semiramide*), or Verdi's Ethiopia (*Aïda*) and Chaldea (*Nabucco*), or Puccini's America (*La fanciulla del West*) and Japan (*Madama Butterfly*) are not really rooted in the specific geographic and human environment the spectator would be entitled to recognize. One of the most famous names linked to exoticism in music is incontestably Debussy's, who was preceded and then surpassed by quite a few talents and geniuses exploiting rhythms, tonalities, melodies, and orchestrations inspired by distant civilizations: Saint-Saëns' *Suite algérienne*, Ravel's *Boléro*, Villa-Lobos' *Chôros*. But mention should also be made of Félicien David, Manuel de Falla, Delius, Stravinsky, Bartok, Milhaud, and Prokofiev.

In the visual arts, exoticism is incarnate in thousands of canvases with a biblical subject, all the *Paradis terrestres*, the *Adorations of the Magi*. Military and political history on canvas similarly incorporate exoticism: marriages, ambassadorships, battles against the Moors and the Turks, the taking of Constantinople, the campaigns of Bonaparte in Egypt. Rubens and Boucher both painted a *Chasse aux lions*, Renoir, Matisse, and many others innumerable *Odalisques*. Douanier Rousseau in his *Le Rêve* and *La Bohémienne endormie* and Paul Gauguin in his *Scène tahitienne* and *Martiniquaise* exalt a tradition that mixes primitivism and expressionism, and suggests a species of surrealism.[31] Similar inspirations are identified in fauvism and cubism. Literary exoticism should also be studied within the framework of artistic exoticism.

Another important aspect of exoticism is illustrated in the so-called literature of escape. Poets of all ages have looked upon their art as a means of making men forget their real and temporal existence. Every accurate definition of literature has included the flight from reality, and the history of what the Anglo-Saxons call *escapism* and the Germans *Lebensflucht* parallels the history of humanity itself. This idea is best expressed in Mallarmé's *Brise marine:*

> The flesh is sad alas! and all books I have read.
> To fly far away!
> I know that the sea-birds are drunk
> With being amid the unknown foam and the skies!
>
> . . . .
>
> I will start! Steamer balancing your masts,
> Leave anchor to reach a nature exotic![32]

Fleeing the *hic et nunc* of the human condition, the duties implied by life, and the concerns and anxieties of existence, has been one of mankind's most constant preoccupations. And this general desire for a spiritual exodus, which I would readily call *exodism*, is realized precisely by exoticism or exotism.[33] Both exodism and exotism are combined in works like Ts-ao Siue-k'in's *Hung-lou mêng* (Dream of the Red Chamber),[34] in the novels of Loti, Stevenson, Cooper, Sealsfield, and Gerstäcker, not to forget Kipling.

Man has always been more or less unhappy with his lot. No matter how fertile his field of endeavor, he dreams of another realm. He dreams of lost paradises and golden ages gone forever, of perfect happiness that he stubbornly seeks and hopes to find on some lost island of his own creation—or of the creation of a poet.

⚵

Exodism will last as long as man will last, while exoticism is inevitably destined to die out during the centuries to come, unless it is transferred into space. One grows accustomed to everything. As soon as all countries know one another, exoticism will disappear, for it is founded on ignorance. Paul Valéry thus explains the mirage of the Orient: "For this noun to produce in the mind its full and entire effect, it is necessary above everything else not to have been in the hazy region that it designates." More and more, long voyages have become part and parcel of the habits of the nations. And they are not even long anymore, unless one chooses to make them so for the sake of pleasure. Also, countries and regions are beginning to resemble one another more and more, and in a yet more disquieting manner the nations of the world are losing their own distinctive character, thus contributing to an impoverishment of the spiritual possibilities of mankind. Economic, political, and intellectual exchanges have built-in dangers in regard to the conservation of cultural autonomies. Peoples will identify themselves with their national traditions as long as they are able to maintain their ethno-psychological and ethno-sociological independence.

In the West, exoticism seems to be a constant of literary history in the sense that it is detectable at all ages in most nations. Even so, it does not sufficiently characterize specific literatures in specific periods to be equated with a movement or a current, like romanticism, though its impact on different cultures in the course of the centuries has been of paramount significance. The confrontation between romanticism and exoticism also shows that a literary movement represents and embodies a definite conception of art, an aesthetic Weltanschauung, while a literary trend manifests itself in externals, in a set of themes and motifs, as in the case of exoticism, or in a set of stylistic particularities, as in the case of euphuism and gongorism. As long as Spanish and Latin American *costumbrismo* was only concerned with the integration in novels and short stories of accurately observed scenes of everyday life, it was considered a trend. As soon as it came to represent a reaction against romanticism and to take roots in a critical doctrine identifying itself with realism, it was a literary movement. In the comparatistic perspective, however, the distinction between movement and trend—seldom acknowledged or noticed by critics—is far less momentous than the study itself of both movements and trends, for they grant students and scholars, as do the studies in our three other basic categories, a synthetic view of literature that is the very purpose of comparatistic inquiry.

PART IV

Genres and Forms

10

Prolegomenon C

IN contemporary literary criticism, *genre* and *form* are, theoretically, perfect synonyms. In practice, however, the term genre is heavily burdened with classical and traditional connotations. A scholar familiar with the millennial European literary patrimony should, therefore, still be reluctant to call the sonnet or the Bildungsroman, the educational novel, a literary genre. He would prefer words like form, species, or subspecies, by which he would mean a category of works written according to similar or identical patterns. To some degree the historical implications that genre still has should be known and understood. Nonetheless, with this observation in mind, we may safely use either term.

Genre is employed in the most diverse cultural contexts.[1] In the study of literature, it currently serves to signify the various rubrics in any comprehensive inventory of literature; it is synonymous with *kind* or *sort*, and it is most frequently related to the notion of a standard form, a matrix or mold. In Western criticism it is quite common to speak of the genre of the ode, the genre of the ballad, the genre of the short story, or the genre of the essay. The literary critic does not hesitate to use the word to point to works with similar qualities of style or tone, or to contrast more sharply the "genre of the sublime" with the "genre of the familiar." In the fine arts, the term sometimes assumes a very particular sense: "genre paintings" represent intimate scenes and subjects taken from everyday life.[2]

Genre designates, first of all, however, the primary categories into which the ancient Greeks and Romans, without formulating any firm doctrine, classified their literary output. They distinguished the epic from the drama, which with the lyric—much later acknowledged as a third genre—formed the classical trilogy. The somewhat stereotyped definitions of these three notions are still found in most contemporary handbooks of literature. The usefulness of these concepts cannot be denied. They are not only historical milestones of European culture, but they still define three basically different methods of conveying thoughts and feelings to the reader, the spectator, or the listener. Events are told (in a third-person epic), or enacted (in a second-person drama), or felt and formulated (in a first-person lyric poem). These three categories of writing originally constituted the general rationale of the theory of literary genres.

Traditionally, each genre existed independent of the other two; each was governed by its own code, recognized and respected by authors. In the course of the centuries, however, literary life grew more complex, and the authority of absolute literary rulers became questionable. To divide the literary body into these classical categories proved to be increasingly artificial. Even some ancients had refused to write their works according to the norms of Aristotelian or Horatian dogma. Toward the end of the eighteenth century it was commonly admitted in Europe that poetical creations not only could be divided into groups other than those suggested in the *Ars poetica*— for example, separated into those having imagination and those having reality as their major source of inspiration—but that they could be split up into a theoretically infinite number of subclasses. The lyric genre could be divided into ten or more species: elegies, hymns, odes, rondeaux, songs, sonnets, ballads and ballades, madrigals, idyls, bucolic and pastoral poems. Today the specialist of the elegy, to cite another example, would have little difficulty in inventing a series of varieties, each of which might in turn become the concern of still more specialized scholars. One could also go so far as to discriminate dramas according to their number of characters or acts. Ionesco's *Le Nouveau locataire* and Pirandello's *Il dovere del medico* could be studied together (both plays in one act), or O'Neill's *Before Breakfast* and Kafka's *Ein Bericht für eine Akademie;* in this latter instance conclusions could be drawn about the one-act monodrama, in which only one character appears.[3] On a different level, a critic may recognize the "rhetorical genre," or on a particular level, he may speak of the "picaresque genre," or of the "euphuistic genre," which brings him rather close to the concept of literary currents.[4] Again we are far from the usual distinction of genre. But in practice any group of works with similar characteristics of any kind may constitute a genre in the broadest acceptation of the word.

Do genres exist in and of themselves? Two hundred years ago this question still made sense to many writers. According to their reply, they aligned themselves with either the Tories or the Whigs of literary criticism. Before the romantic era, it is true, the critic of either group had at his disposal a magic formula to put a speedy end to most literary disputes: *Horatius dixit, Boileau dixit, Pope dixit.* A unanimously recognized authority could always intervene in any problem of criticism and give the final word. And authority had decided that as long as man was going to deal with literature, every work would belong, by its very essence, by its form and content, by its tone or quality, by the social class of its characters, and by the nature of its plot, to a category, that is to a *genre.* Today the time of acceptance of such an autonomous existence or ontological validity for the genres has passed. "Genres exist," Wellek says, "as an institution exists."[5] It is commonly recognized that they are the product of specific civilizations, that they develop and die with them; consequently, all of them are not necessarily represented in all parts of the world, and if some of them are, their rules are not identical everywhere. The Chinese, with all the wealth of their ancient literature, have never cultivated anything resembling the epic as it flourished in India and in Europe. Furthermore, in most works of a certain length, regardless of the historical period, the genres are mixed to various degrees. A tragedy may contain lyrical elements, especially in monologues or in stanzas recited by a chorus, as well as epic elements, such as accounts of events reported by confidants or messengers.

It is true that for centuries poets have conformed to the canons of the genres. However, the evolution of the genres is no less striking than their permanence. They seem to reflect historical periods, states, and stages of literature and culture. Just as the scientist no longer believes in immutable genres and species in nature, the literary scholar notices changes in his own universe. In this respect Darwin's *Origin of Species* (1859) and Brunetière's *Evolution des genres dans l'histoire de la littérature* (1890) follow a similar logic. A scholar like Benedetto Croce markedly influenced contemporary criticism to the extent that in all his major writings he denied genres any a priori existence, granting them at the most an empirical value or significance. He insisted that in literature one must not speak of anything but art, and he ceaselessly asserted that conformity to the laws of a genre remains the feeblest of all artistic criteria. Works may obey general rules of aesthetic cohesion, but they do so in greatly diversified fashions. Croce himself interpreted Dante and Ariosto without having recourse to the concept of the epic. He wonders—in his *Estetica come scienza dell'espressione e linguistica generale* (1902)—how the rule of the three unities, which found general acceptance in seventeenth-century France, could promote or even make possible tragic emotion as it exists in other literatures and other periods. To limit time, space, and action is to incarcerate the spirit and to support the theory that art consists in overcoming technical difficulties. By expounding these views Croce found himself to be in accord with the opinions of August Wilhelm Schlegel (*Comparaison entre la "Phèdre" de Racine et celle d'Euripide*, 1807) and Stendhal (*Racine et Shakespeare*, 1823).

Western tradition shows that art can flow from discipline and be derived from the perfect mastering of a system of conventions. This argument, by extension, is all the more true because art is artifice. And literature abounds in examples of masterpieces rigorously written according to a set of rules. In reply, however, it may also be argued that nobody will ever be able to tell what these works would be like if the rules had not been followed. Are they masterpieces because of the rules or in spite of them? All that can be suggested is that the framework imposed by a genre has not always been useless. This concession in no way threatens the doctrine that literary beauty exists independently of any specific genre.

Literary genology—the study of literary genres—needs a re-examination and re-evaluation. The main source of contradiction or confusion noticeable in genological studies lies in the fact that recent literary forms are often judged against the background of the classical genres, which no longer assume particular forms and shapes. Today no specific cast is assigned to the dramatic, epic, or lyric genre. Rather than forms and shapes, the three genres represent and designate three attitudes, or three modes of communication, which Goethe called "Naturformen der Poesie." But there is obviously a fourth one, the expository or didactic mode, which in our modern perspective may take on the importance of a classical genre. Aristotle could have cited as an example the work of his master Plato. In antiquity, however, the concept of genre applied to poetry exclusively. For us the literary matter, including philosophical writings, may be conveyed to the public in four basic ways, or by four methods, according to the writer's purpose. The author may perform (dramatic genre), narrate (epic genre), sing (lyric genre), or expound (didactic genre). Genres may be organically grouped according to other vantage points. In his well-known *Anatomy of Criticism* Northrop Frye indicates five modes: the mythic, the romantic, the high and the low mimetic, and the ironic. Such a division may be imposed on our tetralogy, or on Frye's own, as he poetically and philosophically presented it in the third essay of his work: "The Mythos of Spring: Comedy"; "The Mythos of Summer: Romance"; "The Mythos of Autumn: Tragedy"; "The Mythos of Winter: Irony and Satire."

A literary work does not necessarily belong to only one of the four genres as thus defined. There are lyrical dramas, dramatic novels, epic treatises, and didactic or philosophical poems. "Petrarch's collection," says August Wilhelm Schlegel—and he means the *Canzoniere* —"is a true and complete lyrical novel,"[6] and the stanzas of Carducci's epic *Ça ira* are sonnets. An epistolary novel does not necessarily and exclusively belong to the epic genre. It may be written in any of the four modes or in several of them to various extents. *Werther* is mainly lyric, *Tom Jones* mainly epic, *The Citizen of the World* mainly didactic, and *Liaisons dangereuses* mainly dramatic—as are so many French nineteenth-century novels. "Balzac's and Flaubert's masterpieces," Henri Peyre writes, "have traditionally been glorified by French critics as the rightful successors to classical tragedy."[7] Nevertheless, the novel is usually said to be the modern form of epic poetry.

A problem in literary genology may sometimes vanish as soon as the notions of genre (that is, the modes of communication) are dissociated from those of form, or kind, or as soon as genology is not considered identical with literary morphology. Current language scarcely distinguishes between the two concepts, and, as we have already stated, genre and form, when used in literary discussions, are equivalent terms. They are synonymous in the most authoritative works. René Wellek and Austin Warren witness to this fact in a text that leads to our conclusion: "Genre," they say, "should be conceived as a grouping of literary works based, theoretically, upon both outer form (specific meter or structure) and also upon inner form (attitude, tone, purpose—more crudely, subject and audience)."[8] Empirically oriented genre and form studies serve above all to coordinate works written in various languages, to bring them closer together or to place them in contrast in order not only to better apprehend their purport and meaning in the course of history, but also to better understand the making of literature.

In the two chapters that follow, the concept of genre represents a coordinating principle. Neither the *Bildungsroman* nor the sonnet are impermeable genres or forms. An apprenticeship novel indeed can and should also be considered a psychological novel, and may at the same time belong to several other species of fiction. Similarly, a sonnet may transcend the genre of the lyric to which it originally was connected and belong to the epic or didactic genre as well. The genres chosen here are defined by two different sets of criteria; the educational novel rather by content and purpose (inner form), the sonnet, rather by size and structure (outer form). In both studies the idea of genre constitutes mainly a frame of reference for literary rapprochements and international confrontations.

11

The "Bildungsroman" in Germany, England, and France

THE novel has only recently come to the foreground on the stage of letters, although it can boast of a noble lineage. If in the course of its development we forget its indebtedness to the pastoral, the comedy, and the drama, indeed, even to lyric poetry, we can claim for it the function that the epic poem used to have in literature. Finding it useful to classify works, the contemporary critic has continued to distinguish between the drama, the lyric, and the novel, the latter today substituting for epic poetry. To be sure, epic poetry has never received a death certificate. Quite a few epic geniuses in the classical sense of the term have left their mark on our own period: Carl Spitteler, Paul Claudel, and Nikos Kazantzakis.

Since the Republic of Letters includes philosophy, criticism, and social, pedagogical and natural sciences, the fourth genre should be remembered here, the didactic, the purpose of which is to set forth knowledge systematically and provide instruction. Evidently the educational novel participates to some extent in this fourth genre. It is readily seen that in the present context, the four genres are conceived of as modes of imparting literary matter, rather than as molds. That the novel represents in effect the narrative mode is illustrated by the fact that a phrase like "art of the narrative" has almost become synonymous with "art of the novel." Several genres or modes, however, usually characterize a single book. Rousseau's *Emile* mingles the didactic, the lyric and the epic mode, and in Goethe's *Wilhelm Meister* perceptive pages and lyrical poems interrupt the flow of the narration, while in both works lengthy dialogues remind the reader of the dramatic genre.

Yet these four basic divisions of genre remain deceptive. While in premodern periods writings were judged by the standards of a single genre—and genre specified a fixed form and a mode as well—today they are often classified according to a complex set of criteria. The contemporary scholar's indispensable nomenclature resembles that of natural history textbooks in that a subtle classification, based upon essential characteristics, leads readily to the identification of a group. A particular animal may at the same time be a mammal, a quadruped, a herbivore, and a pachyderm. For too long a time the literary critic tended to call attention to his elephant by means of one single attribute, sometimes the most typical one, and unfortunately, often only the most picturesque. The beast in question might have been described only in terms of his proboscis, his trunk, and it was thereby implied that the elephant's essence had been recognized.

Classifications in literature overlap at least as much as do those in zoology. A certain book may belong at one and the same time to several categories of works: it may simultaneously be listed as a social novel, a propaganda novel, a regional novel, a historical novel, a rustic novel, a Gothic novel, a psychological novel, a personal novel, and an epistolary novel. Furthermore, the work can be a *Bildungsroman*—an apprenticeship novel. Indeed, the art of the contemporary novel is one of infinite hybridization, and without the benefit of circumspection, the entire species faces the danger of self-destruction. It follows that the Bildungsroman does not at all constitute an isolated category. In varying degrees, its prototypes share in different categories which, heterogeneous themselves, do not form exclusive groups. The first task, therefore, is to define the concept of Bildungsroman. The second is to illustrate this concept by quoting and discussing some of its best-known examples.

I

The term Bildungsroman is in itself most intriguing and warrants the critic's attention. It is essential to remember the primary meaning of *Bildung*. It was a synonym, up to the eighteenth century, of *Bild*, of *imago* or portrait.[1] *Bildung* (education, formation), in the pedagogical sense of the word, is the process by which a human being becomes a replica of his mentor, and is identified with him as the exemplary model. The Bible speaks of man made in his Creator's image. At the same time Bildung, in our literary context, is the secularized metaphor found in the patristic tradition: the church fathers explained the action of divine grace with the image of clay kneaded and shaped by the potter. The art object (das *Bildnis*) is the creation and property of the artist (der *Bilder*, later, der *Bildner*).

Who then is the potter molding his clay in the Bildungsroman? The formative principle we find in the apprenticeship novel is not derived from a doctrine, nor is it taught in a school or explained in a book. Since *Wilhelm Meisters Lehrjahre* (1795–1796), customarily considered the classical example of the Bildungsroman, the agent of Bildung is the world. The man of the world would therefore appear to be the perfect hero of such a novel,[2] and Mrs. Western, the aunt of Tom Jones's Sophia who ceaselessly proclaims that she "knows the world," may be declared Wilhelm Meister's feminine counterpart. The finest knowledge of the world, however, does not entitle anybody to become automatically the ideal character of a Bildungsroman. The criterion is elsewhere: the hero must profit from the lessons of the world. In the adventure novel, events test, punish, or reward the hero; in the apprenticeship novel, they mark him, mature him, or form him in a definitive way, and finally crystallize his character. The Goethean principle of Bildung must be seen in terms of the hero's confrontation with his milieu; the genre, therefore, may be defined as the representation of the interactions between the self and the world, with special reference to the process of the education of the self.

Such a conception of the hero entails profound effects on the structure of the plot. The world is no longer the arsenal for the thunderbolts of fate; it is an arena, or a practice ground, on which man may fortify himself against the reversals of fortune and the uncertainties of life. Instead of submitting to his fate, the hero prepares himself to confront it. In a sense, the Bildungsroman is, therefore, only a sort of pre-novel, a preamble to a novel. At the end of the work, the hero appears armed for the battle of existence, ready to live out his own future novel. The Bildungsroman does not in any way reproduce the essential phases of a man's life or expound the fulfillment of his destiny. The denouement is only provisional. The end of the novel is the beginning of the hero's life. This partly explains the numerous sequels to apprenticeship novels. *Wilhelm Meisters Lehrjahre* was supplemented by *Wilhelm Meisters Wanderjahre;* Goethe further toyed with the idea of a novel to be called *Meisterjahre.* *Agathon* induced Wieland to write *Agathodämon;* Stifter, after his *Nachsommer,* wrote *Witiko;* and Keller's *Martin Salander* may be considered a sort of sequel to *Der grüne Heinrich.* This phenomenon can be observed in literatures other than the German: Stendhal's diary is a continuation of his *Vie de Henri Brulard.*

There is a definite tendency to provide the traditional Bildungsroman with a happy ending, or at least with an ending that does not imply irreparable disasters. Death might occur in the narrative; it can strike any character except the main hero, not even in the final chapter. It would be pointless for a protagonist to wind up in the grave after pursuing his *Bildungsziel*, his educational goal, over hundreds of pages. The novel would lack its raison d'être. Death as a term of the plot is also excluded in another genre for obvious reasons: autobiography. Real or fictitious, a self-portrayal does not require a finite solution; quite like the novel of apprenticeship, it can or even should somehow present an "open end." The two types of narrative have many characteristics in common. To begin with, every Bildungsroman is in effect a more or less skillfully veiled autobiography in which the action is projected against a background of didacticism or philosophy. In both autobiography and Bildungsroman, the author analyzes certain attitudes toward life and emphasizes diverse reactions to events. The heroes in both move in the world of realities that they strive to master, and that they try to judge in a wide context. That is why to a certain extent precursors or models for the Bildungsroman can be seen in the *Confessions* of Saint Augustine and Rousseau, the *Memoirs* of Cellini, the *Vita* of Hobbes, and *Monsieur Nicolas* of Restif de la Bretonne; clearly, it is often the "lived" elements that prevail in apprenticeship novels.[3]

There are variants of the Bildungsroman other than confessional narratives. German lexicons frequently give *Entwicklungsroman* and *Erziehungsroman*—literally, "novel of development" and "novel of education"—as synonyms for Bildungsroman.[4] The first label implies greater attention to development than Bildungsroman, the second less. Of course, one rarely finds a work in which the hero does not develop in some way, for such a protagonist would be psychologically inert, and therefore static. In this respect the picaresque novel (*Schelmenroman*), in which events have no real effect on the souls of the characters, is antipodal to the apprenticeship novel. As to the educational novel, it requires that its plot be designed to accommodate an intentionally formative process in the pedagogical sense of the word. The term itself, Erziehungsroman, insinuates that the young man being educated progresses under the influence of a preceptor, a school, or some force artificially instituted for the purpose of obtaining specific results. The hero of the Bildungsroman, rather than following a program of studies like the hero of the Erziehungsroman, pursues a goal that he himself has perhaps only vaguely formulated, a goal to which he has entirely dedicated himself; the struggle for attaining that goal forms and perfects him, although he remains in his natural milieu, in his professional and social environment.[5]

The history of the word Bildungsroman can easily be traced to the author of *Wilhelm Meister*, although the term is not found in the work. Bildung and its compounds occur so frequently when Goethe speaks of his novel, not only in his late *Gespräche mit Eckermann*[6] but at much earlier dates, that the name of the genre already seems to be implied. Goethe provided the suggestion for the word, if not its exact formulation.

The term Bildungsroman was probably coined for the first time by a scholar, at the University of Dorpat (today Tartu, Estonia), Karl von Morgenstern.[7] In 1803 he already had the idea of completing a study on what he thought of as Bildungsroman, a neologism he was going to use in a course he eventually taught (1810) under the title "On the Spirit and Coherence of a Series of Philosophical Novels."[8] Several years later, in 1819 and 1820, he gave two lectures with the titles "On the Essence of the *Bildungsroman*" and "Toward a History of the *Bildungsroman*."[9] Since Morgenstern's writings did not become widely known, the honor of having first introduced the term was until very recently given to the celebrated philosopher and historian of letters, Wilhelm Dilthey, who may have believed himself to be the inventor of the expression. Bildungsroman became a part of accepted literary terminology after the publication of his *Leben Schleier-machers*, in which he deals with the subject and uses the word.[10]

II

The Germans seem to have a monopoly on the production of the Bildungsroman. It was on the basis of several German works, not only *Wilhelm Meisters Lehrjahre*, that the concept became clear, and a glance at any critical bibliography is enough to convince anyone that most studies on the genre have not only been published in Germany, but deal predominately with the German Bildungsroman.[11] Goethe's novel in particular remains the model on the international level: it has become the living embodiment, the definition of the form, a kind of literary universal—in spite of some doubts expressed in a few recent German studies on whether it really belongs to the genre to which it has served so well as prototype.[12] The extent to which any specific work approaches *Wilhelm Meister* usually decides the rank it occupies in the list of apprenticeship novels.

Nineteenth-century Germany did not produce a historical novel comparable with *I promessi sposi* [The betrothed], a social satire on a par with *Vanity Fair*, or a naturalistic triumph of the magnitude of *Germinal*. It can be fairly stated that German narrative art during that period largely proceeded under the aegis of the Bildungsroman, that is, of *Wilhelm Meister*. It signified a new conception of the novel, which inaugurated the systematic presentation of those slices of life that heretofore had been dealt with only incidentally or exceptionally, those that illustrate the formative influence of events upon an individual's character. The apprenticeship novel is the novel of adolescence, or the first years of manhood, of that stage where the boy becomes a man, or where the child in the man loses its influence. It is the "growing-up novel." In vain would we seek a firm structural principle in *Wilhelm Meisters Lehrjahre* or in the novels of its kind. Events follow events, diverge or converge according to needs that differ from those of the laws of logic. Each episode is rooted in the preceding one and is vaguely continued in the next. All happenings, however, occur without the appearance of organic sequence. The unifying element is to be sought in the hero himself, in his attitudes toward life, and in the consequences he draws from his victories and his defeats. Thus the Bildungsroman remains a sort of record of a spiritual voyage: a new *Pilgrim's Progress*. The interior distance traveled gives the measure of the betterment accomplished. There is a change from uncertainty to certainty, from error to truth, from confusion to clarity, from nature to spirit.

While still a young man, Wilhelm is liberated from paternal tutelage: he sets out on a business trip on behalf of his father. He enters the new phase of his life with all the enthusiasm of a newly independent youth. The last page of the volume shows a mature man, sure of himself and freed from all indecision, a man characterized by firmness of character and suppleness of spirit. He appreciates the arts and the letters, and is ready to fully enjoy his existence. He has found his own way, "his habitual way of questing after happiness," which, according to Stendhal, reveals most accurately a man's character.[13] This miracle of spiritual evolution has been accomplished through a series of crises and incidents, of failures and misfortunes that, instead of rolling off the hero's back or leaving him a mere witness of facts and events, have shaped, molded, and formed him. All these experiences stand in the same relation to Wilhelm as does a chinning bar to a gymnast: they are the instruments that enable him to develop himself, to train himself with a view toward the great tests that mark every human career.

This inner forming of a man, which alone captivates the interest of the reader, is accomplished in several steps and at various levels. First, Wilhelm observes the world; he becomes a witness of human suffering which he attempts to alleviate. He makes the Melina couple's cause his own, makes himself the protector of Mignon and of little Felix, and he is touched by his reading of the "Bekenntnisse einer schönen Seele" [Confessions of a beautiful soul]. It is by his own suffering that he gauges his desires and that his thousand velleities are condensed into a concerted will. He knows the joys of love, but above all he is familiar with the entire roster of its pains, and worse, of its full complement of illusions. He finds Marianne deceiving him, sees himself rejected by the countess; he mourns the death of "sweet Amelia," and, at the end of the novel, resolves to marry Natalie, who, under the camouflage of the most amiable of amazons, had saved his life during a memorable adventure with highwaymen. But Wilhelm also develops by cultivating his acting talents, by playing the most diverse dramatic parts and especially by mixing with wandering troupes of thespians who traipse around the country. An atmosphere emanates from this gypsy company, a theme announced in Scarron's *Roman comique* (1651–1657) and marvelously recreated in Théophile Gautier's *Le Capitaine Fracasse* (1863)—an indication that Goethe's novel developed and opened possibilities beyond the Bildungsroman.

As a child, Wilhelm had adored the marionette theater; as an adolescent he became a frequenter of gatherings of actors in his hometown. He is seen among the artists who group around Philina and later among those led by Serlo, a director of plays worthy of Wilhelm's standards. It is in connection with *Hamlet* that the virtues of the theater in forming character are impressed upon the reader. In fact, in the first version of the novel the hero's evolution centered on his dramatic career, his theatrical vocation; its title indicates as much: *Wilhelm Meisters theatralische Sendung.* Some of its major ideas can be traced to Schiller's *Briefe über die ästhetische Erziehung des Menschen* [Letters on the aesthetical education of man] (1795), the publication of which helped to strengthen Goethe's friendship with Schiller.[14]

Goethe's novel is not intended to show and further a purely rationalistic education. Wilhelm's mind is in no way closed to the universe of mysteries, a universe from which no man can completely escape. Every apprentice has to find his own way through that un-planned and unplannable labyrinth. Thus Wilhelm journeys through a maze of lies and superstitions toward the acceptance of a certain irrationality of the world. As he gradually comprehends what kind of man he is, Wilhelm recognizes his place in the world better than he understands the world at large. Throughout his career he will be able to remember the words he utters at one point: "From youth I have directed the focus of my mind more towards the inner than the outer, and thus it is quite natural that I have learned to know *man* to a cer-tain extent, without understanding or conceiving *men* in the least."[15] The fruit of education is the fulfillment of the Socratic "know thyself." Understanding the world is only a by-product of this process.

⚘

Wilhelm Meister did have precursors. Wolfram von Eschenbach's *Parzival*, for example, displays characteristics of the Bildungsroman, in spite of the fact that the hero moves and develops in a world that is constructed in accordance with the ordinance of divine grace rather than that of human experience. Between the thirteenth-century *Parzival* and the late eighteenth-century *Wilhelm Meister*, a major transposition of values took place. The Bildungsroman appeared in an era when the neopagan imperium had succeeded the Christian. The philosophes, the physiocrats, and the "friends of man" had taken the place of the representatives of a religious doctrine and commu-nity. A comparison of the two works illustrates this laicization of the pedagogic ideal, which in many European countries, including Germany, was completed by the time of the French Revolution. In the seventeenth century, Grimmelshausen's *Simplicissimus* presented an example of a mixed genre. A picaresque novel in tone and structure, it also includes specific features of the Bildungsroman, or at least of a developmental novel: the hero, in following some of the lessons of life, forms his character.

Wilhelm Meister not only had its precursors, it was also, as noted, the model of many novels that followed. Every German novel since *Meister* that expounds a certain Weltanschauung is in some way an apprenticeship novel or strongly reminiscent of the genre. Scores of well-known novelists have practiced their artistry through it. The list includes *Heinrich von Ofterdingen* by Novalis—so often related to or contrasted with Goethe's work—Hölderlin's *Hyperion*, Moritz' *Anton Reiser*, Jean Paul's *Titan*, *Die Flegeljahre*, and *Hesperus*, Eichendorff's *Ahnung und Gegenwart*, Freytag's *Soll und Haben*, Stifter's *Nachsommer*, Mörike's *Maler Nolten*, Gotthelf's *Bauernspiegel*, *Uli der Knecht*, and *Uli der Pächter*, Keller's *Der grüne Heinrich*, Raabe's *Der Hungerpastor*, and Immermann's *Die Epigonen*. Ricarda Huch leads the way to the twentieth century: her *Erinnerungen von Ludolf Ursleu dem Jüngeren* was published in 1893 and her *Vita somnium breve* in 1902. Closer to the present are Stehr's *Nathanael Maechler*, Hofmannsthal's *Andreas oder die Vereinigten*, Hermann Hesse's *Peter Camenzind* and *Das Glasperlenspiel*, Carl Hauptmann's *Einhart der Lächler*, Hans Grimm's *Volk ohne Raum*, and Emma Weiblinger's *Die Ströme des Namenlos*. And one of the most celebrated novels ever written, Thomas Mann's *Der Zauberberg*, constitutes in many respects a Bildungsroman while his *Doktor Faustus* may be called a parody of the genre.

≫≪

Carlyle translated *Wilhelm Meisters Lehrjahre* and published the novel in 1824. He rightly thought *Wilhelm Meister's Apprenticeship* would adequately render the title of the original. Obviously, the Anglo-Saxon world owes to Carlyle the term that still designates the genre. In 1827 he also translated *Wilhelm Meisters Wanderjahre* (*Wilhelm Meister's Travels*, included in Carlyle's *German Romance*). Both novels appeared together for the first time in English in 1839. Before this date, in the second book of his *Sartor Resartus*, published in 1834, Carlyle had applied some principles of Goethe's *Lehrjahre*. Meanwhile Disraeli's *Vivian Grey* (1826–1827) and *Contarini Fleming* (1832) qualified as *Bildungsromane*, and Edward Bulwer-Lytton, in the preface to his novel, *Ernest Maltravers* (1837–1838)—which was preceded by *Pelham* (1828), also an early sample of the genre—connected it to *Wilhelm Meister*. These examples give the proof that the first blossoming of the English apprenticeship novel took place immediately after

Goethe's novel was known, although it may not have been induced exclusively by Carlyle's translation.

During the second half of the nineteenth century, the genre was abundantly exemplified in Great Britain.[16] The extent, however, to which the English apprenticeship novels are Bildungsromane in the traditional sense will always be a debatable question. And the same problem arises for every specimen of any national literature, including the German. Among English samples of that period, Dickens' *David Copperfield* and *Great Expectations* should be remembered, but also Thackeray's *Pendennis*, Meredith's *The Ordeal of Richard Feverel*, George Eliot's *The Mill on the Floss*, and Butler's *The Way of All Flesh*. In the twentieth century, the genre has continued to enjoy the favor of the Anglo-Saxon public, as is attested by the success of novels like *Sons and Lovers* by D. H. Lawrence, *Of Human Bondage* by Somerset Maugham, and *A Portrait of the Artist as a Young Man* by Joyce. Books like Thomas Wolfe's *Look Homeward, Angel*, Sinclair Lewis' *Arrowsmith*, George Santayana's *The Last Puritan*, William Faulkner's *Go Down, Moses*, and Saul Bellow's *The Adventures of Augie March* could also be named. In Denmark, we find *Niels Lyhne* by Jens Peter Jacobsen and *Pelle* by Martin Anderson Nexö; in Holland, *De kleine Johannes* by Frederik van Eeden; in Norway, Sigrid Undset's *Kristin Lavransdatter;* in Russia, Ivan Gontcharov's *Obyknovennaya istoriya* [A common story]. Less intensely, perhaps, than other countries, but with more striking originality, France has been dealing with the Bildungsroman. Her writers have adapted it from the Germans more freely than those of other nations. And here, once again, what seems to be an imitation is often nothing but the result of similar literary concerns. Frequently, therefore, we are faced with a problem of analogy rather than of influence.

III

Wilhelm Meisters Lehrjahre appeared in French five years later than in English, in 1829, and was less accurately imitated in France than in Great Britain. In the French narrative tradition, the hero as such is a given element to start with. He is part of *la donnée* and usually performs all his deeds as a fully developed character. The Bildungsroman, on the contrary, creates the character whose personality is being formed and whose qualities are being developed under the eyes of the reading public. Quite a few French novels of the eighteenth century may be considered vague samples of apprenticeship novels; but the genre in France never evolved into a firm and coherent literary tradition. It had no legal status in French criticism until very recently. In 1938 Albert Thibaudet still had occasion to marvel that the French "novel of young intelligence" had not been written yet.[17] Would not that novel have to be a Bildungsroman?

Thibaudet's phrase closely approaches a definition of the apprentice-ship novel. One could maintain that Paul Bourget's *Le Disciple*, André Gide's *Faux monnayeurs*, and Romain Rolland's *Jean-Christophe*, are *romans éducatifs;* yet they reflect as much an international tradition as a Gallic heritage. In addition, Gide and Rolland especially had a remarkably broad knowledge of German literature.

This Gallic narrative heritage can be traced back, although rather loosely, to Marivaux's great novel, *La Vie de Marianne* (1731–1741). When Countess Marianne relates her birth, youth, and first mature years in twelve long letters, the Marquise, to whom the account is addressed, feels sympathy and curiosity about the fate of her friend. The very subtitle indicates the reason for the appeal the book had to the reader: *ou les aventures de Madame la Comtesse de****. The Marquise weeps at the rebuffs suffered by Marianne as much as the latter weeps at the memory of her tears. Tears and sighs, sensibility and pity constitute the theme and the essence of the novel. Doubtless the heroine's character is formed by the series of tests she relates. But the narrative hardly attempts to illuminate the formative power that both the struggle for an ideal and the wheel of fortune possess. It is instead the extraordinary that endows Marivaux's book with life and movement.

Twenty years after the publication of *La Vie de Marianne*, Jean-Jacques Rousseau wrote, in the form of a dialogue, his second preface for the *Nouvelle Héloïse*. The interlocutor reproaches Rousseau for having thought of such a banal plot: "Not one evil man who makes us fear for the good people , , , nothing unexpected; no 'coup de thé-âtre,' " to which Rousseau replies: "So you require common people and rare events? I believe that I should prefer the contrary."[18] Rousseau's answer marks an essential change in the concept of the novel. From now on, the antithesis between "personnages rares" and "événe-ments communs" confers greatness on a novel. Two titles illustrate this change of attitude, one of them Rousseau's who modestly called his novel *Julie, ou La Nouvelle Héloïse: Lettres de deux amans habi-tans d'une petite ville au pied des Alpes*. Some forty years earlier, in 1722, Defoe had given one of his novels this sensational title: *The Fortunes and Misfortunes of the Famous Moll Flanders, etc., Who Was Born in Newgate, and during a Life of Continu'd Variety for Threescore Years, besides her Childhood, was Twelve Years a Whore, five Times a Wife (Whereof once of her own Brother), Twelve Years a Thief, Eight Years a Transported Felon in Virginia, At last Grew Rich, Liv'd Honest, and Died Penitent. Written from Her Own Memoran-dums*. Rousseau inaugurates a new era for the art of the novel.

The hero of the Bildungsroman is "rare," uncommon, for he profits from the teachings of life. The strangest events lose their strangeness when once they are studied not in terms of their power to produce surprise—the essential quality of *Moll Flanders*—but rather in terms of their formative virtue. This should not be misconstrued to mean that the *Nouvelle Héloïse* directly anticipates *Wilhelm Meister*. It is the confrontation of the two souls that captivates the reader of Rousseau's novel. Even his *Confessions* are not really closely related to the Bildungsroman, as it was "made in Germany." To understand this, it suffices to reread the opening phrases of the third paragraph: "Let the Trumpet of the Last Judgment sound when it will; I shall come, this book in hand, to present myself before the sovereign judge. I shall say aloud: this is what I have done, what I have thought, what I was."[19] Rousseau certainly does not intend to explain at the foot of God's throne how he was formed by his experience, or how his joys and sorrows made him worse or better. In the *Confessions* there is less explanation of the how and why of the development of the hero's character than there is a gradual unveiling of a personality that, according to Rousseau, was fully developed even during adolescence. The work remains essentially an *apologia pro vita sua*, not the account of an evolution or, as the Germans like to put it, of a *Werdegang*. Further, the "penitent" of the *Confessions* is judged pitilessly according to his actions and not according to his intention to profit from events in order to move toward some ideal of perfection. Rousseau is not really concerned with the process of Bildung.

The true French precursor of the Bildungsroman is found in *Emile*. Although its subtitle, *de l'éducation*, confers a treatiselike quality on the book, it has many characteristics of a novel.[20] Could not *Emile* be more properly termed an Erziehungsroman than a Bildungsroman? Emile has a preceptor who apparently guides him according to a preconceived study plan, the basis of the perfect education for his pupil. Rousseau, moreover, scarcely takes his hero beyond the point where Goethe will begin: Emile is something of a *Wilhelm Schüler*, a disciple on the way to becoming a *Wilhelm Meister*, a master of himself.

Looking at the matter more closely, we note that in *Emile* the role of the preceptor is not really that of an educator in the customary sense of the word. His main function is to create certain circumstances and to provoke little incidents that the pupil will have to confront. This doctrine of intellectual midwifery, of Socratic maieutic, proves Rousseau's faith in the essential goodness of man, just as the system applied by Goethe supposes it. In Goethe a clear opposition appears between what Johann Nicolas Tetens called, in 1777, "natural development" and "artificial school development."[21] In spite of his teacher, Emile appears, in many respects, as a self-taught man. It is the great book of nature—the world of the boy and then the world as a young man may experience it—that constitutes the true formative agent in *Emile*.[22] Rousseau does not want to make the child plunge into the furnace of the world—"world" as "société mondaine" with all its artifices; nothing could be more contrary to his principles.

By "world" he means the "natural milieu" of man, which remains his great teacher.[23] Rousseau warns his reader: do not let a library of books make man "neglect the book of the world."[24]

According to Rousseau a triple educative force leads the child to maturity: nature, men, and things. "The internal development of our faculties and of our organs is the education by nature; the use we are taught to make of this development is the education by men; and the acquisition of our own experience of the objects that affect us is the education by things."[25] The gradation of these three forces is of the utmost significance. Education through things—situations and events—is indeed what the Bildungsroman attempts to illustrate, and what *Emile* does in fact illustrate. The hero, having profited from the large and small lessons of the world, is ready for life in the fullest sense of the word at the end of the book. He marries Sophie and makes his appearance in the arena of human society. And like so many authors of this genre, Rousseau composed a sequel, *Emile et Sophie, ou les solitaires*, in which the reader is able to see the fruits of Emile's education.[26]

Other French novels could be included in a list of eighteenth-century Bildungsromane. The author of *La Vie de Marianne* also published *Le Paysan parvenu*—which is actually the history rather of a peasant *parvenant* struggling for his goal. Here Marivaux illustrates the phases of the most surprising of careers. *Surprising* is the key word, however; the reader is more interested in the events than in their effect on the mind of the hero. The work thus does not belong unequivocally to the genre. *Le Paysan perverti* and its sequel, *La Paysanne pervertie*, by Restif de la Bretonne, deserve closer analysis in this regard. They are among the most brilliant illustrations, after *Emile*, of the Bildungsroman in eighteenth-century France, even though they portray an education toward evil, a paysan and a paysanne *se pervertissant*. For generations the books remained a byword for depravity. Restif's novels, however, are not Bildungsromane in the Goethean sense: the lives of the paysan and paysanne are failures. The two works teach how not to prepare oneself for life.

Similar remarks apply to many nineteenth-century French novels that for various reasons do not quite qualify for the genre. The series of frustrations and the final downfall of Lucien de Rubenpré, and not his eagerness to educate himself, captivate the reader of Balzac's *Les Illusions perdues*,[27] and the hero's "education" in *L'Education sentimentale: Histoire d'un jeune homme* is not a successful apprenticeship novel either; the tentative title of the novel was *Les Ratés* [The ne'er-do-wells].[28] The situations by no means crystallize Frédéric Moreau's personality: he lives to enjoy life and believes in the intrinsic value of every hour.[29] Rastignac in *Le Père Goriot*, illustrates more faithfully the principles of a Bildungsroman. His adventures prepare him to face a hostile world, the society of Paris. But neither

Flaubert nor Balzac, nor for that matter, Hugo or Zola, present a world comparable with that of *Wilhelm Meister*'s in their own works. Nor does Stendhal. In *Le Rouge et le noir* and *La Chartreuse de Parme*, he does not present Julien or Fabrice as being altered by their adventures on whatever level they take place. The reader watches both heroes react according to the native bent of their own character. Again the heroes are given, not formed. In both novels the events seem to reveal the characters, rather than to shape them. The work of Stendhal's that comes closest to a Bildungsroman is *La Vie de Henri Brulard*.

☙❧

Although Stendhal, who knew German very well, states in his diary on August 12, 1810, that he read *Wilhelm Meister* and grew quite enthusiastic about it—"Ces idées m'avaient rendu fou"—there is little probability that he found in it a real source of inspiration for his *Henri Brulard*. The novel is an autobiographical narrative centered on the development of the character. Rare are the events that have any intrinsic significance or interest. On the fourth of December, 1835, the following little adventure happens to the hero: in the stagecoach from Rome to Città-Vecchia, he finds himself in the company of a charming lady. She looks at him "sans cruauté," and the affair seems about to take its expected course. But something supervenes, a recollection: the slightly aquiline nose of the lovely passenger reminds the hero of another aquiline nose, that of the Abbé Raillane, who had been the most hated of his preceptors. Brulard is shaken brusquely from his dream and no longer sees the woman's face. He pretends to be sleeping in his corner of the coach. As to the "divine créature," no more space than this is allotted to her in Stendhal's life.[30] The episode is interesting because it illustrates a kind of education. It was not the instruction received from his masters that most affected the character of our writer—*Brulard* would then have been an Erziehungsroman—it was rather the preceptors themselves or, to be more precise, his confrontation with them that left an imprint on his mind. Brulard is, and will be all his life, what his adventures, his milieu, and things have made of him. What separates him from Meister is obvious: in the process of formation Meister is more dynamic than Brulard; Meister tends to act, Brulard is inclined to let things happen.

Most events related in the *Vie de Henri Brulard* are insignificant if considered in themselves. They are quite remarkable, however, if taken in their psychological context, or in the formative effects and consequences they precipitate. Brulard is their inevitable product, or at least their semivoluntary product. His motto: forward or burst, "crever ou avancer." A frenetic passion for independence determines his every reaction to persons and events. Education, however, cannot be simply an affair of choice or of will; it is equally a matter of temperament and heredity. For instance, Brulard illustrates significant repercussions of the Oedipus complex in the literary domain, the genesis of the tastes of a writer, and the history of his moral allergies.

Stendhal's mother, who was of Italian blood, had a definitive influence on his destiny. "I never thought of Beyle save with repugnance,"[31] he says, regarding himself as totally and exclusively the descendant of the Gagnons, the maternal branch of his genealogical tree. This ingenuous offspring of an apparent parthenogenesis execrated everything that might remind him of the man who had dared to be his father. These are the sentiments of the young man as he left the paternal home to study in Paris: "My father received my goodbyes in the Jardin-de-Ville, under the windows facing Montorge Street. He was weeping a little. The sole impression his tears gave me was that it made him look quite ugly."[32] Again, leaving Grenoble was no sacrifice for the future novelist. This city was for him "like the memory of an abominable indigestion."[33] Italy was to be his chosen land.

Stendhal's father was a lawyer in the Grenoble parliament, a man marked by the classical education invariably dispensed to the bourgeoisie by the Jesuits. Accordingly, the son felt he owed it to himself to have other literary preferences. Racine, praised by his parents, "struck him as a total hypocrite"[34] and Virgil, "protected by the priests," horrified him.[35] He turned his reflections toward England: "I was mad about Hamlet,"[36] he declares, thus revealing his affinities with Wilhelm Meister. And Stendhal adds: "So that nothing might lack in the power Shakespeare had over my heart, I believe that my father even said something bad about him to me."[37] The ideas in *Racine et Shakespeare* are a direct expression of the author's character; they are Stendhal's reaction against his background. Quite naturally, he had great enthusiasm for Fielding, and *Grandisson* [sic] made him shed tears. One of his masters in school—he loved none of them—Dubois-Fontanelle, had a predelection for Voltaire, and his father admired Voltaire enough to possess his complete works—good and sufficient cause for young Henri to "sincerely and totally scorn the talent of Voltaire."[38]

On the other hand, father Beyle seemed to understand the works of Rousseau. He only spoke of him "with adoration, while, all the time, cursing him as impious."[39] As a "dangerous" philosopher, Rousseau was taboo. Predictably, this was a stimulus to Stendhal, who writes: "The reading of the *Nouvelle Héloïse* and the scruples of Saint-Preux formed me as a profoundly righteous man. . . . Thus, it was a book read in hiding and in spite of my parents that made me an *honnête homme*."[40] Habits favored by his mother and discouraged by his father became increasingly dear to him. And if he consistently adhered to a few idiosyncrasies, it was because he did not find them bothersome: "Spinach greens and Saint-Simon have been my sole lasting tastes."[41] The spiritual development of Stendhal was a fight, often an unconscious one, against his milieu.

The *Vie de Henri Brulard* is only a rough draft written in haste. Its spontaneity and sincerity are the more pronounced for this, but its artistic value is blemished by repetitions, digressions, illogicalities, and inadvertencies of all kinds.[42] And yet this work may honorably be placed—but certainly not for formal reasons—beside *Wilhelm Meisters Lehrjahre*, a work Goethe had polished and repolished.[43] A common principle unites them: that of inner development. Its nature, its phases, and its results engage the interest of the reader. In both cases the development is accomplished largely by the meaningful confrontation with literature and its relevant backgrounds. Meister lived in the world of the theater and actors, Brulard in the world of books and the people vitally concerned with them, his parents and his masters. In point of age the heroes differ: with Wilhelm it is the first stage of maturity that is depicted; with Henri it is infancy and adolescence. But their fascination for life brings them together. They both feel responsible for their own future. The smiles and tricks of destiny are the products of their own doing.

⁂

The appearance of the Bildungsroman on the scene of European letters ought to be related to the pedagogical preoccupations of the period. And these cannot be fully understood unless viewed in the light of the social revolutions occurring in the eighteenth and nineteenth centuries. The Bildungsroman can surely be defined as the literary expression of a new ideal of education.

Why was Germany rather than any other nation the home and source of this new narrative genre? A partial answer is furnished by the history of education. It was in the area of Swiss and German culture that Rousseau's educational theories found their first active disciples and their first practical applications on a broad scale. It suffices to name Pestalozzi and Fröbel, Humboldt and Herbart. And Rousseau himself, Swiss by birth and temperament, drew as much, if not more, from international sources for the elaboration of his work in the field of education as he did on French ones. Rousseau was the first great writer who expressed with authority the idea that instead of *educating* a child, it was necessary to permit him to *educate himself*. This conviction lay at the base of the diverse Swiss and German systems coming to the fore in the late eighteenth century and at the beginning of the nineteenth. Create the best possible conditions so that the child, good by nature, may exercise his initiative, his will, and his feeling for independence; in sum, let him develop his own personality as a child. A child, after all, is a *child* and not a young adult. The child must form *himself*, not be formed, that was the first article of the new Swiss-German pedagogical programs.

The new systems did not embrace the theory that educators sweep away all obstacles in the paths to be traveled by their Emiles. On the contrary, every human being destined to fulfill himself by himself must spend his childhood and his adolescence in a purgatory, for which Dante's *purgatorio* serves as the model, except that a new humanitarian philosophy is substituted for traditional beliefs of a specific church. Having learned to be a child, one also learns to be a man. And terrestrial happiness is not improvised; it is award and reward at the end of an evolution. The idea of progress in the moral and intellectual areas implies the striving for the ideal, whatever it may be, coping with efforts and tests that dispose man, according to Dante, to "raise himself to the stars," through the mature acceptance of the human condition. These ideas represent the quintessence of the Bildungsroman. The apprenticeship is conceived of as a catharsis. Goethe did not have to wait for the wisdom that went with the *WestÖstlicher Divan* to understand with the Brahman that nothing purifies like knowledge.

Like memoires and confessions (one could comment not only on *Brulard* but on Tolstoy's *Childhood* as well), the Bildungsroman insists on portraying the springtide of life. Popular in Germany since the time of Goethe, whence its influence spread to the most varied countries, the genre, by its episodic and often slowly moving plot, represents, in the history of letters, the German form of the *roman fleuve*.[44] Like the latter, it terminates with the hero's success or triumph. *Wilhelm Meisters Lehrjahre*, the prototype of the species, presents a character who, by his own choice and effort—thereby denouncing the principles of the romance in which the protagonist remains the toy of events—arrives at a happiness "that he would not exchange for anything in this world," to repeat Wilhelm's words at the end of the book.[45] The notion of choice is of central importance not only to Goethe, but in all apprenticeship novels. For example, if Stifter calls the place of action Wahlsteig in *Nachsommer*, the name is obviously symbolic.[46] The Bildungsroman always grants a degree of free play to antagonistic forces—world and individual—that in the course of the confrontation merge into personality, a term that implies moral character. The change and the transformation, Goethe explains, are accomplished by Bildung. The advice that he once gave to Eckermann concerning the means of furthering oneself by the contact with books has not only a specific but a universal significance: "It is good that you gradually familiarize yourself with all that other countries and your homeland have to offer, in order to see where one can really obtain a higher *Weltbildung*, which a poet ought to possess."[47] Here is the concept of Weltbildung through world literature. It is not hard to grasp the double meaning of the word: Weltbildung is a universal education, certainly, which makes us understand the world, the whole; but it also means an education that makes us, indi-

vidually, suited for the world. In this sense the hero of the Bildungsroman integrates himself in the world in order to understand it better
and in order not to be dominated or crushed by it.

These reflections on a literary genre bring us back to the concept of
genre and form. The notion of the Bildungsroman, obviously, cannot
be identified or reconciled with that of any of the three classical
genres. The term genre, therefore, was used only reluctantly in the
preceding pages. And so was the term form, again for a strictly
semantic reason. The Bildungsroman is characterized and defined by
its subject and its purpose rather than by its outline and its structure,
or, as Wellek would say, by its inner rather than by its outer form.
With form, however, outer form is usually meant. This explains why
the word is much more properly used to indicate literary genres that
include in their definition elements of the outer form, such as the
sonnet.

12

The Sonnet in Its European Context

FEW literary terms have ever been clearly and objectively defined. Most words referring to genres, for example, like those used in all areas of letters, are still, and probably always will be, the topic of scholarly discussions. Broad descriptions and approximations are likely to continue to serve in the absence of unanimously approved definitions.

The sonnet, however, seems to be one of the very few terms adequately defined. Generations of textbook authors have commented with delight on its apparently fixed and accurately circumscribed form, and anthology makers have compiled examples from each national literature of the West. It is quite natural that the comparatist yields to the temptation of studying this kind of poetry in its international context in order to verify and, possibly, to justify the common belief in a recognized concept. The rise and development of the sonnet in the nations that have practiced it as a major genre, the architecture of the stanzas, the rhyme schemes and prevailing themes —all these are aspects to be studied if an answer is to be found to the question of whether or not a European sonnet exists, and, if it does, whether or not the sonnet may be defined without taking into account national idiosyncrasies or particular patterns popularized by single poets.

I

The history of the sonnet, from its obscure origins to its most brilliant triumphs, is a fascinating one.[1] Even the durability and luster of its fortunes constitutes a mystery, for one should suspect that the more artificial a genre is the more short-lived it will be. Yet though sonnet rules appear to be quite arbitrary, the genre has passed the test of time gloriously and is widely practiced by contemporary poets. It is now some seven hundred and fifty years old. Two specimens may delimit this span of time and serve, if not as an evolutionary compendium of the genre, at least as one variation of a theme of Louis de Bonald's: "Le sonnet est l'expression de la société." Each example reflects definite trends of a specific *Zeitgeist*, those of the sophisticated, metaphysical-minded, medieval aristocracy, and those of our somehow naïvely, yet brutally materialistic democracies. Both sonnets illustrate in their own ways some of the numerous connections relating literature to other cultural areas and, therefore, they show the interdisciplinary character that comparative studies may assume. One of them is from among the very first sonnets ever written, the other from among the most recent. Between these compositions of Jacopo da Lentino and Mary Ellen Solt, there are hundreds of thousands of sonnets that have justly fallen into oblivion. But there are several thousand, too, of outstanding quality, and a few hundred are masterpieces left by the makers of world literature.

Here is Lentino's sonnet:

> Amor è un desio che ven da core
> per habundanza de grand plaçimento;
> cgl'ogli en prima genera l'amore,
> e lo core li dà nutrigamento.
> ben è alcuna fiata om amatore
> senza vedere so namoramento,
> ma quel amor che strenze cum furore,
> da la vista dig ogli à nasemento.
> Che gl'ogli rapresenta a lo core
> d'onni cosa che veden bono e rio,
> cum è formata naturalemente.
> e l core che di ço è concipitore,
> ymaçina e plaçe quel desio;
> e questo amore regna fra la zente.[2]

From time immemorial poets have said in a less blunt way than Lentino does here that love is a desire that comes from the heart and elevates human existence.

"Ut pictura poesis": why not, for once, take literally this celebrated maxim of Horace that a poem be like a painting? Mrs. Solt's *Moonshot Sonnet* belongs to the so-called concrete poetry genre that is ordinarily based on the combined use of words and designs, and consists mainly of picture puzzles, optic or acoustic puns, and, above all, pictograms and calligrams. This last kind of poem, well-known since the end of the Middle Ages, has been illustrated by Apollinaire in recent times and may be clearly traced back for certain of its aspects to the tradition of emblem poetry. About the sonnet, shown on p. 154, Mrs. Solt comments: "It has not been possible since the Renaissance to write a convincing sonnet on the moon. Looking at the moon photographs in *The New York Times*, it occurred to me that since the scientist's symbols for marking off areas on the moon's surface were presented five to a line and the lines could be added up to fourteen, a visual sonnet could be made of them. The poem is intended as a spoof of an outmoded form of poetry and as a statement of the problem of the concrete poet's search for valid new forms."[3] Mrs. Solt's sonnet, however, is far from marking the end of Lentino's invention.

At least two reasons explain the astonishing success of the genre of the sonnet. The first is of an extrinsic order: two geniuses, Dante and Petrarch, had based their universal reputations in part on this ingenious game of fourteen lines; the poets who succeeded them quite naturally had to follow suit. The other reason is intrinsic in character: the whole history of the sonnet seems to prove that fourteen lines are a most fortunate space for the compact expression of a thought, image, or emotion. This magic number[4] lends itself at the same time to an intriguing play of rhyme. Effects of light and darkness, rest and movement, conciseness and parallelism—everything that aesthetics prescribes or counsels can find its most convincing illustration in a single sonnet. Why is a tennis court seventy-eight feet long and thirty-six wide? Because a certain sporting ideal can best be realized in that space. Why are we tempted to believe that the dimensions of the sonnet and the tennis court are artificial? Because it is difficult to divest ourselves of the superstition of decimal arithmetic, and because we believe the metrical system to be natural, whereas it is simply practical. An analogous superstition has led a part of the intellectual elite to divide literature into centuries. All this suggests that the sonnet is a literary form somehow congenial to the pattern of our intellect. The sonnet is not the conclusion of a theory, but the result of experience or a long series of experiments.

The sonnet was born in Sicily during the first half of the thirteenth century under the aegis of Frederick II, Holy Roman emperor, who presided over a remarkable court at Palermo. He himself wrote poems in the Sicilian vernacular as well as a delightful treatise on falconry in Latin, *De arte venandi cum avibus* [On the art of hunting with birds]. The sonnet assumed its form in Frederick's court, which was nourished by Byzantine and Arab contacts and known for both its literary interests and cosmopolitan spirit. Thirty-

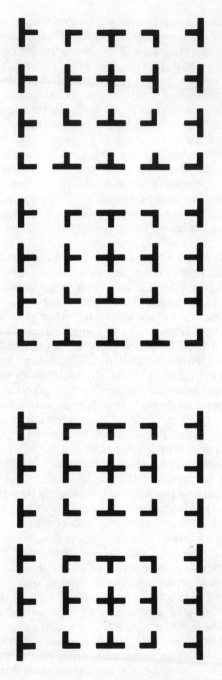

Moonshot Sonnet by Mary Ellen Solt

five sonnets written at the court by several authors between 1220 and 1240 have been preserved.[5] One of these authors, Jacopo (or Giacomo) Notaro da Lentino or Lentini (also called James the Notary), whom we just quoted, seems to have played a principal role and is generally regarded as the first poet to exemplify the form. Two men at the court of Frederick are historically prominent: Rinaldo da Aquino, in whom critics see the brother of Saint Thomas Aquinas, and Pietro della Vigna, the emperor's chancellor, both of whom also wrote sonnets. It is not possible, however, to determine exactly their contribution to the creation of the genre.

Most certainly, Lentino did not invent the formula for the sonnet by himself. It emerged from the Sicilian laboratory, but the first efforts were probably made in other places at other times. One may suppose that from the moment rhyme became an integral part of both Latin and vernacular poetry, attempts were made to explore and exploit the possibilities it offered; these attempts were in favor among both the Italian poets, at a moment when their language was taking new shape, and the Provençal poets, whose influence over vast regions of the Mediterranean basin is well known. In Frederick's Sicily, the *strambotto*, consisting of two quatrains, was a popular form of poetry; many scholars accept the hypothesis that the sonnet is a strambotto lengthened by a double tercet. As to the word sonnet, it derives from the Latin *sonitus* and the Italian *sonnetto*, the respective diminutives of *sonus* and *suono*; hence, it means a little sound or song. The etymology reminds us that this kind of poem was meant to be sung. In both Provençal and Sicilian language *sonet* means song.

In the course of the second half of the thirteenth century, the sonnet came into its own in Italy. Twenty-odd authors of sonnets thrived during this period, including Guittone d'Arezzo, who set the rules for the Italian rhyme scheme, and Balduccio d'Arezzo. Petrarch himself came from Arezzo, a neighboring and rival town of Florence; in 1289 Dante Alighieri, of Florence, took part in the battle of Campaldina between the two cities. From its Sicilian beginnings, then, the sonnet seems to have established itself in Tuscany, where a specific cultural milieu helped poets to investigate the lyrical possibilities of the new form. These were the circumstances under which Dante, in the last decade of the thirteenth century, composed the sonnets he included in his *Vita nuova* (in all he wrote fifty-five sonnets), and under which Petrarch, forty years Dante's junior, wrote those that form his *Rime in vita e morte di Madonna Laura*, commonly styled *Canzoniere*.[6] While Dante, in his *De vulgari eloquentia*, puts the sonnet in the lowest class of poetry, in spite of his own accomplishments, Petrarch was perfectly aware of the literary value of his poems, though he wanted his reputation to rest mainly on his humanistic achievements. In the trecento many poets engaged in sonneteering, but they were all not only inspired but overshadowed by the two giants of Italian literature—all except Giovanni Boccaccio, who, however, did not specialize in the sonnet.

The popularity of the genre also has to be related to a new stylistic trend. In the *dolce stil nuovo* the sonnet became the exercise par excellence in technique and smoothness of language.[7] The subsequent centuries, the quattrocento and the cinquecento, are those of poets like Matteo Maria Boiardo, Lorenzo de' Medici, Leonardo da Vinci, Ludovico Ariosto, Pietro Bembo, Michelangelo Buonarroti, Baldassarre Castiglione, Torquato Tasso, and Giordano Bruno. Later, other names, some famous, represent the genre: Francesco Molza, Cipriano da Rore, Tommaso Campanella, Giovanni Battista Guarini, Giambattista Marini, Giovanni della Casa, who was probably the first to use the enjambment, and two celebrated ladies, Vittoria Colonna and Gaspara Stampa. In the settecento, Pietro Matastasio, Giuseppe Parini, Vittorio Alfieri, and in the ottocento Vincenzo Monti continued the tradition of the Italian sonnet. Subsequent periods witnessed the work of Ugo Foscolo, Giosuè Carducci, Giovanni Pascoli, and Gabriele D'Annunzio. Giacomo Leopardi, however, perhaps the greatest Italian lyrical poet after Petrarch, and probably the most profound commentator on the *Canzoniere*, did not write any poem shorter than fifteen lines. This could hardly hamper the popularity of the sonnet in Italy, where the genre is still very much alive in our own age.[8]

The success of the sonnet in France was so overwhelming that some of the French poets thought they had invented the genre.[9] Indeed, many critics found it difficult to believe in its Sicilian origin; they surmised that the Provence was its real birthplace. An eighteenth-century literary history reads: "The sonnet was born in France and the Italians made vain efforts to appropriate its invention to themselves."[10] A similar assertion was made a hundred years later by Charles Asselineau.[11]

The honor of being the first French sonneteers can most likely be claimed by Clément Marot and Mellin de Saint-Gelais.[12] Both poets had spent some time in Italy about 1520 before reaching their thirtieth year. Marot composed ten sonnets and Saint-Gelais seventeen. Today, however, their tiny collections possess only historical interest. La Pléiade, the famous mid-sixteenth-century school of poets, had a more durable success.[13] Its members naturalized the sonnet in France: Ronsard, Du Bellay, Rémi Belleau, Dorat, Antoine de Baïf, Pontus de Tyard, and Etienne Jodelle. Other poets should also be mentioned, such as Olivier de Magny, Philippe Desportes, Jean Bertaut, Louise Labé, Etienne de la Boëtie, Jacques Grévin, Maurice Scève, Jean de Sponde, Marc de Papillon and, a later figure, their antagonist, François de Malherbe, one of the earliest legislators of the French sonnet. Thus the high water mark of the genre in France came some two or three centuries later than it did in Italy.

The seventeenth century in France was the epoch of the theater.

So-called "petits genres" could not really flourish in the age of
Racine: they were all driven into the artificial asylum of the salon.
This situation is best understood by a comparison of some great
literary figures from other centuries: if Ronsard and Du Bellay had
not written sonnets, the history of French literature—and their roles
in it—would have been radically different from what it is now. But if
Racine, Corneille, and Molière had not written any of their few sonnets, their renown would still be assured. Under Louis XIII and Louis
XIV—apart from these towering figures—sonnets were composed
mainly by rather mediocre authors like Pierre Lemoyne (1602–1671)
and Georges de Brébeuf (1618–1661). If these third-rate artists still
appear in literary textbooks, it is because someone decided one day
that everything in the Grand Siècle was great. It is true that the
list of seventeenth-century French writers who, besides Malherbe,
tried their hands now and then at sonnets in leisure hours could be
considerably expanded: it would include the names of Vincent Voiture and Isaac de Benserade, Mathurin Régnier and François May-
nard, Théophile de Viau and Paul Scarron, Marc-Antoine Girard de
Saint-Amand and La Fontaine, and also Boileau. But even if these
attempts had been crowned with success, the results would have
remained marginal as measured by aesthetic standards. The following century, the eighteenth, is predominantly a period of poetic prose
or, simply, of prose. It is characterized by the *emancipation* from
particular literary forms, rather than the attempt to refine one specific genre.[14] These tendencies and attitudes are visible at the beginning of the following century in the Romantic age.

The second half of the nineteenth century, on the contrary, is the
era of the *cult* of form. In Hugo's works we still find scarcely ten
sonnets, twenty more in Musset's—but most varied in structure and
rhyme patterns—and a lesser number in Vigny's. Besides, who could
expect the Promethean artists of the Romantic period to imprison
their souls behind fourteen bars? To do that, one had to be, like
Wordsworth, English. Gautier, the great promotor of "art for art's
sake," and Leconte de Lisle, the olympian spirit behind the Parnassian
movement, are at the beginning of the rehabilitation of the French
sonnet. To restore the genre to its former glory required the combined
poetic labors of artists like Baudelaire, Théodore de Banville, Heredia,
Saint-Beuve, Sully Prudhomme, Catulle Mendès, Louis Ménard, Nerval, Mallarmé, and Rimbaud.[15] Their labors were continued in the
twentieth century by Emile Verhaeren, Francis Jammes, Apollinaire,
Valéry, and Claudel. On the face of it, the Sicilians gave the French a
permanent genre in the sonnet.

✷

It is surprising that Chaucer, who had traveled in Italy and who
was one of the first Englishmen to become acquainted with the work

of Dante, did not compose a single sonnet.[16] Neither in England nor
in France did the sonnet reach full popularity until the sixteenth
century, and one can find a certain parallel in the evolution of the
form in the two nations. Sir Thomas Wyatt wrote the first English
sonnet approximately at the same time that Marot and Mellin de
Saint-Gelais composed the first French examples. England became
acquainted with the sonnet thanks to *Tottel's Miscellany*, an anthology, published in 1557. This collection included a great variety of
works, in particular poems written a few decades earlier by two
young authors who had visited Italy: Wyatt and Henry Howard, Earl
of Surrey. As far as their roles in the history of the European sonnet is
concerned, these two men can best be compared with Ronsard and
Du Bellay. Sometimes English poets actually did take their inspiration
from the members of the French Pléiade, but more often from the
first Italian masters of the craft. It is true that Spenser, the author of
the *Amoretti*, translated *Les Antiquités de Rome* of Du Bellay, and the
biographers of Shakespeare have stressed his debt to his colleagues
across the Channel.[17] Yet, generally speaking, the English were not
strongly influenced by the French. They always admitted their fealty
to the poets who praised Beatrice and Laura, not to Ronsard, the
singer of Cassandre and Marie. Wordsworth typified this attitude in
his poem *Scorn Not the Sonnet*, when he named seven poets who had
contributed greatly to the sonnet: Milton, Shakespeare, Spenser,
Dante, Petrarch, Tasso, and Camoëns.[18] An astonishing number of
sonnets were produced in sixteenth and seventeenth-century England.
In addition to the authors already mentioned, dozens of poets and
their works would be worth naming, like Sir Philip Sidney, for his
Astrophel and Stella, Thomas Watson, for his *Hecatompathia* and his
Tears of Fancy, Henry Constable for his *Diana*, Michael Drayton for
his *Amours in Quatorzains*, and Samuel Daniel for his *Delia*. Giles
Fletcher, Barnabe Barnes, Thomas Lodge, and William Percy could
also be cited. Evidently, Shakespeare's sonnet cycle was the epicenter
of this poetic movement.

England in the seventeenth century had at least one great genius
to continue the sonnet tradition, Milton, who was preceded by John
Donne and William Drummond. But one must look hard in that
period to find writers who abstained from composing sonnets. Among
poets of renown, only Jonson and Harington showed neither interest
nor faith in the enduring qualities of the sonnet; Jonson used the
form only in a few epigrams. But after Milton's generation, the link
was broken. The sonnet was not really revived in England until the
age of Wordsworth. Thomas Edwards, Thomas Gray, Thomas Warton
the Younger, and Thomas Russell had all sought in vain to repair the
break during the interim. The tradition, nonetheless, existed. It was
slowly restored by the next generations of British and Irish poets, and

during the first half of the nineteenth century it also took root in the United States.

Wordsworth was the only great English romantic who not only excelled in the sonnet, but adopted the genre as one of his major forms of lyrical expression. Shelley wrote a few, as did Byron, Keats, and Coleridge, who published a dozen *Sonnets on Eminent Characters* in the *Morning Chronicle* (December, 1795–January, 1796). But the sonnet never became either an essential part of the work or one of the favorite forms of any of these British poets. In a later period Elizabeth Barrett Browning, on the contrary, founded her literary reputation on the celebrated collection *Sonnets from the Portuguese*, and Dante Gabriel Rossetti is mainly known for his *House of Life*.[19] The nineteenth century also witnessed poets like Aubry de Vere, George Meredith, Algernon Charles Swinburne, and Oscar Wilde at work on the sonnet. Eugene Lee-Hamilton's *Imaginary Sonnets* and *Sonnets of the Wingless Hours* definitely have their place in the history of English lyric poetry. Yeats, Masefield, and Dylan Thomas are among the best known representatives of the sonnet tradition in the twentieth century. As to the United States, names abound: Edgar Allan Poe, John Greenleaf Whittier, Henry Wadsworth Longfellow, Jones Very, Ezra Pound, and Edwin Arlington Robinson. More recently, Malcolm Cowley, Edna St. Vincent Millay, Edward E. Cummings, Robert Frost, and W. H. Auden (of British descent), achieved mastery of the form. There is also Merrill Moore, the most prolific, original, and independent of all American sonneteers.[20]

☙❦

Italy, France, England, Ireland, the United States are not the only countries that adopted the sonnet as a major poetic genre. It flourished in Iberia and South America, and to a lesser extent in Germany.

The sonnet appeared in Spain before it did in France, but the Spanish poets did not take it to their heart in the same way the French did. The form was introduced into Spain by Iñigo López de Mendoza, Marqués de Santillana (1398–1458), the author of *Infierno de los enamorados*, in which he shows himself to be the disciple of Petrarch and Dante. During his rather hectic diplomatic career, he managed to compose forty-two *Sonetos fechos al italico modo*, which are, however, of rather slight value.[21] Nonetheless, these poems prove that the Spanish poets were influenced by Petrarch a hundred years before the French. This advantage in time did not suffice to firmly establish the genre in Spain, although Juan Boscán Almogaver (ca. 1490–1542) sought to strengthen the foothold of the Italian form. Following the advice of the celebrated Venetian scholar Andrea Navagero, who had established himself in Granada, Boscán decided to write sonnets "in the Castilian language," setting an authoritative example for the generation of poets to come.[22] His friend Garcilaso de la Vega (ca. 1501–1536), however, played perhaps as important a part as Boscán in the history of the naturalization of the sonnet in Spain. This soldier and poet had spent time in Naples and had done much traveling before he tragically died (when Ronsard was twelve) in his early thirties.[23] His sonnets were first published in the fourth volume of Boscán's works (1543), which contain fifty-three sonnets composed by Boscán and thirty-nine by Garcilaso.

The second half of the Spanish sixteenth century contributed one great name to the history of the sonnet, Cervantes, but rather few great sonnets. Diego Hurtado de Mendoza (1503–1575), Luis de León (1527–1591), and Fernando de Herrera (1534–1597) were destined to arouse only a few echoes in international letters. Cervantes was of another order, though literary history has, in practical terms, retained but two of his sonnets. The first belongs to the genre of "vers de circonstance." It was an elegiac poem written to mourn the passing of Queen Isabelle of Valois, and appeared in 1569 in a collection of works dedicated to her memory. The future author of *Don Quixote* was only twenty-two when he made this "precious" contribution to the genre. The second noteworthy sample is one of the twenty sonnets included in the novel itself and in its preamble. It is a delightful conversation between Babieca and Rosinante.

Lope Felix de Vega Carpio (1562–1635), a member of the following generation, has better claim than Cervantes to preeminence in the domain of the sonnet. He wrote more than fifteen hundred examples of the form, perhaps as many as seventeen hundred or two thousand —a number very close to that of his plays. If the comparativistic method were wider spread in the Iberian peninsula, some Spanish critic would long since have proclaimed Lope de Vega king of the sonnet, since he created more poems in this genre than Ronsard, Du Bellay, Dante, Petrarch, Ariosto, Shakespeare, Milton, and Wordsworth put together. What is more, his accomplishment in quantity did not diminish the quality of his work.[24] Some two hundred of Lope's sonnets, especially those with religious inspiration, are comparable to the best work of his rivals.

Luis de Góngora (1561–1627) strove to equal or surpass Lope de Vega in his *Sonetos heroicos* and *Sonetos amorosos*, and Francisco Gómez de Quevedo y Villegas (1580–1645) almost succeeded in this goal, thanks to a certain delicateness that Góngora lacked. The achievement of Pedro Calderón de la Barca (1600–1681) cannot be ignored either. Even after the *Siglo de Oro*, the Golden Century, the tradition was maintained by many writers—for example, Juan Meléndez Valdés (1754–1817) and José de Espronceda (1808–1842)— and has been continued to the present day. It has survived by virtue of poets like Miguel de Unamuno, Juan Ramón Jiménez, Salvador Rueda Santos, Jorge Guillén, Rafael Alberti, and the Machado brothers. In all Spanish-speaking countries of Latin America, scores of sonneteers practiced their art throughout the last three centuries: in Mexico, for instance, Sor Juana Inés de la Cruz, in Nicaragua, Rubén Dario, and in Chile, Gabriela Mistral.

Several volumes could be filled by the sonnets of Portuguese poets alone. Francisco de Sá de Miranda (ca. 1485–1558) introduced the sonnet into Portugal, after a long sojourn in Italy (1521–1526). It was Luis Vaz de Camoëns (1524–1580), however, who brought the form to its ultimate perfection during the first Portuguese classical period. He has left some two hundred examples that could profitably be analyzed in an international study of the sonnet.[25] Antônio Ferreira (1528–1569), Diogo Bernardes Pimenta, and Agostino da Cruz (ca. 1540–ca. 1605), are also among the earliest Portuguese sonneteers. The tradition was continued by Rodrigues Lobo, Manuel Maria Barbosa du Bocage, João de Deus Ranus, Antero de Quental, Manuel de Silva Gaio, and Antônio Nobré.

The sonnet also became a favorite lyrical form in Brazilian literature. It was cultivated by Gregório de Matos (1633–1696), Tomaz Antônio Gonzaga (1744–1807), Machado de Assis (1839–1908), Raymondo Correia (1859–1911), Sousa e Cruz (1863–1898), Olavo Bilac (1865–1918), Alphonso de Guimaraens (1870–1921), Alberto de Oliveira (1857–1937). The list could be completed with names like Manuel Bandeira, Vinicius de Moraes, Augusto Frederico Schmidt.[26]

∂∕⌐

In Germany, it took time for the sonnet to gain acceptance, and its early practitioners were often third-raters.[27] Even so, a man like Johann Fischart, the translator and adapter of Rabelais, also counts, among the first German sonneteers with seven samples (after 1575). However, the real integration of the sonnet into German letters had to wait for the pens of Martin Opitz (1597–1639), Georg Rudolf Weckherlin (1584–1653), Paul Fleming (1609–1640), and Philipp von Zesen (1619–1689), decisively supplemented by the works of Andreas Gryphius (1616–1664), and of Hofmann von Hofmannswaldau (1617–1679). In the eighteenth century the form was not generally recognized as a valuable poetical expression by any important critic until the time of August Wilhelm Schlegel. Bodmer and Gottsched, for example, had only scorn for the fourteen-line poem, while Schlegel, in the middle of a famous lecture delivered at Berlin in the winter of 1803–1804, declared that sonnets should particularly interest the Germans: "They were either entirely foreign to German poetry up until now, or they never took root in the soil of our language, and recently some poets have tried to import them, which can be of great importance."[28] For Schlegel and Wilhelm von Humboldt, no less than the romantic school in general, the sonnet represented medievalism—which goes a long way toward explaining its later success in Germany. For the French romantics, on the other hand, the genre bore the mark of the Renaissance. This, of course, suggests at least one reason why the French romantics were not overenthusiastic about the form.

Goethe often showed a reticent attitude toward sonnets, though between 1807 and 1808 he composed seventeen of them; he wrote only twenty-five during his whole career.[29] All of them were love poems in which Petrarch still sang. The fame of the sonnet in German was secured by poets like Bürger, Hölderlin, Joseph von Eichendorff, Gottfried August Rückert, Platen, Franz Grillparzer, Theodor Körner, Heinrich Heine, Nikolaus Lenau, Mörike, Friederich Hebbel, and Paul von Heyse. To this list should be appended a few more recent names: Ricarda Huch, Christian Morgenstern, Rainer Maria Rilke, Stefan Zweig, Rudolph Alexander Schröder, and Stefan George, as well as Georg Trakl, Josef Weinheber, Franz Werfel, and Reinhold Schneider.

☙❦❧

In the Slavic countries, too, the sonnet took hold slowly. In the fifteenth century, the Dalmatian coast, with its main city-state of Ragusa, was a literary center boasting two poets who imitated the Petrarchan sonnet: Šiško Menćetić (1452–1527) and Gjorgje Držić (1461–1501). In Venice a collection of fifty sonnets, *Vila Slovinka* [The slavic fairy] from the pen of the Dalmatian poet Juraj Barković (1548–1628). Poland, where Desportes sojourned when Henri of Anjou reigned as king (September, 1573–July, 1574), experienced the direct influence of France. The oldest Polish sonnets appear in the collection of *Fraszki* [Trifles] by Jan Kochanowski (1530–1584), first published in the year of his death. Kochanowski, who was familiar with the works of Petrarch and Dante, thus founded the sonnet tradition in Poland, followed by Mikolaj Şep Szarzyński (1550–1581) and Andrzey Morsztyn (1613–1693). It was brilliantly carried on by Adam Mickiewicz (1798–1855), notably in his *Sonety Krymskie*. In the twentieth century, Poland continues to find poets who practice the genre.

From the moment Russia found out there was such a form, she began to compose the sonnet. This occurred in the seventeenth century, when she discovered western Europe. Alexander Pushkin, however, was the first great Russian writer to master the fourteen-line poem. Sonnets by Afanasi Afanasievich Fet (1820–1892) and Alexander Blok (1880–1921) are especially important. But poets like Balmont (1867–1943) and Vyacheslav Ivánov (1866–1949) also contributed significantly to the furthering of the genre. Balmont brought attention to himself by his translation of Shelley before composing sonnets himself that are scattered among his numerous volumes of poetry. Despite the attention the sonnet has received in Russia, however, it has not really taken root in Russian soil; it is a form that remains deeply embedded only in the traditions of the West. Other linguistic regions also testify to the permanence and omnipresence of the sonnet in European letters: Czechoslovakia, for instance, with Jan Kollár (1793–1852), Sweden with Per Daniel Amadeus Atterbom (1790–1855), Norway with Johan Sebastian Welhaven (1807–1873), and Iceland with Thornsteinn Erlingsson (1858–1914).

II

Of all the questions concerning the nature of the sonnet as an internationally homogeneous poetic form, only one can be answered with any degree of conclusiveness: it has fourteen lines. To know how to count to fourteen, however, is not sufficient to identify a regular sonnet. A series of formal or structural factors, varying from one particular literature to another, is involved. If the critic is Italian, for example, he will insist that the fourteen verses be divided into an octave and a sestet, which are further broken down into quatrains and tercets. The rhyme scheme for the earliest Italian sonnets is *abab/abab/cde/cde*. Guittone d'Arezzo recommended *abba/abba/cde/cde*, or, in the tercets, *cdc/dcd*. The rhymes, for the Italian, are five (or four) in number and should be arranged according to one of these schemes. In practice, a good deal of freedom was permitted nonetheless. Antonio da Tempo, one of the first critics to include an extensive treatment of the sonnet in a treatise on poetics (1332), accepted sixteen legitimate patterns; one of his most noticeable variants was that the rhymes of the quatrains could be embraced (abba), a scheme that Dante and Petrarch had already used, and many other writers followed. The line usually consisted of eleven syllables, a meter the early French poets reduced by one. The first definitions of the sonnet were obviously empirical, since they derived immediately from the examples furnished by the *Vita nuova* and the *Canzoniere*.

When the English took up the form, they recognized that the fourteen lines could be divided in a different fashion. Not that they imagined they were improving the Italian sonnet; rather, they wisely admitted that the ear of a British islander is slightly different from that of a peninsular Italian—though the first sonnets were written by Italians on an island: Sicily. However, there was a much more serious reason for this change: a fundamental difference in the phonetic structure of the two languages.

The English kept the two quatrains, but they changed the two tercets into a quatrain to which they added a couplet. The formula, rendered stylish by Wyatt, is *abba/abba/cddc/ee*. The octave and the sestet (*cdd/cee*) are still clearly visible. Surrey, and then Shakespeare, carried Wyatt's idea of a final couplet much further and also tended to modify the number of rhymes (seven instead of five). The number of differentiated vowel sounds, simple or diphthongized, is considerably higher in English than in the Romance languages. As a consequence, there are more groups of rhymes in English, but fewer voices within each specific rhyme group. The English poet writing in the *italico modo* had to overcome this additional obstacle arising from the relative scarcity of rich rhymes, while the Italian, as well as the Spanish, the Portuguese, and the French had cornucopiae at their disposal. Yet a tendency to restrict the number of rhymes (three instead of five) is also occasionally found, notably in Surrey's work. Furthermore, the arrangement of the rhymes is sometimes changed from the Italian, ending up with this seven-rhyme formula: *abab/ cdcd/efef/gg*, or, for three rhymes: *abab/abab/abab/cc*. Spenser had the idea of the following hybridization: *abab/bcbc/cdcd/ee*, a solution with five rhymes, unless the poet thought to replace *ee* by *cc*, which reduced the number of rhymes to four. Spenser's interlacement of the rhymes clearly brings Dante's stanzas to mind and the rhyme patterns of the *Divina commedia*.

The Frenchman is inclined to remain faithful to the Italian origins of the sonnet in that he likes to keep two quatrains and two tercets. The leading poets of the Pléiade who had launched the sonnet in France tended to generalize this scheme: *abba/abba/ccd/eed*. It was one that later changed into another commonly used in the so-called "French" sonnet, characterized by the variant in the tercets: *ccd/ede*. Malherbe fixed this rhyme pattern, although Du Bellay had already given numerous examples in his *Regrets*, and more than a third of the pieces in *Les Antiquités de Rome* are "French" sonnets. The form was cultivated in the century of Louis XIV, almost at the exclusion of any other, and Voiture's *Sonnet à Uranie* and Benserade's *Job*, which were the poems at issue in the famous "Querelle des sonnets," follow this model.[30] Were we to treat the sonnet on the international level, we would be obliged to define it as a poem of fourteen lines, arranged so that we can always recognize an octet or two quatrains in the first eight lines, followed either by two tercets (romance literatures) or a third quatrain and a couplet (English sonnets). All the forms mentioned justify acceptance of this rule.

Of course, there is also the problem of terminology in dealing with the genre. One part of the critical world advises calling these English fourteen-line poems sonnets, the other prefers to consider them mere quatorzains. The term quatorzain—actually a decatetrastich, or poem in fourteen lines—has been used especially to name pieces consisting of three quatrains with alternate rhymes completed by a couplet and having seven pairs of rhymes in all. In practice, though, the distinction between these quatorzains and the original sonnet is hardly made, at least in the Anglo-Saxon world, and even purists forget it at times. Everybody speaks of the *sonnets* and not of the *quatorzains* of Spenser, Shakespeare, and Daniel. Moreover, the distinction is not constantly applicable: one would have to concern oneself with all the intermediary forms.

Sonnet or quatorzain, we are far from having exhausted the subtleties of the sonneteers. There are many subspecies among the sonnets, and one of them may be called the "American sonnet," in which the stanzas are handled with absolute freedom. Merrill Moore shows patterns like these: *abba/cddce/fe/gfg* (*Old Men and Old Women Going Home on the Street Car*—the modern version of Ronsard's *Quand vous serez bien vieille*), *abcdeed/ffbacff* (*Waring to One*), *aa/bbccddef/egfg* (*Village Noon: Mid-Day Bells*), and *ababa/cbcdd/eebb* (*Unkown Man in the Morgue*). Granted, the total of Moore's lines is almost always fourteen. But this is the observation of an accountant only, and does not take other basic elements of the sonnet tradition into consideration. Julien August Brizeux (1806–1858), the author of a useful French translation of Dante, is known as the creator of the "sonnet à rebours," a subspecies for which both Verlaine and Baudelaire furnished specimens.[31] One of the principal forms of the Brizeux sonnet is *abb/acc/deed/deed*. The first of Verlaine's *Poèmes saturniens* followed this pattern. Mallarmé found a further refinement. He wrote a "French backward sonnet," beginning "Ma faim qui d'aucuns fruits," in which the rhymes are arranged *aab/cbc/deed/deed*. It would not be difficult to find similar forms in English literature. Samuel Taylor Coleridge's *Work Without Hope*, is divided into a sestet and an octave with this rhyme scheme: *ababbb/ccddeeff*, and one of the earliest examples of this sort of sophisticated sonnet is by Thomas Carew (1594–1640). The rhyme scheme for his *Song* is *a/ba/bcc//d/ed/eff/aa;* here, too, the sestet precedes the octave.

Such observations have led quite a few critics to reject any definition of the sonnet that prescribes in any way the division into stanzas or sections, or the arrangement and number of rhymes. For them only one absolute criterion is left, that of fourteen lines. It would follow that Milton unwittingly wrote a sonnet when he had his chorus recite a poem of fourteen lines to end *Samson Agonistes*, and that Mallarmé did the same in his *Don du poème*, as did Conrad Ferdinand Meyer in his *Chor der Toten*, and Vladimir Nabokov in *Pale Fire*, wherein a passage of fourteen lines (247–260), separated from its context, forms a poem of a striking unity.[32]

Why is only the first of these poems a sonnet in the classical sense? The reply is to be found in the general notion we have of what a sonnet should be. Essentially, it is the genre of the "difficulté vaincue," a challenge to the poet's artistry and a call for all his technical skill. A framework of rhymes and verse division is provided for the poet who then agrees to fill it in. It is a Procrustean mold into which a thought or sentiment of a certain quality has to be compressed. Seven rhymed couplets, however, do not constitute such a mold, and any fourteen lines from Corneille's or Racine's dramas do not justify Boileau's statement that one single faultless sonnet is worth a long poem: "Un sonnet sans défaut vaut seul un long poème."[33]

The fateful number of fourteen would be quite arbitrary if we discounted the importance of European tradition. A stubborn critic could espouse the cause of other numbers, eleven or seventeen, for example, or thirteen; but we would continue to write, read, and appreciate fourteen-line sonnets. It is a matter of tradition, and in all probability no tradition survives unless it corresponds to some secret need in man's psyche. Although a poet may seem quite flexible on many points, he does not compromise when it comes to the sonnet. Why is the tradition so strict about what appears to be only arithmetic? All the sonnets of Shakespeare have fourteen lines, with the exception of one (No. 126), which has twelve. Byron's *Sonnet to Lake Leman* has thirteen. In *Das Glasperlenspiel* (1943, *Magister Ludi*), Hesse also includes a poem of thirteen lines. Apollinaire's well-known poem *Les Colchiques* has the misfortune to include one too many lines, and the arrangement of the strophes and the rhymes (*abaccaa/ ccddb/baa*) does not recall Petrarch, nor do the fifteen liners— which the author calls sonnets—by the *enfant terrible* among the sonneteers, Merrill Moore. These poems did not so far win universal acceptance as sonnets. On the other hand, if we analyze *Les fiançailles*, another poem by Apollinaire, we notice that it is a "sonnet à rebours," in the laxest manner, an acephalous sonnet, since it lacks one tercet. Its schema: *abb/cdcd/efef*. No one would call these atrophied or emaciated poems sonnets except, sometimes, their authors. They are simply related forms. The "curtal sonnet," first practiced by the British poet Gerard Manley Hopkins (1844–1889), has eleven lines, the last being half the length of the others (*abc/abc/dbcd/c*); it also represents a kind of shortened "à rebours" sonnet. Many other variations of pseudo-sonnets are to be found in other literatures—German and Spanish, for example—though they appear less frequently in Slavic poetry. Criticism has framed a particular notion of the sonnet, a concept based on firm principles. To a certain extent, however, their application is still subjective. As a result, the exact contours of the sonnet remain blurred and indistinct.

Some of the rules for sonnet writing continue to be closely connected to the laws governing prosody in the various literatures. In Italy, the hendecasyllable line was the early verse for the sonnet; in England, it was the decasyllable line; in France, the alexandrine quickly gained the upper hand. License was taken very early in every country. The French poets were most liberal in the realm of meter. *Les Antiquités de Rome* presents sonnets of both twelve and ten syllables. Benserade's *Job* and Corneille's verdict, which settled the "Querelle des sonnets," are written in octosyllabic lines. The closer we approach the contemporary period, the more variants we meet. In Rimbaud's *Rêve pour l'hiver*, the second and fourth verses of the quatrain are six-syllable lines, as are the third lines of the tercets. *Sur une dame blonde*, a Petrarchan theme par excellence, was composed by de Banville on the French scheme in tetrameter.

One of the basic principles of the sonnet is to confer a standard length on a given emotion or thought. Obviously this length depends not only on the number of lines, but also on their own length. Some sonneteers went so far as to write monosyllabic lines. Such sonnets, quite obviously, are materially ten times shorter than sonnets consisting of decasyllabic lines. Here are examples of such sonnets composed by rather obscure English, French, German, Brazilian, and Cuban virtuosi:

"I	Fort	Mit	Deus	Mi
Through	Belle	Prall-	Vê	Fe
Blue	Elle	Hall	Que	Que
Sky	Dort!	Sprüht	Meus	'Di
Fly	Sort	Süd	Ais	...¡ Ni
To	Frêle	Tral-	Não	Sé
You.	Quelle	Lal-	São	De
Why?"	Mort!	Lied,	Mais	Tí !
"Sweet	Rose	Kling-	De	¿Dó
Love	Close	Klang	Dó	Más
Feet	La	Singt;	Por	Vas ?
Move	Brise	Sing-	Ti,	¡ Oh
So	L'a	Sang	Ó	Bien!
Slow!"	Prise.	Klingt.	Flor!	¡ Vien !....

The Sicilian invention has here become the para-sonnet, a play, not a song—an amusement for the *poeta ludens*.

As for the *poeta canens*, he has usually referred himself, although most flexibly, it is true, to one of the standard meters and to one of the six main types of sonnet that have grown on European soil. These types may be recapitulated with their characteristics as follows:

1. Italian or Petrarchan: *abba/abba/cde/cde*
   abba/abba/cdc/dcd
   (Octave also: *abab/abab*)

2. Ronsardian: *abba/abba/ccd/eed*
   French: *abba/abba/ccd/ede*

3. English, Elizabethan, or   *abab/cdcd/efef/gg*
   Shakespearean:
   Spenserian: *abab/bcbc/cdcd/ee*[34]

It must be recognized that the national titles given particular forms of the sonnet do not imply that other countries did not also employ those patterns, or that in the given country these were the only forms used. Germany used mostly two forms, the Italian and the French. And in a famous sonnet to the sonnet entitled *Das Sonett*, August

Wilhelm Schlegel defined the formal characteristics of the poem by utilizing a variant of the Petrarchan sonnet (*abba/abba/cde/dce*).[35] In England the sonnet of the Elizabethan age was preferably Shakespearean, in the Victorian age, it was more often Petrarchan. Whether the poet uses the Ronsardian or the Spenserian or the Petrarchan form, or even the Schlegel variant, the goal implicit in the genre is to produce the most powerful poetic effect possible with a minimum of means—or, at least, of space—and to offer the most lively contrasts molded into the most perfect unity.

The sonnet consists of two different strains of verse systems, a major and a minor. These two systems are in balance. In the classical sonnet one system is an ensemble of eight lines, the other six, whereas in the English sonnet one is composed of twelve, the other of two. In the English sonnet, however, which seems to lack equilibrium, the major system almost always contains secondary contrasts; and the final couplet, a sort of epigrammatic close, tends to contrast itself with the twelve preceding lines or to complete them in a striking fashion. The contrast, in either kind of sonnet, is further supported by the use of rich rhymes, which differ in the two systems in timbre and tonality. The antithesis, though not abrupt, is unexpected. Nonetheless, the two parts complement each other like the two panels of a diptych (the Pindaric ode is a triptych): unity in the midst of diversity. As to the general movement of thoughts, especially in early sonnets, it often resembled that of a syllogism; the sestet was a particular application of a more general statement made in the octet.

The distinctive characteristics of the sonnet, however, do not relate to form alone. It has to be seen in the correspondence between content and rhyme patterns. Their function is to stress and emphasize the ideational or emotional antithesis between the two systems. The idea a sonnet is designed to express should possess certain intrinsic qualities, and it too must be developed according to a fairly well-established set of rules. The Petrarchan tradition requires that the central idea arise from an antithesis, that the emotion be engendered by a juxtaposition. This explains why the structure of thought in both the continental and the British sonnet is relatively simple and homogeneous. It corresponds, *mutatis mutandis,* to that of most classical literary works: after the presentation of the subject, the author proceeds to explain or illuminate the theme; after having posed the question, the poet answers or eludes it. These are the functions respectively of the octave and the sestet, or of the quatrains and the couplet in the English sonnet. The first system is rather objective in nature, the second rather subjective, or vice versa. The octave treats the problem, explains the situation, expounds facts, and shows the ideal; the sestet resolves, concludes, dissipates doubts, formulates a declaration, or applies a principle, or conversely. The passage from the octave to the sestet marks the turning point of the sonnet; the

thought or the emotion takes another direction. At this precise moment—Milton usually has it in the middle of the eighth line—a contrast or a change of scene occurs, and the poem moves on to its last
line, which should in some way contain the "substantifique moëlle"—
the very philosophy—of the piece, or the most condensed expression
of the emotion described or evoked. Consequently, the final line
tends to evolve into a proverb, a maxim, or an apothegm. A hundred
years after Petrarch poets started confusing the sonnet with the epi-
gram[36]—one reason the English changed the pattern of the sonnet to
end it with a couplet, a sort of distich characteristic of epigrammatic
poetry; the couplet detaches itself clearly from the body of the three
quatrains. Both the continental and the British sonnet contain a cli-
max, a surprise or a shock, the feeling of a fatal reversal, most often a
thought or a final formula resembling a *pointe*, a bite in the last lines
—*in cauda venenum*. We are tempted to take the word pointe in the
choreographical sense, too, where pointe designates a position of
balance on the *extreme* tip of the toe: the *extreme* line of the sonnet
commands each movement of its thirteenfold body; the fourteenth
line expresses its soul, it contains its motif. This structure, however,
is not an exclusive characteristic of the sonnet. Comparable procedures can be found in the drama, the epic, and the novel.

One of the earliest French sonnets, the work of Mellin de Saint-
Gelais, illustrates in an oversimplified manner the conception of
pointe. Saint-Gelais writes about a capricious lady, his friend. Thirteen lines of comparisons—"There are not as many barks in Venice
. . . bears in Savoy . . . swans on the Thames," and so forth—lead to
the pointe (here, somewhat anticlimactic): "As my girl has whims
in her head."

> Il n'est point tant de barques à Venise,
> D'huîtres à Bourg, de lièvres en Champagne,
> D'ours en Savoie et de veaux en Bretagne,
> De cygnes blancs le long de la Tamise,
>
> Ni tant d'amours se traitant en l'église,
> Ni différents aux peuples d'Allemagne,
> Ni tant de gloire à un seigneur d'Espagne,
> Ni tant se trouve à la cour de feintise,
>
> Ni tant y a de monstres en Afrique,
> D'opinions en une République,
> Ni de pardons à Rome un jour de fête,
>
> Ni d'avarice aux hommes de pratique,
> Ni d'arguments en une Sorbonnique,
> Que m'amie a de lunes dans la tête.

Such linear structures, however, in spite of examples by even Du Bellay—for instance, No. 79 in *Les Regrets*—are rare in Romance litera-

tures because they do not allow for any stinging antitheses in thought or contrasts in emotion between the octave and the sestet, a generally respected rule.

Most frequently the last line contains some striking figure of speech, including at times puns and conundrums. Francisco de Quevedo finishes his *A Roma sepultada en sus ruinas* with "El fugitivo permanece y dura" ("That which is transitory lasts and remains"). And Luis de Góngora concludes the eighteenth sonnet of his collection with, "O bella Clori, o dulce mi enemiga" ("Oh beautiful Clori, oh my darling enemy"). Frequently, too, the closing line garners its force not from linguistic and rhetorical techniques, but from the intrinsic power of the thought, expressed in images. Usually, more than one line is necessary for the elaboration of the conclusion, which is often clearly detached from the rest of the poem. Goethe, explaining in a sonnet his neglect of it, compared himself with a sculptor who prefers to carve his statue out of a block of wood rather than to create it by gluing pieces together—what the sonneteer necessarily has to do. This contrast is expressed in his final couplet:

> Ich schneide sonst so gern aus ganzem Holze,
> Und müsste nun doch auch mitunter leimen.[37]

An emotional conclusion occurs in Thomas Gray's *On the Death of Richard West:*

> I fruitless mourn to him that cannot hear
> And weep the more because I weep in vain.

Sometimes an unexpected image produces the effect in which the main value of the sonnet resides. When a poet forgotten by today's public, Guillaume Colletet (1598–1659), wished to ridicule a "water-drinking poet" to whom he was devoting a sonnet, he began by praising the Muses for whom the Hippocrene fountain was sacred, but ended by saying that they did not themselves drink from that spring. They preferred red wine:

> Les tonneaux de vin grec échauffent leur repas
> Et l'eau n'y raffraîchit que le cul des bouteilles.

Surprise was also at times a poetic forte of Baudelaire, who used it to good purpose in many of his creations. Addressing his mistress in one of the poems of *Les Fleurs du mal, La Géante,* he expresses the desire to slumber nonchalantly in the shade of her breasts, like a hamlet at the foot of a mountain:

> Dormir nonchalamment à l'ombre de tes seins
> Comme un hameau plaisible au pied d'une montagne.

The genre of the sonnet would appear to be peculiarly suited to formulating isolated ideas and sentiments. Yet literary history shows that sonnet sequences and cycles are as numerous as they are famous. Dante's *La vita nuova* does not consist entirely of sonnets, but in it we have one of the first models for the cyclic mode. Each sonnet expresses a single complete thought or feeling, which is in perfect harmony with the whole sequel. Petrarch, in his *Canzoniere*, did still more than Dante to open this new poetic vein. Interestingly enough, the Italian version of the *Roman de la Rose*, contemporary with the two Tuscan poets, is also a sonnet cycle. "Sonnetaria" were abundant in France. Here, Du Bellay's *Olive* (1549) inaugurated the movement and, shortly afterward, Ronsard composed his *Amours de Cassandre*, *Amours de Marie*, and *Sonnets pour Hélène*. Desportes wrote *Amours d'Hippolyte*, Marc de Papillon, *Amours de Théophile*, to mention only works of the sixteenth century. Sidney's *Astrophel and Stella* appeared at this time in England, as did Spenser's *Amoretti*, Watson's *The Tears of Fancy*, Barnes's *Parthenophil and Parthenophe*, and Giles Fletcher's *Licia*, among other sonnet sequences. But the hundred and fifty-four sonnets of Shakespeare's cycle (printed in 1609) end for several decades a period of fertile sonneteering in the English-speaking world. In the nineteenth century, however, the sequence tradition again came brilliantly to life in the creations of Rossetti, notably in his *House of Life*. Meredith wrote *Modern Love*, a collection that may be compared, or contrasted, with Elizabeth Barrett Browning's *Sonnets from the Portuguese*. In 1909 Lee-Hamilton's *Sonnets of the Wingless Hours* were published, and his *Mimma Bella* posthumously. Rupert Brooke added his name to this list with *1914*, a sequel in which the same patriotic feelings are expressed as in Wordsworth's *Sonnets Dedicated to National Independence and Liberty*. In these works each sonnet keeps its individuality and maintains its intrinsic value; at the same time the poet continues faithful to the cyclic tradition, binding each poem to the meaning of the series.[38]

⚘

Conclusions about the sonnet as a major genre may be drawn on the level of literary history and on that of criticism. Originating in Sicily during the first half of the thirteenth century, and formulated first by Jacopo da Lentino, though he certainly benefited from collective experiments, the sonnet was not long in imposing itself upon the majority of Italian poets, among whom it promptly enjoyed unabated popularity. In Italy, the tradition of the sonnet is unbroken. The genre swept over Spain, Portugal, France, the Netherlands, and England in that order. Polish literature furnishes examples before German letters, in which the sonnet, after sporadic attempts and some exceptional results in earlier periods, reappeared only with the rise of romanticism. The first significant Russian, Scandinavian, and Balkan sonnets were written in the nineteenth century, although a few Dalmatian poets had been among the earliest imitators of the

Italians. England taught North America the sonnet—not the rhyme
schemes, since most sonneteers in the United States preferred Petrarch's form to Shakespeare's—just as Spain and Portugal were the
tutors of Latin America.

The importance of our subject can be measured by examining
the position the sonnet holds in the international Republic of Letters.
At least five major literatures would be most harmfully mutilated if
the sonnet were subtracted from their list of creations: the Italian,
Portuguese, Spanish, French, and English. In other nations, in spite
of transitory triumphs, the significance of the sonnet has been marginal, though not necessarily in the works of some specific poets. Had
we to describe the spreading of the sonnet in Europe in only a few
words, we would begin by advising the reader to look at the map.
Keeping in mind that part of Scandinavia and part of the Balkans
were culturally isolated from the rest of Europe for a considerable
period of time, we suggest that the length of the seacoasts in each
country almost adequately reflects the sonnet's impact and momentum. Perhaps it would suffice to say that the diffusion of the sonnet
in each literature reflects the degree of its latinity. It would be
pleasant if literary history were so simple.

Studies on literary genres may also include comparative poetics.
Fixed or semifixed forms other than the sonnet, such as the madrigal,
the rondeau, the ode, and the ballad, would also lend themselves to a
comparative approach. The task would be to throw light on problems
concerning the rhythm and melody of the lines and of the poem as a
whole, showing why authors using a certain language tended to
choose certain structures. It would be necessary to describe, on an
interlingual basis, the relations between an emotion and its expression, between an idea and its incarnation. The most immediate goal
of comparative studies in fixed forms is to complete the conclusions
concerning the homogeneity of European civilization. If these forms
impress by their general spread, it is perhaps not overadventurous
to defend the hypothesis that ideas, too, infinitely more flexible and
adaptable, likewise widely circulated in several lands. It is a part of
the comparative task of the literary critic to discern, beneath accidental diversities, the essential identity of these forms and ideas.

PART V

Motifs, Types, Themes

13

Prolegomenon D

Scholars in literary theory and criticism make use of various devices to disguise their little hesitations about the validity of their exegeses. One device appears in their books regularly. It consists of creating an ad hoc vocabulary for a specific study. While new terms are sometimes explained and even defined, they often remain ambiguous, and they might become altogether unintelligible when put into certain contexts that could be perfectly understood if commonly accepted words were to replace these fallacious barbarisms. Unfortunately, the import of even commonly accepted words has become eroded, a circumstance that does not ease the critic's task. He now has to give well-established expressions some restricted and exclusive sense. Words, however, may lead to equivocal interpretations when artificially trimmed of their natural semantic ramifications: they may tacitly and insidiously undermine the otherwise solid structure of a logical demonstration. This imprecision is the main source of the misunderstanding encountered in the relatively new field of literary inquiry called thematics or thematology.[1]

In any study concerned with textual criticism and interpretation, we find words referring to specific components of works, to meaning and matter: problem, idea, thesis, theme, motif, type, archetype, topic, subject, fable, story, plot. Still another set of expressions is: leitmotiv, topos, recurrent image, objective correlative. With such a technical terminology the critic designates formal—that is, linguistic, stylistic, or structural—devices. The words of the first series have entries in *Webster's New Collegiate Dictionary* and in most standard lexicons as well. Those of the second series do not; they belong to the generally recognized terminology of the specialist.[2] The majority of critics, sometimes rightly, use many vocables of the first series synonymously, while others make occasional distinctions—for instance, opposing idea and problem, theme and motif, story and plot, or type and archetype. As to the terms of the second category, they are either borrowings from the fine arts and therefore have to be taken metaphorically, or, though partly of ancient origin and usage, they are words not generally understood in the same way that they were in their historical settings. This precariousness of the technical vocabulary should sufficiently explain the insecurity that students and scholars feel and show when dealing with problems of thematics.

The English use and meaning of the words *theme* and *motif* are the subject of the first section of this chapter; the second section expounds the thematological system developed mainly by the Germans and widely agreed on in international criticism; and the final section considers some expressions other than theme and motif. No attempt is made in this part of the book to have English freshmen change their perfectly legitimate terminology. Within the Anglo-Saxon world, a theme obviously represents the central idea, the ultimate purpose for which a piece of literature is written. If asked about the theme of *Murder in the Cathedral*, no young citizen of the United States having spent his savings in college tuitions and fees would answer: Thomas à Becket. The archbishop of Canterbury is the topic, the subject, whereas the theme, as he is daily told, represents the basic problem emerging from the specific treatment of that topic or subject.

If, however, these English freshmen, and others enjoying *otium cum dignitate*, wish to be introduced to comparative literature and want to confront several critical systems, and if, therefore, they decide to leave, temporarily at least, the sphere of American and British attractions, they necessarily would have to forget, provisionally to be sure, about the set of thematological concepts they learned and to deviate radically from their accustomed orbit of thought. They would have to gravitate, tentatively, around other notions than those they previously heard of, to explore other ways of thinking, to test other literary reasonings, to grasp other national logics. This willingness and readiness would stamp them as virtual comparatists, and allow them to understand this final part of the book.

The entire prolegomenon is intended to introduce the reader to the fourth category of comparatistic inquiry. Motifs, types, and themes of major significance in any national literature necessarily trancend political and linguistic borders; although not losing in this process all of their specifically autochthonous characteristics, they tend to assume universal relevance. Naturally, the comparatist will be inclined to concern himself with the occurrence and frequence, the permanence and variations of motifs, types, and themes in several literatures rather than with the history and function of these thematological elements in one cultural patrimony. Nonetheless, the comparatist will most frequently begin by pursuing his queries along national lines, and, as a basic premise for the extension of his literary horizon, detect motifs, types, and themes in the countries of their origin. We will, therefore, explore the English and the Swiss origins of the Thomas à Becket and the William Tell traditions before studying their international implications. Such an analysis can hardly be pursued, however, for a theme like suicide.

I

Current thematological terms as used within single cultural areas may lead to interminable controversy in international criticism. A firm, universally respected thematological system of expressions does not exist as yet, although more and more comparatists are adopting the German view and terminology. The system, however, has not yet been organically explained, and it can only be understood as a whole after studying the critics who use it and after commenting on its various parts. In brief, two languages are spoken in thematics: one understood readily by everyone, the other by the specialist only; except for the initiated, the second is an esoteric language. Both languages are equally capable of showing the relationships between the thematological elements of a specific work. The desirability of the more technical terminology, however, is strongly felt as soon as more than one critic, even within the border of a national literature, comments on specific thematological issues.

In international studies an agreement on a unified vocabulary and system of concepts is an absolute necessity. Such an agreement, however, does not even exist on the national level. *Webster's Collegiate* defines motif as follows: "In literature and the fine arts, a salient feature of a work; especially the theme or dominant feature."[3] If one term serves to define another, they might somehow be identical in meaning. In many other contexts theme and motif are interchangeable words. Handbooks provide ample exemplification. In *Current Literary Terms* by A. F. Scott, a motif is said to be "a particular idea or dominant element running through a work of art, forming part of the main theme." Further, theme is "the subject on which one speaks"; more often the term is used "to indicate a central idea."[4] Theme, it should be noticed, has still another meaning, fundamentally different from all others. This meaning is stressed in Thrall, Hibbard, and Holman's *A Handbook to Literature*, where theme "in poetry,

drama and fiction" is called "the abstract concept which is made concrete through its representation in person, action, and image in the
work." The first meaning,—a subject or topic of discourse—applies
rather to nonfiction prose. In the work just quoted, "motif (motive),"
on the other hand, becomes "a simple element which serves as a
basis for expanded narrative; or, less strictly, a conventional situation, device, interest, or incident employed in folklore, fiction, or
drama."[5]

Although no common accord exists among English and American
critics about the difference between theme and motif, a certain
tendency seems to prevail in the Anglo-Saxon world to see the abstract
in theme and the concrete in motif, just as the vast majority of college instructors, as tradition wants it, teach their students. This tacit
consensus among instructors and scholars is reflected in the works
of Kenneth Burke, especially in his thematological diptych,[6] and Mon-
roe C. Beardsley, for whom a theme is "something named by an abstract noun or phrase: the futility of war, the mutability of joy,
heroism, inhumanity."[7] Eugene H. Falk also corroborates these interpretations. "Theme," he explains, "may be assigned to the ideas that
emerge from the particular structure of such textual elements as
actions, statements revealing states of mind, feelings, gestures, or
meaningful environmental settings. Such textual elements, I designate by the term *motif;* the idea that emerges from motifs by means of
an abstraction, I call the theme."[8]

There is certainly no reason to quibble over words as long as the
general intentions and interpretations lead to similar final goals. In
Burke's, Beardsley's, and Falk's system, theme and motif have lost
their interchangeability. Other English or American authors hardly
make any distinction between the two concepts. If one cannot speak
of an Anglo-Saxon set of thematological definitions, at least one
notices a current Anglo-Saxon terminology. The mere fact, however,
that a large number of scholars still feel the need for defining the
thematological vocabulary they are using eloquently expresses their
insecurity.

II

That which the three Anglo-Saxon critics say about the *theme*
applies to the German word *Motiv*, and what they say about *motif*
applies to *Stoff*. Although the thematological problem should not be
quite that simple, the tendency—particularly in the German-speaking
countries as conceived as a unit, a homogeneous linguistic area, a
"Sprachraum"—is to associate the Motiv with the abstract and Stoff
with the concrete. Other characteristics implicit in what I shall call
the German system, which gives high promise to becoming coherent
and consistent, distinguish that system from any other thematologi-

cal organon. Since many comparatists of whatever linguistic groups are inclined to accept it, despite a few still unanswered questions, the German system deserves special attention; it has been adhered to in this book.[9]

The three basic thematological elements in the German system are the *Rohstoff* ("raw material"), *Stoff* ("theme"—in the Anglo-Saxon system usually called motif), and *Motiv* ("motif"—in the Anglo-Saxon system usually called theme). A terminological table of these elements should help to clarify the following pages; it shows which English and French words are or should be currently used in scholarly works on thematics to translate the three German words:

Rohstoff	raw material inorganic literary matter	matière première matière littéraire inorganique
Stoff	theme	thème
Motiv (Kernmotiv, Zentralmotiv)	motif, motive, (central motif)	motif (motif central)

Rohstoff consists of all the parts of discourse, of words designating objects, qualities, actions, and ideas. Taken for themselves, for their intrinsic meaning, these units of speech—concrete or abstract—and whatever they stand for, their life and their use, interest the linguist, the philologist, and the grammarian more than the thematologist, who is concerned with criticism. They are found in literary and in non-literary works: the stones that served as the raw materials to pave the streets of Athens might be those used to build the monuments of the Acropolis; their shape and function decide their value.

Stoff—stuff, reminds one of matter, material substance—is the logically (and there are many logical systems) or chronologically *organized* Rohstoff. While *Rohstoff* consists of all immediately apprehensible particles, *Stoff* consists of rationally comprehensible wholes. The intelligibility of these wholes is based on cause-effect or yesterday-today relations. Stoff constitutes a self-sufficient story or episode. It includes characters and proper names. The reader is faced with life —or a slice of life—as it really is or as it is imagined to be.

Beyond Rohstoff and Stoff, beyond words and beyond facts and events, there might loom a fundamental human problem of which one specific narrative is just one single and unique illustration. While spontaneously aware of all the elements of Rohstoff and Stoff included in the book, the reader does not necessarily, and often not without effort, see the possibility of such a deeper interpretation. Nor does the author always have the intention to say more than the story does. If, however, the writer relates the happenings he reports to some major human issue or to several of these issues, if he connects particular junctures of events to conditions inherent in human nature—to

"Urverhältnisse des Daseins," as Ernst Robert Curtius says—if with single facts he proves a general truth, if in his work the contingent reveals the essential, then he adds to his Stoff a Motiv.[10] Stoff makes sense, but like any concatenation of facts, it is per se meaningless. As soon, however, as the writer interprets these facts by imposing upon them a structure, as soon as he gives them meaning, he is concerned with a Motiv. The Motiv is the human dimension of the Stoff.

The literary Motiv refers to purposefully organized Stoff. While Stoff is articulated, the Motiv is structured. Thus conceived it includes at least three elements that are specifically named, or at least clearly recognizable, in the course of the work: the agent, the agency, and the action considered in its result. The fate of an individual figure in a work (Stoff element), no matter how mediocre or strange his life and deeds may appear, has a relationship to the destiny of mankind, which the reader identifies with his own. This individual figure becomes the model—recognized as real or potential—of the reader's own life and deeds.

We touch here upon an essential aspect not only of thematology, but of literature at large. The efforts of the serious creative writer differ from those of the hack writer in that they are generated and sustained by the power of inner necessity. Psychologically, the process of molding the figures of the imagination and their respective situations into a structured work constitutes a process of liberation. The creative act frees the writer of his problem of subjective involvement in what is so compellingly envisioned by him, a problem concomitant to his self-assumed role of interpreter of the human condition. Palpably, the situation imaginatively perceived not only provides the initiating force—the motivation—for the verbal depiction: it *is* in effect the Motiv. To see the term motif in this light is to restore its original meaning to it. The Latin verb *movere* signifies to spur or urge on, to cause something to happen and to move it forward. Herein lies the true nature and function of the motif, while the theme (Stoff) tends to be factual and therefore literarily static.

A progression should be noticed: most literary works are likely to contain a motif, or even motifs, that may or may not be explicitly expressed, and which, in each case, is difficult to formulate accurately. Every literary work, in the broadest sense of the word, has a theme or themes, or at least thematical elements. There are possible exceptions, mainly in strictly lyric poetry, where the motif usually derives from one particular situation or from single objects or persons rather than from a sequence of facts. Although thematology in the lyric deserves separate treatment, one aspect of it should be touched upon here. A definite distinction exists between a "fictional" or "narrative" motif and a "lyrical" motif. The lyrical motif is of an emotional nature, and it initiates intuitional and not logical or chronological developments. Since the quintessence of a lyric poem consists in pre-

senting, formulating, and communicating emotions, a lyric Motiv does
not, like the epic one, spur on an action; instead, it induces the poet
to find the adequate form. Stress is laid on formal elements, whereas
the thematological elements pertain mainly to content. The complex-
ity of this problem can also be recognized in works other than poems,
as, for instance, in one of Samuel Beckett's plays, *En attendant Godot*
(*Waiting for Godot*). The motif is quite apparent: all human expectation is either vain or disappointing. The theatrical, thematical incarnation of the motif, however, is of a relatively static order; Stoff is almost eliminated, and the episodes are most insignificant. Refrains
are substituted for action: "What do we do now?" "Wait for Godot."
Estragon and Vladimir, two major characters, are in the same psychological situation at the beginning and at the end of the play. They
are not really figures of a developing plot, and their recurring formulas—per se mere *Rohstoff*—become *motival topoi*. These formulas express the fundamental idea of the work.

❧❦

All three parts of the thematological system before us have frequently become the subjects of scholarly studies, especially in German criticism. The concept Rohstoff, however, has seldom been
properly delineated; it remains the neglected element in the trilogy.
This neglect is explained by the fact that thematics obviously is
centered on Stoff and Motiv. As a consequence, critics have sometimes
mistaken Rohstoff for Motiv, forgetting that abstract qualities and
ideas are in themselves nothing but raw materials.

One authority to be mentioned in discussing Stoff is Wolfgang
Kayser. He says, or insinuates, that those concrete or abstract elements of a work that also exist outside of that work in a nonliterary,
nonaesthetic tradition and have influenced that work are Stoff.[11]
Elisabeth Frenzel explains the difference between Rohstoff and Stoff
in this manner: Stoff consists of the "fable" itself, of the "story" that
exists prior to the work, while Rohstoff consists of the isolated components of that "fable" or "story."[12] Gero von Wilpert interprets Stoff
similarly: it is the story as it can be told, or, in his words, "der erzähl-
bare Inhalt."[13] Stoff is necessarily expressed in specific characters,
places, and times. Its distinctive quality is to be concrete; it is an
incarnation, that of a Motiv.

The Motiv, on the contrary, is abstract by nature. Kohlschmidt
and Mohr state that the term does not designate any specific part of
the literary work, but is the basic situation—or set of situations—
that may be illustrated in many ways by Stoff;[14] Stoffe, themes,
therefore, could be defined as individualized Motive, motifs, and
capable of being individualized in an indefinite number of ways. Motiv
means potential Stoffe. It is a soul susceptible to be reincarnated in
many Stoffe, and the themes, therefore, are the bodies of a literary

metempsychosis. This confirms what has already been stated: the number of possible Motive, though not small, is limited, while the number of their possible manifestations, Stoffe, is theoretically infinite.[15] A corollary is that the Motiv is objective in its character; it is the depersonalized and de-individualized substratum of the work, while Stoff has the opposite characteristics. Curtius says: "The motif is on the objective side; the theme belongs to the subjective side;"[16] the theme is the actualization of the Motiv. (In the Anglo-Saxon perspective, motif in these sentences would stand for theme and theme for motif.)

Kayser and Wilpert are also in agreement when they speak of the Motiv as a typical and meaningful situation.[17] Situation is a key word. For them the Motiv is a dramatic situation (not just a quality), "dramatic" being taken in its etymological sense of active (drama, action). It is not surprising, therefore, that both critics also insist on the relationship between Motiv and Beweggrund, or motif and motivation, to return once more to the psychological facet of the question. The Motiv is said to be the ideational motif that not only inspires the writer to choose a certain Stoff and to give that Stoff an artistic form,[18] but to make the characters act; more than that: to make them act the way they do. In any typical human situation (Motiv), there is an immanent tension that is explained in the work, and that grows and is finally relieved, happily or tragically. In other words, the Motiv decides the general evolution of the Stoff, the movement of the plot.[19] To direct this movement is one of the basic functions of the Motiv, a function suggested by the name itself.

In his essay "Thematics and Criticism"[20] Harry Levin reasons very much along these lines, as does Stephan Gilman, who is quoted by Levin. Gilman, like some other scholars, calls certain motifs "theses," and his notion of theme includes some nuances not considered by most German thematologists. Using the traditional Anglo-Saxon terminology, Gilman says: "The critic recognizes the theme [theme here means Motiv] as profoundly vital, as a sense of life, clearly distinguishable from those specific intentions, ideas, or lessons which, being consciously proposed, may fairly be called theses."[21] German scholars would here choose the words Kernmotiv or Zentralmotiv. In the theoretical part of his Un Problème de littérature comparée: les études de thèmes, Raymond Trousson adopts this view without any reservation. What is a theme [he says "thème"]? His answer is: "Let's agree to call theme a particular expression of a motif [he says "motif"], its individualization or, perhaps, the result of the passage from the general to the particular."[22] And what is a motif? "A background, a broad concept designating either a certain attitude . . . or a basic situation, still impersonal, the actors of which have not as yet been individualized."[23]

Madame Bovary may serve to illustrate the interrelationship between the three basic thematological elements and to point to the usefulness of a coherent system in the field.[24] What is the *theme* of the novel? The word, taken for that which common language suggests, means the subject or topic of the work. In a sense, however, everything in a work is subject matter. The thematologist, as a literary critic, wants to explain that the subject—"that which is said"—can be studied on three main levels. His inquiry and his answer as well are threefold. On the level of Rohstoff, the subject matter of *Madame Bovary* consists of an unhappy lady, goodhearted and incompetent husband, egoistic and uninspired lovers, a party in a castle, a pharmacy, and many other things, concepts, happenings. These elements are put together to make a coherent story, and we have the Stoff, the theme in the technical sense, of the novel. But judged from a different point of view, Stoff is also subject matter; it is the plot: Emma's acquaintance with Léon and with Rodolphe, her attitudes toward Charles, her trips to Rouen, her stealing arsenic in Mr. Homais' shop, her suicide, all the phases of her life seen in their organic sequence. This time each phase explains the other.

When the thematologist wants to determine the subject matter on the level of Motiv, he notices that Flaubert's work is concerned with man's wretchedness and despair because of vain wishes and desires. The subject, then, is "the tragedy of dreams,"[25] of the woman between several men. These are general situations (Motive) that the novelist wants to illustrate with the aid of Stoff (the cast, the setting, the events considered as a whole: in short, the fable), and he uses *Rohstoff* (words, expressions, ideas, notions, phrases, isolated incidents seen as separate units of the work: in short, particles of the fable). All these elements of Rohstoff become literarily meaningful only in the context of Stoff and Motiv. This again shows that thematology is not an a priori science. It is a study in functional variations.

III

Various little and large *tesserae* in the thematological mosaic have as yet received little attention. And even a most prominent piece in that mosaic, such as motif, may belong to two distinct categories. Next to the motif in which we recognize the organizing principle of the whole narrative, there might be secondary motifs, or submotifs, since a work is not necessarily built according to a merely linear architecture. Critics who call motif what is in fact a submotif have to find another term for the authentic motif, as defined in these pages. They therefore speak of the central or principal motif that clearly pervades an entire work—in German the Kernmotiv or Zentralmotiv[26]—as opposed to the more or less peripheral motifs. It is also quite common to call motifs certain particular situations, specific features, or devices found either in one work (the one-legged sailor in Joyce's *Ulys-*

ses)[27] or in several works (folklore). This terminology seems to be a borrowing from the fine arts, notably painting. On closer analysis, however, these motifs are really topoi or recurrent images. In addition to this category of motifs, the concepts of the literary type, the leitmotiv, and the objective correlative should retain our attention.

A literary type may be defined as a written incarnation of either a motif or a theme in the form of outstanding figures, be they mythical, fictional, or historical. The examples of Thomas à Becket and Pietro della Vigna will clarify the thematological notion of type. The general topic in all works concerned with their lives is destroyed friendship. As such, this topic belongs to the domain of Rohstoff. It is a static idea, which in itself does not suggest a situation profiled enough to be a motif. Stoff consists of an illustration of this idea by way of a logically, chronologically, or psychologically understandable narration of the destruction of a specific friendship: that between Thomas à Becket and King Henry II, that between Pietro della Vigna and Emperor Frederic II. As to the Motiv, it has to be seen in the basic moral situation underlying the plot; seen there, the Motiv takes on a meaning that transcends the factual events. Thus, in both examples one may see this Motiv: friendships between kings and their favorites are transitory.[28] But a certain Stoff may express several Motive. Becket also symbolically represents a man's struggle between his sense of duty and his feelings as a former protégé, and in Pietro della Vigna we see a man's confrontation with a suspicious and vengeful benefactor. Nor are these the only motifs that serve as substrata for the two themes, or the two stories.

A literary type may be defined as a personification of either a theme or a motif, a character that has become a metaphor. Whether a type refers to Stoff rather than to Motiv depends mainly on its real historical existence. Historical figures are usually thematical types that limit the poet's freedom of treatment, while fictional and especially mythical figures well suit the role of motival types. Becket and Vigna are closer to Stoff-types; Faust and Don Juan, Oedipus and Prometheus are basically Motiv-types. This implies that the latter four are likely to offer more original thematical ingredients in each new treatment than the two former. Motiv-types are also more frequently used metaphorically than Stoff-types.[29] A man may be considered a Don Juan (he is one of the numerous possible incarnations of a definite Motiv), whereas nobody can become a Becket, a figure too highly individualized to ever have a double. His metaphorical character is scarcely evident, though similar figures may be compared with him. Historical characters cannot easily be disentangled from well-known, reliably reported facts, which have become part of a cultural heritage. This is to say that the genuine literary type is the Motiv-type. Nevertheless, some promising attempts have been made to convert Stoff-types into a Motiv-type, especially in contemporary drama. Whenever it has been done with success, specific theatrical

devices revealed this essential change of treatment to the audience
at the rise of the curtain: the new Stoff stresses the symbolic character of the hero who is to transcend history. The distinction between
the two categories of types deserves the attention not only of the
thematologist: Motiv-types have often been promoted, by general
consent, to the rank of *Urtypen,* archetypes or prototypes.[30]

⤛⤜

A few decades ago, Curtius brought to the attention of scholars
a number of literary processes almost as old as our civilization. The
characters in the picture writing of ancient peoples may be considered the first topoi. Today, not only similar images, but identical
expressions and analogous ideas recur regularly in various works.
Curtius observes this phenomenon in a wide range of texts from
antiquity to modern times, but particularly up to the Renaissance. He
calls his inquiry *Topik,*[31] which should be translated topology. Topology is the study of a sort of literary stock in trade transmitted by
tradition, a sort of repertory from which poets and rhetors have
drawn as needed. The Greeks—one remembers Aristotle's *Topics*—
called these entities *koinoi topoi,* or commonplaces, while the Romans
—Cicero, one would say today, holds the copyright on the Latin translation—called the same devices *loci communes.*

In ancient literature we find set invocations to nature or to the
Gods, consecrated oratorical expressions, or certain oppositions and
rapprochements of words and ideas. The topoi appertain simultaneously to the realms of stylistic figures and thought patterns, a
dualism that the Germans have recognized and tried to clarify by
their insistence on the distinction between "formale Topoi" and
"inhaltliche Topoi," or form and content topoi—a too rigorous distinction, as some scholars have pointed out.[32] Curtius offers a rich
array of examples.

The first topoi are stereotypes, comparable to hieroglyphics. When
the introductory verses of epic poems promise in similar words
"adventures as yet undreamed of by mortal men," the authors are
not plagiarizing, but using such speech topoi as naturally as we today
use single words. Homer's "rosy-fingered dawn" is a speech topos,
while "the fair mendicant" or "the fear of the night" belong to the
common thesaurus of metaphors and allegories of the Middle Ages.
Lovejoy wrote a book with the title *The Great Chain of Being* and Voltaire included in his *Dictionaire philosophique* an article "Chaîne des
êtres créés." This is a timeless topos. Articles and books have been
written on topoi, like *locus amoenus,* or *naturae cursus.*[33] Many
topoi, however, are even more complex and sophisticated. The *puer
senex,* for example (literally the old child, that is, the ideal of the
young man who combines the zest for life with mature sagacity), is
an image that has remained vivid for two millennia in scores of
variations.

In literature the notion of leitmotiv (leading motif) is closely connected with that of topos. It is the term designating a recurring musical theme, for which the French have expressions like *élan vital* or *idée fixe*, the latter invented by Berlioz. One of the major functions of the leitmotiv—most successfully applied in Wagner's *Tristan*, *Siegfried*, and *Götterdämmerung*—is its allusion to characters, situations, and happenings in order to create or re-create specific emotions. This function was exactly that of the ancient and medieval topos. From the point of view of the thematologist dealing with literature, "leitmotiv" is a misnomer. It is not a motif, but a thematical element, because it refers to particular facts and particular heroes. Moreover, instead of "leading" the characters, it accompanies them: it is in literature a *Geleit-topos* or *Begleit-topos*, an "accompaniment-topos," not a *leit-motiv*.[34]

Also connected with the notion of leitmotiv is that of objective correlative. In his *Geburt der Tragödie aus dem Geiste der Musik* (1872, *The Birth of Tragedy from the Spirit of Music*) Nietzsche explains in chapter 17 that often in ancient tragedy heroes speak more superficially than they act, as do some characters of Shakespeare, notably Hamlet. Commenting on this discrepancy, Nietzsche says that the substance, or the "myth," of the play did not find its "adequate objectification" (*die adäquate Objektivation*), an expression rightly translated by Francis Golffing with "adequate objective correlative." In his essay on "Hamlet and His Problems" (1921), T. S. Eliot, who incidentally was also fascinated by Wagner, gives this comment:

> The only way of expressing emotion in the form of art is by finding an *objective correlative;* in other words, a set of objects, a situation, a chain of events which shall be the formula of that particular emotion; such that when the external facts, which must terminate in sensory experience, are given, the emotion is immediately evoked. If you examine any of Shakespeare's more successful tragedies, you will find this exact equivalence; you will find that the state of mind of Lady Macbeth walking in her sleep has been communicated to you by a skilful accumulation of imagined sensory impressions; the words of Macbeth on hearing of his wife's death strike us as if, given the sequence of events, these words were automatically released by the last event in the series. The artistic *inevitability* lies in this complete adequacy of the external to the emotion; and this is precisely what is deficient in Hamlet.[35]

The leitmotiv, as Wagner used it, *inevitably* establishes a complete correspondence of the character appearing on stage with the emotion that character is supposed to evoke.

One aspect of thematology is *Stoffgeschichte*, meaning the history of major thematological elements.[36] Themes and motifs, types and topoi, studied in their developments, in their variations, and in their persistence, explain and illustrate fundamental preoccupations of man. Since literature represents the faithful reflection and expression of these preoccupations, theme and motif studies belong to the *Geistesgeschichte* of humanity, the history of ideas. The ramifications of "Stoff- und Motivgeschichte," therefore, touch upon the most diverse domains, including those of social philosophy and ethnic psychology.

Theme and motif studies, however, like any other kind of inquiry, have their weaknesses. A complete history of a topos, a motif, a theme, or a type must necessarily take into account mediocre works as well as masterpieces, and often only segments of masterpieces are relevant to the specific problem treated. Although Walter Muschg wrote a valuable *Tragische Literaturgeschichte* structured according to motival and thematical principles, histories organized along these lines are usually limited in their scope and can hardly replace broad investigations of the literary world. Such studies only incidentally yield valid interpretations of the unfolding of a certain historic phase, or furnish the full explanation of an artistic conception. Their all too frequent deficiency is that they seldom coordinate, subordinate, or organize elements in a hierarchical structure. Often elements that are drawn together by the apparent logic of similarity remain profoundly disparate in relation to their aesthetic virtues. Irremediably bound to detail, which it finds difficult to transcend, Stoffgeschichte rarely takes off on flights from the terrain of analysis; its worth lies in its ability to throw a vivid light on particular aspects of human history.

At the beginning of this century, Benedetto Croce and, following his example, Fernand Baldensperger expressed their reservation toward Stoffgeschichte as a literary method. "Books," remarked the Italian critic, "which hold strictly to this order of research necessarily assume the form of the catalog or bibliography."[37] Such a structure, however, does not apply to thematology as a whole. The most evident value of Stoffgeschichte is instrumental in nature. All art, every discipline, presupposes tools; those of thematology proper are the repertoires of themes and motifs as furnished by Stoffgeschichte. Frenzel's *Stoffe der Weltliteratur* proves the usefulness of such lexicons. This work is not a simple alphabetical enumeration of major topics; each of them—one should not expect all-inclusiveness—has its history there. Frenzel's book presents, with bibliographical references, innumerable suggestions for analyses, rapprochements, and studies to be applied to thematic evolutions; it also unveils fascinating aspects of comparative criticism.[38] Stoffgeschichte is only a branch of thematology. This distinction should contribute to the rehabilitation of thematology itself.

14

Thomas à Becket in European Fiction and Drama

THOMAS à Becket (1118–1170), the archbishop of Canterbury, represents one of the most striking yet ambiguous figures of an age marked both with brutality and elegance, heroism and refinement. In Franco-Norman countries, including England, the twelfth century was especially characterized by the struggle between the nobility and the clergy, for the powers of the secular state were limited by the prerogatives of the Universal Church. As chancellor for Henry II, Becket fought for the state; as primate of England, he defended the church. From an intimate friend of the king, he evolved into his irreconcilable foe. These are the roots of the tragedy of Becket.[1]

The first phase of his life hardly presents the historian with an insoluble enigma: he was a clever diplomat, a perfect man of the world, a political genius. But the second phase remains full of mystery. What was he? An ambitious and obstinate prelate and a traitor to the king? A proselyte enamored with asceticism and a champion of the rights of God? Or was he a saint? Posterity has not only attempted to analyze and explain his radical and surprising change of character, but has also put it to aesthetic use. Many of the writers concerned with Becket have looked beyond the apparent contradictions of his life and have seen the greater, more profound unity that lies behind the surface paradoxes of his character.[2] They have viewed his eventful and passionate career as an evolution rather than as an abrupt revolutiontionary transformation: the deeds and thoughts of the chancellor allow us to foresee those of the archbishop.

Becket's drama remains inseparable from its historic and traditional setting. To isolate it from this background often amounts to destroying its substance. Transpositions of historical characters from their real framework into an imaginary one is a most delicate enterprise. Such characters, although typical for a specific human situation, are bound to act in their historical circumstances and to keep their real personalities.[3] Pietro della Vigna (Peter of Vinea, also Pier delle Vigne, ca. 1190–1249) helps illustrate this thematological and aesthetic rule. Chancellor and confidant of the Holy Roman Emperor Frederic II, he eventually lost his monarch's favor[4] and, in many respects, became another Becket. But he was still *other* than Becket. Both tragedies stem partly from a ruined friendship, but undue stress upon the similarities conceals the importance of very significant diferences between the two. Becket exemplifies political ambition as the source or perhaps the pretext of saintliness; or, as some historians have suggested, he is the champion of the temporal power of the church. Pietro della Vigna, for his part, appears to have been the victim of a cruel and unjust emperor, who, according to tradition, drove his former friend to suicide. Both Becket and Vigna have become the heroes of literary works that are thematically similar though different in many other important respects; they are both literary types shaped by a specific historical Stoff. The subject matter of these pages will be limited to Thomas à Becket.

☙❧

The popularity Saint Thomas à Becket enjoyed in England is well known. His fame rapidly crossed the Channel, all the more easily since a vast continental territory was then under English suzerainty. For centuries in all parts of Christendom his image was as popular as that of Saint Francis of Assisi or of any apostle of Christ (including Thomas Didymus), and Canterbury became the Santiago de Compostela of the North. Hardly had his martyrdom been accomplished and the first miracles achieved, when poets and biographers set to work on his eternal fame. One of the first poems about Becket is that of a French cleric's, Guernes de Pont-Sainte-Maxence, who wrote *Vie de saint Thomas le martyr* immediately after the assassination. Simultaneously, four different *Lives*—the four oldest biographies of the saint—were written; a compilation of them was printed in Paris more than two centuries later, in 1495. This *Historia quadripartita* became the principal source for scores of historians. But the works on Thomas were not limited to Franco-Norman countries; they multiplied throughout Europe. *Tômas von Kandelberk* shows the migration of the Stoff toward the German lands, and *Thómas saga erkibyskups*, re-edited in 1965, testifies to the appearance of Saint Thomas in Scandinavia. Both works were written by fourteenth-century authors.

The *Canterbury Tales* were in several ways associated with Becket. Chaucer organized his book, which helped consolidate the theme in England, around Saint Thomas' sanctuary. According to tradition the idea came to the author when he saw the thousands of pilgrims flocking past his home at Greenwich making their way southeast to the shrine, "The holy blisful martyr for to seeke."[5] But if the fortune of saints is forever safe in heaven, it is not always so on earth. In 1538, when Henry VIII prohibited the cult of the rebellious archbishop, the sellers of devotional articles closed their shops, and the famous center of pilgrimage fell into a state of lethargy.

Memories of the saint lingered in other places, however. In 1588, for example, a certain Thomas Stapleton published in France a Latin work entitled *Tres Thomae* in which he related the lives of the apostle Thomas, Thomas More, and Thomas à Becket. But it was not until Europe became more vividly interested in the Middle Ages—a date that coincides with that of the beginnings of modern historiography—that the story of Chancellor Thomas was revived. He underwent his resurrection as a political figure before he regained his crosier and miter. The circumstances of his death had to be studied, and he was again certified a martyr of the church, a title he had barely retained except in liturgy.

There is a second reason for the return of the chancellor-primate. In almost all European countries, romanticism posed the problem of the relations between church and state with singular acuity. On the continent, Augustin Thierry renewed the interest in Thomas à Becket through his *Histoire de la conquête de l'Angleterre par les Normands*, printed in 1825, when the infatuation for the medieval was at its apogee. In the nineteenth century Thomas remained, with Joan of Arc, the only canonized Christian to play a significant role in Europe as a literary type. Not that he conducted himself as a saint in all the works in which he appeared, or that he was of that breed of saints who always please those who give the aureoles. A detailed analysis of the works inspired by Thomas shows him in turn as a heretical doctor, a haughty pastor, an acute diplomat, and a stubborn martyr.

Four works illustrate four of the numerous variations or interpretations of the Becket theme. *Thomas: A Novel of the Life, Passion, and Miracles of Becket,*[6] by Mrs. Shelley Mydans, is closest to the historical truth. The author based her story on firsthand documents. Although the form is fictional, her biographical novel is both a scientific and a literary consecration of an eight-hundred-year-old tradition. The second work, however, *Der Heilige*[7] by the Swiss novelist and poet Conrad Ferdinand Meyer, an eminent figure in nineteenth-century German literature, is not a traditional story of one saint among others, but tells of *the* saint of a specific epoch—that which prepared the rise of psychoanalysis—tries to explain sainthood. With the third work, T. S. Eliot's, we enter a different sphere; his pageant is centered on the last act of Thomas' life. The title, *Murder in the Cathedral*[8] (1935), causes a sensation in a manner similar to the cry of a newsboy: a prince of the church assassinated in the House of God. The fourth study is of a Thomas à Becket who maintains his secular family name; it is Jean Anouilh's drama, *Becket; ou, l'honneur de Dieu.*[9] The contemporary French writer has demonstrated, unintentionally to be sure, that brilliance may guarantee the success of a "comédie de boulevard," while history, obviously, assures that of a historical play.

A profitable reading of this chapter supposes knowledge of these four books. They are studied here in two sections, first the novels, then the dramas. All four are equally intended to illustrate aspects of thematology, which forms the last of our four basic categories of studies in comparative literature.

I

The works of Mrs. Mydans and Meyer are to be taken as historical narratives, novels or romances. A basic difference, however, distinguishes them: the American novelist presents the actions and reactions of Thomas as being dictated by the spirit of the age that he himself helped to form; the Swiss writer, although the plot develops in a historical setting, traces Thomas' behavior to his individual character and personality. According to Mrs. Mydans, Thomas was shaped by circumstances and caught in the gears of national destiny. As the head of the opposition, he was condemned to die. The stern edicts "I will bend your neck" and "Submit or else you will die" were the replies of Henry II not to a lost friend but to a political antagonist, a defender of the Church. Becket clearly reveals himself as the leader of a state within the state: "I cannot," he declares, "not without the sanction of the Pope and of the Universal Church, forego the basic tenet of canonical election! Shall I, as father of our island Church, place her in schism from the rest of Christendom? It cannot be. I shall not."[10] Historical facts and political situations are the first and last causes of the martyrdom of the archbishop.

Meyer's Thomas, on the other hand, seems to be only accidentally involved in history, no matter how deeply he was entrenched in it. According to Meyer's version, not the public affairs but an event in the characters' private lives rendered the antagonists irreconcilable. Young Grace, the chancellor's daughter (Meyer assumes Thomas had been married to a Moorish princess), who had been corrupted by Henry and then killed in the course of events, becomes central to the plot. Thomas is shown as the champion of the church, but even more as a man who becomes a saint because of his personal desire for vengeance. In this quite personal struggle, the king proved to be the stronger. Not so much the chancellor and archbishop, but the man and former friend had to die. "A mediating formula which would have secured and guaranteed in equal parts the English royal power and the rights of the merciful church would have been already at hand, thanks to the chancellor's wisdom . . . But the hearts of both men no longer knew each other, and when they wished to take the final step for their reconciliation, the ghost of their dead love stepped between them as pure hatred."[11] Meyer's motivation is fictional, Mrs. Mydans' historical. Obviously, their works represent two different kinds of historical novels.

❧

Mrs. Mydans' *Thomas* is a work that exceeds four hundred pages, a length that permits a certain liberty of movement.[12] We can accordingly expect that the author will emphasize the development of action as well as of character, and, indeed, she builds a novel in the classic sense of the term. Nevertheless, Mrs. Mydans raises some doubt concerning the literary genre to which her work belongs. The book, she admits in the preface, falls into the category of the novel, since most of the conversations are imaginary and certain characters, notably those of the family of Elured Porre—an infinitely useful group for the evocation of the medieval spirit and the mood of the time—are creatures of pure invention. She could have invoked other and more commanding reasons of a formal order, for the whole structure of the book is suited for fiction, not history. *Thomas* represents a model for the historical novel.

The work is divided into five books—"Murder and Miracles" (119 pages), "Thomas of London" (90 pages), "The Chancellor" (70 pages), "The Archbishop" (82 pages), and "The Exile" (68 pages)—and the entire volume comprises twenty-five chapters and an epilogue. The very succession of these titles reveals the author's rejection of a rigorously chronological development, or of a history in the technical sense of the word. The murder and the miracles—the denouement of the plot—are narrated at the beginning—along with the account of Thomas' youth. The martyr is, then, first depicted at his death and at his birth, an architectural procedure unlikely ever to be used in history, which explains one particular event by those that precede or accompany it. The historical narrative as a genre almost necessarily presents a linear organization of events.

The four knights who have just assassinated the archbishop appear in Mrs. Mydans' opening scene in the north wing of the transept of his cathedral. "Our job is done," they conclude. And already the blood of the martyr is working its first miracles. As we shall see, Meyer begins in much the same way. In the opening of *Der Heilige*, the feast of the saint is being celebrated, an occasion that becomes the catalyst for the whole account of Becket's life and death; and it is reported at the feast how Becket's intercession stopped a conflagration that threatened to destroy a convent. However, as soon as Meyer really begins to tell Thomas' story, he strictly follows the historical order of events, which he pursues to the end of the book. In Anouilh's *Becket,* the same method as Mrs. Mydans' is used, but no more extensively than in Meyer's *The Saint.*

After Mrs. Mydans' presentation of the murderers, a change of scene occurs: Mary, a nun and the oldest sister of Thomas, enters into conversation with the prior of an abbey, the friend and former confessor of her glorious brother. From this conversation we learn details concerning his boyhood. Then another leap forward occurs—forty years—and the reader is told of the punishments that strike the saint's executioners. Other miracles are related simultaneously, and then Mary suddenly takes the floor again, providing other memories of Becket's adolescence. Later young Thomas himself becomes the beneficiary of a miracle—the wheel of a mill stopped turning at the moment he was to be dragged under it by the current—and quite naturally other miracles, worked by the martyr, are again woven into the narrative. At eighteen, Thomas leaves for Paris; he will be twenty-three at the end of this first book. From this point, historical chronology is followed more closely.

Though not employing usual historiographical devices or techniques, *Thomas* gives the impression of absolute historical accuracy. As Thucydides, Tacitus, Plutarch, and Suetonius had already realized, historians are not mere scribes or record keepers. In writing their works they followed the impetus of their genius. By the eighteenth and nineteenth centuries, aesthetic preoccupation had come to dominate the books of historians such as Gibbon, Carlyle, Taine, de Tocqueville, Ranke, and Klyuchevski. Yet in the course of the ages the principal rules applied in historical composition hardly underwent any basic change affecting the general structure of a work of history while those of fiction were, and still are, in constant flux. What makes Mrs. Mydans' book especially valuable for a study in *Stoffbehandlung* (treatment of themes) is the fact that by resorting to merely novelistic resources she creates the impression not only of fictional reality, but of absolute historicity as well. Her work is the result of extensive study in sources, which have been exploited with literary intuition.

Nevertheless, it becomes evident upon closer analysis that Mrs. Mydans had to subordinate historical truth to artistic truth in many ways, and as a novelist in the traditional sense of the word, she had to resolve the problem of unity. In real life, most people who exercise some influence on our existence leave and enter the scene haphazardly; experience shows that their entrances and exits escape consistent control. In *Thomas,* however, characters do not step onto the stage at the will of historical circumstances, but at the need of the plot. Their roles, however naturally played, are those of heroes of the theater, who appear, pose, produce their effect at the propitious moment, leave, and return. The heroes in *Thomas* do in fact return, at least those who do not perish en route, like Gilbert Becket, Thomas' father, and Theobald, his predecessor in the primatial see of Canterbury. The four assassins of the first pages are revived in the last, and Ranulf de Broc, their commander, is never lost from view. The name of Grimm appears in chapter 5, and reappears in the last chapter of the novel. The Elured tribe, as well as the principal representatives of the higher clergy, might stimulate similar observations. Not all these characters accompany Thomas throughout his life in reality, but the reader feels that they do. Indeed, the circular form of the narrative sustains the impression that Thomas lived his entire life surrounded by an immutable group of friends and enemies, partisans and opponents. In brief, novelistic technique and artistic imagination take precedent over history.

Meyer, too, does not finish his novel without organizing a general parade of the characters. Those who belong to the frame of the story quite naturally close the plot, since they opened it: the narrator, John the cross-bowman (Hans der Armbruster); a priest, the canon Burkhart; and Sir Kuno, an equally minor character. Saint Meinrad himself, who gave his name to the inn mentioned in the beginning, is indirectly evoked at the end of the story because it is at Einsiedeln, Meinrad's hermitage, that the narrative closes. Also reappearing are the sorceress, who Thomas refuses to condemn ("die schwarze Mary"), and who seems to have become a woman who serves the chancellor's daughter, Grace; Trustan Grimm, a London worker among Thomas' following in one of the first chapters, later the cross-bearing monk of the archbishop at the time of the murder; Hilde, the fair, love of young Hans, who returns to the stage on two occasions, as does Sir Rollo, Henry's master-at-arms. In Mrs. Mydans' and in Meyer's works, not only the protagonists play a continuous organic role in the drama, but many secondary characters do also by means of their repeated interventions, thereby giving unity to the two novels, the sort of unity that historiography can never attain.

Mrs. Mydans also makes ample use of all sorts of thematological devices on every level of her work. Throughout the book she scatters recurring images, topoi, and symbols directly related to Rohstoff, Stoff, and Motiv, but often relevant to major parts of the main motif. The end of a friendship that brings death to Thomas is symbolized and dramatically announced in many ways. The spider, harbinger of unhappiness, weaves its web from one end of the narrative to the other. Mary, for example, relates scenes from her youth to Prior Robert: "That was the year winter came so late and great gray spiders set their webs in the garden long past their time." The archbishop dreams of seeing a spider at the bottom of his chalice, and that spider becomes an obsession: "No more visions came to him—only some nightmare dreams: of spiders once again, of murderers." At the end of Thomas's solemn debate with Henry at Montmirail in the presence of the clergy and the French and English nobility, the defeated archbishop allows his eye to wander: "He glanced beyond the crowd to where a barren tree stood in a shaft of sun and saw a lone leaf dangling, held by some spider's web perhaps, from a dead limb." Prophecies are enunciated, renewed, and accomplished. "In Harbledown the priest dreamed of a horned man. In Burgate Church a worm was found coiled like a serpent in the sacred host. The priest at Godmersham took up his scrying bowl and polished it, anointed it, saying the secret words, and called the boy in so that he might scry, and asked him what the future showed him, what he saw. The shadows in the bowl, the moving shapes, were clear. He saw a crown, a tree, a knife. What was to come?" On the following page, the same symbols recur: "Some people who read portents thought they knew what was to come. The scrying boy had seen a knife, the moon had worn a crown, the Archbishop had stumbled when he reached the altar stone."[13] The atmosphere is one of mystery and tragic terror.

Stylistic and structural elements suited to enhancing the literary value of the work abound. At the same time, the constant concern for the particular and the local seems to suggest that the author has personally visited even the smallest place of which her novel speaks. Mrs. Mydans knows the mores of the century as well as the liturgy, the laws of the land, and of the church. She has evoked an age that is at once grandiose and subtle, and depicts an epoch that was splendid and rude, upon which history has not yet pronounced its last word.[14]

≫≪

Meyer makes a different use of history. He supplies a mere two or three dates, while Mrs. Mydans mentions some fifty of them, a difference that gives a partial measure of the historical involvement of the two works. The crossbowman Hans, Meyer's narrator, when asked if his chronology is not off, says expressly: "Don't bother me with vain numbers."[15] Meyer, for instance, does not inconvenience himself in any way by placing the canonization of Thomas later than it took place; Mrs. Mydans indicates, with the historians, 1173, a little more than two years after the murder in the cathedral (December, 1170). The historian who reads the novel—Meyer calls it "eine Novelle," a novelette—is struck by its legendary tone. The annals of England furnish him nothing but setting and events, and hardly contribute to the shaping of the characters. Becket's historical situation thereby frees the author from having to invent the place of action,

the protagonists, and the reasons for their dispute. Meyer found in
history his point of departure, the outline of the plot; the rest is
legend or invention.[16]

Historical accuracy simply does not fit into the overall structure
of Meyer's narrative. He tells his story not as a historian, but as a man
—an intelligent albeit somewhat simpleminded one—who had witnessed the events. Hans, the narrator, has himself been involved in
them and judges from a personal point of view, reporting facts as well
as rumors and impressions. On a gloomy winter day, he comes to
Zurich for business, and while warming himself at his host's fireplace,
he declares the best time of his life were the years spent in the service
of Henry II and Thomas à Becket. It is a frame story concerned with
Saint Thomas, and thus in two senses a *Canterbury Tale.*

Artistic unity is guaranteed by the title figure for Thomas, and it is
Thomas who really fascinates the reader. His portrait may seem
somehow monolithic—although most dramatic—when contrasted
with Mrs. Mydans' mighty fresco. One can sympathize with the fate
of Hans, but all the other characters are pale, overshadowed by the
brilliance of Thomas. The king himself remains in the background,
and becomes a king who scarcely thinks, a slave to his rage and a
victim of his destiny. In one of the final scenes, for example, Henry
is informed by Hans that the four barons have left Normandy for
England and that their swords will not spare the rebellious prelate.
What measures ought he to take?

> "Catch up with the four of them and bring them back to
> me". . . .
> "They will not hear me". . . .
> "That is your affair. . . . If a hair of that worthy head is dis-
> turbed, you will pay for it and dangle from the nearest gal-
> lows!"[17]

This is surely not the most judicious way to settle important matters
of state. In the meantime the four barons arrive at Canterbury followed by Hans, whose charge is to make them return to Normandy.
They rush into the cathedral threatening the archbishop: "The King
wishes that you die!"[18] The moment seems to have come for Hans to
fulfill his mission and to speak to them in the name of the king. But he
has forgotten why he went to Canterbury. Instead of presenting the
royal message to the murderers, he tries to protect the victim by
throwing himself against him. In other words, the plot becomes
incoherent as soon as the limelight leaves Thomas. These weaknesses,
however, should not be overemphasized, for the value of the book
lies in the organic development of the main character, not in the
logical sequence of a set of minor events.

Meyer's Thomas is a saint who is anything but saintly. Dickens
had already evoked this sort of man rather unsympathetically in
Hard Times: A Child's History of England (1854):

I will make, thought King Henry Second, this Chancellor of mine Thomas à Becket, Archbishop of Canterbury. He will lead the Church, and, being devoted to me, will help me correct the Church. Now, Thomas à Becket was proud and loved to be famous. He was already famous for the pomp of his life, for his riches, his gold and silver plates, his waggons, horses and attendants. He could do no more in that way than he had done; and being tired of that kind of fame (which is a very poor one) he longed to have his name celebrated for something else. Nothing, he knew, would render him so famous in the world as the setting of his own utmost power and ability against the utmost power and ability of the King.[19]

For Meyer, too, pride and vainglory led the archbishop to his canonization. "Thou art ambitious, ambitious, ambitious!" cries Henry to his chancellor who in turn declares: "One can also grow weary of the world without piety."[20] It is not sheer coincidence that Meyer's work appeared in the same year, 1879, as Nietzsche's *Menschliches, All-zumenschliches* (*Human, All-Too-Human*). An ideational relationship can and ought to be established between these two works. In Meyer's book Thomas is a saint who is not more than a man. He is hardly an *Übermensch;* on the contrary, his feelings and reactions are plainly *menschlich*, if not *allzumenschlich*.

Accordingly, it is legitimate to ask whether Meyer's saint is really Christian. Once installed in his celestial glory, he works miracles for his friends and enemies, aiding the first and chastising the second, as if he were still on earth. The affairs of the kingdom deteriorate rapidly, apparently at the intercession of the blessed martyr. Fair Hilde, whom Hans has sought to take as his wife, hopes for a cure from a serious illness by the force of Thomas' holy relics; but as she touches them, she dies. The "blisful martyr" of Chaucer's *Tales*, the benevolent saint of tradition, becomes a "revengeful heathen"[21] who knows no other law save that of retaliation. At war with his sons, and besieged on all sides, the king throws himself upon the tomb of the saint and flagellates himself. He kneels before the marble cut by a Saxon artist and begs his former favorite to leave him at least Richard, "Coeur de Lion." He only has the time to formulate this vow before the treason of the son is reported to him. Meanwhile, writes Meyer, "Lord Thomas smiled on his gravestone."[22] In life and in death Thomas à Becket appears a jealous and intractable personality, somewhat sly, suspicious, and mystical. A thematological similarity is noticeable with the legend of John the Baptist; Herod's wife, Herodias, dies while kissing the head brought before her of the martyr whose execution she had ordered.

Thomas' vindictive spirit explains the tragedy of the broken friendship. "Present or absent," says Hans, "Thomas still pursued the King." If the chancellor assures his Lord that he has pardoned him for Grace's loss, he does not convince the reader. Thomas never pardoned anything. After his daughter's death, an insurmountable resentment made him refuse to concern himself thenceforth with the royal infants, whose tutor he had been. One day, however, the impossible reconciliation seemed to be accomplished; the king and the primate of England met with a few knights in a lonely countryside and were at last to give each other the kiss of peace. But this was not to be. The lips of Henry reminded Thomas of a crime. He turned his face away from the king with disgust, and "regarded him with horror." He had once declared to Hans, who had just invented a new crossbow: "I love thought and art, and I like it when intellect triumphs over the first, and the weaker strikes and conquers the stronger from afar."[23] *From afar:* even from beyond the tomb. Thomas' supreme vengeance was that he got the most glorious title, that of martyr, and Henry the most abject one, that of executioner. But Henry VIII will avenge Henry II in turn, for the history of mankind, as is well known, consists of a long series of reprisals.

In *Der Heilige,* Thomas' secret desire for power is the reason for his unforgiving attitude, which causes the fatal break with the king. In his position as chancellor, but more so as archbishop, he can combine his ambition with asceticism, a virtue commanding respect. Furthermore, ambition becomes the motivation for his asceticism, as Meyer shows when he narrates the life of the saint, and even more effectively when he pictures his physical appearance. In these descriptions Meyer repeatedly applies adjectives like pale, colorless, and their synonyms to Thomas' face.[24] Other descriptive examples confirm that in *Der Heilige*—as we have seen in Mrs. Mydans' *Thomas*— the topoi, the recurrent images, at least the most striking ones, are related to elements of the motif. Both novelists disclose an equal concern for thematological unity.

II

The tragic hero and the saint: although neither Eliot's nor Anouilh's play is a tragedy in the traditional and technical sense of the word, the dichotomy between the tragic and the saintly deserve attention, for it poses the problem of how to treat the Becket theme dramatically. A tragic play, as Maxwell Anderson remarks accurately, must lead to and then move away from a central crisis.[25] This movement should depend upon a discovery that affects the thoughts and emotions of the major character and thereby impresses a new direction on the plot. The tragic fault of which Aristotle speaks seems to be a permanent element of occidental classical theater. An experience opens the eyes of the hero who recognizes a fatal error—his own.

It seems that these principles cannot be applied to a hero who is a saint, and who frequently, especially in the medieval tradition, is by birth or by baptism a perfect man, and in many ways a rather static character. Yet because the struggle for perfection makes a saint, his life may nevertheless offer dramatic possibilities, though these may not necessarily be tragic. Tragedy is the theatrical representation of the defeat of the hero by the gods. He is the victim of a superior power that mysteriously seems to fix the steps of his descent to the infernal regions; his death is a fall. The death of a saint, on the contrary, is a triumph, for he is on the side of the superior power.[26] Unless we confuse tragedy and tragicomedy, *Trauerspiel* and *Schauspiel*, the lives of saints, and particularly those of martyrs, cannot be the basis of anything but Schauspiele.[27] If Corneille styles his *Polyeucte* a "Christian tragedy," he is pretending to forget the first principles of the ancient theater. Unless Polyeucte is damned, there is no fall. What tragic element is there in eternal joy? For the man who doubts the reality of divine happiness or for the man whose thoughts move outside what theology calls the economy of salvation, Polyeucte is defeated; but this is not the sense of Corneille's work. If at the foot of the altar of the false gods, Polyeucte were to lose all instead of gaining all, then he would be acting within a tragic sphere. No such action, however, occurs in the play. Divine grace is the antidote of the fatalism of the ancients, and in a Christian conception of life, the drama of Calvary abolishes the rite of tragedy. The Christian periods of literary history knew the liturgical drama, the mystery play, and the miracle play, a tradition especially strong in France, Germany, and England. It was the Renaissance, essentially pagan in form if not always in thought, that established the hegemony of tragedy on European soil. "Christian tragedy" has become a contradiction in terms.

There is no reason for discussing here the question of the causes for which Thomas died. The historian George Greenaway has this to say: "There will always be divergent opinions as to whether or not Becket really died a martyr for the freedom of the Holy Church against the tyranny of the secular power, but there can be no doubt that he died in defence of his archiepiscopal prerogatives and the rights of the church of Canterbury."[28]

✳

Eliot attaches himself to medieval tradition. *"Murder in the Cathedral,"* says Hans Galinsky, "is not a drama in the narrow sense, but rather a play, a *mystery play*. The drama, in a stricter sense, represents events as they are happening *hic et nunc*; in the mystery play, something that has happened before happens again; the hero, once more experiences his sufferings. Thomas *performs his own history*."[29] Eliot's work represents a genre fundamentally different from most other Becket plays, like those of Douglas Jerrold (1829), Richard Cattermole (1832), George Darley (1840), Aubrey de Vere

(1876), Alfred Tennyson (1879), Raoul Konen (1909), Eugen Linz (1934, based on Meyer), Jean Anouilh (1959), and of some twenty other playwrights.

The spirit of the mystery play, as well as significant elements of its technique, relates Eliot's work to the Middle Ages. *Murder in the Cathedral* is divided into two contrasting parts, and this binary architecture was usual in old pageants. The chorus, however, is primarily reminiscent of the ancient tragedy, at least for those readers and spectators unfamiliar with medieval literature. The tradition of the chorus had not at all been discarded in medieval theater, where one of its more important functions was to bind together, almost in Senecan fashion, the acts or "tableaux." This use of the chorus was still current in sixteenth-century France—for example, in Alexandre Hardy's *Didon se sacrifiant*—but it disappeared almost entirely in the classical periods in both France and Germany; the few noticeable exceptions include Racine's *Esther* and *Athalie*, and Schiller's *Braut von Messina*.[30]

Substitutes for the chorus have been attempted in many great literatures, especially in England, in whose dramatic tradition Eliot's play should be studied. Of special importance for the history of the chorus is the pantomime in *Gorboduc* by Sackville and Norton, an example adapted later by Shakespeare—or his unidentified collaborators—for his *Pericles* and his *Henry V*, and imitated by the fool in *King Lear*. The technique of Kyd, in *Spanish Tragedy*, is essentially the same, and so is Molière's in the intermissions of *Le Bourgeois gentilhomme*. During these interludes the spectator lets his tension slacken, while he is maintained in the atmosphere of the play. The action does not advance. A similar function will later be assumed by the chorus in great operas such as *Die Zauberflöte*, *Nabucco*, and *Fidelio*, except that there the intervals, lyric in nature, are integrated parts of the acts. In Elizabethan and French seventeenth-century drama the tasks of the chorus were often taken over by messengers or confidants, or at times by the heroes themselves. One of these tasks was to introduce new characters to the audience, as when Hamlet says: "This is one Lucianus, nephew to the King," and Ophelia in turn reacts like a literary critic: "You are as good as a chorus, my lord."[31]

Eliot's work opens with a long complaint by the poor women of Canterbury, a group that recites almost one third of all the verses, and thereby constitutes the chorus proper. Thomas, who pronounces a sermon during the intermission, represents a second chorus. Finally, the knights, having accomplished their murder, go to the front of the stage to explain and justify their actions in choric fashion. To a certain extent, therefore, Eliot's play represents a rehabilitation of the chorus.

Eliot used a medieval device to deal with a medieval subject; both form and content belong to the past. Written for the Canterbury Festival of 1935, *Murder in the Cathedral* was intended to be staged in a church, and as a result Eliot's work is linked with the drama of the "sacrifice" of the Mass. In the Mass and in Eliot's play a chorus of participants seeks not merely to commemorate the death but to re-enact the murder of Christ or the martyrdom of Thomas. Past and present join together; there is no displacement of time between the present and the past, between the actual fact and the re-enacted fact. Thus the genre itself implies anachronism, though its object and its setting are legend or history. And no one should be surprised at hearing the Tempters, perfectly oblivious to the flow of time, pronounce these words:

> Man's life is a cheat and a disappointment;
> All things are unreal,
> Unreal or disappointing:
> The Catherine wheel, the pantomime cat,
> The prizes given at the children's party,
> The prizes awarded for the English Essay,
> The scholar's degree, the statesman's decoration.[32]

The originality of a mystery play lies neither in the general outline of its plot nor in its denouement. Eliot's work, consequently, is basically a new presentation and a new interpretation of an old theme instantly recognizable by the audience. When in the opening scene the women of Canterbury say they are awaiting the return of their archbishop who has been absent for seven years, they do not intend to supply facts; they want to create and re-create an atmosphere:

> Since golden October declined into sombre November
> And the apples were gathered and stored, and the land became
>   brown sharp points of death in a waste of water and mud,
> The New Year waits, breathes, waits, whispers in darkness.
> While the labourer kicks off a muddy boot and stretches his
>   hand to the fire,
> The New Year waits, destiny waits for the coming.[33]

To wait: the verb is repeated four times—and eight times more in the sequel to the initial chant—orchestrated by words of tragic resonance: *points of death, whispers in darkness, destiny*. Already the predominant motif is announced, although vaguely and mysteriously. The expression "to deny his master" arises twice in this context. The Christian sees Saint Peter stretching his hands toward the fire that the soldiers have lighted, the spectator sees Thomas condemned to betray one of his two Lords. The dilemma is part of the central theme: forced to choose between Henry and Christ, Thomas chooses Christ, and so incarnates a fundamental Christian tenet and illustrates a fundamentally Christian motif, namely, that Christ has no rivals. Around this motif are grouped the main thematological elements of the play.

Since Thomas' life is so familiar to the audience, there are more allusions and insinuations in the play than full accounts, and the events that lead to the catastrophe are suggested rather than dramatically rendered. At the simple words *"hungry hawk"*[34] the imagination soars, for the audience connects them with biographical details, with Thomas' hunting parties, and his friendship with the king. But Thomas himself is given a chance to tell his remembrances:

> Thirty years ago I searched all the ways
> That lead to pleasure, advancement and praise.
> Delight in sense, in learning and in thought,
> Music and philosophy, curiosity,
> The purple bullfinch in the lilac tree,
> The tiltyard skill, the strategy of chess,
> Love in the garden, singing to the instrument,
> Were all things equally desirable.[35]

With this Faustian theme Eliot, like Meyer, stresses the humanity of Thomas' personality. But fate determined that Becket would study theology, despite his more secular inclinations:

> While I ate out of the King's dish
> To become servant of God was never my wish.[36]

Theology—to reason with the unbelievers—seems to be here the true source of Thomas' distress. It was at the origin of the fatal ambition that led to his glory and to his fall. This is not, to be sure, how Thomas himself interprets the mysteries of his destiny.

There are allusions to political issues, both temporal and churchly, which motivate the action. Eliot's Thomas, however, is above all a mystic with an existentialist tendency. To be is to act, and to act is to suffer. In his first appearance on the stage, Thomas shows himself as a man torn between acting and suffering:

> They know and do not know, what it is to act or suffer.
> They know and do not know, that action is suffering
> And suffering is action. Neither does the agent suffer
> Nor the patient act. But both are fixed
> In an eternal action, an eternal patience.[37]

These verses are taken up again, word for word, by the fourth Tempter, and Thomas returns to the same idea at the end of the first part: "I shall no longer act or suffer, to the sword's end."[38]

In Eliot's view, however, Thomas is less a philosopher than he is a saint. He gives this image of himself when his last hour comes. The murderers entering the cathedral ask for *"Becket*, the traitor to the

King,"[39] and each of the three stanzas of their poem contains this provocative verse drawn from the Old Testament: "Come down Daniel to the lions' den." A saint does not react with arguments *ad hominem*. "*Henry*, the traitor to Christ and to his Church," a worldly minded archbishop would have retorted. But the taunt receives a reply worthy of a martyr:

> No traitor to the King. I am a priest,
> A Christian, saved by the blood of Christ,
> Ready to suffer with my blood.
> This is the sign of the Church always,
> The sign of Blood. Blood for blood.
> His blood given to buy my life,
> My blood given to pay His death,
> My death for His death.[40]

Placed between earthly and spiritual interests, the Christian has already made his choice. Thomas will not "deny his master." The motif of Eliot's work is a lesson in Christianity, according to the tradition of the mystery play.

※

Jean Anouilh's *Becket ou l'honneur de Dieu* is a drama of another kind. "Ou l'honneur de Dieu," obviously, is intended as a subtitle, an opposition to "Becket." Does the author really deal with the honor of God? Or are we rather concerned with the honor of Becket? This tragic dilemma may be more appropriately expressed by a simple question: *Becket or the honor of God?* Anouilh's answer is: *Becket*. Nothing in the play is done *ad majorem Dei gloriam*. This assertion is sustained by the constant recurrence of the topos "honneur de Dieu" in a purely political context, and also by subtle allusions to "la tentation de la sainteté."[41]

Like Meyer, Anouilh read the story of Henry and Thomas in Augustin Thierry's work, and was impressed by this scene: "Kneeling on the stone of the tomb and stripping himself of his clothing, he [Henry II] placed himself, with his back naked, in the *posture* in which a short time ago his judges had placed the English for having welcomed Thomas upon his return from exile or for having honoured him as a saint."[42] The word *posture* must have inspired a master of stagecraft like Anouilh. The gestures of the monks striking the king— a tableau seen as soon as the curtain rises—are to become in the final scene the gestures of the barons killing the archbishop before they again become those of the monks. In the history of the theater, there is hardly a more fascinating image. Thus a direct and intense relationship is established between sin and chastisement, crime and punishment.

One should, therefore, expect to see the central motif of the work in that relationship. This expectation, however, proves to be vain, for the play appears to have a false departure: the announced *Motiv* remains totally unexploited. The ingenious invention is derived, it seems, from Anouilh as a stage director and not from Anouilh as a playwright. The substance of his drama lies in a broken friendship, the absurdity of existence, the service to state or church as source and pretext for ambition. The thematological elements are not focused on a main motif, and Anouilh's unconnected imagery has to be taken at its face value.

Anouilh's *Becket* also confronts the critic with the problem of the relationship between history and the historical play. Thomas à Becket belongs to history and historical legend, that is, legend inseparable from its historical setting. When Thomas appears as a theatrical figure, he represents a literary type related to *Stoff*, to a predefined theme. One may disengage Thomas from history or tradition and endow him with an imaginary, a symbolic existence. Such a change, however, has to be made without equivogue, as Alfonso Sastre does in his *Guillermo Tell* (see chapter 15). Anouilh clearly chose the historical Becket and, like Meyer, Mrs. Mydans, and Eliot, created some nonhistorical secondary characters useful to the plot. His dramatis personae are all supposed to act in historical or in well-known legendary surroundings, and nothing in the play contradicts this natural assumption, which scenery and costumes fully justify. The play belongs to Anouilh's "pièces costumées," his historical series.

Becket ou l'honneur de Dieu is based on medieval characters and events; nonetheless, the spirit of the time, the true cultural environment in which these characters act, is absent from the play. A drama is not historical because of the plot alone or the theatrical devices employed. According to elementary laws of artistic cohesion, a historical drama should faithfully reflect a specific age, a specific phase of our civilization. The author does not have to create a new world, but to re-create a preexisting one.

To the cultured audience, the protagonists are known from history, which presents Henry II as one of the most respected monarchs of the second half of the twelfth century. In *Becket* he is a bon vivant, and Thomas is one of his boon companions. The king exalts one ideal however, the honor of the realm, which is formulated in his discourses but not illustrated in his actions or attitudes. On several occasions, for example, Anouilh compares Henry Plantagenet with a child. In the second act, one of the sallies of the monarch is preceded by this commentary: "The King, *excited like a little boy.*" When Louis, King of France, speaks, his eyes are *"sparkling with intelligence,"* and he has an air of superiority that could be tolerated only by French superpatriots. "If the King of France began to be afraid of the King of England, there would be something wrong in Europe." Louis greets the court with gracious condescension and a sophisticated smile, while the semibarbaric Henry is suddenly "overcome by an inextinguishable, joyous laughter."[43] He thus scarcely does honor to his tutors. His father, Geoffrey Plantagenet, count of Anjou, had given him two teachers: Adelard of Bath and later the famous scholar William of Conches. Historians have presented Henry as a promoter of arts and letters.[44] But Anouilh demands from the spectator that he forget what he knows about Henry's life and character. He uses a perfect stage technique, it is true, and he shows a sequence of brilliantly organized scenes. While this may assure the success of the play, it is not enough to characterize it as a work of art that, considered as a whole, necessarily represents a synthesis of all its constituent elements. Here, history is such an element; Anouilh left it out.

What qualities are to be found in Henry, aside from his genius at chasing women? He is cowardly, afraid of even the boy who serves at mass. "He is perhaps a dwarf. With these French, one never knows." When he converses with Thomas about the affairs of the kingdom, he cannot help advancing the most ridiculous ideas. Of his son, crowned as Henry III at the age of fourteen, he says: "A little imbecile, sly as his mother." To a priest and archbishop he gives this advice: "Never get married, Becket!"[45] Many of Anouilh's scenes are filled with this kind of Parisian-café wit.

The action develops in a spiritual, intellectual, and social climate foreign to the times of the Plantagenets. "It simplifies life to know that one will be hung at the slightest initiative": this is the reflection of a conscript in a French barracks, not of a King of England. When the peasant's daughter trembles with fear before him, refusing to reply to the simplest question, he asserts his superior rank by addressing her father with these words: "Dog, how old is she? (*The man trembles without replying, hemmed in.*) Your son is mute too [he had just entered the hut]. Did you have him with a deaf female?"[46] Henry's language is that of a fishwife. It is to be regretted that Anouilh does not give his characters—if not more finesse—at least more common sense. When the King of France or the King of England came to have dealings with charcoal burners—as in the scene just alluded to —they comported themselves like fathers of the people, distant and benevolent. Not that they were necessarily moved by any humanitarian sentiment, but all monarchs knew the rudiments of the art of government. From the moment a newly crowned king sat on his throne, the palace was dominated by the fear of a revolution; today, from the moment a newly elected president of a republic takes office he thinks of reelection. The famous *oderint, dum metuant*, however ("they may hate, provided they fear"), belongs to the Roman Emperor Caligula, but Caligula the Madman, not to Henry II. The scene in the hut of the poor fellow supposes a monarch entirely deprived of intelligence; and the brother of the girl, if logic ruled, ought to have plunged his knife between the royal ribs instead of using it to scratch the hand of the chancellor, as in Anouilh's play. Frequently, no more psychology exists in *Becket* than in a fairy tale. The portrait of Thomas reveals similar weaknesses.[47]

While mystery plays, as reenactments, presupposes anachronism, historical plays generally do not admit to it. For aesthetic reasons, certain events can transcend historical order, an artistic freedom that Meyer takes advantage of as he permits himself license in regard to chronology. Anouilh, however, writes against the spirit of an age.[48] In *Becket*, moreover, factual anachronisms abound. Thomas, for instance, is alluded to as the inventor of a game that became a success in England a half-millennium later: "Suppose I taught you that governing can be as amusing as a cricket game?" If the reader wants to know why the United Kingdom has developed into the powerful nation it is, he may learn it from Anouilh: more than a century before the Swiss Confederation was even founded (1291), the English succeeded in recruiting mercenary regiments there, "three thousand Swiss fantassins." One character is presented "with his quid of tobacco that he will not spit out, even to drink bouillon"; tobacco did not come to Europe until after the discovery of America.[49]

An author's respect for medieval culture certainly does not require the characters to speak the vernacular language of the time, but in his use of terms like "psychologue," "esthétique," and "international," Anouilh violates the essential spirit of the Middle Ages. Many words in our daily vocabulary are free of historic connotations, while others are filled with overtones of the past. Certain expressions are to be rejected as being alien to one period or suggestive of another. What is true for specific words is true also for particular conversational topics. It is obvious that questions concerning the sex of angels were of no concern either to theologians of the Middle Ages, or of any other age. That such a question did not interest "learned priests," as Henry pretends, but at the most jokers like Anouilh's Henry himself, is confirmed by another famous Thomas who lived a hundred years after Thomas à Becket, Thomas Aquinas. He mentions it only incidentally in his *Summa*, the sum of theological concerns up to his time. Aquinas' statement will always appear as a truism for any Christian: because angels have no material existence, and therefore no bodily functions, they may, to make themselves visible, assume the physical aspect they like. In biblical times, they most frequently appeared as males; in the Baroque most often as females, the contour of their breasts matching the ornamental patterns used in the fine arts; and, finally, romantic writers in their turn, used to style as angels the sweetest of their female characters. Plain ambiguity (intentional transpositions or allegories) has become one of the most savoury spices of the modern theater; ambiguous ambivalence (scorn or ignorance of history or tradition) deprives a play of the piquancy of its literary flavor.

The repertoire of contemporary drama offers scores of plays that do not respect history, though they are dealing with historical events. Should we conclude that the Western stage is in decline? Such general pessimism is in no way justified. Frankly, parahistorical characters, but not insidiously antihistorical ones, may perfectly incarnate the main motif of a work. Anouilh reminds us that after the theatrical revolution of the last decades, not all of its aesthetic rules have as yet been satisfactorily reformulated.

☙❧

The preceding pages show how a specific theme can be treated in works of the most diverse literary genres. For Mrs. Mydans, Thomas à Becket was the Stoff, the theme of a historical novel, while Meyer wrote a historical romance, Eliot a mystery play, and Anouilh a drama. Most naturally these works would stem from the writer's concern with artistic order; they should possess that aesthetic virtue that makes all their parts cohere into an organic whole. Such literary cohesion is most efficiently achieved by means of the motifs, themes and types; but they in turn impose a set of rules on novelists and playwrights. The Becket theme, or any other historical theme, demands of the writer a knowledge of history in its broadest sense. Anouilh fails to fulfill this requirement. In many respects *Becket ou l'honneur de Dieu* appears to be a paraliterary artifact, a hybrid in the realm of letters, a camelopard, a body clothed with a borrowed skin.

By its very nature a historical theme poses the problem of liberty in creative literature. Despite the demands that history imposes upon the writer, artistic freedom still exists, limited though real. The author may organize the matter furnished by history and tradition to achieve a specific artistic effect. He may pose accents and counterpoints, create from whole cloth characters who complete the picture or the action. Like Mrs. Mydans, he can base the work on fact, on a narrative as transmitted by a cultural heritage. Lyricism and mysticism may sublimate the subject; this is the formula adopted by Eliot, who possesses the art of dramatizing the story of Thomas to the point where he virtually overcomes historical distance. But novels and dramas can also include new interpretations of historical data. Within the framework set by events and defined by the hero's nature, the genius of the poet discovers or invents his motif, the stimulus for the action he presents. Thus Meyer's motif refers to the desire for vengeance or power, Anouilh's—although rather loosely—to the man promoting his own honor by serving in turn two masters, the king and God. These motifs, which could warp the perspective of the historian, guide and widen the scope of the literary artist, whose work must at once both include and transcend history.

15

A Mythic Type: William Tell

THE legend: in the heart of the Alps lived a herdsman and hunter, William Tell, whose abode was tucked away in a valley not far from the lake that later was called Lake of the Four Cantons—the first four states of the Swiss Confederation. In those days, the House of Hapsburg exercised its despotic power over the region through a governor, or bailiff, whose name was Gessler. To test the worthy people of Altdorf, the main town of the Uri district, he had a pole with a hat on top erected in the public square. Persons passing by were required to salute the hat as a sign of their respect for Gessler and the Austrian Government. It happened one day that Tell, crossing the square with his little son Walter, ignored the hat. By chance the bailiff happened to be in Altdorf, and the "rebel" was hauled before him. As punishment for his crime, Tell was commanded to shoot an apple from his boy's head. Superb marksman that he was, he accomplished the difficult feat. But Gessler, a mordant and observant man, demanded to know of Tell why he had put two arrows into his quiver. Tell replied that had the first arrow injured his son, the second would unfailingly have pierced the tyrant's heart.

After Tell proudly confessed his intention, the legend continues with his arrest and eventual escape. Gessler and his retinue set out to take Tell to the prison in the governor's chateau, which was located in Küssnacht at the other end of the lake. Scarcely had they left the

208

shore when a storm came up. Now Tell was not only an expert with the crossbow but also with the rudder of a boat, as Gessler well knew. So the prisoner was charged with the responsibility of steering the craft safely to its destination. They were still a considerable distance from Küssnacht when Tell maneuvered the boat toward shore. Suddenly seizing his crossbow and the one remaining arrow, Tell jumped onto the rocky ground. After preventing the others from also gaining the safety of the bank by giving the bark a mighty push, he escaped. Gessler's men successfully defied the angry waves, however, and happily reached Küssnacht. In order to get to his château, Gessler had to pass through a wooded ravine, known as the "hollow lane," which Tell in the meantime had reached on foot. Hidden behind an elderbush, he shot his arrow through the despot's heart as he rode on this solitary path; and so died the man who had oppressed a people destined for a peaceful and simple way of life.

Many literary and extraliterary materials enter into the composition of the story: Tell's insubordination, the shot at the apple, the murder of the governor. On another level, there is the glorification of the bow as both an implement to practice an artful sport and as a symbol and guarantee of personal independence, as the ultimate assurance of political liberty. Various possible modes of treatment, therefore, offer themselves to the poet: he can feature the idyll of the highlander, illustrate the skill of the archer, or show the ideology of the revolutionary. And, indeed, all these approaches can be found in the numerous works dealing with the legend.

The Tell saga will here be viewed from three different perspectives. First, the legend itself, centering on Tell's masterly shot, will be discussed; the tracing of the growth and metamorphoses of the story or fable in several European countries is a study in Stoff. The second part of the chapter considers the Tell Motiv as it developed from the fusion of folktales with historical facts. This Motiv, the thought behind the story, may be expressed in several ways, two of them being that oppression leads to the murder of the oppressor, and, in revolutionary terms, the oppressor should be eliminated by the oppressed. Two writers, the German Friedrich Schiller and the Spaniard Alfonso Sastre, demonstrate two different modes of treating the motif: their works about Tell are in effect variations on a theme. Finally, the Tell tradition will be viewed as illustrating that *Stoffgeschichte*, rather than merely contributing to the writing of literary history at large, may shed light on particular aspects of civilization and particular evolutions of culture.

❦

Tell, let it be noted, may play the double role of a Motiv-type and of a Stoff-type. He is a Motive-type when he embodies the idea of national liberator, of those who free their country from usurpers of the people's sovereignty. But Tell can also be considered a model of marksmanship; in this case an apple and a crossbow are his emblems, which obviously are borrowed from the story and belong to the Stoff only. Similarly, Narcissus symbolizes a person endowed with the qualities psychoanalysts refer to when they speak of narcissism; they are using certain elements of the Narcissus story, elements of Rohstoff and Stoff. Here the emblem is a mirror. The complete mythological story of Narcissus itself, however, contains a Motiv: egoism is self-destructive. Becket, in contrast with Tell and Narcissus, exists only in his historical setting; he is inseparable from his real life and from the annals of Great Britain. For this reason, he is not ordinarily identified with a striking symbol of specific qualities or a representative performer of a specific action. In other words, he remains only a Stoff-type identified with the main character of a plot; he is not the personification of the general thought expressed by that plot.

The thematologist does not limit his field of research to one culture, although motifs, types, and themes originate in single national traditions. He studies the thematological elements and their constant interplay whenever they occur in any significant work. To him this kind of literary inquiry represents one of the four ways leading to a synthetic view of literature. A thematologist is indeed a comparatist.

I

Historians have never found any evidence of the existence of a man called William Tell who was involved in events like those recounted above; nor have they established that the Hapsburgs really intimidated the herdsmen of Uri. And we search in vain for documents that pertain either to a Gessler or to the assassination of a governor. The archives contain no trace of a hat, an apple, or a storm at the time the story was supposed to have happened. The adventures of the great patron of Switzerland, then, belong to a legendary patrimony that may be traced back to European sagas. Like those of most sagas, its origins remain diffuse and obscure, and the history of its rise and growth rests largely on oral tradition echoed in literary works, opinions, and rumors. Nevertheless, a network of probabilities surrounding the beginnings of such tales and sagas is frequently detected; these probabilities pertain to other epochs and their contribution to the creation and success of the heroic figure.

The most significant book relating events later echoed by the Tell story was written by Saxo Grammaticus (ca. 1140–ca. 1220), Saxo "The Literate," who was one of the earliest writers and historians of Denmark. In his *Gesta Danorum*, finished probably near the end of the first decade of the thirteenth century, the feats of an archer called Toko—or Palnatoke—are reported. This stalwart was in the service of King Blue Tooth, a figure of the tenth century. One day Toko, claiming superior prowess with the bow, boasted to his jealous comrades that his arrow would not miss an apple atop a stake. Clearly enough, Toko, like other prototypes of Tell, is a sort of *miles gloriosus*. The king, aroused by such brashness, ordered Toko to place his apple on the head of his own son.[1] There was no refusing the order; nor did the arrow miss its target. But Toko had held several arrows in reserve. "Why these other arrows?" asked the king. The fearless archer did not deign to lie about their purpose: "To avenge myself in case I should have missed the apple." This tale, with its striking similarity to the Tell legend, probably constitutes the latter's embryo form. Indeed Toko was deemed worthy of literary treatment centuries later, most notably in a Danish tragedy, Oehlenschläger's *Palnatoke*. This play was performed in 1808, four years after Schiller's Tell drama, and published in 1809. A decade later it appeared in a German translation, the foreword relating Toko to Tell: "The appleshot episode depicted in this work took place three hundred years earlier in Denmark (Palnatoke) than in Switzerland (William Tell)."

Tell, of course, has more ancestors than just Toko. They can be found in various works about European folk traditions, especially those on Scandinavia.[2] As far back as the early eleventh century, the king and martyr Saint Olaf forced one of his heathen chiefs, Einridi, to shoot a wooden tablet off his son's head; and King Harold Sigurdarson made a famous marksman, Hemingr, perform a similar feat, although in this case it was the hero's brother rather than his son who held the target on his head, the target being, of all things, a hazelnut. Other sources in which the theme occurs are a series of more or less related legends like the *Wilking Saga* and the *Thidrek's Saga* (thirteenth century). In this latter story, the anonymous author has the seventh-century archer Egill—presaging Toko—hit an apple on his son's head. In England, the apple episode is incorporated into the story of Wayland Smith, and in Germany into that of Wieland der Schmied and Dietrich von Bern.[3]

Tell's remarkable shot supposedly took place on November 18, 1307, a date arbitrarily invented by the Swiss chronicler Aegidius Tschudi.[4] Around 1425, a German, Punker,[5] takes a hand at crossbow shooting, and is imitated toward the end of the same century by a legendary Holstein hero, Henning Wulff—or Wulffen. This was the time when the famous William of Cloudesley made his appearance in an English ballad (1536) together with Adam Bell and Clym of the Clough.[6] One might even point to Robin Hood, who died in 1247, as a distant member of the Toko-Tell family; he certainly possessed some of the sterling qualities with which the Danish and the Swiss heroes were endowed: skill with the bow, love of liberty and justice, and a predilection for an independent and rustic life. This love of justice and independence compelled Robin Hood to steal from the rich in order to give to the poor, just as it prompted William Tell to rouse and liberate the oppressed as well as to slay the tyrant. It is difficult to reject the theory that these fables moved south from their apparent Scandinavian birthplace and settled at the foot of the Alps. The origin of the Tell legend coincides with the development of commerce over the famous Saint Gotthard Pass. Merchants from northern nations, traveling in increasing numbers through Switzerland on their way to Italy, might well have narrated the story to the tavern owners of Altdorf, who in turn entertained their guests with it.[7] Unfortunately no such tales are reflected in any written document.

The history of Switzerland itself may supply a more plausible explanation for the birth of the Tell legend. The modern tourist taking his obligatory sightseeing tour through lovely Bern, Lucerne, or Zurich, is hardly apt to realize that the Swiss Confederation toward the middle of our millennium was one of the great military powers in Europe. The battles against the Austrian army at Sempach (1386)— one remembers Walter Scott's ballad "The Battle of Sempach"—and at Näfels (1388) consolidated the franchises the Swiss had already secured, and the war against Charles the Bold of Burgundy, who was defeated at Grandson, Morat, and Nancy (1476–1477), popularized the reputation of the Swiss as soldiers and mercenaries. Twenty years later, after a series of victories over the troops of Maximilian I (*Schwabenkrieg*), Switzerland cut its last ties with the German Empire. When the peace was signed in Basel in 1499, the country had reached the peak of its military fame. The origin of the Tell saga seems tied up with the growth of Swiss influence within the European community. It became impossible to imagine such a courageous people without a leader, such a heroic country without a hero. The faith in Tell was most efficiently strengthened by launching him into the orb of religious practices and beliefs. Chapels were built in his honor, the oldest being probably that of Tellsplatte, at the place where the liberator of Switzerland escaped from Gessler's boat. This chapel called Tellskapelle and officially dedicated to Saint Sebastian, patron of archery, is first mentioned by the Swiss chronicler Brennwald in the early sixteenth century.

While some historians claim the beginnings of the oral Tell tradition go back to the fourteenth century, the first account of Tell's deeds is dated about 1470; it is included in the so-called *Weissbuch von Sarnen* [White book of Sarnen]. Some hundred and eighty years had already elapsed since the birth of Switzerland. Ironically enough, the *Weissbuch* also asserts that the people of Schwyz, Uri's neighbors and allies, were of Norse descent, a legend once as firmly believed as that of Tell. The anonymous author quite innocently suggests, at least to the mind of the modern reader, that the citizens of Uri may well have stolen their Tell story from the ancestral patrimony of their closest friends who once emigrated to Helvetia from the land of Toko. In any case, to maintain that a certain William Tell has played a pivotal role in the history of the Swiss fight for independence, without being able to point to a shred of evidence of that famous figure in official or private documents, is to assume a position that defies common sense.

The story of either Toko or one of his kinsmen, real or imaginary, vaguely embedded in the historical and geographical setting of early Switzerland, put an end to a people's quest for a hero. Once discovered or invented, this hero did rather well. In the age of Enlightenment, however, doubts arose. A Swiss author and correspondent of Voltaire, Uriel Freudenberger, was one of the first to be struck by the similarity of the Tell story and the sagas of the north. In 1760 he published a critical pamphlet, *Der Wilhelm Tell, ein dänisches Märchen* [William Tell, a Danish tale], which the inquisitors of Altdorf promptly burned. This booklet, translated into French by one of Albrecht von Haller's sons, inspired some passages of the *Essai sur les mœurs:* "We must agree," Voltaire wrote, "that the story of the apple is quite suspect. It seems someone thought it necessary to decorate the cradle of Swiss liberty with a fable." In the nineteenth century a group of historians, notably Joseph Eutych Kopp and Marcel Beck, defended Freudenberger's viewpoint. Nevertheless, a few patriots continue to this day to believe in the hero's deeds.

II

So far we have been concerned with the parahistorical or legendary *Tell-Stoff;* we have discussed a theme proper for fictional works. Stoff that receives literary treatment is often supplemented by a Motiv, the exception occurring when the theme is presented for its intrinsic value as a story or a tale. This is to say that themes treated in narratives, no matter how skillful may be the telling of facts and happenings, alleged or real, do not necessarily develop a well profiled Motiv in the thematological sense of the word. The Motiv springs from the writer's imagination and his particular perception of the events, not merely from the events themselves. It should be noted, furthermore, that legendary themes frequently undergo a more flexible literary treatment than historical ones, for they are by nature suited to expressing a greater variety of motifs.

The motif of a people's liberation from its oppressors may be substantiated by themes drawn from history or from imagination. Tyrants have always provoked tyrannicides in the most casual manner. After reading the story of Aod and Jehu in the Bible, Calvin was not at all at a loss for examples to support his theory that political sedition may be commanded by God. In all periods of history despots,

some of them at least, have found their assassins. Rome was delivered
of Caligula by Cassius Chaerea. It had rebels like Gaius Gracchus and
more famous ones like Brutus, whose deeds have been celebrated by
countless writers. There was Arminius, the liberator of what later
became Germany, whom we encounter as the hero of Kleist's *Her-
mannsschlacht* [Hermann's battle]. European belles lettres from the
end of the seventeenth century contain interesting references to the
Neapolitan leader Masaniello. Charlotte Corday killed Marat in his
bath, and Andreas Hofer led the uprising of the Tyrol against Napoleon. Indeed, William Tell belongs to the international history of
conspiracies and revolutions. *Histoire des conspirations et révolu-
tions* (1754) is, fittingly enough, the title of a work by François
Dupont du Tertre, in which the murderer of Gessler occupies an
honorable place.

It was a fortunate combination of circumstances that caused Tell
to remain a popular example of the legendary type of patriotic hero.
The parahistoric nature of his existence in no way affected the durability of his success. Curiously enough, Switzerland, one of the first
modern nations to be structured in accord with a democratic ideology, was also one of the last to seek its roots in the realm of myth.
Could it be that liberty *is* a myth? Surely it is the mythological orientation that becomes important for the interpretation of William Tell
as a literary type. The ensuing discussion of the Tell motif will be
confined to two examples: Schiller's play *Wilhelm Tell* (1804), and
Guillermo Tell tiene los ojos tristes (1962, *Sad are the Eyes of William
Tell*), a drama in seven scenes by the Spanish author Alfonso Sastre.

✵

Schiller stresses the legendary—and mythological—character of
Wilhelm Tell throughout his drama. First, he groups the individual
episodes, whether traditional or invented by him, around a motif too
visibly preestablished to be considered historical. Secondly he intro-
duces supernatural elements that decisively influence the course of
the action. In some instances the personal intervention of God is
openly proclaimed, and in his monologue at the narrow pass, Tell,
while waiting for his victim, goes so far as to declare himself the
executioner appointed by heaven to avenge the wrong done him, the
instrument of divine justice on earth. "There is a God who punishes
and saves," he states, and an instant later his arrow strikes Gessler's
heart with the same precision as the first had pierced the core of the
legendary apple. In both cases, superior forces were at work, as so
many interpreters of the story have pointed out. Emily Dickinson,
for example, who was familiar with Schiller's drama, impressed and
inspired by the marksman's deed and fate, jotted down six stanzas in
his honor, pointing her pen of praise to the omnipotent Lord who
rescued the oppressed from the oppressor:

> Mercy of the Almighty begging—
> Tell his Arrow sent—
> God it is said replies in Person
> When the cry is meant.

And Tell's cry was meant, for "God helped" as Schiller says.[8] In his play, Providence hovers over the life of the hero, as did the spirit of Yahweh over the waters in the days of creation. To a large extent religious faith substitutes for patriotic exaltation, or is mixed or juxtaposed with it. Schiller's work is not, by intention, simply a historical account of the deeds of a medieval figure. Rather, the events, the characterizations, the language, indeed all elements that enter into the composition of the drama are determined by the motif the author imposes upon the raw materials and the theme of the legend. As a result, his *Wilhelm Tell* should not be compared with his historical plays like *Don Carlos, Maria Stuart, Wallenstein,* or with *Die Jungfrau von Orléans.* Schiller's biographers have shown that as a professor of history he courted Clio almost as much as Melpomene. In her *De l'Allemagne,* Madame de Staël devotes a chapter to German historiography in which the two major names mentioned are Friedrich Schiller and Johannes von Müller (1752–1809).[9] Müller drew the inspiration for his account of the Tell story mainly from sixteenth-century sources, including Tschudi. Both Tschudi and Müller provided Schiller with thematic information. Having himself never traveled to the Swiss cantons, he took his local color from maps, books, and, presumably, from Goethe's personal descriptions.

It was, of course, Schiller the poet and folklorist, not the professional historian, who wrote *Wilhelm Tell.* The play opens with the melody of the *Kuhreih* or *ranz des vaches,* a herdsmen's tune popular in several versions in many parts of the Alps. Schiller's song may be considered a variation of the theme of Goethe's poem *Der Fischer,*[10] which transports the spectator into the fabulous world of nymphs and nixes:

> Out of the depths there comes a call:
> Beloved youth, you are mine!
> I lure the sleeper,
> I draw him to me.[11]

It is, therefore, not the world of reality in which the characters move and in which their actions take place, but the realm of myth: they must be judged accordingly.

The first act makes evident the absurdity of attempting to foist a realistic interpretation on the drama. As the shepherds return home after a long day in the mountain pastures, the waves of the lake give warning of an approaching storm. Baumgarten, one of the pillars of a neighboring community, comes rushing onto the scene, fleeing from the henchman of an Austrian bailiff. The idyll turns into tragedy when the spectator learns that somebody has just been killed. Baumgarten reveals himself as the assassin of a government official.

In such cases—as long as nations are or claim to be policed—moral and legal questions arise that must be answered: the question of culpability in relation to the motivation for the deed. But fables and dreams transcend the concepts of good and evil. The murder merely illustrates the wrath of the oppressed, which generates the plot. In *Wilhelm Tell* the matter of blame and guilt and of moral responsibility is of little relevance. One might even venture to suggest that the poet's sporadic moralizing, often in the form of proverbs, is intended to hide the lawlessness to which the first major character coming onto the stage readily admits. The action develops in an atmosphere of myth. Man is a child of nature; his passions are legitimate as long as they stem from a sense of justice—in the present instance, as long as they express the feelings of the enslaved shepherds. Baumgarten, just like Tell, is a noble savage whose moral laws are determined by instinct.

If one maintained that Schiller, believing in a historical Tell, wanted to stage a true event, the history of the liberation of Switzerland from Austrian authority would come close to being a burlesque. To a man deprived of any mythical sense, or to a realist knowing the social and historical context of the events presented in the play, Schiller's opening scene would seem a travesty. Listening to Baumgarten's story, he could scarcely detect any reason why this somewhat trivial adventure should become the pretext of a people's rebellion against the legitimate political authority. Schiller invites him to imagine that an emissary of one of Gessler's colleagues has ventured onto Baumgarten's pastureland to count the livestock and to assess the tax. This anonymous visitor has found Baumgarten's wife rather charming. She even has told him that her husband is at work in the woods, and so the conversation is prolonged. Since the collector has traveled a long distance, he has asked Frau Baumgarten to prepare a bath for him. To be sure in the early fourteenth century the word "bath" was not really part of the everyday vocabulary at three thousand feet above sea level. The woman has wondered how she can provide the required service. The two have continued to chat; propositions, undoubtedly, have been advanced. The Hapsburg functionary has finally proceeded to his ablutions, and Frau Baumgarten has set to reflecting that she would enjoy the company of a clean man for the first time in her life. To the realistic observer it would seem that what has happened has been a matter of a little adventure arranged in advance and tacitly accepted by the parties involved; and he would go on interpreting Baumgarten's expository report in his own way. He would see in the abrupt change of the lady's attitude the cause of the tragic turn of the story. Let the Austrian bathe by himself, she suddenly thinks, and she secretly escapes from the house. She runs into the woods and explains the situation to her husband, declaring herself in danger of committing a mortal sin. The Austrian had demanded something of her, she says, that was simply not acceptable; he had demanded "Ungebührliches," things "that are not done." While the unlucky bather is still happily splashing in his kettle, Herr Baumgarten, followed by his chaste spouse, rushes into this first bathroom in the history of Swiss hostelry. Evidently an employee of the state is always wrong in wasting time soaping himself for a woman who, as the incident shows clearly, is not worth the bubble. The all-too-well-mannered guest pays dearly for his romantic inclination. The host's reasoning is simple: all Herr Baumgartens have the right to split the skull of any individual for whom Frau Baumgartens may have prepared a bath in a cheese tub. The skull is very properly split: "And with my ax I blessed his bath for him."[12] The fame of the adventure was quickly bruited around the region and, Austria being a civilized country, the murderer was pursued. Of the three characters in this scene, the first, the tax collector, is an imbecile, the charming lady of the house a traitoress, and her husband an outlaw.

Obviously, we cannot view *Wilhelm Tell* through the eyes of a realist. These events could hardly motivate the liberating action of the central hero. Understood as a mythical play, however, the work is great. Its relations to Greco-Roman, but far more evidently to Judeo-Christian mythology quickly become apparent to anyone who detects in the Baumgarten scene reminiscences not only of classical antiquity, but of certain biblical passages, like those relating the stories of Susannah and Bathsheba. Schiller, however, was more rigorous than Yahweh in repressing lustful thoughts though much less in preventing crime. The tax collector's murderer proudly proclaims:

> God and my ax prevented him
> From accomplishing his evil desires.[13]

Schiller's drama is meaningful and justifies Baumgarten's appearance before the audience as a man above reproach, a "Biedermann," to be viewed only as a mythical character. In a realistic setting, Baumgarten would be merely an assassin. Schiller's entire work was composed in the spirit of myth. Tell is a mythical type.

᭞᭞

Alfonso Sastre's treatment of the Tell story differs radically from Schiller's. Whereas *Wilhelm Tell* is placed within a historical framework, *Guillermo Tell tiene los ojos tristes*[14] is a symbolic and basically ahistorical play. The events that allegedly took place in Switzerland in the late thirteenth and early fourteenth centuries are presented as reflections of events in contemporary Spain. Sastre's work is reminiscent of paintings that show scriptural scenes with figures from widely separated periods, as for example the Dominican monk who witnesses the conversation between Gabriel and Mary in Fra Angelico's *Annunciation*, or the Spanish gentleman who consoles the holy women in El Greco's *Descent from the Cross*. All these paintings are bent on presenting the mystic and mythic character of the work of art. For them, symbols, by their very nature, transcend history. And the same is true of Sastre's play.

Sastre intended to endow his drama with allegorical qualities, for he saw a parallel between the situation of medieval Switzerland and the dilemma of twentieth-century Spain. The eyes of Tell, simultaneously triumphant and tragic, are veiled with sorrow from the first scene to the last; they show the solitude of the anarchist, the isolation of the revolutionary, and they reveal the author's individual conception of tragedy.[15] To underscore the allegorical tone and mode of the play and its ability to represent two widely separated epochs at the same time, Sastre avoids concessions to historic particularities in language and decor for the production of his drama. In his stage directions he says: "This *William Tell* can be played with modern clothing and uniforms against an abstract background. Not wishing to go that far, one might use conventional costuming without reference to particular epochs and such simple functional architecture as would best serve the needs of the text." And to illustrate clearly the symbolic meaning of the drama, Sastre specifies: "The police and the men of the Governor's escort are armed with firearms. The people fight against them with their arrows and pikes. This contrast is intentional." Historical allusions, however, abound in the play. In the fourth scene, for example, after the reading of the edict obliging the inhabitants of Uri to salute the famous hat on Gessler Square, the herald adds the date of the edict, the eighteenth of November, 1307. This date, arbitrarily given by Tschudi as that of Tell's memorable shot, might also be related by the spectator to what occurred on the banks of the Ebro between the twenty-sixth of July and the eighteenth of November, 1938 during the Spanish Civil War. Medieval history serves as a setting and a camouflage for contemporary events and situations.[16]

But the treatment and even the denouement have undergone considerable change in Sastre's drama. In quite a few other plays of his, such as *Prologo patetico*, *El pan de todos* (The Community Bread), *En la red* (In the Net), *Escuadra hacia la muerta* (The Condemned Squad), Sastre deals in one way or another with the problem posed by the dilemma of theory-action. This dilemma dominates the problem of motivation as posed by the legend: why did Tell kill Gessler? And in so doing, was he a hero? Heroism supposes the risk of placing one's life in danger for altruistic reasons, for a person or a cause. In Sastre's plot, however, Tell seems to behave most unheroically. On the square of Altdorf, his refusal to obey Gessler's orders concerning the hat amounts to a simple boast. When the situation turns serious, his courage leaves him. Like the traditional Tell, he is careful not to defy the command to shoot at the apple on his son's head, thereby exposing himself to the danger of slaying his own flesh and blood. He vaunts to the guards of being a rebel, but is found wanting when the moment comes to prove it. In Schiller's play there is no personal risk either; the heroism of the brave man is based on his sniping at the governor from ambush: "There the elderbush hides me from him."[17] This is premeditated murder, plain and simple. Gessler Plaza, Altdorf, was the only possible backdrop for a heroic deed. But Schiller's Tell is a figure of myth: he is a hero thanks to poetry and dramatic subterfuge. In Sastre's play, Tell is not depicted as a hero. He is an ordinary man. Not one heroic act in the traditional sense is performed, only a natural, spontaneous reaction to tyranny is portrayed. In the final scene of the German drama, Tell is saluted by the crowd: "Long live Tell! The Marksman and the Saviour!"[18] In the Spanish play he is proclaimed a hero in spite of himself. He himself disclaims being one. To his friend Stauffacher he remarks that people are wrong in regarding him as a hero: "I beg you to tell them all that I deny being their liberator. I felt impelled to do something. If at the same time the country was liberated, it's not of my doing. I have nothing to do with it. It's your business."[19]

Guillermo Tell obviously does not act like Wilhelm Tell. One of the most important differences between the two plays resides in the denouements. After Tell refused to salute the hat, Sastre has him arrested and makes him suffer the punishment we are familiar with. But then Sastre surprises his audience with a coup de théâtre. Tell has a moment of weakness. He hesitates to shoot in the direction of his son Walty, thereby causing Gessler to grow impatient:

GOVERNOR:	Either you shoot or my escort will fire on both of you! Either you shoot . . . !
TELL:	I'm going to shoot, Governor.
	[*He aims again. He shoots. All eyes turn to* WALTY *who reels and falls heavily to the ground. Shouts.*]
ONE PERSON:	How horrible! [*Murmurs among the crowd.*]
ANOTHER:	Right in the head! [*More angry murmurs.*]
YET ANOTHER:	He's dead! [*More murmurs and an angry cry.*]
TELL	[*trying to make his way toward his son. Shouts*]: What's happened? What's wrong? [*The* SECOND MAN OF URI *stops him.*]
SECOND OF URI:	Be calm, friend.
TELL:	What's happened?
SECOND OF URI:	You failed. Your son is dead. [TELL *utters a terrible cry like the howl of an animal.*]

TELL   [*shouting wildly and desperately*]: Death to
              the Governor! [*He fires his crossbow at the*
              GOVERNOR *who falls wounded.*] Death to all
              tyrants! [*A great surge of movement, cries,*
              the people fighting against the GOVERNOR'S
              GUARDS.]
ONE: Death to all tyrants!
ALL: Death!
ANOTHER: The signal! The signal! The Governor is dead!
YET ANOTHER: Set fire to the forest! The Governor is dead![20]

In spite of their mythical or symbolic character, both Schiller's and
Sastre's dramas show some realistic elements. In Schiller's, realism
appears mainly in the medieval setting, and in Sastre's, in the motivation and the logic of the final action. Both Wilhelm Tell and Guillermo
Tell kill Gessler to revenge themselves. In the German play he pretends to be a hero, but he certainly should not be one if he were not
transfigured by the dramatist; in the Spanish play, he denies being a
hero, but he might well be one, though a most unconventional one.
His action springs from the noblest rage and is performed with the
spontaneity of the righteous man; he is a heroic anti-hero, so to speak,
and comes close to being the "positive hero" called for by socialist
realism.[21]

A crime demands to be expiated, or at least pardoned, and pardon
implies a prior wrong. In Schiller's presentation, mythical and mystical as it is, Tell's hands are pure.[22] This is not so, however, in many
other works expressing more realistic concerns, like Eugenio d'Ors y
Rovira's, for example; the last part of his *Guillermo Tell* (1926) is
entitled "El perdón supremo" ("The Supreme Forgivingness"), and
it is the emperor himself who absolves Tell from guilt. In Jeremias
Gotthelf's story, *Der Knabe des Tell* [Tell's son] (1846), it is God who
grants forgiveness. Here Tell, tormented by remorse, takes refuge in
the confessional of the church in Altdorf. The penitence imposed consists of his renouncing all the advantages that his action could bring
to him.[23] Let Tell again take up his rank of simple citizen, the priest
decrees.

Is Tell innocent or guilty? This is not in itself the crucial question:
mythical types and legendary figures will always be laws unto themselves. They are a priori heroes just as martyrs are a priori saints.[24]
Many works treating the Tell theme have accordingly discarded the
ethical problem completely. A much deeper literary insight is gained
by our recognizing that the two plays, based on the same motive—the
liberation from the oppressor by the oppressed—are centered on radically different characters; a Wilhelm is not a Guillermo. One and a
half centuries separates two antithetical conceptions of heroism: the
two "heroes" symbolize two different worlds.

III

The legendary and allegorical nature of the Tell story is one of the major reasons for its widespread popularity. Its reception in various nations and epochs is the subject of a study in Stoffgeschichte in the broadest sense of the term.

As a hero of political independence, Tell was welcomed in the cabarets and cafés of the Hapsburg domain during the nineteenth century, not only in reactionary circles, but in all homes where people loved to play cards. In territories under Austrian control, like those that today constitute Hungary and Czechoslovakia, playing cards, instead of having on them images of kings, their valets and ladies, pictorially told the story of Tell and his companions, that is, of Swiss liberation, while the court of Vienna kept on playing "the royal game," chess.

Though it is most flattering for a hero to provide inspiration to the designers of playing cards, the French philosophe Abbé Raynal thought it a more honorable tribute to Tell to set a monument of stone. He therefore had an obelisk erected (1783) on a little isle in the Lake of the Four Cantons to commemorate the deeds of the founders of Swiss liberty, Stauffacher, Fürst, Melchtal, and Tell. A wise and learned man, Raynal turned out to be a poor physicist: Tell's arrow was placed at the top of the monument, but it proved useless as a lightning rod when in 1796 a thunder bolt struck and felled the obelisk. Raynal's intention was clear, however. His statue was dedicated to the Swiss heroes, but above all, to *liberty*. Once again, Tell was a type and symbolized a people's love of independence.

Tell also signified the embodiment of ideals of freedom during the French Revolution, when his name cropped up constantly in the discourses of the Jacobins. One of them cried out one day: "Let the children of William Tell and the friends of Marat be united by eternal bonds!"[25] Unimpeachable sources document Tell's popular fame in France at that time. Under Robespierre, the village of Château Guillaume, in the Indre Department, was named simply William Tell; another village, Châteaumeillant, in the Cher, became Tell-le-Grand; and Saint-Martin-en-Bresse, in Saône-et-Loire, assumed the name Tell-les-Bois. A political district of the city of Paris was named William Tell, and the hero's bust graced the meeting hall of the Jacobins. When Bonaparte's army invaded Switzerland in 1798, it was proposed that a vast central Canton be created and called Tellgau, that is Telle-govia.[26] Tell finally came to be used as a first name for males. It took its place—along with Socrates, Aristotle, Shakespeare, Bacon, Voltaire, and Rousseau—in republican calendars in which lay saints had been substituted for those the Roman Church had taken the trouble to canonize.[27]

The Swiss rebel also played a role, although a modest one, in the

Russia of Nicholas I. The cultured Decembrists, and likewise Alexander Herzen and his group, and at the beginning of the twentieth century Gorki and Ivánov, were all among the admirers of Tell, whose noble deeds were known to them mainly from Schiller's play.[28] When in 1834 a political suspect, Nicholas Platonovitch Ogarev, was arrested and accused of having attempted to murder the czar, he was asked to account for his allusions and references to the Swiss hero, for in a letter to Herzen, he had given particularly free rein to his enthusiasm for the famous crossbowman. "The investigation commission," it is reported, "saw in Ogarev's reference to the famous drama of F. Schiller proof of the existence of a conspiracy within the [Herzen] circle to assassinate the Czar. The letter, with part of it underlined by the commission . . . was presented to Ogarev, Herzen, and the other prisoners with the demand of explanation."[29]

⧉⧉

   The Stoffgeschichte of Tell also has a directly literary aspect. During the French Revolution the director of the Comédie Française received subsidies from the state for the performance of plays apt to exalt the Parisian spirit of liberty. As a result, titles like *Brutus, Gaius Gracchus,* and *William Tell* were often seen on the public posters. The Tell play performed in Paris was the work of a French forerunner of Schiller, Antoine-Marie Lemierre. It had been given for the first time in 1766. Then in 1790, a quite popular author, Sedaine, wrote the text for Grétry's opera with the same title as that of Lemierre's drama, *Guillaume Tell.* Both works radiate an atmosphere of patriotic exaltation. In addition, a long idyll was composed in this period, the Chevalier de Florian's *Guillaume Tell; ou, la Suisse libre,* which has striking touches of the heroic-epic genre. As for Rossini's world-famous opera, which may be claimed by French and Italians alike, it was first performed in 1829.[30]

   During the nineteenth century the French produced a great variety of treatments. We find the Tell Motiv and Mérimée's *La Jacquerie* and in Nerval's *Léo Burckhart.* Lamartine paid tribute to Tell in his little narrative *Guillaume Tell,* and Victor Hugo in several poems of *La Légende des siècles.* Stendhal, on the other hand, seems to have doubted the legendary aspect of the story. "I am a great admirer of William Tell," he insists in his *Souvenirs d'égotisme,* "although ministerial writers claim that he never existed."[31]

   In England, where Roger Ascham's celebrated treatise *Toxophilus* (1545), "lover of the bow," testifies to British fondness of archery, Tell was introduced into belles lettres toward the end of the eighteenth century. Before then he had been mentioned only in travel and history books, like those of Addison and of the traveler and painter William Coxe. One of the first imaginative works about Tell in Great Britain was written by a "Kentish Bowman" who has remained anonymous; this drama, *William Tell*, dated 1792, was dedicated "to all the Archers of Great Britain." A few years later William Godwin narrated the story in the ninth chapter of his *Fleetwood* (1805), and in 1808, Eugenius Rock's play *William Tell* was published, but was never performed. In 1825, James Sheridan Knowles's extremely romantic drama was staged at Drury Lane. The much celebrated actor Macready, who gave Knowles the idea for the undertaking of the work, was assigned the main role. Like Schiller, Knowles and his friend Macready had never been to Switzerland. They chose to make Tell a winegrower and his friends Savoyards, as did Sedaine and Grétry in their opera. In the same year (1825), Henry R. Bishop's opera *William Tell* was staged in London—and Carlyle published his *Life of Schiller*. Charles Timothy Brooks translated Schiller's drama into English in 1833. The first American play on Tell probably is *The Patriot; or Liberty Asserted*, published anonymously in New York in 1794, preceding by two years the premiere of William Dunlap's opera *The Archers; or, the Mountaineers of Switzerland*.

The history of the Tell *Stoff* in the literature of the German-speaking lands has been the object of several studies.[32] The first manuscript of a poem, the *Tellenlied*, by a still unidentified author, is dated 1501, although as we have seen the first Tell chronicle in *Das Weissbuch von Sarnen*, preceded it by thirty years. The first play seems to be the *Urner Tell-Spiel*, dated 1511. Both Germany and Switzerland can boast of an abundance of writings of all sorts about William Tell. In 1672 an especially interesting piece, *Dialog in der Hölle* [Dialogue in hell], appeared in Leipzig under the veil of anonymity. The dialogue takes place between Tell and Masaniello. Classical and baroque plays abound. One of the most recent treatments is Max Frisch's *Wilhelm Tell für die Schule* (1971).

All these uses of the Tell legend indicate that each work founded on our motif is clearly rooted in a popular tradition of long standing. And there will probably be no shortage of authors ready to perpetuate that motif, though it is unlikely any will ever eclipse the glory of Tell's "official" poet, Schiller.

☆

Each country has produced its rebels, each tyranny its revolutionaries. William Tell is one of the few figures among them who enjoys international fame. He is the prototype par excellence of an oppressed people's liberator. Several reasons account for his maintaining this position: most importantly, his marvelous career is unencumbered by trivial statements of contemporary witnesses; and his life is not imprisoned on parchment. He can dole out his lessons lavishly in accordance with the poet's inspiration and ideological goals. The symbolic force of the plot diminishes any and all documentary evidence: legend surpasses history just as myth triumphs over reality. These general principles characterize a whole series of modern dramas that develop mythological themes. Jean Cocteau in his *Orphée*, Tennessee Williams in his *Orpheus Descending*, Hofmannsthal and Giraudoux in their *Electra* and *Electre* respectively, and O'Neill in his *Mourning Becomes Electra* are in many ways closer to the Tell Stoff than are authors of historical plays.

Myth permits transpositions and reworkings because it harbors a more profound truth, a more essential one than that embodied in a specific historic event, whatever its scope and repercussions may be. History signifies the particular; myth, the general. The one is theme and belongs to the realm of facts, the other is part of ideas and ideals, of the literary motif; the one presents heroes, the other engenders them. As a mythic type, William Tell does not have to prove his historical existence. Both the poet and the critic are in this particular instance only secondarily interested in factual evidence; they share Gottfried Keller's view that the question of Tell's existence hardly deserves an answer:

> Whether it all happened?
> It ought not to be asked here,
> The pearl of each fable is the meaning,
> The core of truth lies fresh herein,
> The ripe kernel of all Folk sagas.[33]

William Tell is indeed a type: he is the Liberator, the Tyrannicide, "ein Narr der Freiheit," as Thomas Mann dubbed him, "a fool in the cause of freedom." In the mythological tradition he presents himself as a new Prometheus who stole from tyrannic gods the torch of liberty.

Both Becket and Tell demonstrate that a literary type is never the Stoff itself or the Motiv itself. A type belongs to one of these two basic thematological elements without being identified, however, with either one. On the one hand Becket, a historical figure, belongs to the Stoff rather than to the Motiv; he is generally considered the principal character of a particular story. Tell, on the other hand, is more than that. As a mythical type he transcends his own circumstances to become the incarnation of an idea of central relevance to mankind. He is a Motiv-type, as all mythical figures tend to be.

Moreover, this chapter and the preceding one urge us to believe that studies in thematics, the fourth category of comparatistic inquiry, presuppose a comprehensive knowledge of the political, historical, and philosophical background of the society that engendered the themes and motifs under examination. Thematology, therefore, cannot be separated from the history of ideas, a premise confirmed by our third thematological analysis, that of suicide as an element of literary themes.

16

Suicide: Elements of
Literary Themes

"THE pure philosophical act is killing oneself; this is the real beginning of all philosophy; all the need of the philosophic disciple goes therein, and only this act corresponds to all stipulations and criteria of transcendental action."[1] A century and a half after Novalis made this statement in his *Fragmente*, Albert Camus expressed a somewhat similar thought at the beginning of *Le Mythe de Sisyphe:* "There is only one really serious philosophical problem: suicide. To judge whether life is or is not worth living is to reply to the fundamental question of philosophy. The rest—does the world have three dimensions, does the mind have nine or twelve categories—comes after."[2] The problem, however, is not a matter of metaphysical speculation alone. Many books that lack Novalis' and Camus' philosophical inclination have been written on suicide,[3] and throughout the world it is the cause of twice as many deaths as murder.

The question of suicide presents itself in the history of mankind with tragic insistence. It has stirred the attention and conscience of those concerned with the human condition. In more recent years suicide has become the object of psychoanalytical and sociological research; it is an important subject, too, in the history of ideas; and since it frequently assumes the function of a motif or a theme in major literary works, it becomes the subject of thematological analysis. Special attention will be given here to *Die Leiden des jungen*

Werther [The sufferings of young Werther] (1774) and *Madame Bovary* (1857). The three sections of this chapter deal with three approaches to the problem of suicide: the psychoanalytical-sociological, the historic-philosophical, and the literary.

I

Freud was the first to study seriously and fruitfully the psychology of suicide. In 1920 he published *Jenseits des Lustprinzips* (*Beyond the Pleasure Principle*), a book that had momentous repercussions. The impulse for self-destruction and the antagonism between life and death instincts were not, however, totally new discoveries: Freud simply approached scientifically certain problems that until then had been fair game for dilettantes. What Freud called the death instinct was already present in the Christian image of the Pelican tearing its breast to nurture its young. Furthermore, Saint Ambrose had observed bees killing themselves. And according to some sources, as John Donne relates, scorpions under certain circumstances sting themselves mortally.[4] Legends notwithstanding, psychoanalysis is concerned with the examination of the instinct for self-destruction in man, and it tries to find with objective methods the keys to the troublesome mysteries that surround suicide. In contrast with the answers given by psychoanalysis to these mysteries, those provided by literature are not scientific. The literary response tends to remain on the intuitive plane: what is the man who raises a revolver to his head thinking about—or the man who is about to jump before an onrushing train, or the man who leaps from the rooftop of a twenty-story building?

Freud and his disciples deal with these events as data, as raw material; writers deal with them as human tragedies. They both examine motives. While the psychoanalyst tries to establish general rules of man's behavior, however, the novelist wants to scrutinize a person's destiny. For the one, a suicide is an object of science, for the other, he is an object of compassion. The writer evokes rather than explains a state of mind. Literature and psychoanalysis, often assuming complementary functions, may ask the same questions, but they formulate answers on different levels.

The motivation for suicide, in both psychology and literature, has often been traced to solitude or abandon, or to ennui, the *taedium vitae*, which affects men in all periods of history. Ennui might result from an inability to integrate oneself into a social milieu, be it only a family circle, or it might be the final symptom of a madness. Sometimes it stems from the feeling of being misunderstood, or from the frustrations of repeated failure. For those who need but never achieve fame, suicide—or at least the thought of it—can provide momentary renown: the honor of being written about in a local newspaper. In the scene where he idly proposes to put an end to his life, Tom Sawyer epitomizes the psychology of many a desperate man. Deprived of the affection of those around him, the candidate for suicide savors the attention that will be showered upon him after his would-be death. Tom gets ready to throw himself into the Mississippi because his aunt does not love him; he imagines that when she hears the bad news she will cry out: "Oh, if I had only loved him more!"

In other cases a variety of disappointments and ill fortune accumulate to the point where even a patient man like Job curses his existence. Voltaire insists that such situations and attitudes have been observed only among civilized men. "Savages," he says, "do not dream of killing themselves out of disgust with life: this is a refinement of people of good parts," an opinion Rousseau also expresses in his first discourse. But anthropologists have shown how mistaken Voltaire and Rousseau were on this point. Ennui, often combined with the malady of Werther, may strike any man, oriental or occidental, civilized or savage, and disappointment in love in all its forms—jealousy, indifference, and betrayal—remains one of the most clearly recognized motivations in life on all parts of the globe. It also remains the literary motif most frequently exploited in world literature.

⧓

For the sociologist, questions concerning suicide do not become less complex. In his statistics he distinguishes between suicides, attempts at suicide, and simulated attempts. If these three classes are lumped together, the list of persons involved, in the majority of western countries, contains an equal number of men and women. Yet two or three times as many men as women carry through their attempts and succeed in killing themselves. Men, in contrast with women, love the pistol or the hangman's noose, almost infallible mechanisms of death that practically guarantee success. The psychological reasons for this striking difference are obvious: the woman's natural aversion, by far more coercive than the man's, to any sort of brutality, especially that involving bloodshed. The sociologist records these facts: prudently, even wisely, a woman by preference chooses rather dubious means, less radical engines of destruction than a man. She opts for poison or drowning, thereby obtaining a slower and smoother escape from this world—an escape that at the same time permits the opportunity for possible resuscitation. In the age of the telephone, the ambulance, and the helicopter, not to speak of the medical marvels of modern hospitals, the female suicide must frequently be considered the result of an overly zealous attempt. Hope, unconscious most of the time, is often rewarded: the doctor, the police, and the precariousness of methods combine to restore the order of things. Is it too bold to suggest, as some legislation does, that some of these "saved" women deserve at least a light reprimand?

Sociologists took charge of the problem of suicide as soon as their science was constituted into a scholarly discipline during the nineteenth century. Their predecessors were largely found in England. In 1757 John Brown published a curious essay, *An Estimate of the Manners and Principles of the Times*, in which he speculated on the causes of suicide; and in 1790 the monumental two-volume work of Charles Moore, *A Full Inquiry into the Subject of Suicide*, appeared. These studies and many others did not fail to influence the literary treatment of the theme. Continental scholars such as Adolph Wagner, Alfred Legoyt, and Enrico Agostino Morselli were among the most intelligent precursors of the celebrated sociologist, Emile Durkheim.[5] Durkheim took advantage of the work of statisticians and ethnopsychologists who had been providing some useful data since the eighteenth century concerning the frequency of suicide in all the nations of Europe. His immediate predecessors, however, formulated untested hypotheses rather than scientific or practical conclusions. Suicides, as their texts indicate, were particularly frequent among prostitutes and dipsomaniacs; they were much more common in times of economic crisis than in the midst of moderate prosperity; they were relatively rare in wartime, or in any other period that engaged the vital forces of the population in major national issues. These premises are still the rule. Statistics and probability theory even allow predictions of future suicides: *The Statistical Abstract of the United States*[6] reports quite prosaically that for forty years the annual number of Americans who grew weary of life was almost constant (slightly declining if related to the rate of population growth): 18,323 for 1930, 21,325 for 1965, 22,630 for 1970. Ethnopsychological laws predict that these will be the approximate figures for years to come. As to the rank the United States occupies in this particular death race, it is plain average.

Until very recent years suicide according to the mores and conventions of society, was regarded as ignominious—the main reason why suicide statistics turn out to be inexact and misleading. An undetermined and indeterminable number of suicides necessarily slip into the category of illnesses and accidents. Furthermore, the concept of suicide is open to interpretations that vary significantly. Since it is usually defined as the act of voluntary and intentional self-destruction, persons killing themselves while not in full possession of their faculties obviously do not commit that act. They are, nonetheless, included in the figures quoted. The problem of suicide prompts still more delicate questions: does a person who sacrifices himself for a cause, or allows himself to die by failing to take preventive measures, or order his own death commit suicide? The notion of suicide, therefore, presents many variations, and these correspond to the thousand variants in the thematological treatment of suicide in literature. In

Wallenstein, Max Piccolomini, seeking death at the head of his troops, shows one of these variations:

> You have chosen your own destruction.
> Those who go with me, be ready to die.[7]

Thomas à Becket, in T. S. Eliot's play, illustrates a kind of passive suicide. As he allows himself to be assassinated without defending himself, it is possible to maintain that he, too, qualifies as a tacit accomplice. Is this not simply another form of voluntary death? In order to justify the murder, the Fourth Knight in Eliot's pageant suggests to his colleagues that since the archbishop foolishly ordered the door of the cathedral to be opened while they were still "inflamed with wrath," they should "render a verdict of suicide while of Unsound Mind." If Thomas is free of guilt, they should be too.

II

Though moralists and theologians of all lands have often debated the question of suicide in a most lively manner, they are far from having reached unanimous conclusions. Contrary to what one might suppose, the opinion that suicide constitutes in itself a sin, an immoral act, does not date back to the earliest Christians. Saint Augustine, whose view was later shared by Thomas Aquinas, was the first to declare with authority that there was no hope for eternal salvation for those guilty of their own death.[8] This judgment was ratified by the second Council of Arles (452), the second Council of Orléans (533), and that of Braga (563). The statements of the Church, however, were not founded on the Holy Scriptures. Yahweh, doubters reasoned, could not be the instigator of a crime when he gave the hopeless Samson enough strength to destroy the temple of the Philistines; Samson crushed himself voluntarily along with the enemies of his people under a mass of stones—a theme treated by Milton and often discussed by his critics. When Jonah requested his companions to throw him into the rolling waves to appease the wrath of the Lord, he was seeking his own death. It was not a simulated suicide since he could not expect to be rescued by some providential Leviathan. The Bible offers no real judgment upon the morality of suicide. No formal condemnation is ever expressed, while some passages could be interpreted as approbatory.[9]

For centuries Christianity was unanimous in condemning suicide, while at the same time it venerated as saints Pelagia and Sophronia, Dominica and her two daughters, and other "martyrs" who killed themselves in order to prevent being raped. These pious women sinned without knowing any better, a valid excuse and a happy fault. It is the Christian version of the Lucretia motif, which later found another thematic reincarnation in Lessing's *Emilia Galotti*. In theory, Catholic philosophy since Augustine, and all other Christian confessions as well, have considered suicide to be immoral. The Albigenses, however, or Cathari—the religious sect founded in central France after the failure of the Crusades—included suicide among their tenets; they were condemned as heretics.

In more modern times some books that have treated the subject are remarkable either for their intransigence or for their heterodox and subtle theories. Two of these works—they both transcend mere theology—are well known to literary critics. In the seventeenth century, John Donne, dean of Saint Paul's in London, accepted the moral legitimacy of voluntary death in his *Biathanatos*.[10] About a hundred years later, in 1736, the Jesuit Johannes Robeck defended a similar viewpoint in a more convincing and systematic manner in his *Exercitatio philosophica de . . . morte voluntaria* [A philosophical treatise on . . . voluntary death].[11] This one work occupied Robeck during his entire life. After composing his thesis and perfecting and refining his manuscript to meet the most precise models of the day, his own arguments in favor of suicide appeared so convincing to the reverend father that he felt compelled to go sailing alone on the Weser River in order to drown himself quietly—thereby demonstrating the personal conviction with which he had written his book. Fortunately for his memory, he had charged a friend with the task of prefacing and publishing his work. Not logic, however, but a strange metaphysical curiosity constrained a lady of London to kill herself, as Louis Racine, the son of Jean, reports.[12] After reading Sherlock's *Immortality of the Soul*, she wanted to determine whether there was really a future life; mankind is still awaiting her news.

In the world of antiquity an even deeper concern about suicide existed than in the Judeo-Christian tradition. Whole generations of Greeks, fascinated by the suicide of Dido and of Sappho, saw the plays of Sophocles and Euripides, many of which included the suicide theme: *Oedipus, Antigone, Heracles, The Supplices*. During the classical period—fifth and fourth century B.C.—Greece was far from favoring suicide, despite these examples from its mythological or legendary tradition; suicide was tolerated and praised, however, in subsequent times, as in the Hellenistic or Alexandrian period—third and second century B.C.

The change from the classical period can only be understood with the historical and sociological context in which it took place. Aeschylus, Aristophanes, Aristotle, and Plato thought of the "polis" as the citizen's universe. Each citizen was precious to the self-enclosed community to which he was essentially committed. Plato (429–347) even found philosophical reasons—shared by Pythagoras—for condemning suicide in his *Laws*, although he foresaw some possible exceptions. After Alexander's conquest of Asia (334–323), public life was increasingly influenced by the cosmopolitan spirit, and the city ceased to be the necessary frame of a Greek's existence. As a result, a decrease in personal responsibility brought about an increase in the number of suicides, an inverse relationship confirmed by modern sociological studies. A similar evolution can be noticed in Rome from the republic to the empire, though great men of both these periods left their names and examples in the history of suicide: Lucretius, Cato, Seneca, Marcus Aurelius.

Of wide diffusion in Greece and Rome, the Stoic philosophy founded by Zeno (ca. 320–250) held suicide as one of its fundamental notions. Death may be desirable or at least a matter of indifference, and suicide may not seem unwise to anyone who considers irrelevant whatever affects the body alone. Death is the harbor for all: a good captain should *steer* his ship toward the harbor rather than reach it by chance—and with delay. There was also the school of the Cyrenaics, which flourished during Zeno's youth; its most illustrious master, Hegesias, explained his doctrine so eloquently that he is said to have driven several of his disciples to suicide. His surname was Peisithanatos, Counselor of Death. In his *Decline and Fall of the Roman Empire* Gibbon shows some practical implications and later results of the Stoic view. He speaks of the "bolder effort" that was required to escape from the tyranny of the caesars. "This effort," he says, "was rendered familiar by the maxims of the Stoics, the example of the bravest Romans, and the legal encouragements of suicide. The bodies of condemned criminals were exposed to public ignominy . . . but, if the victims of Tiberius and Nero anticipated the decree of the prince or senate, their courage and dispatch were recompensed by the applause of the public, the decent honours of burial, and the validity of their testaments."[13] A man like Horace (65–8) granted men not only the right to live but also the right to die. Two lines of the *Ars Poetica* (in Ben Jonson's translation, lines 665 and 666) explain this point of view:

> He that preserves a man against his will
> Doth the same thing with him that would kill him.

It is as criminal to take away life as it is to take away death.

Many cases of self-destruction reported by ancient history offer some insight into contemporary philosophical and political attitudes toward suicide. Socrates, contrary to the often expressed opinion, did not commit that act. He was his own executioner, true, but he was only carrying out the verdict of a political body. The Athenians, who forced him to sip the hemlock, did not join his name to a contradiction in terms, to a voluntary death imposed from without. Better examples can be studied: those of Hamilcar and Hannibal, of virtuous Lucretia and mighty Cleopatra, of Demosthenes and Lucan. After the battle of Philippi, as Plutarch reports, Brutus killed himself, and so did Cassius who used the same dagger he had plunged into Caesar's chest. At his joyous funeral banquet Petronius, the "arbiter elegantiarum," had his veins opened and then, a moment later, closed—to make the pleasure last longer, some claim, while others suspect that he did so to yield momentarily to a last hesitation. Apicius, the famous gourmand, poisoned himself because he reckoned that the two or three millions that remained to his name were not sufficient to nourish an honest man. There is also Nero himself, who, after driving so many people in his entourage to suicide, was himself driven to it; in conformity with Stoic doctrine, he commanded one of his slaves to kill him.

A history of the concept of suicide would also include thinkers like some of the Church fathers and philosophers like Plotinus (205–270), who deeply influenced a number of them, mainly Augustine. In his *Treatise on Suicide* Plotinus rejects the idea of taking one's own life; if a period be allotted to all by fate, he maintains, to anticipate the final hour would be imprudent. The Koran of the Moslems condemns suicide as a crime worse than homicide. Centuries later, however, with the Renaissance, the principles of the Stoics were renewed. The Belgian scholar Justus Lipsius found himself in almost perfect agreement with one of his most famous contemporaries, Montaigne, who, like many ancients, guaranteed to man the fundamental liberty of disposing of his days according to his wishes, though this latitude is reserved notably for those gravely threatend by all sorts of reversals of fortune. Epicurus had already revolted against the illogic of complainers who say it would be better not to have been born. If they spoke thus out of conviction, he queried, why were they still alive? The *Essais* give ample space to the question,[14] the answer to which was simple and obvious: "The sage lives as long as he should, not as long as he can." Nature "has ordained only *one* entrance to life and a hundred thousand exits." "Life depends on the will of others, death upon our own will." Montaigne's remarks directly reflect a text of Seneca who, in his chapter "On Providence," wrote one of the most eloquent apologies for suicide to be found in world literature. Man's complaint is invariably the same: many things happen that are sad and dreadful and hard to bear. Seneca registered God's answer:

> "Because I could not keep you from them I have given your minds armor to withstand them all; bear them manfully. In this respect you may surpass god, for he is exempt from enduring evil, while you rise superior to it. Scorn poverty: no one is as poor as he was at birth. Scorn pain: either it will go away or you will. Scorn death: either it finishes you or it transports you. Scorn Fortune. I have given her no weapon with which to strike your soul. Above all, I have provided that nothing

should detain you against your will. The way out lies open. If you do not wish to fight you may flee. Of all the things which I have intended as necessary for you, therefore, I have made none easier than dying. I have placed the soul on a downgrade, where it is pulled by gravity. Only observe and you will see what a short and speedy road leads to freedom. I have imposed no such long delays at your going as at your coming. Otherwise, if a man were as slow in dying as in being born, Fortune would have held enormous power over you. Let every occasion and every situation teach you how easy it is to renounce Nature and throw her gift in her face. At the very altars and the solemn rites of sacrifice, while you are praying for life, study death. Huge bulls fall by a trivial wound, and the blow of a human hand fells powerful animals. A thin blade severs the joints of the neck, and when the connection between head and neck is so cut, the whole great mass collapses. The soul is not deeply buried and need not even be rooted out with steel; there is no need to probe for the vitals with a penetrating wound, for death lies near the surface. I have appointed no specific spot for the lethal blow; wherever you choose you are vulnerable. The process called dying, whereby the soul departs from the body, is so short and swift as to be imperceptible. Whether the noose strangles the throat, or water suffocates the breath, or the hard ground that breaks the fall crushes the skull, or fire sucked in blocks respiration—whatever the means, it is fast. Are you not ashamed? You have been fearing this so long, and yet it happens so quickly."[15]

Like Socrates, Seneca had been sentenced to kill himself by opening his veins. His former pupil, Nero, was his judge. Seneca's wife wished to share the cruel fate. They cut their arms with the same stroke.

After Montaigne, the two most notable philosophers of the golden age of the Netherlands, Spinoza and Geulincx, treated the subject in several of their works. Thinkers and writers of both the Enlightenment[16] and the Romantic period liked to take up the discussion. Voltaire's definitive opinion on suicide is found in the article "Caton" in his Questions sur l'Encyclopédie. When Voltaire was in England (1726–1729), Addison's Cato (1713) was still one of the most frequently performed tragedies. David Hume, early in his career, composed an Essay on Suicide, which was not published, however, until 1789—as though to tell generations beginning with that fatal year that a man of honor does not lower himself to having his head forced to the guillotine block: Brienne, Condorcet, Babeuf, and Pichegru escaped that fate through suicide. In his essay Hume strives "to restore men to their native liberty by examining all the common arguments against suicide, and show that that action may be free from every imputation of guilt or blame, according to the sentiments of all ancient philosophers."[17] Once the Revolution was over, Madame de Staël started arguing against Hume. After her rather lenient and romantic attitude expressed in her early study, *L'Influence des passions* (1796), she moved to a more orthodox Christian point of view in *Réflexions sur le suicide* (1812). The action of destroying oneself, she concluded, does not in itself bear "any character of devotion." It cannot, consequently, "merit enthusiasm."[18] This, however, is only a mild form of condemnation. And she probably did not foresee that five years later she would die from taking—to whatever extent her free will was involved—too large a dose of opium.

Arthur Schopenhauer reached a conclusion roughly similar to Madame de Staël's in *Die Welt als Wille und Vorstellung* (*The World as Will and Idea*).[19] He notes that suicide is contrary to the moral perfection that man ought to strive for. But whoever kills himself commits only an error, not a crime. Schopenhauer devotes to the theme of suicide the thirteenth chapter of his *Parerga und Paralipomena*, where he disagrees with the Christian attitude. Why should voluntary death be forbidden? he asks; the great number of suicides tends to establish that we are definitely not in "the best of all possible worlds," and that God must have been in error to think, after the days of creation, that his work was good.

Authors unknown today kept the general public informed about the history of suicide, although a work like Stäudlin's *Geschichte der Vorstellungen und Lehren vom Selbstmorde* [The history of the notions and doctrines of suicide], published in Göttingen in 1821, still has more than informative value. The great apologist for suicide in modern times was Friedrich Nietzsche. The title of a section of his *Menschliches, Allzumenschliches* (1878, *Human, All-Too-Human*) reads: "Vom vernünftigen Tod" ("On reasonable death"), and that of a chapter in his *Also sprach Zarathustra* (1883, *Thus Spake Zarathustra*): "Vom freien Tod" ("On free death"). Almost all twentieth-century philosophers have touched upon the question of suicide. With the exception of those who relate their system to Christian tradition, like Karl Barth and Gabriel Marcel, all of them seem to agree that suicide properly defined should be legally permissible and does not violate ethical canons.

Because enough people came to believe that suicide not only affected public order and welfare, but frequently conflicted with the basic attitudes or moral principles of certain societies, it became a matter for legislation. It was readily classified, under the influence of Christianity, as murder pure and simple. It was therefore necessary that tribunals punish it. The early penalties devised were the mutilation of the body, confiscation of goods and properties, and burial without holy rites (*sepultura asinina seu canina*).[20] This attitude, which is frequently reflected in most literatures of the Middle Ages, had scarcely changed by the eighteenth century. To draw a few examples from the French, Montesquieu, in letter 76 of his *Lettres persanes*, felt that the matter deserved discussion,[21] as did the Abbé Prévost in *L'Histoire de M. Cleveland*, Toussaint in *Les Moeurs*, and d'Argens in his *Lettres juives*. Jean-Jacques Rousseau treated the ethics of suicide in two letters of his *Nouvelle Héloïse* (part 3, letters 21 and 22) but did not consider the legal aspect of the question.

The idea of prosecuting a suicide may appear absurd today. Schopenhauer already observed: "What punishment can frighten a man who seeks death? And if we punish an attempt at suicide, we are punishing the clumsiness through which the attempt failed."[22] We recognize here the argument already employed by Beccaria in the thirty-second chapter of the book that made his fame, *Dei delitti e delle pene* (1764, *On Crimes and Punishments*). To punish a suicide, Beccaria remarks, is to punish either an unfeeling corpse or its innocent offspring. It is to whip a statue. Until very recently traces of these antiquated juridical notions could still be observed here and there in the corpus of laws across all of Europe. The United Kingdom, for example, did not abolish measures against suicide until 1961, some two centuries after Prussia and France abrogated punishment for suicide in 1751 and 1790 respectively. In the United States, suicide was a crime under the common law. In those jurisdictions, few in number, that have not abolished common-law crimes, suicide is still criminal.[23]

III

Crucial as it is in the history of human behavior and thought, the problem of suicide most keenly concerns the literary critic, since the Rohstoff of literature necessarily deals with sociological, psychological, moral, and philosophical aspects of human life. Suicide provides a frequent theme or basic motif in works of all literary genres.

In literary history and criticism the question of suicide arises in the most diverse contexts. It often becomes a primary concern of a biographer, for an impressive number of authors have voluntarily killed themselves. The English poet Thomas Chatterton took arsenic in his garret in Holborn, a suicide reenacted in the play of Vigny and in the opera of Leoncavallo—both entitled *Chatterton*. Benjamin Robert Haydon, author and painter, cut his throat in his studio; Thomas Lovell Beddoes, author of *Death's Jest-Book*, chose poison for his suicide, and so did Paul Lafargue, socialist writer and son-in-law of Karl Marx; and Gérard de Nerval was found hanged one pale winter morning from the grating of a courtyard. Other examples abound—the French Chamfort, the Spaniard Mariano José de Larra, the Russian Mayakovski, the Austrian Stefan Zweig, the German Heinrich von Kleist, the Italian Cesare Pavese, the English Virginia Woolf, the American Ernest Hemingway—without counting those who, feeling the temptation, have, according to the verse of Stéphane Mallarmé, escaped suicide, or, in his own words, have "Victorieusement fui le suicide beau," or those who have been discouraged in their project by one of Wolfgang Borchert's most prosaic statements: ". . . ich scheiss auf deinen Selbstmord," which means: "I couldn't care less about your suicide."[24]

These deaths, however, are the concerns of literary biography. Criticism, on the contrary, should be primarily occupied with the function or relevance of suicide in particular works. After antiquity, Dante was the first to present the literary potentialities of voluntary death in a work of genius. Those who, in the words of the *Divine Comedy*, had caused their own death out of their free will are now transformed into trees shading the nests of wicked harpies. In the thirteenth canto of the *Inferno*, the poet, remembering the hero of the *Aeneid* and his visit to Dido beyond the Styx, penetrates into this lugubrious "forest of the suicides," where those who rebel against themselves and their gods reside. On the other hand, Cato—Dante, at times, likes casuistry—is not to be found in hell: he is the warder of *Purgatorio*. Petrarch, although living in the French Provence and rather close to the Albigenses—for whom suicide was legitimate—never sympathized with their ideas in his writings. When he was tempted to put an end to his days on earth out of love for his Laura, he was saved, as he asserts in his twenty-ninth sonnet to her, by this reflection: he would only be exchanging his present unhappiness for the greater miseries of eternal sorrows.

Yet the official Christian doctrine on suicide did not prevent the development in the fifteenth century of the theme of Romeo and Juliet, the unhappy lovers whose memory, from Masuccio to Keller, has been perpetuated across the ages with singular vigor. Shakespeare, who staged their tragedy in 1595, wrote many other plays in which there were suicides: *Anthony and Cleopatra* (also the theme of Dryden's *All for Love*), *Othello*, and *Julius Caesar*, where the suicide takes place behind the curtain; Shakespeare's *The Rape of Lucrece* also has suicide as a theme. Corneille's heroes kill themselves in *Médée* and *Rodogune*, Mairet's in *Sophonisbe* and *Cléopâtre;* Rotrou wrote *Crisante* and *Antigone*. Racine, in *La Thébaïde; ou, les frères ennemis* succeeded in convincing four characters to willingly shuffle off their mortal coils. English drama and perhaps more strikingly German and French took up the suicide theme again in later periods. In the final act of Schiller's *Die Räuber* Franz Moor hastens to join his forefathers by strangling himself with the cord of his hat—quite a performance. One of the most dramatic scenes composed by Schiller is in the fourth act of *Maria Stuart*, where Mortimer, the heroine's lover, stabs himself for no reason other than mere love.

Victor Hugo also has a feeling for this sort of tragic death: Doña

Sol shares the phial that Hernani is condemned to drink; for, in the theatre, characters may retire from the world just to astound the spectator. Hugo delights in serving some of his heroes death-dealing beverages before sending his audience off to the café: Guanhamara poisons himself at the end of *Les Burgraves* and Ruy Blas, before the curtain falls, swallows the poison cup in one gulp. Suicide sometimes surprises the survivors, at least on the stage, where it happens to serve as a deus ex machina; but often it is extensively prepared for with thematological intentions.

This preparation for the final deed is usually finer and subtler in the novel than in the drama, where characters necessarily develop in a rather rapid series of events and where, as a rule, only concise psychological analyses are possible. A glance at English literature of the Restoration and the Enlightenment shows Aphra Behn treating the theme of suicide in *Oroonoko; or, the Royal Slave*, a work that dates back to 1688. The reasons a savage advances before committing suicide—death rather than slavery—differ markedly from those an Englishman might present. A Londoner, according to the fourth letter of Goldsmith's *Citizen of the World*, "dies when he fancies the world has ceased to esteem him," a statement that could be related to Boswell's fourteenth *Hypochondriack* essay. But there are thousands of novels dealing with suicide: it plays a secondary role in F. Scott Fitzgerald's *The Great Gatsby*, and a major one in Oscar Wilde's *The Picture of Dorian Gray* and Bryant's *Monument Mountain*. In literatures other than Anglo-Saxon, it is featured in Foscolo's *Ultime lettere di Jacopo Ortis* (*The Last Letters of Jacopo Ortis*) echoed in Leopardi's poem *Gentilezza del morir*. And with what poignancy is the suicide of Anna Karenina depicted, and that of the heroes of *Il trionfo della morte* by Gabriele D'Annunzio, and that of Jean Cocteau's *Les enfants terribles*.

Lyric poetry has also availed itself of the theme, which appears, to quote a few examples from English writers, in the sixteenth song of Young's *Night Thoughts;* in a poem, *The Suicide*, by Thomas Warton, and in another, *Against Despair*, by his brother Joseph; in the nineteenth century, in Keats's *Ode to a Nightingale*, Tennyson's *The Two Voices*, Matthew Arnold's *Empedocles on Etna;* and in our times, in Siegfried Sassoon's *Suicide in the Trenches*.

These and other writers have centered the most diverse works on suicide, and many of them, especially in modern times, show man's liberation from his feelings of entrapment and bondage. Freely chosen, death represents the supreme proof of man's free will and superiority to blind destiny. In Schiller's *Die Braut von Messina* (*The Bride of Messina*), for example, Don Cesar proudly states, "Free death alone breaks the chain of fate,"[25] before stabbing himself in the final scene. And Kirillov, in Dostoevski's *The Possessed*, resolved to put a bullet into his brain declaring that by killing himself he was going to prove his absolute independence. Suicide became part of Karl Jaspers' existentialist system: it represented the ultimate triumph of men enslaved by modern society. Quite a few contemporary authors see in the possible choice between life and death a source, even a condition of human happiness.[26]

Thematological treatment of suicide can also be traced in non-European literatures. Suicides occur notably in eighteenth-century Chinese fiction, in *Hsing shih yin yüan chuan* [The tale of conjugal union to arouse the world] and in *Hung lou mêng* [Dream of the Red Chamber] written respectively by P'u Song ling (1640–1715) and Ts'ao Chan (ca. 1717–1763). In Japanese literature suicide was most frequently treated by the dramatist Chikamatsu Monzaemon (1653–1725).[27] Even a very large book would not suffice to encompass a theme with such strongly marked variations. We shall, therefore, now concentrate upon its treatment in two famous novels.

☆

Incontestably, *Werther* remains the classic novel of suicide.[28] When it was first published it was stigmatized as the major cause of that wave of "suicidomania," which became apparent then and swept over Europe during the Romantic period. The origins of the "Werther fever" seem to coincide both with the publication of Goethe's book and with the computation of statistics by early sociologists. In the last quarter of the eighteenth century, they endeavored for the first time to record all cases of suicide reported to them. Before then, the number of real suicides must have been markedly different from the official figures, based as they were on occasional estimates; and since then, as we have indicated above, a degree of discrepancy still exists. This is to say that suicide was presumably as frequent before *Werther* as after; instead of producing this wave, Goethe's work probably was carried by it and owed its success to it. Germans died of Werther fever long before the hero of Wahlheim appeared on the literary scene. Dozens of books and booklets against suicide appeared in Germany during the fifty years preceding the publication of Goethe's novel, their authors clearly motivated by the conditions surrounding them. As a result, at least two later generations recognized their own sentiments in *Werther*. Goethe, in other words, did not render suicide fashionable; rather, as an expression of the spirit of his time, he succeeded in crystallizing particular feelings and applying them to a tragedy that each reader thought might well be or might become his own.

Preoccupations similar to those observed in Germany existed in other countries. In 1761 Appiano Buonafide and in 1773 Jean Dumas epitomized their fellow citizens' concern about the suicide problem by publishing *Istoria critica e filosofica del suicidio* and *Traité du suicide ou du meurtre de soi-même*, and we have already mentioned

Johannes Robeck's (1736) and John Brown's (1757) works. The year Werther's story was first published, in 1774, The Royal Humane Society was founded in London "for the recovery of persons apparently drowned," obviously not only after a shipwreck on the Thames. Many other facts prevent us from being surprised that Goethe's work was favorably received in Great Britain.[29] Here, too, the theme of the novel matched a sociological phenomenon that, in turn, favored the success of the book; in this instance, as in so many situations in human existence, effects and causes are interwoven and often mysteriously blended and intermixed.

The primary motif of *Werther* is easily identified: he who can renounce love, loves not; he who has to renounce it, renounces life, commits suicide. The relationship between motif and motivation is also apparent: a frustrated love that leads to self-destruction defines Werther's situation and prompts the plot. The primary motif is supported by a series of incidents or events and by numerous reflections, allusions, and images, which give the entire work an intense thematological unity. In the first letter of this epistolary novel, the hero refers to his failure to respond to the love once proffered by a certain Leonore. The reader understands that this untold story took a fatal turn for the girl. From the beginning of the novel, then, Goethe sounds the tragic note of the composition: death. The thematological elements multiply: words, phrases, analogies referring to suicide. When Lotte plays the piano, Werther becomes conscious of suicide as the solution if his love should be rejected. A few days later, he recalls a strange tale, that of the *Magnetenberg*, the mountain of Magnets. Every boat that approached it, according to the legend, was suddenly deprived of all its iron parts; at the foot of the mountain, the bottom of the river was strewn with cadavers and jetsam. The magnet represents Lotte, the fiancée of Albert. The problem is treated more directly in the letters of August 8 and 12.

The literary devices at the service of the motif are used in the most diverse manner; there are, for example, recurrent images, like that of our earth as man's prison. Werther never ceases complaining that he is enclosed and circumscribed (*eingeschränkt*), just as Goethe himself does at times, for instance, in the little poem *Einschränkung*. Only death can free Werther from the barriers (*Schranken*) that surround him.[30] One day he speaks of flowers gathered into a bouquet and thrown into the river that carries them off (August 10); on another, he describes a solitary stroller who plunges into the turbulent water and has his body crashed against the rocky shores (August 15). Images foreshadow his eventual death: in Werther's words, only the tomb will be able to put an end to his ills (August 30). There are also simple exclamations: "And now I could plunge a dagger into my heart!" (March 15) and striking comparisons that again suggest death as the remedy for man's enslavement: horses biting their reins to catch their breath; a man opening his veins to enjoy eternal liberty (March 16). Some events at Wahlheim are understood as allegories: a peasant lad who acknowledges no rival and resorts to the ultimate, the absolute solution. "Read this account, Wilhelm," Werther concludes, "and imagine that it might well be the story of your friend!" (September 4). Any Ossianic hero—Werther reads to Lotte a long passage from Macpherson's work—must have enough courage and friendship to fulfill the wish of a chief who has become unable to fight, even if that wish is to plunge the sword into the body of his chief. As Werther approaches his final decision he speaks, on the third of November, of the hope to awaken no more. Man, he reckons, is only happy when he loses his mind, when he becomes mad like "der glückliche Unglückliche"—the happy unhappy one—or dies. Our hero ends by declaring: "I have the courage to die" (December 12). Melancholy does not deprive him of the power of action. "It would be better for me that I should go," he says in the same letter, and in fact he will voluntarily pass away. In his farewell letter to Lotte, he writes: "I want to die." Throughout the novel the reader has thus been prepared for a necessary end: one theme and one motif pervade the entire work, and Werther's suicide can be explained not only psychologically but philosophically, morally, and artistically as well.

Goethe is careful not to include in his book all the classical arguments in favor of suicide. He invokes only two of them—not those that tradition discusses most frequently, but those that are in perfect harmony with the character of the hero and the circumstances of the plot. The first argument is that of a psychologist and philosopher. Werther is the victim of a fatal malady. His troubles do not result from temporary misfortune from which he might easily recover. In ordinary life people usually overcome their feeling of despair because they spontaneously recognize that the cause of their unhappiness is transitory. Many suicide victims, however, seem to succumb to such a momentary feeling. Had they resisted their impulses, they might—after a period of readjustment—have resumed their quiet or even happy lives. Werther's despair is of another nature. His desire to die is not an ephemeral temptation but a disposition of the spirit—a kind of illness. Because of the disease he must commit suicide. Suicide results from his mental affliction in much the same way that a sneeze results from a cold or a fever from influenza or death from leukemia; such reasoning recurs in several of Werther's letters (August 12 and 28; December 4). Consequently, it is absurd to hold Werther any more responsible for his death than one would hold a cancer patient responsible for his. In psychoanalytic terms, Werther's death instinct predominates over his will to live. Once his physical and emotional ills become more than he can withstand, and once he realizes that he has the power to end his suffering, suicide inevitably follows. Had Goethe insisted on this argument alone, he would have had to discuss the question of Werther's liberty, suicide being voluntary self-destruction.

But to justify his suicide, Werther presents a second argument, of a moral, religious, and biblical order. Indeed, *Die Leiden des jungen Werther* may be conceived as a value allegory of the passion of Christ. To support the analogy one has first to consider the numerous quotations from Scripture and the striking allusions to the events surrounding the drama of Golgotha. The letter of the fifteenth of November directly suggests this order of ideas, and that of the thirtieth of the same month takes away any remaining doubts concerning the religious attitude of the main figure. We are dealing with a kind of mystical suicide: "Father whom I know not! Who wert once wont to fill my soul, but Who now hidest Thy face from me! Call me back to Thee! Be silent no longer! Thy silence cannot sustain a soul which thirsts after Thee. What man, what father, could be angry with a son for returning to him unexpectedly, for falling on his neck and exclaiming: Here I am again, my father! Forgive me if I have shortened my journey to return before the appointed time!"[31] This is much the same thought as Alzire's who says in Voltaire's play, written almost forty years before *Werther*:

> What crime is it, before this jealous God,
> To hasten the moment he prepares for us all?[32]

The sacrifice of Werther will be accomplished in his room, converted into a kind of private chapel: the Bible or the missal will be represented by the work of one of the first heralds of the new literature, the *Emilia Galotti* of Lessing, a kind of romantic gospel; and the Eucharistic elements, the holy bread and wine, will be on the altar.[33] Like Christ, Werther returns to his Father: his suicide, far from being immoral, is a religious act.

The frequency and insistency with which motif devices recur throughout the novel is partly explained by the fact that *Young Werther* reflects one of Goethe's most memorable personal experiences. Goethe had just been promoted to doctor of law when, in 1772, he went to Wetzlar, seat of the supreme court of the empire. There he fell in love with Charlotte—or Lotte—Buff, became acquainted with her fiancé, Johann Christian Kestner—Albert in the novel—and saw again one of his former fellow students, Carl Wilhelm Jerusalem. After Miss Buff's refusal to fully reciprocate his feelings, Goethe abruptly left Wetzlar in grief and bitter disappointment, while Jerusalem, who also experienced an unhappy love, committed suicide. Goethe, as we can see, took the essential raw material for his novel, not only for its plot, but even for its motif, simple and intense as it is, from his own life and from his immediate surroundings.[34] Both these sources merge, most harmoniously, with Jerusalem as Goethe's perfect substitute in the second part of the work: Goethe is rebuked by

Fräulein Buff, and Jerusalem, rebuked by another lady, draws for both disappointed lovers the deadly consequences.[35] This basic accord greatly helps to clarify the striking unity of *Werther*, which is achieved by the pervasiveness of a series of thematological elements, all of which center around the primary motif.

❧

In French literature *Madame Bovary* remains the novel of suicide par excellence.[36] Even though its author was an enthusiastic admirer of Goethe, prompting a French writer and critic to dare to say that "Goethe est le générateur de Flaubert,"[37] *Madame Bovary* can hardly be compared with *Werther*.[38] The thematological function of suicide is fundamentally different from one novel to the other, though Flaubert's inspiration, it is true, is also somehow rooted in experience. His experience, however, is not personal in the same sense that Goethe's is, and the fact that his friend, Maxime Du Camp is the author of *Mémoires d'un suicidé* (1853) cannot be put to any immediate connection with the Bovary theme. The most that can be said is that Flaubert, as he states in his *Oeuvres de jeunesse*, was "born with the desire to die," just as every man is, according to Freud. Emma's death could have echoed this general desire, which explains nothing. The kind of death Emma had to suffer is not immediately related to the basic meaning of the story. Wertherism has necessary connections with suicide, Bovaryism only loose ones. In one work, suicide is part of the motif, in the other, part of the theme. This is not to say that a motif always directly relates to the author's life. Despite a great number of exceptions, however, this seems to be a kind of pragmatic rule, or at least a frequent occurrence.

In *Madame Bovary* three episodes announce the denouement. The first takes place at the Bovary's. Emma has just received from Rodolphe, her lover, the letter putting an end to their affair. She reads it, supported against a window ledge in the attic. Then she looks around her, "with the wish that the earth might crumble into pieces. Why not end it all? What restrained her? She was free. She advanced, looked at the paving-stones, saying to herself, 'Come on! Come on!' "[39] But Charles, her husband, calls her to dinner, and the trance is over.

The second episode is more directly bound to particular circumstances of Emma's suicide. As soon as the Bovarys arrived at Yonville, the main setting of the novel, they make the acquaintance of Mr. Homais, the pharmacist. It is thus quite natural that Flaubert should describe his shop. The insistence, however, with which certain details are presented causes the reader to guess spontaneously that he is being familiarized with the scene of subsequent important events. This account is at the beginning of the second book. When the third starts, once again, we stop in Homais' shop, and this time for a passage of four pages. Emma is asked to see the pharmacist before returning home from Rouen. Homais is in the process of admonishing his apprentice, Justin, who dared to put jam in a dish that had been standing close to a jar of arsenic. Both Emma and the reader learn where the key to the "laboratory" is kept, and even the exact location of the poison: "In the corner, to the left on the third shelf." When the fatal hour sounds, Emma will go once more to the pharmacy: she will persuade Justin to let her enter the "laboratory" without Homais' knowledge. In Flaubert's words: "She went straight to the third shelf, so well did her memory guide her, seized the blue jar, tore out the cork, plunged in her hand and withdrawing it full of a white powder she began eating it."[40] This memory that guides her betrays premeditation.

The third incident occurs when Madame Bovary is about to start a new love affair with Léon, then a clerk in Rouen, a few hours ride from Yonville. Charles invites his wife to the theater at Rouen, which is giving *Lucia di Lammermoor*, Donizetti's opera based on Walter Scott's *The Bride of Lammermoor*. Since Scott ranked among Emma's favorite authors,[41] the novel helps her to understand the libretto—in spite of many differences—and her heart vibrates to the spectacle of Lucia's unhappy love for Edgar. Forged letters convince Lucia of Edgar's unfaithfulness, and, as a result of the deception, she marries Arthur. After the wedding ceremony, she learns the truth, loses her mind, assassinates Arthur on the very night of their nuptials, and kills herself. Edgar, unable to survive this catastrophe, also commits suicide. Flaubert presents Emma attending the play with Charles and Léon, faced between Arthur and Edgar, as it were. She had not united her life to some great soul, to a generous heart—like Lucia to Edgar's—but preferred "the soilings of marriage and the disillusions of adultery."[42] She recognizes on the stage the reason for her own pain. But before Donizetti's lovers die in a cloud of coloratura arias, before Edgar sings his "morir voglio" and plunges the dagger into his heart, the three spectators leave the theater, which has become filled with "intolerable heat." Emma's suicide is put off until later. It will take place a few months hence at Yonville, in the Bovary home. These three episodes are really meaningful only in the light of the final act, which they foreshadow. Emma is now likely to commit suicide. The reason, however, has still to be seen in the theme, in the story as it is told, and in the plot as it develops, not in the motif, that is, not in the ultimate sense of the work.

The reason for Emma's suicide leads us back to the basic thematological differences between Goethe's and Flaubert's works. Throughout his novel, Flaubert prepares the tragic ending, but with not more than hints to the specific form that it is to assume. In his first plan of the novel he noted: "Illness. Her death." The reworked plan indicates: "Suicide. She will steal some arsenic from the pharmacist. Agony . . . Death."[43] This change in plot construction clearly

shows that Emma's suicide is not of a primary and essential thematological relevance. Furthermore, *Madame Bovary*, in contrast
with *Werther*, nowhere sets forth a philosophy of suicide. Nor is there
any discussion of the moral problem of whether man has the right to
dispose of his own life as he sees fit. While Goethe's hero reveals
tendencies that from the beginning of the story drive him inevitably
toward his ultimate fate, the destiny of Flaubert's heroine, apart from
the scenes just described, is far from being so inexorable; Emma's
destiny does not possess the same sense of necessity, the same logic of
certainty. The German novel accumulates a considerable mass of
"evidence," indirect, to be sure, but as convincing as an accumulation
of indexes in a courtroom; they can be seen in the development of the
main characters, the succession of events and images, the organization of symbols, the multiplication of allusions, and the continuous
crescendo of sentiments. All these elements lead to the conclusion that
Werther must either commit suicide or defy the logical, unifying
thread of the work, and deprive it of its ultimate meaning as well.
Any other ending is excluded. In *Madame Bovary*, on the contrary,
many other alternatives are possible. However strong the reader's
suspicions are concerning Emma's end, suicide clearly does not serve
the motif of the story.

Suicide bestows a remarkable tension on Flaubert's work. The
motif, however, only demands Emma's fall, not her death; her psychological development, in other words, could have admitted other conclusions, probably less effective artistically, but logically possible.[44]
It would have been permissible for Flaubert to have had recourse to
solutions analogous to those chosen by his successors, like Theodor
Fontane, Leopoldo Alas, Sinclair Lewis, and George Moore, the
authors respectively of *Effi Briest*, *La Regenta*, *Main Street*, and *A
Mummer's Wife*. An author can bring misery to his characters in
many ways: Emma might even have multiplied her escapades; she
might have died in the most ordinary way, just as any other lady of
small virtue. But Flaubert's solution, like Goethe's, lays stress upon
the tragic element. It should be observed, nonetheless, that two conceptions of fatality separate the two novels: in both the reader knows
that the leading character is destined to perish; in *Werther*, however,
he also knows *how* the hero will meet his fate. This "how" is essential
in *Werther*, and suicide thereby becomes part of the motif; in *Madame Bovary* it is just one possible "how": it belongs to Stoff. In
antiquity two deities swayed human life, Ananke (necessity, fate),
and Tyche (chance, fortune). Ananke decided on Werther's death,
Tyche on Emma's.

❧❦

In the preceding pages a basic principle of thematology has been
illustrated: a single idea or action—and, consequently, the typo-

logical performer of that action—may have diverse literary functions in different works. To define the function of an idea or action is equivalent to deciding whether it falls into the category of raw material, theme, or motif.

In many works suicide appears as a fact or notion independent of any epic narration, dramatic plot, or lyric emotion: it is Rohstoff, like a subject of inquiry in psychology, sociology, religion, or legislation. Rohstoff, however, is essential to the study of literature. Without knowing the many implications of suicide in all sectors of human thought and activity, no suicide theme or motif can be fully understood. Similarly, all other concepts related to human existence have to be put into their proper context. The study of literature cannot be separated from philosophy, history, ethics, and aesthetics.

Suicide Stoffe are plentiful, with the drowned lady, to note briefly one variation, as one of the most frequent ones. The literary possibilities of that theme—used also in *Werther* (letter of August 12)— have been exploited by scores of writers. In the first pages of *La Peau de chagrin* (*The Wild Ass's Skin*), Balzac writes: "Each suicide is a sublime poem of melancholy. Where will you find, in the ocean of literature, a surviving book that can equal the genius of this snippet: *Yesterday, at four o'clock, a young woman threw herself into the Seine from the top of the Pont des Arts.* In the face of this Parisian laconism, dramas, novels, everything grows pale."[45] Shakespeare's Ophelia, tragically destroyed by a sweet madness, drowns herself while seeking to decorate a willow with flowers. At present, in the majority of Western literatures, the drowned lady, decked in the splendors of an unconquerable love, is surrounded with an aureole of pathetic lyricism that a masculine suicide, unless performed by a member of the Werther tribe, almost always lacks. Ophelia captivated the imagination of quite a few painters and a considerable number of poets. Stefan George takes up the theme in three poems; Thomas Hood in *The Bridge of Sighs* (1844); Rimbaud in *Ophélie* (1870); and Brecht in *Vom ertrunkenen Mädchen* (1927). And before the Parisians had their miniature Eiffel Towers on sale in all the souvenir stores and gift shops of their city, the tourist could acquire the "Inconnue de la Seine," the mortuary mask of a girl whose body had been fished out of the river on a foggy winter morning.

As to the suicide Motiv, its use in *Werther* supersedes its use in all other novels, with the possible exception of *Anna Karenina*. A comparison between these two works would show how diversely a concept may become part of a literary theme or motif. However, the thematological study of suicide also corroborates a statement already made: motifs are limited in number; themes may abound.

A study of concepts and phenomena that are as important as that of suicide also shows that literature, if not confined to technical analyses, expresses man's philosophy and image of the world. Literature is the most direct and most adequate reflection of an entire civilization. As for the concept of suicide, despite numerous philosophers and moralists, the preachings of the Stoic school, and many examples of how self-destruction can be effected, the peoples of the Western world have long conceived of life as the toy of destiny. Man is born by chance and he dies by chance. Through technological and scientific innovation, however, twentieth-century man has left fewer aspects of his life to the workings of fate, and has brought more of his environment and more of his destiny under his control. He is able to meet the threat of exploding population—since the natural checks, epidemics and famine, are almost eliminated—through birth control and family planning. Moreover, in his effort to deprive chance of its spoils, he is moving toward greater control over a wider area of his experience by subjecting death to his own will. In other words, the time may come when the individual can himself decide to prolong a still meaningful life or shorten the last stage of his decay. Voluntary euthanasia or the painless suicide of the hopelessly lonely and incurably sick has already become a subject for heated discussion in both political circles and society at large—and also the theme of a most sarcastic satire, *The Suicide Academy* (1968), by Daniel Stern. Sooner or later, it seems, medicine will give the legal assent to those tormented by the quest for death. Blind destiny loses its empire over birth and death. To be or not to be: that is a question to be answered by two pills.

The idea of personal control of one's own death is far from new. In his *Utopia* Thomas More presents a community in which mercy killing has been regulated by law and in which unhappy and unhealthy persons may commit suicide provided permission has been granted by the state. "If a person suffers from a disease which is both incurable and continually excrutiating, the priests and magistrates come and urge him to make the decision not to nourish such a painful disease any longer. He is now unequal to all the duties of life, a burden to himself and to others, having really outlived himself. They tell him not to hesitate to die when life is such a torment, but in confidence of a better life after death, to deliver himself from the scourge and imprisonment of living or let others release him. This, they say, he would do wisely, for by death he would lose nothing but suffering."[46] This view, which long ago had been adopted by Plato,[47] was expressed throughout the centuries by a few men known for their wisdom and integrity. They have finally provoked the first fundamental change in people's attitude toward suicide. Today suicide does not receive nearly the same degree of censure it would have engendered in most European countries just a few years ago.

Like suicide, many themes and motifs treated in literature are so universal, and so deeply affect man's most profound concerns with his own existence, that the historical analyses of such themes and motifs

—Stoff- und Motivgeschichte in the original sense of the word—may prompt conclusions that demand major modifications of human life and thought. Such conclusions, however, transcend literature proper, for they belong to the study of culture itself.

With these chapters we have scanned our comparatistic horizon and have determined the four cardinal points that symbolize the four categories of comparatistic inquiry, focusing on each of them for a while. Our intention was not to scrutinize all corners of the literary universe, but rather to become aware of the four basic types of comparatistic problems by examining two or three examples in the four sections. Our division of the entire comparatistic matter into four parts does not imply that there are sharp borderlines between them. The study of the analogies between Rousseau's doctrine and eighteenth-century North American thought might at the same time permit us to trace common themes and motifs in a specific body of French and American works, and the research on the sonnet as a literary genre could also lead to conclusions on definite influences. After all, there are not only four but thirty-two points of the compass, all of which, however, refer to some cardinal points. If after perusing these pages, the reader can better orient himself on the vast ocean of our civilization, they will have served their main purpose, which is to introduce comparative literature.

Notes

TITLES are usually cited in their original language. In the *text* foreign titles are translated in parentheses unless readily understood even by a monolingual English-speaking reader. I also mention in parentheses translations that are easily available. In the *notes* foreign titles are not translated.

All translations of foreign passages are mine unless otherwise noted. Quotations in a foreign language in the *text*, if not understandable with a slight smattering of the language quoted, are translated in parentheses. Longer quotations, except those that are paraphrastically explained, are translated in the *notes*.

A large percentage of the notes are annotated bibliographically.

1. The Historical Perspective

1. Chaucer was bilingual. His personal circumstances led him to write in English rather than in Norman-French. Petrarch wrote extensively in Latin, but today his fame rests mainly on his *Canzoniere*. The first authority to be consulted on Chaucer is F. N. Robinson. See especially his edition of *The Complete Works of Geoffrey Chaucer* (Boston and New York, 1933), which has an extensive scholarly and bibliographical apparatus.

2. "You should welcome." This is the first line of the poem in which one also finds a delimitation of German territory: "From the Elbe to the Rhine and Hungary." See Friedrich Heer, *Mittelalter* (Zurich, 1961), trans. Janet Sondheimer, *The Medieval World: Europe 1100–1350* (London, 1962).

249

3. "Rien ne m'a induyt que l'affection naturelle envers ma patrie." One of the most recent studies on the genesis of modern patriotism is Jean Lestocquoy's *Histoire du patriotisme en France, des origines à nos jours* (Paris, 1968). See also, Rabindranath Tagore, *Nationalism* (New York, 1917), and Hans Kohn, *The Idea of Nationalism: A Study in Its Origins and Background* New York, 1944). The question of nationalism is connected with that of races, which has been studied by Friedrich Otto Hertz, *Rasse und Kultur* (1905), trans. A. S. Levetus and W. Entsz, *Race and Civilzation*, rev. ed. (New York, 1970). Two important eighteenth-century documents on nationalism are Henry St. John Bolingbroke's *A Letter on the Spirit of Patriotism* (1736) and Johann Georg von Zimmermann's *Von dem Nationalstolz* (1758, *On National Pride*, translator unknown).

4. Still, in 1650 Racine, on a trip to the Rhone Valley, noticed that in Lyons a language other than that of Paris was spoken, and in Valence he felt as much in need of an interpreter as a Frenchman in Moscow. See Sanche de Gramont, *The French: Portrait of a People* (New York, 1969), chap. 5, "The Universal Tongue." In the course of history, some languages have again transcended their national borders. Not only do they define a nation, or nations, but they play eminent roles in international affairs, cultural and economic. In 1784 the Comte de Rivarol published his famous *Discours sur l'universalité de la langue française* at a time when Italian was still a major language at the court of Vienna and in music. Today English has strong positions on five continents and in business, and prophets already seem to know the importance of Chinese in tomorrow's world.

5. "The Name and Nature of Comparative Literature," in *Comparatists at Work, Studies in Comparative Literature*, ed. Stephan G. Nichols, Jr. and Richard B. Vowles (Waltham, Mass., 1968, p. 15).

6. See Michel Devèze, *L'Europe et le monde à la fin du XVIIIᵉ siècle* (Paris, 1970).

7. See Arturo Farinelli, "Gl'influssi letterari e l'insuperbire delle nazioni," in *Mélanges d'histoire littéraire générale et comparée offerts à Fernand Baldensperger*, 2 vols. (Paris, 1930), 1:271–290.

8. Characteristically enough, small countries have paid a relatively high tribute to the international study of literature. Denmark, as Brandes shows, Holland (e.g., Jerrit Kalff, *Westeuropaeische letterkunde*, 2 vols. [Groningen, 1923–1924]), Hungary (e.g., Mihály Babits' history of European literature in the nineteenth and twentieth centuries, originally published in Budapest, 1935; German translation, *Geschichte der europäischen Literatur im 19. und 20. Jahrhundert* [Bern, 1947]), and Switzerland (e.g., the works of Fritz Strich and Walter Muschg) seem to be more keenly aware of the artificiality of literary divisions according to nations.

9. *Portraits contemporains*, new ed. rev., 5 vols. (Paris, 1889–1891), 3:367; *Nouveaux lundis*, 13 vols. (Paris, 1870–1914), 13:184.

10. Quoted by Claude Pichois and André-M. Rousseau, *La Littérature comparée* (Paris, 1967), p. 15 and by René Wellek, "The Name and Nature of Comparative Literature," in *Comparatists at Work, Studies in Comparative Literature*, ed. Stephan G. Nichols, Jr. and Richard B. Vowles (Waltham, Mass., 1968), p. 7. Also in 1968, Ulrich Weisstein published his *Einführung in die Verlgleichende Literaturwissenschaft* (Stuttgart), a book that includes an extensive study on the history of comparative literature

(pp. 22–88). Simon Jeune gives a lengthy bibliographical description of the *Cours de littérature comparée;* see his *Littérature générale et littérature comparée* (Paris, 1968), p. 35, note 13.

11. A bibliography of similar works would include Johann Gottfried Eichhorn's *Allgemeine Geschichte der Cultur und Litteratur des neueren Europa,* 2 vols. (Göttingen, 1796–1799), and his *Geschichte der Litteratur von ihren Anfängen bis auf die neueste Zeit,* 3 vols. (Göttingen, 1805–1811).

12. Villemain's *Cours de littérature,* however, seems of somewhat mediocre critical value, a "banal compendium digne d'un rhétoriqueur," according to Baudelaire. *Critique littéraire et musicale,* comp. Claude Pichois (Paris, 1961), p. 407.

13. See Bibliography, p. 306.

14. Giovanni Battista Vico is one of the founders of ethnic psychology. See Jules Chaix-Ruy, "J.-B. Vico, précurseur de la psychologie sociale et de la psychologie des peuples," *Revue de Psychologie des Peuples* 24, no. 3 (1969): 291–322. Related to the concerns of comparative studies are those of the *Review of National Literatures* (Jamaica, New York, since 1970), "a forum for scholars and critics concerned with literature as the expression of national character and as a repository of national culture in its most vital and most readily communicable form" (ed.). The comparatist, however, studies literature in its international rather than in its national context.

15. The International Comparative Literature Association was founded in 1955, the year in which its first congress also took place, in Venice. On the occasion of the World's Fair of 1900 in Paris, an international congress was organized. Its theme was "Histoire comparée des litteratures." There are also French (since 1954), Japanese (since 1954), American (since 1960), German (since 1968), Canadian (since 1969), Philippine (since 1969), and Hungarian (since 1971) associations of comparative literature.

2. The Meaning of World Literature

1. Since the end of the eighteenth century, quite a few major German writers have shown lively interest in oriental studies. In 1808, for example, Friedrich Schlegel published his *Über die Sprache und Weisheit der Inder.* At an earlier date Herder attempted to explore the mind of the universe, when he wrote *Ideen zur Philosophie der Geschichte der Menschheit* (1784–1791); Herder, however, was also one of the first to popularize the notion *Volksgeist* and to be considered a promotor of German nationalism. See Edgar B. Schick, *Metaphorical Organicism in Herder's Early Works: A Study of the Relation of Herder's Literary Idiom and his World View* (The Hague, 1970), and Robert S. Mayo, *Herder and the Beginnings of Comparative Literature* (Chapel Hill, 1969). The case of Hegel, "Hegel in Comparative Literature," has been studied in a special issue, ed. Frederick Weiss, of *Review of National Literatures* 1 (1970): 2. In literatures other than the German, similar trends are noticeable, especially in the English romantic school. Even Lamartine, one of the least cosmopolitan writers of nineteenth-century France, sometimes shows this sort of universalism, as, for example, in his poem *Ressouvenir du Lac Léman.* Geneva is said to be the European Palmyra:

Elle voit en ses murs l'Ibère et le Germain
Echanger la pensée en se donnant la main.

2. In many countries studies have been written on the concept of *Welt-literatur* and its history. Richard Green Moulton, *World Literature and Its Place in General Culture* (New York, 1911); Fritz Strich, *Goethe und die Weltliteratur* (Bern, 1946), esp. pp. 393–400, trans. C. A. M. Sym, *Goethe and World Literature* (London, 1949); Luigi Foscolo Benedetto, "La letteratura mondiale," in *Uomini e tempi: Pagine varie di critica e storia* (Milan and Naples, 1953), pp. 3–20; Helmut Bender and Ulrich Melzer "Zur Geschichte des Begriffes *Weltliteratur*," *Saeculum* 9 (1958): 113–123; Haskell M. Block, ed., *The Teaching of World Literature* (Chapel Hill, 1960; René Etiemble, "Faut-il réviser la notion de Weltliteratur?" in *Proceedings of the Fourth Congress of the International Comparative Literature Association*, ed. François Jost, 2 vols. (The Hague, 1966), 1:14–26; Hans Joachim Schrimpf, *Goethes Begriff der Weltliteratur: Essay* (Stuttgart, 1968); Árpaád Berczik, "Die ersten ungarischen Verkünder der Weltliteratur und der Vergleichenden Literaturwissenschaft," *Zagadnienia Rodzajoów Literackich* [The problems of literary genres] 11, No. 2 (1969): 155–173; I. Neupokoeva, "The Comparative Aspects of Literature in *The History of World Literature*," in *Proceedings of the Fifth Congress of the International Comparative Literature Association*, ed. Nikola Banašević (Amsterdam, 1969), pp. 37–43.

3. "La storia particolare delle nazioni sta per finire, la storia europea sta per incomminciare." Mazzini adds: "All'Italia non è concesso di starsi isolata in mezzo al moto comune" ("Italy cannot stay isolated in the midst of this general movement"), *Opere*, ed. Luigi Salvaterelli, 3 vols. (Milan and Rome, 1939), 2:118.

4. "Ich sehe mich daher gerne bei fremden Nationen um und rate jedem, es auch seinerseits zu tun. Nationalliteratur will jetzt nicht viel sagen, die Epoche der Weltliteratur ist an der Zeit, und jeder muss jetzt dazu wirken, diese Epoche zu beschleunigen" (*Gespräche mit Eckermann*, ed. Ernst Merian-Genast, 2 vols. [Basel, 1945], 1:214). Parts 1 and 2 first published in 1836 and Part 3 in 1848.

5. It follows that in Goethe's perspective, courses on "masterpieces of world literature," frequently offered in American universities, would bear a slightly tautological title. *World* literature, being the *value* literature or *Wert*literatur, necessarily consists of masterpieces alone.

6. "Es ist aber sehr artig, dass wir jetzt, bei dem engen Verkehr zwischen Franzosen, Engländern und Deutschen, in den Fall kommen, uns einander zu korrigieren. Das ist der grosse Nutzen, der bei einer Weltliteratur herauskommt und der sich immer wieder zeigen wird" (July 15, 1827, *Gespräche*, 1:245). Goethe explains his cultural universalism in other passages, e.g., in the collection of his maxims, or *Sprüche:* "Es gibt keine patriotische Kunst und keine patriotische Wissenschaft. Beide gehören wie alles hohe Gute der ganzen Welt an und können nur durch allgemeine freie Wechselwirkung aller zugleich Lebenden in steter Rücksicht auf das, was uns vom Vergangenen übrig und bekannt ist, gefördert werden" ("There is no national art and no national science. Both belong to the sublime good of the entire world and can only be developed through

a general and free interaction of all human beings of the same period with constant consideration of that which has been left to us and of that which we know from the past" (*Goethes Werke in sechs Bänden* [Leipzig, 1940], 6:492).

7. Many passages in Goethe's work lead more directly to comparatism, for instance, some statements in the *Gespräche mit Eckermann*. On Dec. 3, 1824, Goethe urged his friend to study English literature, saying that most of German literature derived from the English. He adds: "Unsere Romane, unsere Trauerspiele, woher haben wir sie denn als vom Goldsmith, Fielding und Shakespeare?" (*Gespräche*, 1:120). Here Goethe seems to suggest dissertation topics to students in comparative literature.

8. *Journal d'André Gide* (Paris, 1948), p. 814. Gide adds: "Je crois que Renard ne se peignait pas moins fermé qu'il n'était en réalité" ("I think that Renard did not describe himself as less exclusive than he actually was").

9. These tendencies can be studied in René Wellek, *A History of Modern Criticism*, 5 vols. (New Haven and London, 1965), esp. vols. 2 and 3.

10. Quoted by André Gide in "Dostoïevski d'après sa correspondance" (1908), in Gide's *Oeuvres complètes*, 5 vols., ed. Martin-Chauffier (Paris, 1933) 5:65.

11. "Sur la multiplicité des livres," in *Oeuvres complètes de M. de Bonald*, ed. Abbé Migne, 3 vols. (Paris, 1859), 3:1125.

12. "Faut-il reviser la notion de *Weltliteratur*" (*Proceedings of the Fourth Congress*, ed. Jost, 1:14).

13. Etiemble's ideal certainly was materialized by a man like Albrecht von Haller. One should assume—and scholars know—that he read considerably more books than he reviewed: from 1747 to 1777 he discussed in the *Göttingische Anzeigen* some 1,200 literary works written in all European countries. See François Jost, *Essais de littérature comparée*, vol. 1, *Helvetica* (Fribourg, 1964), pp. 143–146.

14. "The American Scholar," in *Nature, Addresses, and Lectures, and Letters in Social Aims* (Boston and New York, 1929), p. 113.

3. A Philosophy of Letters

1. During the last quarter of the nineteenth century, the term and its equivalents were used in a great part of Europe, like "comparative anatomy" or "comparative linguistics." In France *comparatif* stood sometimes for *comparé; comparatiste, comparatisme* are of more recent date. The Germans shifted from *vergleichende Literaturgeschichte* to *vergleichende Literaturwissenschaft*. *Komparatist* and *Komparatistik* (earlier *Komparativistik*) are relatively current words. The English and Americans, before saying *comparatist*, used *comparativist*, but they are still reluctant to accept *comparatism, comparativism*, and now for the first time, I believe, one finds in this book *comparatistics*, which is a quite practical expression. This is not to say that the term comparatistics more adequately reveals the reality behind it; at least it eliminates the puzzling "comparative." Generally, however, scientific terminology remains symbolic and needs interpretation. Thus "physics," which etymologically refers to "science of nature," is not concerned with medicine, chemistry, biology, agricul-

ture, astronomy, or zoology, though obviously all these disciplines are branches of the "natural sciences." Similarly, literature is excluded from the "fine arts," which could suggest that literature is not *fine*, an *art*, a *fine* art, or a fine *art*.

2. *Yearbook of Comparative and General Literature* (Bloomington, Ind., 1968), pp. 5–16.

3. Werner P. Friederich with David H. Malone, *Outline of Comparative Literature from Dante Alighieri to Eugene O'Neill* (Chapel Hill, 1954).

4.   Nunc hos, nunc illos percontor; multa vicissim
            Respondent, et multa canunt et multa loquuntur!
            (*Ad Iacobum Columna*, from *Epystole Metrice*)

5. I. Neupokoeva testifies to this statement when she writes: "A great part in diachronous comparative analysis is played also by an inner national element, for example, a comparison of Anatole France's novels with the novel of the French Enlightenment or of the epic novel in Russian Soviet literature with that of Leo Tolstoy's." "The Comparative Aspects of Literature in the *History of World Literature*," in *Proceedings of the Fifth Congress of the International Comparative Literature Association*, ed. Nikola Banašević (Amsterdam, 1969), p. 40.

6. *Comparative Literature: Matter and Method* (Urbana, Ill., 1969), p. 1. However, Edwin Koppen, though reluctantly, answers in the positive his question: "Hat die Vergleichende Literaturwissenschaft eine eigene Theorie?" in *Zur Theorie der Vergleichenden Literaturwissenschaft*, ed. Horst Rüdiger (Berlin and New York, 1971), 41–65.

7. "On the Study of Comparative Literature," *Oxford Slavonic Papers* 13 (1967): 1–13.

8. Some authors of classical definitions insist more than I do on the inclusion in the discipline of studies on the interrelations between literature and the other branches of human knowledge. Henry H. H. Remak writes: "Comparative literature is the study of literature beyond the confines of one particular country, and the study of the relationships between literature on the one hand and other areas of knowledge and belief, such as the arts (e.g. painting, sculpture, architecture, music), philosophy, history, the social sciences (e.g., politics, economics, sociology), the sciences, religion, etc., on the other. In brief, it is the comparison of one literature with another or others, and the comparison of literature with other spheres of human expression" ("Comparative Literature, Its Definition and Function," in *Comparative Literature, Method and Perspective*, p. 1). Aldridge's condensed formula reads: "Comparative literature can be considered the study of any literary phenomenon from the perspective of more than one national literature or in conjunction with another intellectual discipline or even several" (*Comparative Literature, Matter and Method*, p. 1). The "ut pictura poesis" belongs to the domain of the theory of general aesthetics and literary criticism at large. It was already widely examined from Horace to Lessing by many illustrious minds. Since comparative literature, especially in the United States, has "absorbed" general literature, the question is rather often taken up by American comparatists. But it obviously is not exclusively the comparatist's concern. Moreover, practical illustrations of such relations are usually confined to one single literature: there are studies on the paintings and writings of William

Blake, the paintings and writings of Eugène Fromentin. These are questions of English and French literature respectively. Inquiries in the history of ideas are more likely to include several literatures, and are, therefore, more genuinely comparative in nature. My chapter on Rousseau belongs to this category of studies.

9. Marius-François Guyard, *La Littérature comparée*, Foreword by J.-M. Carré (Paris, 1951), p. 5.

10. *La Littérature comparée* (Paris, 1931), p. 23.

11. "Wenn unsere Zeitschrift sich auch zunächst den Interessen der deutschen Literatur widmen soll, so vergessen wir doch nicht, dass jede Nationalliteratur nur ein Zweig am Baum der Weltliteratur ist und allein aus dieser heraus in ihrer wahren Bedeutung erfasst werden kann" (*Deutsche Monatshefte* 1 (1878): 112).

12. This viewpoint is clearly stated by both Van Tieghem and Carré. Van Tieghem: "Le mot *comparé* doit être vidé de toute valeur esthétique et recevoir une valeur scientifique" ("The word *comparative* should be emptied of all its aesthetical value and receive a scientific value"), (Guyard, *Litterature comparée*, p. 21). Carré: "La littérature comparée ne considère pas essentiellement les oeuvres dans leur valeur originelle, mais s'attache surtout aux transformations que chaque nation, chaque auteur fait subir à ses emprunts" ("Comparative literature does not, essentially, consider the works in their original value; the discipline is mainly concerned with the transformations that each nation, each author imposes upon its borrowings"), (Ibid., p. 6). According to the traditional French school, new criticism and comparative literature are obviously incompatible theories.

13. René Wellek and Austin Warren, *Theory of Literature*, 3rd new rev. ed. (New York, 1962), p. 49.

14. Karl Marx and Friedrich Engels, *The Communist Manifesto*, trans. F. Engels (New York, 1948), p. 13. See also, idem, *Über Kunst und Literatur*, 2 vols. (Berlin, 1967), selected texts.

15. Earlier, Louis de Bonald said: "La littérature est l'expression de la société" (*Du style et de la littérature* [1806], in *Oeuvres complètes, de M. de Bonald*, ed. Abbé Migne, 3 vols. [Paris, 1859], 3:976). A note explains: "La société se prend ici pour la forme de constitution politique et religieuse" ("Here society means the form of a political and religious structure"). *Expression*, Bonald says, means "représentation, production au dehors d'un objet."

16. *Typological* is a key word in Soviet comparatism. It refers to any characteristic grouping of elements of literature, to works, for instance, that belong to a same genre or movement. See M. B. Chrapčenko "Typologische Literaturforschung und ihre Prinzipien," in *Aktuelle Probleme der vergleichenden Literaturforschung*, ed. Gerhard Ziegengeist (Berlin, 1968), pp. 17–46.

17. "Study of Comparative Literature," in *Oxford Slavonic Papers*, p. 1. The same thought is expressed in Zhirmunsky's "Methodologische Probleme der marxistischen historisch-vergleichenden Literaturforschung," in *Aktuelle Probleme*, p. 1: "Wichtigste Voraussetzung für eine historischvergleichende Erforschung der Literaturen verschiedener Völker bildet die marxistische Auffassung von der Einheit und Gesetzmässigkeit des Gesamt-

prozesses der sozialgeschichtlichen Entwicklung der Menschheit, durch die auch die gesetzmässige Entwicklung der Literatur oder der Kunst als einer ideologischen Überbauerscheinung bedingt wird." What Zhirmunsky is maintaining here is that the development of art and literature takes place according to fixed laws and is parallel to the socio-historical development of mankind. Thus society is the necessary substratum of literature and literature an accidental superstratum—"Überbauerscheinung"—of society. An abundant library of studies exists on the theory of comparative literature written by Soviet authors, such as Irina Grigor'evna Neupokoeva's *Problemi vzaimodeistviia sovremennykh literatur; tri ocherka* [*Problems of the interrelation of modern literatures;* three essays] (Moscow, 1963); Herman Ermolaev's *Soviet Literary Theories 1917–1934; The Genesis of Socialist Realism* (Los Angeles and Berkeley, 1963); and the collection of articles entitled *Vzaimosviazi i vzaimodeistvie natsional' nykh Literatur* [*Interrelations and interactions of national literatures*] (Moscow, 1901).

18. See Ermolaev, *Soviet Literary Theories.* The official definition of socialist realism as given in the bylaws of the Soviet Writers' Union made known May 6, 1934, reads: "Socialist realism being the basic method of Soviet imaginative literature and literary criticism, demands from the artist a truthful, historically concrete depiction of reality in its revolutionary development. At the same time this truthfulness and historical concreteness of the artistic depiction of reality must be combined with the task of the ideological molding and education of the working people in the spirit of socialism." Realism is also interpreted in Harry Levin's "On the Dissemination of Realism" and in Béla Köpeczi's "Le Réalisme socialiste en tant que courant littéraire international," in *Proceedings of Fifth Congress,* ed. Banašević, pp. 231–241 and 371–377 respectively.

19. See Victor Erlich, *"Russian Formalism. History-Doctrine,* 2nd ed. (The Hague, 1965).

20. Author of *Comparaison n'est pas raison: La crise de la littérature comparée* (Paris, 1963), trans. Herbert Weisinger and Georges Joyaux, *The Crisis of Comparative Literature* (East Lansing, Mich., 1966).

21. Author of *Sociologie de la littérature* (Paris, 1964), trans. Ernest Pick, *Sociology of Literature* (Painesville, 1965). See also Lucien Goldmann, *Pour une sociologie du roman* (Paris, 1964).

22. Chinese and Japanese criticism, interestingly enough, is concerned with European literature to an even smaller extent than European criticism is with the literatures of Asia.

23. The testimony in Friedrich Schlegel's *Über das Studium der griechischen Poesie* [On the study of Greek poetry] is one of the most convincing: "Wenn die regionellen Theile der modernen Poesie aus ihrem Zusammenhang gerissen, und als einzelne für sich bestehende Ganze betrachtet werden, so sind sie unerklärlich" ("If the individual parts of modern poetry are torn out of their context and considered as autonomous entities, they remain inexplicable").

24. Nietzsche's text reads: *"Glück der Zeit.*—In zwei Beziehungen ist unsre Zeit glücklich zu preisen. In Hinsicht auf die *Vergangenheit* geniessen wir alle Culturen und deren Hervorbringungen und nähren uns mit dem edelsten Blute aller Zeiten, wir stehen noch dem Zauber der Gewalten, aus deren Schoosse jene geboren wurden, nahe genug, um uns vorüber-

gehend ihnen mit Lust und Schauder unterwerfen zu können: während frühere Culturen nur sich selber zu geniessen vermochten und nicht über sich hinaussahen, vielmehr wie von einer weiter oder enger gewölbten Glocke überspannt waren, aus welcher zwar Licht auf sie herabströmte, durch welche aber kein Blick hindurchdrang. In Hinsicht auf die *Zukunft* erschliesst sich uns zum ersten Male in der Geschichte der ungeheure Weitblick menschlichökumenischer, die ganze bewohnte Erde umspannender Ziele. Zugleich fühlen wir uns der Kräfte bewusst, diese neue Aufgabe ohne Anmaassung selber in die Hand nehmen zu dürfen" (*Menschliches, Allzumenschliches,* 2 vols. [Berlin, 1967], 2:93, trans. Helen Zimmern and Paul V. Cohn, vols. 6 and 7 [1909–1911], *The Complete Works of Friedrich Nietzsche,* 18 vols. [Edinburgh and London, 1909–1913]).

4. Prolegomenon A

1. Some studies on translation are: Jiří Levý, *Die literarische Übersetzung: Theorie einer Kunstgattung* [The literary translation: theory of a genre] (Frankfort on the Main, 1969); Edward Balcerzan, *Styl I Poetyka Twórczosci Dwujezycznej Brunona Jasienskiego: Zagadnien Teorii Przekladu* [Style and poetics in the bilingual work of Brunon Jasienski: Problems of the Theory of Translation] (Wroclaw, 1968); E. S. Bates, *Intertraffic: Studies in Translation* (New York, 1967); Revzine and V. J. Rosensveïg, *Osnovy obshchego i machinnogo perevoda* [Principles of general and mechanical translation] (Moscow, 1964); G. Rába, "La traduction poétique, sujet de littérature comparée," in *Acta litteraria* (Budapest, 1962); Horst Frenz, "The Art of Translation," in *Comparative Literature: Method and Perspective,* ed. Newton P. Stallknecht and Horst Frenz (Carbondale, Ill., 1961); William Arrowsmith and Roger Shattuck, eds., *The Craft and Context of Translation* (Austin, 1961); Horst Rüdiger, "Übersetzung als Stilproblem," *Geistige Welt* 5 (1951).

2. "Typologische Literaturforschung und ihre Prinzipien," in *Aktuelle Probleme der vergleichenden Literaturforschung,* ed. Gerhard Ziegengeist (Berlin, 1968), p. 29.

3. "Comparative Literature," *The Georgia Review* 13, no. 2 (1959): 180–181. Brown is also the author of "The Relations between Music and Literature as a Field of Study," *Comparative Literature* 22, no. 2 (1970): 97–108.

4. "On the Study of Comparative Literature," *Oxford Slavonic Papers* 13 (1967): 1–13.

5. Ibid., p. 7.

6. "German and English Romanticism," in *Confrontations,* by René Wellek (Princeton, 1965), pp. 11–12.

7. Ibid., p. 33.

8. The terms and notions of *influence, imitation,* and *originality* were the theme of the Fourth Congress of the International Comparative Literature Association. See *Proceedings* of the congress, ed. François Jost, 2 vols. (The Hague, 1966) 2:697–1365, esp. Elmer Hankiss, "Literary Influence: Action or Interaction?" (pp. 1221–1226). See also Arthur O. Lovejoy, *The Great Chain of Being* (Cambridge, Mass., 1936); Ihab H. Hassan, "The Problem of Influence in Literary History," *Journal of Aesthetics and Art Criticism* 14 (1955–1956): 66–76; Haskell M. Block, "The Concept of Influ-

ence in Comparative Literature," *Yearbook of Comparative and General Literature* 6 (1957): 30–37; Joseph T. Shaw, "Literary Indebtedness," in *Comparative Literature, Method and Perspective* (Carbondale, Ill., 1961), pp. 58–71; Anna Balakian, "Influence and Literary Fortune," *Yearbook of Comparative and General Literature* 11 (1962): 24–31; A. Owen Aldridge, "The Concept of Influence in Comparative Literature," *Comparative Literature Studies* 1 (1963): 143–146; D. Ďurišin, "Die wichtigsten Typen literarischer Beziehungen und Zusammenhänge," *Aktuelle Probleme*, ed. Ziegengeist, pp. 47–59; James Thorpe, ed., *Relations of Literature Study: Essays on Interdisciplinary Contributions* (New York, 1969); Saburo Ota, "What Is Influence?" *Tamkang Review* 1 (1970): 109–119. Claudio Guillén has treated "The Aesthetics of Influence Studies" in his book *Literature as System: Essays toward the Theory of Literary History* (Princeton, 1971). See also Jan Bialostocki, *Ut pictura Poesis—Dichtung und Malerei: Forschungen zu einem kunsttheoretischen Problem* (Frankfort on the Main, 1971). A good example of a study on a single author's attitude toward the arts is Emily Stipes Watts's *Ernest Hemingway and the Arts* (Urbana, Ill., 1971).

5. Immanence or Influence? Jean-Jacques Rousseau and North American Thought

1. "Je n'ose parler de ces Nations heureuses qui ne connaissent pas même le nom des vices que nous avons tant de peine à réprimer, de ces sauvages de l'Amérique dont Montaigne ne balance pas à préférer la simple et naturelle police, non seulement aux *Lois* de Platon, mais même à tout ce que la philosophie pourra jamais imaginer de plus parfait pour le gouvernement des peuples" (*Premier discours*, in *Oeuvres complètes de Jean-Jacques Rousseau*, ed. Bernard Gagnebin and Marcel Raymond, 4 vols. [Paris, 1959–1969], 3:11–12, note). The role played by the American Indians in the social and political philosophy of Rousseau can hardly be overrated. The *Deuxième discours*, i.e. *Discours sur l'origine de l'inégalité parmi les hommes* (Discourse on the Origin of the Inequality of Men), refers repeatedly to the Indians. Voltaire, in his turn, has them in mind when he sends to Rousseau—who had given him a copy of the second discourse—the well-known letter of Aug. 30, 1755: "Il prend envie de marcher à quatre pattes, quand on lit votre ouvrage. Cependant, comme il y a plus de soixante ans que j'en ai perdu l'habitude, je sens malheureusement qu'il m'est impossible de la reprendre, et je laisse cette allure naturelle à ceux qui en sont plus dignes que vous et moi. Je ne peux non plus m'embarquer pour aller trouver les sauvages du Canada. . . ." ("One feels like walking on all fours when one reads your work. However, since I have lost the habit for more than sixty years, I feel unfortunately enough that it is impossible for me to resume it, and I leave that manner to those who are more worthy than you and me. I can neither embark to join the savages of Canada. . . ." (*Voltaire's Correspondence*, 107 vols., ed. Theodore Besterman [Geneva, 1957], 27:230).

2. *Proposals*, facsimile reprint ed., Introduction by William Pepper (Philadelphia, 1931), p. 11. Rousseau, assuming a private tutor for each infant, clearly takes up a theoretical and idealistic point of view; Franklin speaks of a practical realization. For a parallel between Rousseau and

Franklin, see A. Owen Aldridge, *Benjamin Franklin et ses contemporains français* (Paris, 1963), p. 153.

3. *Proposals*, p. 10.

4. Some studies exist, like Howard Mumford Jones's *America and French Culture* (Chapel Hill, 1927); François Jost, "La fortune de Rousseau aux Etats-Unis: Esquisse d'une étude," in *Studies on Voltaire and the Eighteenth Century*, ed. Theodore Besterman, 86 vols. to date, vol. 25 (Geneva, 1963), pp. 899–959. The most recent study is that of Paul M. Spurlin's, *Rousseau in America, 1760–1809* (University, Ala., 1969).

5. A similar problem arises in South America. In *Epic of Latin American Literature*, Arturo Torres-Ríoseco thinks that Rousseau's impact on that continent "constitutes one of the most fascinating chapters in Spanish American cultural history." (Berkeley and Los Angeles, 1959), p. 46. The author refers especially to Fernández de Lizardi, José María de Heredia, Andrés Bello, Estaban Echeverría, Domingo Faustino Sarmiento, Jorge Isaacs, and Ricardo Palma.

6. Paul M. Spurlin, *Montesquieu in America, 1760–1801* University, Ala., 1940); Mary-Margaret H. Barr, *Voltaire in America, 1744–1870* (Baltimore, 1941); John Dunn, *The Political Thought of John Locke: An Historical Account of the Argument of the "Two Treatises of Government"* (Cambridge, 1969).

7. Some translations, instead of being imported from England, were printed in America itself. Charles Evans, in *American Bibliography: A Chronological Dictionary of All Books, Pamphlets, and Periodical Publications Printed in the United States of America from the Genesis of Printing in 1639 down to and Including the Year 1820* (Chicago, 1910), vol. 6; (1925), vol. 9; (1931), vol. 11, gives these titles: "Sentiments on Government, Law, Arbitrary Power, Liberty, and Social Institutions," in *Illuminations for Legislators, and for Sentimentalists*, ed. Robert Bell, 8 vols. (Philadelphia, 1784), vol. 3; *Letters of an Italian Nun and an English Gentleman* (Philadelphia, 1794)—an apocryphal work that had a considerable success; the fifth edition was dated 1796, the same year in which the work was also printed at Worcester, Mass.; *The Confessions of J. J. Rousseau, Citizen of Geneva: Part I: To Which Is Added the Reveries of a Solitary Walker; Part II: To Which Is Added a New Collection of Letters from the Author*, 2 vols. (New York, 1796); *Eloisa, or, a Series of Original Letters, Collected and Published by J. J. Rousseau, Citizen of Geneva; The Sequel of Julia; or, the New Elisa (Found Amongst the Author's Papers after his Decease; 3 vols. (Philadelphia, 1796); *A Dissertation on Political Economy: To Which is Added a Treatise on the Social Compact; or, The Principles of Politic Law* (Albany, 1797).

8. Bernard Faÿ, *L'Esprit révolutionnaire en France et aux Etats-Unis à la fin du XVIIIᵉ siècle* (Paris, 1925); Norman Foerster, *Nature in American Literature: Studies in the Modern View of Nature* (New York, 1958).

9. Chinard associates himself more directly with the reciprocal point of view: "Il n'est pas possible d'entreprendre une étude, nous ne disons pas complète, mais simplement exacte de Jean-Jacques, si l'on ne tient pas compte de l'influence exercée sur sa formation par les récits de voyage" ("It is not possible to undertake any study of Jean-Jacques, not a complete one, but simply an accurate one, without taking into consideration the

influence of travel accounts on his development"), (*L'Amérique et le rêve exotique* [Geneva, 1934], p. 342).

10. *The Noble Savage* (New York, 1928), p. 2.

11. The Declaration of Independence says: "We hold these truths to be self-evident, that all men are created equal; that they are endowed by their Creator with certain unalienable rights, that among these are life, liberty and the pursuit of happiness."

12. "Quiconque ose dire: *hors de l'Eglise, point de salut*, doit être chassé de l'Etat" (*Oeuvres complètes*, 3:366).

13. The wealthy southern planters had their sons educated in England, where they were exposed to all cultural trends of the time. Their role as intermediaries, however, seems to be rather modest.

14. This epithet is also the title of an anonymous article published in the *Saturday Review* of London (Dec. 3, 1864): 694–695.

15. William Girard, *Du transcendentalisme considéré sous son aspect social* (Berkeley, 1918), p. 192. Anton Huffert writes: "There is no evidence that he [Thoreau] ever read Rousseau directly. He was acquainted with his ideas only through secondary sources" (*Thoreau as a Teacher* [New York, 1951], p. 151).

16. *Rousseau in America*, p. 45. Spurlin's book was preceded by an article, "Rousseau in America, 1760–1809," *The French American Review* 1 (1948): 8–16.

17. *Rousseau in America*, p. 69.

18. "What is an American?" in *Letters from an American Farmer* (London, 1782) and (London and Toronto, 1912), pp. 40–41. Crèvecœur himself translated his own work and published it in French in 1783: *Lettres d'un cultivateur américain.*

19. *Sketches of Eighteenth Century America: More "Letters from an American Farmer,"* ed. Henri L. Bourdin et al. (New Haven, 1925), p. 104.

20. *Histoire philosophique . . .* , 6 vols. (Amsterdam, 1770). The last volume of Raynal's work includes a physical, economic, and political description of the American colonies.

21. "Somme indigeste et incohérente des idées de Voltaire, Rousseau et Diderot" (A. Feugère, *Un précurseur de la Révolution, l'abbé Raynal* [Angoulême, 1922], p. 101).

22. The rather outdated books about Crèvecœur—Julia P. Mitchell's *St. John de Crèvecœur* (New York, 1916) and Howard C. Rice's *Le cultivateur américain* (Paris, 1933), the latter the more complete concerning the subject treated here—do not emphasize any kind of influence by Rousseau upon Crèvecœur.

23. The *Contrat* is likewise cited in *The Principles of Government* by Nathaniel Chipman, published in 1793.

24. *The Complete Writings of Thomas Paine*, ed. Philip S. Foner, 2 vols. (New York, 1945), 1:4.

25. Ibid., p. 299. See also Harry H. Clark, "Thomas Paine's Relation to Voltaire and Rousseau," *Revue Anglo-Américaine* 9 (1932): 305–318 and 393–405.

26. In his essay on "Rousseau and the Sentimentalists," however, James Russell Lowell points out the influence of Rousseau on Jefferson as well as on Paine (*The Complete Writings of James Russell Lowell*, 13 vols. [Boston

and New York, 1897], 2:232–271). The case of John Adams has been studied by Zoltán Haraszti, *John Adams and the Prophets of Progress* (Cambridge, Mass., 1952). See chap. 5, "Rousseau and the Man of Nature."

27. See Carl L. Becker, *The Declaration of Independence: A Study in the History of Ideas* (New York, 1922), esp. pp. 28–30 and 256–259.

28. Adrian H. Jaffe, *Bibliography of French Literature in American Magazines in the Eighteenth Century* (East Lansing, 1951).

29. Any systematic study of Rousseauism in America has to take account of the studies done by scholars like Henri Roddier, *Jean-Jacques Rousseau en Angleterre au XVIIIᵉ siècle* (Paris, 1950) and, of equal importance, Jacques Voisine, *Jean-Jacques Rousseau en Angleterre à l'époque romantique* (Paris, 1956); see also Maurice Cranston, "Rousseau's Visit to England, 1766–67," *Essays by Divers Hands, Being the Transactions of the Royal Society of Literature*, new series, ed. Peter Green, 36 vols. to date, vol. 31 (London, 1962), 16–34; Annie Marion Osborn, *Rousseau and Burke: A Study on the Idea of Liberty in Eighteenth Century Thought* (London, New York, and Toronto, 1940).

30. In this work were republished *La Nouvelle Héloïse, Emile*, and the *Contrat social*.

31. *Quarterly Review* 3 (1810): 198.

32. The *political* ideas of Coleridge must be excluded; his biographers are right to declare that he was only a "lukewarm admirer" of the *Contrat*.

33. *Brook Farm: Historic and Personal Memoirs* (Boston, 1894), pp. 42–43.

34. "Non par une vaine cérémonie, mais par le travail et la culture, seul signe de propriété" (*Oeuvres complètes*, 3:352). Rousseau always carefully distinguished *propriété* from *possession*.

35. The question of the sources of American transcendentalism is a complex one. It owes more to German romanticism than to Rousseau, for the philosophical tradition that leads from Rousseau to the transcendentalists passed through Kant and Hegel. See Walter L. Leighton, *French Philosophers and New England Transcendentalism* (Charlottesville, 1908) and Henry A. Pochmann, *New England Transcendentalism and St. Louis Hegelianism* (Philadelphia, 1948).

36. Thoreau calculated that the worker must give up fifteen years of his life to pay for the luxury of a house. He asks: "Would the savage have been wise to exchange his wigwam for a palace on these terms?"("Economy," in *Walden; or, Life in the Woods* [Boston and New York, 1906], p. 34).

37. Ibid., p. 36.

38. Rousseau, however, not only knew the political institutions of ancient Greece and Rome, but also knew perfectly that some Swiss cantons came very close to his democratic ideal. It even seems likely that Switzerland partly inspired his political doctrine. See François Jost, *Jean-Jacques Rousseau Suisse*, 2 vols. (Fribourg, 1961), 1:285–308.

39. "L'homme est né libre." Rousseau adds: "Et partout il est dans les fers." The *Contrat social* opens with these words. See also book 1, chap. 4, *De l'esclavage*, to which the abolitionists sometimes referred. One should also note a similar latent and virtual power in the *Contrat* and in *Uncle Tom's Cabin;* the authors employ chemically different explosive formulas,

for Harriet Beecher Stowe was scarcely in direct contact with the works of Jean-Jacques.

40. See in this connection George Hendrick, "Influence of Thoreau and Emerson on Gandhi's Satyagraha," in *Quest for Gandhi* (New Delphi, 1970), pp. 173–189.

41. *Democratic Vistas. Leaves of Grass* (New York, 1855), p. 60.

42. Whitman's manuscript is preserved in the Trent Collection of Duke University. The most inclusive biographies are Gay Wilson Allen's, Roger Asselineau's, and Frederik Leth Schyberg's, the authors, respectively, of *The Solitary Singer* (New York, 1955), *Walt Whitman après la première édition des Feuilles d'Herbes* (Paris, 1954), and *Walt Whitman* (Copenhagen, 1933), trans. Evie Allison Allen, *Walt Whitman* (New York, 1951).

43. Cited by Esther Shephard. *Walt Whitman's Prose* (New York, 1936), p. 173.

44. *Democracy and Poetry* (New York, 1911).

45. *Miscellanies* (Boston and New York, 1893), pp. 131 and 133.

46. Ibid., p. 136.

47. "S'il plaît au Souverain de conserver la présente forme de Gouvernement . . . S'il plaît au peuple d'en laisser l'administration à ceux qui en sont actuellement chargés" (*Oeuvres complètes*, 3:436).

48. Skeptical attitudes in this respect have been expressed by many authors. In 1832 Frances M. Trollope wrote: "Rousseau, Voltaire, Diderot, etc. were read by the old federals, but now they seem known more as naughty words than as great names" (*Domestic Manners of the Americans* [New York, 1904], pp. 281–82.) And Howard M. Jones notes: "The popular notion that the representative institutions of America owe much to Rousseau does not appear to be historically sound" (*America and French Culture*, p. 572.)

6. Russia in French Letters: Milestones of a Discovery

1. *La Littérature russe en France* (Paris, 1947).

2. On Russian influence on French literature see Charles Corbet, *A l'ère des nationalismes: L'opinion française face à l'inconnue russe (1799–1894)* (Paris, 1967); Michel Cadot, *La Russie dans la vie intellectuelle française (1839–1856)*, (Paris, 1967); René Marchand, *Parallèles littéraires franco-russes* (Mexico City, 1959); Albert Lortholary, *La Mirage russe en France* (Paris, 1951); Dimitri S. von Mohrenschild, *Russia in the Intellectual life of Eighteenth-Century France* (New York, 1936); Liubov Jakobson, *Russland und Frankreich in den ersten Regierungsjahren der Kaiserin Katharina II* (Berlin, 1929); G. Lozinski, "La Russie dans la littérature française du moyen âge," *Revue des études slaves* 9 (1929): 71–88; Friederich W. J. Hemmings, *The Russian Novel in France, 1884–1914* (London, 1925); Abel Mansuy, *Le Monde slave et les classiques français au XVIe et XVIIe siècle* (Paris, 1912), chapters entitled "Rabelais et les Slaves," "Montaigne," "La Russie dans la littérature française au XVIIe siécle"; Charles de Larivière, *La France et la Russie au XVIIIe siècle* (Paris, 1909). Important materials on the subject have been published in Russia during recent years. In 1947, for example, there appeared in Leningrad *Vol'ter: stat'i i materialy* [Voltaire: articles and materials], a work by several

authors that sheds new light on Franco-Russian cultural relations in the eighteenth century.

3. See, among other studies, M. S. Anderson, *Britain's Discovery of Russia, 1553–1815* (London, 1958).

4. See Vef Lehmann, *Der Gottschedkreis und Russland: Veröffent-lichungen des Instituts für Slavistik* (Berlin, 1966); E. Reissner, *Alexander Herzen in Deutschland* (Berlin, 1963); P. N. Berkov, *Die deutsch-russische Begegnung im 18. Jahrhundert und Leonhard Euler* (Berlin, 1958).

5. Many French writers, without ever taking the trouble of a journey to Saint Petersburg, had their disciples in Russia. Allen McConnell furnishes an example in his article "Helvetius' Russian Pupils," *Journal of the History of Ideas* 24 (1963): 373–386.

6. *Projet d'une compagnie pour la découverte d'un passage aux Indes par la Russie, présenté à Sa Majesté l'Impératrice Catherine II, in Oeuvres complètes de Jacques-Henri Bernardin de Saint-Pierre,* 12 vols., ed. L. Aimé-Martin (Paris, 1818), 2:329–558. The author's illustrious friend, Rousseau, took equal pleasure in pursuing "projects"; see Charles de Larivière, "Jean-Jacques Rousseau et la Russie," *Annales de la Société Jean-Jacques Rousseau,* XX (1931): 193–212.

7. *Observations sur la Russie,* in *Oeuvres complètes,* 2:271–361.

8. I follow the Paul Gautier edition of 1904, referred to as *Dix années.* There exists a translation by Doris Beik, *Ten Years of Exile* (New York, 1972). Gautier did not have the appropriate manuscripts at hand, and no definitive critical edition exists. There is no evidence that Madame de Staël knew *L'histoire de la Russie* (1783) by Pierre-Charles Levesque, *L'histoire physique, morale, civile, et politique de la Russie à l'époque ancienne et récente* (1783–1785) of Nicolas-Gabriel Leclerc, *Histoire ou anecdotes sur la révolution de la Russie en 1762* (1797) by Claude-Carloman de Rulhière, *Mémoires secrets* (1800) by Charles-François Masson, or the French translation (1801–1810) of Heinrich Friedrich Storch's *Historisch-statistisches Gemälde des russischen Reiches* [Historical and statistical survey of the Russian Empire], 9 vols. (1797–1803).

9. Gautier quotes Pushkin's opinion of Madame de Staël's work: "De tous les ouvrages de Madame de Staël, *Dix années d'exil* est un de ceux qui à juste titre doivent attirer l'attention des Russes. La pénétration de ses vues, la nouveauté et la variété de ses remarques, la reconnaissance et la bienveillance qui guident la plume de l'écrivain, tout, dans ce livre, fait honneur à l'esprit et au sentiment de cette femme extraordinaire" ("Among all the works of Madame de Staël, *Ten Years of Exile* is one of those that should attract the attention of the Russians. The penetration of her views, the newness and variety of her remarks, the gratitude and kindness that lead the writer's pen, everything in this book does honor to the mind and sensibility of this extraordinary woman"), (*Dix années,* p. xviii). Pushkin refers to Trachevsky's study on de Staël in Russia in the *Istoritcheskii Viestnik* [Historical review] of October, 1894. Pushkin also alludes to *De l'Allemagne* in *Evgéni Onégin* (1825–1833).

10. Sergei Semeonovitch Uvarov is said to have composed an essay on the French authoress, whom he knew personally. According to George Soloviev, this essay was placed in the Historical Museum of Moscow. Madame de Staël had many other Russian friends and correspondents.

Soloviev's article, "Madame de Staël et ses correspondants russes. Lettres inédites en français," *Cahiers staëliens*, new series (1962): 6–30, as well as a few other studies that appeared in the same journal, and in the Moscow serial publication *Literaturnoe Nasledstvo* [Literary heritage], notably the volumes published in 1936, 1937, and 1939. Karamzin translated a novella of Madame de Staël's, *Zulma*. *Mirza* had a Russian edition in 1801, *Delphine* in 1804, and *Corinne* in 1809.

11. Cf. Comtesse Jean de Pange, "Le grand voyage de Madame de Staël d'après un carnet de route inédit," *Connaissance de l'étranger: Mélanges offerts à la mémoire de Jean-Marie Carré* (Paris, 1964), pp. 347–362 (hereafter cited as *Notebook*).

12. *Notebook*, quotations on pp. 348, 304, 314 respectively.

13. Ibid., p. 288.

14. The idea of aesthetic relativity was rather new in France. In 1770 Voltaire wrote that "la langue russe, qui est la slavonne, mêlée de plusieurs mots grecs et de quelques-uns tartares, paraît mélodieuse aux oreilles russes" ("the Russian language, which is Slavic, mixed with several Greek and Tartar words, seems melodious to Russian ears"); the Englishman, too, he added, and the German as well, find their native tongues beautiful. However, "un Allemand, un Anglais qui aura de l'oreille et du goût sera plus content d'*ouranos* que de heaven et de himmel, d'*anthropos* que de man" ("a German, an Englishman who has the ear and the taste would be more satisfied with *ouranos* than heaven and himmel, and with *anthropos* than man"), ("Harmonie des langues," *Questions sur l'Encyclopédie*, 70 vols. [Paris, 1770] 7:316). Voltaire thought this was not the right place to praise the absolute harmony of the French language; he does it, unrestrainedly, in other parts of his work.

15. *Notebook*, pp. 279 and 351.

16. Ibid., quotations on pp. 298 and 359.

17. *Dix années*, p. 325.

18. *Mémoires secrets sur la Russie pendant les règnes de Catherine II et Paul I*, 4 vols. (1863 ed.) 2:129.

19. *Dix années*, pp. 363–364.

20. "La civilisation des Esclavons ayant été plus moderne et plus précipitée que celle des autres peuples, on voit plutôt en eux jusqu'à présent l'imitation que l'originalité: ce qu'ils ont d'européen est français; ce qu'ils ont d'asiatique est trop peu développé pour que leurs écrivains puissent encore manifester le véritable caractère qui leur serait naturel" ("Observations générales," *De l'Allemagne*, ed. Jean de Pange, 5 vols. [Paris, 1958], 1: 18).

21. *Dix années*, quotations on pp. 315 and 341. The phrase "Soyez Russes dans l'âme" illustrates, on the literary level, Madame de Staël's anti-Napoleonic philosophy. The expression epitomizes the attitude of a "Modern" as opposed to that of an "Ancient" in the famous quarrel. See *Review of National Literatures*, III, no. 1 (1972), *special issue: Russia: The Spirit of Nationalism*.

22. Ibid., p. 300.

23. *Notebook*, p. 357.

24. *Dix années*, p. 293.

25. *Le Cousin Pons, Etudes de moeurs: Scènes de la vie parisienne*, in

Oeuvres complètes de Balzac, ed. Marcel Bouteron and Henri Longnon, 40 vols. (Paris, 1912–1938), 18:131. In *Cousine Bette* (1847), Balzac gives to a character "l'insouciance particulière aux Slaves qui leur donne un incroyable décousu dans la conduite, une mollesse morale" ("the specific carelessness of the Slavs that gives them an unbelievable inconsequence in their conduct, a moral apathy"). Mickiewicz's lectures appeared in Paris in 1866: *Les Slaves: Histoire et littérature des nations polonaise, bohême, serbe et russe (1840–1842).* In his study on "Balzac in Russia" (*Literaturnoe Nasledstvo* 31 and 32 [1937]: 149–372), the Russian scholar Leonid Grossman summarizes in his Analytic Table of Contents Balzac's relationship to Russia: "Indifference of the writer toward Russian culture and his tremendous influence on the further development of our literature." For more complete information about the literary inspirations Balzac had received, especially from the Latin, the Germanic, and the Slavic world, see Fernand Baldensperger, *Les Orientations étrangères chez Honoré de Balzac* (Paris, 1927) and Geneviève Delattre, *Les Opinions littéraires de Balzac* (Paris, 1961).

26. In the United States the English translation of *The Kreutzer Sonata* was an object of censorship. Postmaster General John Wanamaker saw an attack against marriage in the work, and prohibited it from being sent through the mail. See "The Postmaster General and the Censorship of Morals," *Arena* 2 (October, 1890): 540–542.

27. The American Vogüé was William Dean Howells. While conducting the "Editor's Study" in *Harper's Magazine* (January, 1886 to March, 1892), which also had a British edition, he read Vogüé's *Le Roman russe* (Paris, 1886)—but unlike the French critic, he clearly preferred Tolstoy to Dostoevski—as well as Ernest Dupruy's anthology *Les Maîtres de la littérature russe* (1885), which was translated into English the following year by Nathan Haskell Dole.

28. Valerie A. Tumins, "Voltaire and the Rise of the Russian Drama," in *Studies on Voltaire and the XVIII Century,* ed. Theodore Besterman, 86 vols. to date, vol. 27 (Geneva, 1963), 1689–1703.

29. From October, 1883 to June, 1886. Later Vogüé published a study on Gorki. *Le Roman russe* has had several editions, the most recent published in Lausanne in 1972, *suivi d'une étude sur Maxime Gorki.* The standard translation of Vogüé's work is by H. A. Sawyer, *The Russian Novel* (London, 1913). I am referring to the first edition.

30. We must not forget the state of criticism at the time when *Le Roman russe* appeared. In the foreword one reads: "On ne trouvera point dans ce volume l'histoire d'une littérature, un traité didactique et complet sur la matière. Un pareil ouvrage n'existe pas encore en Russie, il serait prématuré en France" ("This book is neither meant to be a literary history nor a didactic and complete treatise on the subject. As yet, such a work does not exist in Russia: it would be premature in France"), (*Roman russe,* p. vii).

31. The work of Stefan Zweig, "Dostoyevsky," in *Drei Meister* (Leipzig, 1927), published in French translation in 1928, was surpassed only by that of Henri Troyat in 1940. Zweig published his study on Tolstoy in 1928, *Drei Dichter ihres Lebens: Casanova, Stendhal, Tolstoi* (also translated into French), and Troyat published his in 1965. One of the most recent

monographs concerned with the impact of Russian novelists on various writers is Jean Weissgerber's *Faulkner and Dostoïevsky* (Brussels, 1968).

32. *Roman russe*, p. xii.

33. Ibid., p. liv.

34. On the subject of Dostoevski's realism, consult Donald Fanger, *Dostoyevsky and Romantic Realism: A Study of Dostoyevsky in Relation to Balzac, Dickens, and Gogol* (Cambridge, Mass., 1965); for Tolstoy's realism, see George Lukács, "Tolstoy and the Development of Realism," a chapter in his *Studies in European Romanticism* (New York, 1964). Lukács' book is a revision of a study in Russian originally published in 1939.

35. *Roman russe*, p. xxxviii.

36. The father of the novelist was a doctor in Moscow at the Poor Hospital; the conditions of Dostoevski's birth and childhood symbolize his destiny and his message.

37. *Roman russe*, pp. xliv–xlv.

38. Ibid., p. liii.

39. Ibid., p. xlviii. Twenty-two years earlier, in 1864, Taine predicted that Germany, rather than Russia, would assume the intellectual leadership in Europe in the near future. "De 1780 à 1830," he says, "l'Allemagne a produit toutes les idées de notre âge historique, et pendant un demi-siècle encore, pendant un siècle peut-être, notre grande affaire sera de les repenser"("From 1780 to 1830, Germany has produced all the ideas of our age, and for half a century, possibly for an entire century, our great task will be to think them over anew"), (*Histoire de la littérature anglaise*, 4 vols. [Paris, 1864], 4:277).

7. Prolegomenon B

1. See Harry Levin's *The Broken Column: A Study in Romantic Hellenism* (Cambridge, Mass., 1931).

2. See Viktor M. Zhirmunsky, "Az irodalmi áramlatok mint nemzethözi jelenségek" [Literary currents as international phenomena], *Helikon* (Budapest) 14, no. 2, XIV (1968): 183–202.

3. See, for example, Manfred Gesteiger, *Französische Symbolisten in der Literatur der Jahrhundertwende, 1869–1914* (Bern, 1971).

4. Some currents, and schools, too, that are based on common principles and appear at times in different countries, do not have the same names. Russian formalism and the French "l'art pour l'art" movement are related phenomena. See Victor Erlich, *Russian Formalism* (The Hague, 1969). In East European areas the literature that centers on country life— literary populism—has different names, all designating a similar movement; in Rumania it is called *poporanism*, in Poland *ludomania*, and in Russia *narodnicism*. See Stan Velea, "Quelques considerations sur le *poporanisme* dans les littératures russe, roumaine et polonaise" *Proceedings of the Fifth Congress of the International Comparative Literature Association*, ed. N. Banašević (Amsterdam, 1969), pp. 269–275.

5. In *Mauvaises pensées et autres*, Paul Valéry warned the critics against such rigorous and artificial classifications: "Il est impossible de penser—sérieusement—avec des mots comme classicisme, romantisme,

humanisme, réalisme. . . . On ne s'enivre ni ne se désaltère avec des étiquettes de bouteilles" ("It is impossible to think seriously with words like classicism, romanticism, humanism, realism. . . . Labels of bottles do neither intoxicate nor quench thirst"), ([Paris, 1943], p. 35).

6. Georg Brandes has written one of the finest literary histories of the nineteenth century, arranging the materials according to movements and trends. See his six-volume work *Hovedstromninger i det 19de Aarhundredes Litteratur* (Copenhagen, 1871–1887), trans. Diana White and Mary Morison, *Main Currents in Nineteenth-Century Literature*, 6 vols. (New York and London, 1901–1905). Brandes' method has been applied to specific literary areas by Karl Dietrich, *Die osteuropäischen Literaturen in ihren Hauptströmungen vergleichend dargestellt* [The literatures of East Europe presented in their main currents in a comparative way] (Tübingen, 1911). Among more recent books and articles on the significance of movement studies are those by Henri Peyre, *Les Générations littéraires* (Paris, 1948), three by H. P. H. Teesing, *Das Problem der Perioden in der Literaturgeschichte* (Groningen, 1949); "Die Bedeutung der vergleichenden Literaturwissenschaft für die literarhistorische Periodisierung," in *Forschungsprobleme der vergleichenden Literaturgeschichte*, ed. Kurt Wais (Tübingen, 1950); and "Die Magic der Zahlen. Das Generationsprinzip in der vergleichenden Literaturgeschichte," in *Miscellanea Litteraria*, ed. H.Sparnaay and W.A.P.Smit (Groningen, 1959); Jost Hermand, "Das *Epochale* als neuer Sammelbegriff," in his *Synthetisches Interpretieren* (Munich, 1969); and Claudio Guillén, "Second Thoughts on Currents and Periods," in *The Disciplines of Criticism: Essays on Literary Theory, Interpretation, and History* (New Haven and London, 1968); and Herbert Dieckmann, "Reflections on the Use of Rococo as a Period Concept," in *Disciplines of Criticism*. Particular movements have been the object of numerous studies. René Bray's *La Formation de la doctrine classique en France* (Lausanne, 1927) has become a standard work; René Wellek wrote "The Term and Concept of Classicism in Literary History" and "The Term and Concept of Symbolism in Literary History," in *Discriminations: Further Concepts of Criticism* (New Haven and London, 1970) and Franklin A. Ford analyzed another current: "The Enlightenment: Towards a Useful Redefinition," in *Studies in the Eighteenth Century*, ed. R. F. Brissenden (Toronto, 1968).

8. A Lesson in a Word: "Romantic" and European Romanticism

1. *PMLA* 24 (1924): 229–253. The word and concept of romanticism has been studied by Ian Jack, *English Literature 1818–1832*, vol. 10 (New York and Oxford, 1964), pp. 406–421, in *Oxford History of English Literature*, 10 vols. to date. An extensive work on the question of romanticism itself is Giovanni Laini's *Il romanticismo europeo* (Florence, 1959). See the article by Henry H. H. Remak, "A Key to Western European Romanticism?" *Colloquia Germanica* 1 (1968): 37–46; his "West European Romanticism: Definition and Scope," in *Comparative Literature: Method and Perspective*, ed. Newton P. Stallknecht and Horst Frenz (Carbondale, Ill., 1971), pp. 275–311; and his essay "Trends of Recent Research on

West European Romanticism," in *Romantic*, ed. Hans Eichner (Toronto, 1972), pp. 475–500; the article of Cornelis de Deugd, "The Unity of Romanticism as an International Movement," in *Proceedings of the Fifth Congress of the International Comparative Literature Association*, ed. N. Banašević (Amsterdam, 1969), pp. 173–191; the survey by Lilian R. Furst, *Romanticism* (New York, 1969); and Raymond Immerwahr's *Romantik: Genese und Tradition einer Denkform* (Frankfort on the Main, 1971). See also Henri Peyre, *Qu'est-ce que le romantisme?* (Paris, 1971), and the reference work of A. C. Elkins, Jr., and L. J. Forstner, eds., *The Romantic Movement. Bibliography—1936–1970*, 7 vols. (Ann Arbor, 1973).

2. *Concepts of Criticism* (New Haven and London, 1963).

3. "Concept of Romanticism," in *Concepts of Criticism*, p. 131. For Wellek, there certainly is a "romantic age"; *The Romantic Age* is the title of vol. 2 of his *History of Modern Criticism*, 5 vols. to date (New Haven).

4. The most important of these studies are: (a) *English:* Logan Pearsall Smith, "Four Words: Romantic, Originality, Creative, Genius," in *Society for Pure English* (Oxford, 1924); Irving Babbitt, *Rousseau and Romanticism*, 2nd ed. (New York, 1960), pp. 18–21; Gustav Becker, "Die Bedeutung des Wortes *romantic* bei Fielding und Smollett," *Archiv für das Studium der Neueren Sprachen und Literaturen* 110 (1903): 56–66; Erik Erämestsä, *A Study of the Word "Sentimental" and Other Linguistic Characteristics of Eighteenth-Century Sentimentalism in England* (Helsinki, 1951); (b) *German:* Article on "romantisch" in Jacob and Wilhelm Grimm, *Deutsches Wörterbuch* (Berlin, 1852, and ff); Franz Schultz, "*Romantik* und *Romantisch* als literaturgeschichtliche Terminologie," *Deutsche Vierteljahrsschrift für Literaturwissenschaft und Geistesgeschichte*, 2 (1924): 349–366; Richard Ullmann and Helene Gotthard, *Geschichte des Begriffes "Romantisch,"* in *Deutschland vom ersten Aufkommen des Wortes bis ins dritte Jahrzehnt des neunzehnten Jahrhunderts* 13, *Germanische Studien*, Heft 50 (Berlin, 1927); Max Deutschbein, "Romantisch und romanesk," in *Festschrift M. Förster* (Leipzig, 1929); English and German romanticism have been compared by Eudo C. Mason, *Deutsche und englische Romantik: Eine Gegenüberstellung* (Göttingen, 1959), chap. 1; and by René Wellek, "German and English Romanticism," *Confrontations* (Princeton, 1965); (c) *French:* Alexis François, "Le mot romantique," *Annales de la Société Jean-Jacques Rousseau* (Geneva, 1909); idem, "Encore le mot romantique," *Bibliothèque universelle* (Geneva, 1918); idem, "Où en est romantique?" in *Mélanges Baldensperger* (Paris, 1929); Daniel Mornet, *Le sentiment de la nature en France, de Rousseau à Bernardin de Saint-Pierre* (Paris, 1912). Some of the conclusions of these and other studies have been included in Henri Roddier's edition of *Les Rêveries du promeneur solitaire* (Paris, 1960), p. 73, note 1, and App. 4, pp. 199–222; (d) *Italian:* Carla Apollonio, *Romantico: Storia e fortuna di una parola* (Florence, 1958). For the contrasts between the words "classic" and "romantic," see Friedrich Kainz, "Klassik und Romantik," *Deutsche Wortgeschichte*, ed. Friedrich Maurer, 3 vols. (Berlin, 1959), 2:229–409. Baldensperger's study has a more genuinely international character: "Romantique: Ses analogies et ses équivalents, tableau synoptique de 1650 à 1810," *Harvard Studies and Notes in Philology and Literature* 19 (1937): 13–105. For further studies on the international implications of *romantic*, see my "Romantique: la

leçon d'un mot" (*Essais II*, pp. 181–258, and pp. 403–9) as well as its sequel: Hans Eichner (ed.), *Romantic and Its Cognates. The European History of a Word* (Toronto and Buffalo, 1972).

5. In the *Romaunt of the Rose* (ca. 1330) Robert Mannyng of Brunne wrote these lines: Frankysche speche ye cald romaunce/So sey this clerkes & men of Fraunce. See also Walther von Wartburg's classical work, *Französisch etymologisches Wörterbuch*, article on "Romanice." Most of the English romances belong to the fourteenth century, and many of them are translations or adaptations from French originals.

6. In his *Dictionary*, Samuel Johnson has only *romantick*. The termination fluctuates in the period. Sterne, in chap. 12 of book 1 of *Tristram Shandy* wrote *Cervantick*, and in chap. 10, book 3 we read *Cervantic*.

7. *Immortality of the Soul* (London, 1659), p. 228.

8. *Le Berger extravagant* (London, 1662), p. 6.

9. *Essai sur l'origine des romans* (London, 1672), p. 29.

10. Evelyn to Pepys, Sept. 19, 1682. *Diary and Correspondence of John Evelyn*, 4 vols. (London, 1854), 3:269.

11. *Poems on Several Occasions* (London, 1705), p. 15.

12. Gilbert Burnet, *Contra Varillas* (London, 1687), p. 98; John Strype, *Memorials of Thomas Cranmer* (London, 1694), p. 465; Edward Stillingfleet, *Sermons* (London, 1710), p. 91.

13. *An Account of a Journey into Wales, in Two Letters to Mr. Lower*. Letter dated July, 1756. *Works*, 2 vols. (Dublin, 1774), 2:754.

14. *Remarks on Several Parts of Italy* (London, 1705), p. 2.

15. *Spectator* (May 25, 1711).

16. *The Complete Poetical Work of James Thomson*, ed. J. Logie Robertson (London, 1908), p. 164; *Autumn*, lines 878–880. Previously, Thomson used the expressions "a romantic mountain, forest-crowned" (Ibid., *Summer*, line 459) and, speaking of clouds, "romantic shades" (Ibid., *Summer*, line 1375).

17. George Shelvocke, *A Voyage around the World, by the Way of the Great South Sea* (1726), ed. W. G. Perrin (London, Toronto, Melbourne, and Sydney, 1928), p. 143. Shelvocke speaks of the landscape of Juan Fernandez, where all one sees or hears "is perfectly *romantic*. The very structure of the island, in all its parts, has a certain savage, irregular beauty, which is not to be expressed" (Ibid., p. 143).

18. *The Diary of John Evelyn*, ed. E. S. De Beer, 6 vols. (Oxford, 1955), 4:177.

19. *Hymn* (London, 1751), p. 19.

20. Written on June 4, 1786. *Warton's Poems on Various Subjects* (London, 1791), p. 235.

21. Ibid.

22. *Clarissa; or, The History of a Young Lady*, 8 vols. (Oxford, 1930), 2:39. In a certain sense, Richardson is even one of the most mediocre propagators of the dashing kind of romanticism that will be represented by the romantic school, since all his work seeks to illustrate conventional morality. However, he does not call romantic, i.e. extravagant, as it was customary in his time, a lady who would follow the impulses of her heart rather than the rules of social conventions; but Mrs. Hervey does, since

she tells her niece Clarissa: "What a romantic picture of a forced Marriage have you drawn, Niece!" (Ibid., 2:242). Clarissa herself does not think she is a romantic for refusing to marry Mr. Solmes. Talking of those family members who want to force her to do so, she states: "And these, my dear Miss Howe, are they, who, *some* of them at least, have called me a romantic girl!" (Ibid., 2:294). Richardson had shown a similar attitude, which is that of Fielding's *Tom Jones*, in his *Pamela*. This novel, he explains, in the opening sentence of the preface to the second volume, was "written to Nature, avoiding all romantic flights, improbable surprises, and irrational machinery" (*Pamela*, 2 vols. [London, 1930], 2:vii). We also find, a generation after Richardson, the word *romanticity*. Cf. Elizabeth Blower, *George Bateman*, 3 vols. (London, 1782), 3:139: ". . . gave an air of romanticity to the scene, which greatly pleased them."

23. *To Bower*, in *Annual Register* (London, 1775), p. 164.

24. In John Heneage Jesse, *George Selwyn and his Contemporaries, with Memoirs and Notes*, 4 vols. (London, 1843), 4:123. Letter of May 8, 1779.

25. *The History of Tom Jones: A Foundling* (London, 1749); quotations: 1 and 2. book 6, chap. 7; 3 and 4. book 7, chap. 3; 5. book 7, chap. 11; 6. book 13, chap. 3; 7. book 13, chap. 6; 8. book 15, chap. 2.

26. In his famous *Dictionary of the English Language* (1755) Samuel Johnson mainly insists on the pejorative meanings of the word. See under *Romantick*. When La Place translated Fielding's novel *Histoire de Tom Jones; ou, l'Enfant trouvé*, 2 vols. (London, 1750), he had *romanesque* at his disposal, not yet *romantique*.

27. *The Letters of Sir Walter Scott*, ed. H. J. C. Gierson, 12 vols. (London, 1787–1817), 8:39, letter of April 4.

28. Dennys Jasper Murphy (pseud. C. R. Maturin), *The Fatal Revenge of the Family of Montorio: A Romance*, 3 vols. (London, 1807), 1:110.

29. *History of Modern Criticism*, 2:110–111.

30. *After Strange Gods: A Primer of Modern Heresy* (New York, 1933), pp. 26–27.

31. *Neues und ausfürliches Dictionnarium oder Wörterbuch in dreien Sprachen*.

32. *Fragmente aus seinem Nachlasse*, in *Sämtliche Werke*, ed. Karl Rosenkranz, 12 vols. (Leipzig, 1838–1842) 11:224.

33. *Iris*, 8 vols. (Berlin, 1775–1777) 6:284.

34. *Goethes Werke in sechs Bänden* (Leipzig, 1940), 6:388.

35. Ullmann and Gotthard, *Geschichte des Begriffes "Romantisch,"* p. 26. "Das Wort . . . war verständlich im Munde des Publikums" ("The word . . . was understood and used by the public"). Tieck, one of the chief promoters of German romanticism, used the word romantisch in his earliest works. In *William Lovell* (1795–1796) we read: ". . . die finstern Gewölbe eines romantischen Haines" (". . . the dark vaults of a romantic grove") and ". . . der Mond goss durch die roten Vorhänge ein romantisches Licht" (". . . the moon poured a romantic light through the red curtains"), (*Frühe Erzählungen und Romane*, ed. Marianne Thalmann [Munich, 1963], p. 365).

36. *Romantic* in the original. *Remarks*, p. 2.

37. *Lettres d'un Français*, 3 vols. (The Hague, 1745), 2:203.

38. *Etat de la Corse,* par Mr. James Boswell, Ecuyer, trans. S. D. C., 2 vols. (London, 1769), 1: 33.

39. Denis Diderot, *Correspondance,* ed. Georges Roth, 16 vols. (Paris, 1955–1970), 2: 292, 294.

40. Cf. Antoine Léonard Thomas, *Essai sur le caractère, les moeurs et l'esprit des femmes dans les différents siècles* (Paris, 1772). "Jamais le mot *romanesque* ne dut être si à la mode" (p. 161).

41. *Lettres inédites de l'Abbé Nicaise,* ed. Eugène de Budé (Paris, 1886), p. 35.

42. *Obermann* (1804). I quote from the two-volume 1833 edition, prefaced by Sainte-Beuve (Paris) 1: 258.

43. Ibid., 1: 262.

44. Ibid., 2: 65.

45. *Rêveries . . .*, ed. Joachim Merlant, 2 vols. (Paris, 1910), 1: 232. In the same place Sénancour speaks of "la situation romantique du château de Chillon."

46. *Obermann,* 1: 74–75.

47. *Liberty,* part 4, lines 257–259.

48. *Obermann,* 2: 326.

49. *Spettatore* 11 and 12 (1814), quoted in Apollonio, *Romantico,* p. 133.

50. *Spettatore* 3 (1814), quoted in ibid., p. 119.

51. *Spettatore* 24 (1814), quoted in ibid., p. 134.

52. *Della composizione dei paesaggi sul terreno,* trans. Giovanni Agrati (Milano, 1819), pp. 87–88. The English translation (London, 1783, p. 141), is most inaccurate.

53. *Della ragione poetica* (London, 1806), p. 171.

54. *Dell'istoria della volgar poesia* (Venice, 1731), pp. 315–346.

55. *Della novella poesia* (Verona, 1732), p. 80.

56. *Poesia di Ossian, Figlio di Fingal, antico poeta celtico,* trans. Melchiorre Cesarotti in 1772, 4 vols. (Bassano, 1810) 4: 45.

57. *Compendio* (Bassano, 1774), p. 14.

9. Literary Exoticism

1. England has produced hundreds of good novels with her former colonies as setting and background, including George Orwell's *Burmese Days,* E. M. Forster's *A Passage to India,* and D. H. Lawrence's *The Plumed Serpent.* See among other studies that of Robert F. Lee's *Conrad's Colonialism* (The Hague, 1969). In France, too, many writers, like Paul Morand and Pierre Benoit, published novels concerned with exotic traditions. For studies concerning French colonial literature, see Marius Leblond, *Le Roman colonial: Après l'exotisme de Loti* (Paris, 1926); R. Lebel, *Histoire de la littérature coloniale en France* (Paris, 1931).

2. The phrase can be traced to Epictetus's *Dissertations,* "Encheiridion," part 33, chap. 6.

3. See his *Mostellaria,* part 1, chap. 1, line 41.

4. *Nouvelle Héloïse, Oeuvres complètes,* 4 vols. (Paris, 1959–1969), 2: 472; part 4, letter 11.

5. *Oeuvres de François Rabelais,* ed. Abel Lefranc, 7 vols. (Geneva, 1955), 6: 85, book 4, chap. 2.

6. Exoticism is based upon a principle of relativity. At least one of the compared terms must be familiar to the reader. Only specialists of the Near East will read with profit, for example, T. Eric Peets' *A Comparative Study of the Literature of Egypt, Palestine, and Mesopotamia* (London, 1931).

7. See P. Sykes, *The Quest for Cathay* (London, 1936); Arnold N. Rowbotham, *Missionary and Mandarin: the Jesuits at the Court of China* (Berkeley and Los Angeles, 1942).

8. In 1863 a Chinese named Peng-kwei-fen wrote these lines: "Depuis vingt ans que nous avons des relations avec les étrangers dont plusieurs connaissent notre langue et peuvent l'écrire, voire même lire nos livres classiques, au contraire, parmi nos mandarins et lettrés il n'y a personne qui connaisse la culture étrangère" ("For twenty years we have maintained relations with the foreigners. Some of them know our language and are able to write it and also read our classics. Among our mandarins and literate people, however, nobody knows the foreign culture"). Interestingly enough, Peng-kwei-fen, in speaking here of "the foreign culture," assumes there are only two cultures: the Chinese and the non-Chinese. Cited by André Chih, *L'Occident "chrétien" vu par les Chinois vers la fin du XIXᵉ siècle, 1870–1900* (Paris, 1962), p. 28.

9. The essential book on British taste for exoticism in the seventeenth and eighteenth centuries is Beverly S. Allen's *Tides in English Taste (1619–1800)*, 2 vols. (Cambridge, Mass., 1937). A succinct bibliography on the cultural relations between Europe and the Far East includes: Henri Cordier, *Bibliotheca sinica*, 5 vols. (Paris, 1905–1925); Tung-Li Yuan, *China in Western Literature: A Continuation of Cordier's Bibliotheca Sinica* (New Haven, 1958); and Godfrey R. Nunn's *East Asia: A Bibliography of Bibliographies* and *South and Southeast Asia: A Bibliography of Bibliographies* (Honolulu, 1967 and 1966 respectively). Some major studies on important aspects of the question are: Pierre Martino, *L'Orient dans la littérature française au XVIIᵉ et au XVIIIᵉ siècle* (Paris, 1906); H. Belevitch-Stankevitch, *Le Goût chinois en France au temps de Louis XIV* (Paris, 1910); Hosea B. Morse, *The International Relations of the Chinese Empire*, 3 vols. (London, 1910–1918); Adolf Reichwein, *China und Europa: Geistige und künstlerische Beziehungen im 18. Jahrhundert* (Berlin, 1923), trans. J. C. Powell, *China and Europe: Intellectual and Artistic Contacts in the Eighteenth Century* (London and New York, 1925); André Malraux, *La Tentation de l'Occident* (Paris, 1926), trans. Robert Hollander, *The Temptation of the West* (New York, 1961); Geoffrey Francis Hudson, *Europe and China: A Survey of Their Relations from the Earliest Times to 1800* (London, 1931); Chisaburo Yamada, *Die Chinamode des Spätbarock* (Berlin, 1935); Ernest Richard Hughes, *The Invasion of China by the Western World* (London, 1937); Eduard Horst von Tscharner, *China in der deutschen Dichtung bis zur Klassik* (Munich, 1939); Elisabeth Selden, *China in German Poetry from 1773–1883* (Berkeley and Los Angeles, 1942); Peter Venne, *China und die Chinesen in der neueren englischen und amerikanischen Literatur* (Zurich, 1951); William P. Appleton, *A Cycle of Cathay: The Chinese Vogue in England during the Seventeenth and Eighteenth Centuries* (New York, 1951); Herbert Franke, *Sinologie* (Bern, 1953); Jurgis Baltruvaitis, *Le Moyen âge fantastique: Antiquités et exotismes*

dans l'art gothique (Paris, 1955); Hajime Nakamara, *Ways of Thinking of Eastern Peoples: India, China, Tibet, Japan* (Honolulu, 1964); Kuo Heng-Yuu, *China und die Barbaren: Geistesgeschichtliche Standortbestimmung* (Pfullingen, 1967). On the relations between Japan and the Western world, see Donald Keene, *The Japanese Discovery of Europe: Honda Toschiaki and American Literature*, 2nd ed. (Princeton, 1966); George B. Samson, *The Western World and Japan* (New York, 1950); Earl Miner, *The Japanese Tradition in British and American Literature* (Princeton, 1958); Armando M. Janeira, *Japanese and Western Literature, A Comparative Study* (Rutland, Vt., and Tokyo, 1970).

10. C. Dana Rouillard, *The Turk in French History, Thought and Literature, 1520–1660* (Paris, 1940). The interest in Near Eastern countries in no way means that the sense of local color was accurately conveyed. Molière, for example, in *Le Bourgeois gentilhomme* and Racine in *Bajazet* following the example of numerous writers, gave a very fanciful staging of the Turks. Among all the European dramatists, Lope de Vega excelled in introducing exoticism into the theater. The locale of his plays changes from Spain to Bohemia, to Turkey, to Morocco, and to the Americas as well. Voltaire's *Zaïre*, his *Mahomet, L'Orphelin de la Chine* (compare with Arthur Murphy's *The Orphan of China*), and his *Alzire, ou les Américains* all transport the spectator to foreign continents, just as John Dryden, in his *Indian Queen* and his *Indian Emperor*, had done sixty years earlier (1664 and 1665). In these plays of Voltaire and Dryden, the characters are nearly always poorly disguised Europeans, and one could not pretend Lope de Vega did any better in this respect.

11. See Sir Hamilton Gibb, "The Influence of Islamic Culture on Medieval Europe," *Bulletin of the John Rylands Library* 38 (1955): 82–98. For oriental influences upon European romanticism, see Raymond Schwabe, *La Renaissance orientale* (Paris, 1950). For France, and for later periods: Giuditta Podestà, *L'Oriente dimensione dell'anima romantica* (Geneva, 1966), and Hassan El Nouty, *Le Proche-Orient dans la littérature française de Gérard de Nerval à Maurice Barrès* (Paris, 1958).

12. *Mille et une nuits*, 10 vols. (Paris, 1704–1712). Galland not only undertook the first translation, but also prepared the first printed edition of the work. The Arabian text (incomplete) appeared for the first time at Calcutta in two volumes (1814–1818). One of the most informative works on the literary questions concerning the Arab world is that by C. Brockelmann, *Geschichte der arabischen Literatur*, 2 vols. (Weimar, 1898–1902; 2nd ed. 1943–1949).

13. *Crise de la conscience européenne*, 3 vols. (Paris, 1934). Hazard's study has been completed by his *La Pensée européenne au XVIIIe siècle*, 3 vols. (Paris, 1946). Both works contain extensive bibliographical notes, though a reasonably complete bibliography of the voyages would require a separate study. See also Geoffroy Atkinson, *The Extraordinary Voyage in French Literature before 1700* (New York, 1920); idem, *The Extraordinary Voyage in French Literature from 1700 to 1720* (Paris, 1922); idem, *Les Relations de voyages du XVIIe siècle et l'évolution des idées: Contribution à l'étude de la formation de l'esprit du XVIIIe siècle* (Paris, 1924); idem, *La Littérature géographique française de la Renaissance . . . Description de 524 impressions publiées en français avant 1610 et traitant*

des pays et des peuples non européens . . . (Paris, 1927); E. G. Cox, *A Reference Guide to the Literature of Travel,* 2 vols. (Seattle, 1935–1936). There is also the fictitious travel: P. B. Gove, *The Imaginary Voyage in Prose Fiction: A History of Its Criticism and a Guide for Its Study* . . . (New York, 1941, London, 1961); Percy G. Adams, *Travelers and Travel Liars* (Berkeley and Los Angeles, 1962). See also Harold F. Watson, *The Sailor in English Fiction and Drama, 1550–1800* (New York, 1931), a book that also has to be considered a study in a theme.

14. See E. Pons, "Le Voyage, genre littéraire au XVIIIᵉ siècle," *Bulletin de la Faculté des Lettres de Strasbourg* (Feb. 1 and March 1, 1926).

15. The role of the missionaries is of paramount importance in the establishment of the first lasting contacts between the great civilizations. Whether intellectual or semi-intellectual, they transmitted to their homelands relatively faithful accounts of the state of the culture, the mores, and the customs of a country. Examples of such reports are to be found in *The Jesuit Relations and Allied Documents: Travels and Explorations of the Jesuit Missionaries in New France 1610–1791,* 73 vols., ed. Reuben Gold Thwaites (Cleveland, 1896–1901). Extracts appeared in the *Mercure de France,* and a one-volume abridged version has been edited by Edna Kenton (New York, 1925). See also Jean-Baptiste Du Halde, *Description géographique, historique, chronologique, et politique de l'Empire de la Chine et de la Tartarie chinoise* (1735), which appeared also in English (1738).

16. *Emile, Oeuvres complètes,* 4 vols. (Paris, 1959–1969), 4:826.

17. See Hoxie N. Fairchild, *The Noble Savage: A Study in Romantic Naturalism,* (New York, 1938); A. Arinos de Mello Franco, *O Indio Brasileiro e a Revolução Francesa: As origens brasileiras da teoria da bondade natural* (Rio de Janeiro, 1937); W. Sypher, "The West Indian as a Character in the Eighteenth Century," *Studies in Philology* 36 (1939); see René Gonnard, *La Légende du bon sauvage: Contribution à l'étude des origines du socialisme* (Paris, 1946); J. Robert Constantine, "The Ignoble Savage, an Eighteenth-Century Literary Stereotype," *Phylon* 27 (1966): 171–179.

18. Gellert, *Sämtliche Schriften,* part 1, *Fabeln* (Leipzig, 1767), p. 23. This confusion is reminiscent of the earliest periods of contacts between Europe and China, when Cathay was all but indistinguishable from Japan and India.

19. See Harold Jantz, "Schiller's Indian Threnody," in *Schiller 1759/1959. Commemorative American Studies,* ed. J. R. Frey (Urbana, Ill., 1959). This sort of exoticism existed in the land itself of the Indians, the most celebrated example being Longfellow's *Song of Hiawatha.* See Stith Thompson, "The Indian Legend of Hiawatha," *PMLA* 37 (1922): 128–140.

20. See A. Leslie Willson, *The Mythical Image: The Ideal of India in German Romanticism* (Durham, 1964). This work contains a useful list of "Travel Literature and Works on India," pp. 244–248.

21. Arthur E. Christy, "Emerson's Debt to the Orient," *Monist* 38 (1928): 38–64; idem, *The Orient in American Transcendentalism; a Study of Emerson, Thoreau, and Alcott* (New York, 1932).

22. Preface to his translation of *Voyages du Capitaine Robert Lade en différentes parties de l'Afrique, de l'Asie et de l'Amérique* (Paris, 1744).

23. *Voyage en Orient: De Paris à Cythère*, 2 vols. (Paris, 1883), 2:337.
24. Defoe's *History of the Pirates* appeared from 1724 to 1728. He also planned to write a history of the great navigators.
25. See Martha P. Conant, *The Oriental Tale in English Literature in the Eighteenth Century* (New York, 1966).
26. There are scores of studies on the exoticism of the senses. A bibliography would have to begin with Friedrich Brie's *Exotismus der Sinne: zur Psychologie der englischen Romantik* (Heidelberg, 1920) and then continue with A. Hayter's *Opium and the Romantic Imagination* (New York, 1968).
27. See Ray W. Frantz, *The English Traveller and the Movement of Ideas, 1660–1732* (Lincoln, Nebr., 1932); Robert R. Cawley, *The Voyagers and Elizabethan Drama* (Boston, 1938).
28. *The Essays*, trans. Charles Cotton (Chicago, London, Toronto, and Geneva, 1952), p. 93. "Il n'y a rien de barbare et de sauvage en cette nation, à ce qu'on m'en a rapporté, sinon que chacun appelle barbarie ce qui n'est pas de son usage. . . . Ils sont sauvages, de mesme que nous appelons sauvages les fruicts que nature, de soy et de son progrez ordinaire, a produicts" (*Essais*, 3 vols [Paris, 1969], 1:254).
29. At all cultural levels exoticism may be connected with eroticism. In the expression "exotic dancer," exotic is almost synonymous with erotic.
30. Pierre Jourda wrongly uses the term *exotisme* in the title of a work that treats the *foreign* influences in nineteenth-century French letters. In fact, only some of his chapters make any reference to the subject. See *L'Exotisme dans la littérature française depuis Chateaubriand: Le romantisme.* (Paris, 1938). The same can be said of the study by Frida Weissman, *L'Exotisme de Valery Larbaud* (Paris, 1966). Mrs. Weissman's book deals with Larbaud's intellectual relations with various European countries. Obviously the word exoticism is, in these instances, out of place. Jean-Marie Carré does not use it in *Les Ecrivains français et le mirage allemand* (Paris, 1947).
31. See the following works: Jean Alazard, *L'Orient et la peinture française au XIXe siècle, de Delacroix à Renoir* (Paris, 1930); Roger Bezombes, *L'Exotisme dans l'art et la pensée*, Preface by Paul Valéry (Paris, 1953). As to primitivism, the study of George Boas and Arthur O. Lovejoy is most relevant: *Primitivism and Related Ideas in Antiquity* (New York, 1935).
32. Stéphane Mallarmé, *Poems*, trans. Roger Fry (London, 1936), p. 63. The French original reads:

> La chair est triste, hélas! et j'ai lu tous les livres.
> Fuir! là-bas fuir! Je sens que des oiseaux sont ivres
> D'être parmi l'écume inconnue et les cieux!
>
> . . . .
>
> Je partirai! Steamer balançant ta mâture,
> Lève l'ancre pour une exotique nature (Ibid., p. 62)!

33. See Gove, *Imaginary Voyage*. The utopia may also be studied in connection with exoticism, although it represents more genuinely exodism, mostly with satirical purposes. Among the early examples are Thomas

More's *Utopia* (1516), Tommaso Campanella's *Civitas Solis* (1602), Francis Bacon's *New Atlantis* (1626), Cyrano de Bergerac's *Etats et empires de la lune* (1656) and *Etats et empires du soleil* (1662). The genre has been cultivated in modern times, particularly in Anglo-Saxon literature, for example, by Samuel Butler (*Erewhon*, 1872), and by H. G. Wells (*A Modern Utopia*, 1905). Besides Glenn R. Negley's and J. Max Patrick's well-known anthology of imaginary societies, *The Quest for Utopia* (New York, 1952); some judicious studies on the subject have been published, such as Northrop Frye's "Varieties of Literary Utopias," *Daedalus* 94 (1965): 323–347.

34. Trans. Chi-chen Wang (New York, 1958).

10.   Prolegomenon C

1. One of the most recent and most comprehensive general studies on genre is Klaus W. Hempfer's *Gattungstheorie* (Munich, 1973). See also Franz J. Böhm, "Begriff und Wesen des Genres," *Zeitschrift für Aesthetik* 22 (1928): 186–191; Paul van Tieghem, "La question des genres littéraires," *Hélicon* 1 (1938): 95–103; Pierre Kohler, "Contribution à une philosophie des genres," *Hélicon* 3 (1938): 233–245; Jean Hankiss, "Les genres littéraires," *Hélicon* 2 (1939): 115–226; C. Vincent, *Théorie des genre littéraires* (Paris, 1940); Irene Behrens, *Die Lehre von der Einteilung der Dichtkunst, vornehmlich vom 16. bis 19. Jahrhundert* (Halle, 1940); Guillermo Diaz-Plaja, *Teoria y historia de los géneros literarios* (Barcelona, 1940); J. J. Donohue, *The Theory of Literary Kinds* 2 vols. (Iowa City, 1943–1949); Mario Fubini, "Genesi e storia dei generi letterari," in his *Critica e poesia* (Bari, 1956), pp. 143–274. For short general discussions of genres, see Ulrich Weisstein, *Einführung in die vergleichende Literaturwissenschaft* (Stuttgart and Berlin, 1968), chap. 6. A great number of monographs and articles have been published on specific genres, e.g.: W. J. Entwistle, *European Balladry* (New York, 1939); C. M. Bowra, *From Virgil to Milton* (New York, 1945); Ludwig Rohner, *Der deutsche Essay* (Neuwied and Berlin, 1966); Heinrich Dörrie, *Der heroische Brief* (Berlin, 1968); Peter Boerner, *Tagebuch* (Stuttgart, 1969); Ralph Freedman, "The Possibilities of a Theory of the Novel," in *The Disciplines of Criticism*, eds. Peter Demetz, Thomas Greene, and Lowry Nelson, Jr. (New Haven, 1968). The multilingual Polish journal in comparative literature *Zagadnienia Rodzajòw Literackich* [The problems of literary genres] published in Lódz, edited by Stefania Skwarczyńska, and now in its fifteenth year, is a major source of information. See, for example, "The Beginnings of Genological Thinking: Antiquity-Middle Ages," and "Genological Notions in the Renaissance Theory on Poetry," 12, no. 1 (1969): 5–23, and no. 2 (1969): 5–20, by Teresa Michalowski.

2. See E. Seybold, *Das Genrebild in der deutschen Literatur: Von Sturm und Drang bis zum Realismus* (Stuttgart and Berlin, 1968).

3. The variety and continuity of studies in genres, especially in the field of the drama, may be illustrated by two titles: Hans Schwab, *Das Schauspiel im Schauspiel zur Zeit Shakespeares* (Vienna and Leipzig, 1896); and Robert J. Nelson, *Play within a Play: the Dramatist's Conception of his Art, Shakespeare to Anouilh* (New Haven), 1958).

4. Euphuism, gongorism, marinism, and *préciosité* are literary movements. At the same time, however, they provide certain works with specific stylistic features, and may be considered genres.

5. "Genre Theory, the Lyric, and Erlebnis," in *Festschrift Richard Alewyn*, ed. Herbert Singer and Benno von Wiese (Cologne and Graz, 1967), p. 392.

6. "Petrarcas Sammlung, ein wahrer und vollständiger lyrischer Roman" (*Vorlesungen über Schöne Literatur und Kunst*, 3 vols. [Heilbronn, 1884], 3:204). Ralph Freedman provides examples closer to our times; see *The Lyrical Novel: Studies in Hermann Hesse, André Gide, and Virginia Woolf* (Princeton, 1963).

7. *Literature and Sincerity* (New Haven, 1963), p. 162. In his Postscript to *Clarissa*, Richardson calls his novel a "dramatic narrative."

8. *Theory of Literature*, new rev. ed. (New York, 1962), p. 231.

11. The *Bildungsroman* in Germany, England, and France

1. See article "Bildung" by Jacob and Wilhelm Grimm, in *Deutsches Wörterbuch*, 16 vols. (Leipzig, 1860), 2:22.

2. In regard to the sense that Goethe attached to the word *Bildung*, cf. *Goethe Handbuch: Goethe, seine Welt und Zeit in Werk und Wirkung*, ed. Alfred Zastrau, 2nd ed. (Stuttgart, 1955), columns 1209–1211. See also Hans Weil, *Die Entstehungsgeschichte des deutschen Bildungsprinzips* (Bonn, 1930); Ilse Schaarschmidt, *Der Bedeutungswandel der Worte "bilden" und "Bildung"* (Königsberg, 1931); and Ludwig Kiehn, *Goethes Begriff der Bildung* (Hamburg, 1932).

3. See, for example, Roy Pascal, *Design and Truth in Autobiography* (Cambridge, Mass., 1960); Wayne Shumaker, *English Autobiography: Its Emergence, Materials, and Forms* (Berkeley and Los Angeles, 1954); and M. J. Temmer, "Jean-Jacques Rousseau's *Confessions* and Gottfried Keller's *Der grüne Heinrich*," *Revue de Littérature Comparée* 44, no. 2 (1970): 155–184. The classic work on autobiography is that by Georg Misch, who devoted almost sixty years to exploring the subject. The some three thousand pages published to date are divided into six volumes, but the last of them barely reaches the High Middle Ages—an outstanding example of *Gründlichkeit: Geschichte der Autobiographie*, 6 vols. (Bern and Frankfort on the Main, 1907–1962). For the intrinsic relation of biography to the *Bildungsroman*, see J. A. Garraty, *The Nature of Biography* (New York, 1957). One of the few studies that considers the problem of biography from a comparatist point of view is A. Owen Aldridge's "International Influences upon Biography as a Literary Genre," in *Proceedings of the Fourth Congress of the International Comparative Literature Association*, ed. François Jost, 2 vols. (The Hague, 1966) 2:972–981 and "Biography and Realism," *Les Problèmes des genres littéraires*, XI (1969): 5–21.

4. The *Künstlerroman* ("artist-novel") represents a particular type of *Bildungsroman* by virtue of the personality and profession of the hero, not because of the structure of the plot. However, a Künstlerroman is not necessarily a Bildungsroman, as Thomas Mann's *Doktor Faustus* illustrates. But each Bildungsroman presents a sort of *Lebenskünstler*, an artist at living. See Maurice Beebe's *Ivory Towers and Sacred Founts: The*

Artist as Hero in Fiction from Goethe to Joyce (New York, 1964), and his "Le Roman d'artiste: E. T. A. Hoffman et Balzac," in *La Littérature narrative d'imagination: Des Genres littéraires aux techniques d'expression* (Paris, 1961), pp. 137–155; Wolfgang Mohr, "Tristan und Isolde als Künstlerroman," *Euphorion* 43 (1959): 153–174. A related problem is treated by Ronald Peacock, *The Poet in the Theatre* (New York, 1946).

5. *Selbsterziehungsroman* would come close to being a synonym for Bildungsroman. A particularly useful and recent publication on the picaresque novel is Robert Alter's *Rogue's Progress: Studies in the Picaresque Novel* (Cambridge, Mass., 1964). See also Claudio Guillén, "Toward a Definition of the Picaresque," in *Proceedings of the Third Congress of the International Comparative Literature Association*, ed. W. A. P. Smit (The Hague, 1962), pp. 252–266.

6. Eckermann reports on April 20, 1825: "Man sagt mit Recht, fuhr Goethe fort, dass die gemeinsame Ausbildung menschlicher Kräfte zu wünschen und auch das Vorzüglichste sei. Der Mensch aber ist dazu nicht geboren, jeder muss sich eigentlich als besonderes Wesen bilden, aber den Begriff zu erlangen suchen, was wir alle sind. Ich dachte dabei an den *Wilhelm Meister*" (*Gespräche mit Eckermann*, 2 vols. [Basel, 1945] 1:143).

7. Cf. Fritz Martini, "Der Bildungsroman: Zur Geschichte des Wortes und der Theorie," *Deutsche Vierteljahrsschrift für Literaturwissenschaft und Geistesgeschichte* 31, no. 1 (1961): 44ff.

8. "Ueber den Geist und Zusammenhang einer Reihe philosophischer Romane," *Dörptsche Beyträge für Freunde der Philosophie, Literatur und Kunst* 3, no. 1 (1816): 180–195. In the passage in question, Morgenstern does not refer to Goethe, but to Klinger, whose drama *Sturm und Drang* gave its name to a literary movement and who, moreover, spent half his life at Dorpat, where he died in 1831. Goethe, according to his diary (Dec. 6, 1821), read the *Dörptsche Beyträge*. Klinger's novels, excepting perhaps *Fausts Leben, Taten und Höllenfahrt*, are unknown today.

9. "Über das Wesen des Bildungsromans," and "Zur Geschichte des Bildungsromans." Cited by August Langen, "Der Wortschatz des 18. Jahrhunderts," in *Deutsche Wortgeschichte*, 2nd ed., ed. Friedrich Maurer and Fritz Stroh, 3 vols. (Berlin, 1959), 2:59. The first of these lectures was published in *Inländisches Museum* 1, no. 4 (1820/1821) and 2, nos. 5 and 6 (1821), and the second in *Neues Museum der teutschen Provinzen Russlands* 1, nos. 1–3 (1824/1825).

10. Dilthey states: "Ich möchte die Romane, welche die Schule des Wilhelm Meister ausmachen (denn Rousseaus verwandte Kunstform wirkte auf sie nicht fort), Bildungsroman nennen. Goethes Werk zeigt menschliche Ausbildung in verschiedenen Stufen, Gestalten, Lebensepochen. Es erfüllt mit Behagen, weil es nicht die ganze Welt sammt ihrer Missbildungen und den Kampf böser Leidenschaften um die Existenz schildert; der spröde Stoff des Lebens ist ausgeschieden" ("I would like to call *Bildungsromane* those novels that make up the school of *Wilhelm Meister* [the related artistic form of Rousseau did not influence them]. Goethe's work shows the education of men in different stages, characters, and periods of life. It is a gratifying work because it does not depict the whole world with its deformations and abnormities, and the struggle of

wicked passions for existence; the brittle elements of life are ignored"), (*Leben Schleiermachers* [Berlin, 1870], p. 282).

11. The first work to consult on the subject, in fact an "état présent" of the problem, is Lothar Köhn's *Entwicklungs- und Bildungsroman: Ein Forschungsbericht* (Stuttgart, 1968). Earlier studies are: Paula Stolz, *Der Erziehungsroman des wechselnden Bildungsideals in der zweiten Hälfte des 18. Jahrhunderts* (Munich, 1925); Erich Jenisch, "Vom Abenteuer- zum Bildungsroman," *Germanisch-Romanische Monatsschrift* 14 (1926): 339–351; Melitta Gerhard, *Der Deutsche Entwicklungsroman bis zu Goethes "Wilhelm Meister"* (Berlin, 1926); Ernst Ludwig Stahl, *Die religiöse und humanistisch-philosophische Bildungsidee und die Entstehungsgeschichte des deutschen Bildungsromans im 18. Jahrhundert* (Berlin, 1934); Charlotte Kehr, *Der deutsche Entwicklungsroman seit der Jahrhundertwende* (Dres- den, 1938); Berta Berger, *Der moderne deutsche Bildungsroman* (Bern, 1942); Hans Heinrich Borcherdt, *Der Roman der Goethezeit* (Urach and Stuttgart, 1949), chap. 3, "Der Bildungsroman der Hochklassik und Hoch- romantik"; Alfred Schotz, *Gehalt und Form des Bildungsromans im 20. Jahrhundert* (Erlangen, 1950); Roy Pascal, *The German Novel*, 2nd ed. (London, 1965), part 1, "The Bildungsroman"; Herbert Seidler, "Wand- lungen des deutschen Bildungsromans im 19. Jahrhundert," *Wirkendes Wort* 11, no. 3 (1961): 148–162; Joseph Strelka, "Goethes *Wilhelm Meister* und der Roman des Zwanzigsten Jahrhunderts," *German Quarterly* 41 (1968): 338–355.

Some studies deal with individual apprenticeship novels: Friedrich Wilhelm Schröder, *Wielands "Agathon" und die Anfänge des modernen Bildungsromans* (Königsberg, 1904); Max Wundt, *Goethes "Wilhelm Meister" und der Entwicklungsroman des modernen Lebensideals* (Berlin and Leipzig, 1913); Rudolf Lehmann, "Anton Reiser und die Entstehung des Wilhelm Meister," *Jahrbuch der Goethegesellschaft* 3 (1916): 116–134; A. Hauser, *Gottfried Keller: Geburt und Zerfall der dichterischen Welt* (Zurich, 1959); Georg Berger, *Die Romane Jean Pauls als Bildungsromane* (Leipzig, 1923); Joachim Miller, *Vergleichende Studien zur Menschen- auffassung und Menschendarstellung Gottfried Kellers und Adalbert Stif- ters* (Leipzig, 1930); Ludwig Arnold, *Stifters "Nachsommer" als Bildungs- roman* (Giessen, 1938); Gerhard Köttgen, *Wilhelm Raabes Ringen um die Aufgabe des Erziehungsromans* (Berlin, 1939); Heinrich Stolte, *Gottfried Keller und sein "Grüner Heinrich"* (Gotha, 1948); Günther Miller, *Aufbau- formen des Romans: Dargelegt an den Entwicklungsromanen Gottfried Kellers und Adalbert Stifters* (Groningen and Djakarta, 1953); Jürgen Scharfschwerdt, *Thomas Mann und der deutsche Bildungsroman: Eine Untersuchung zu den Problemen einer literarischen Tradition* (Stuttgart and Berlin, 1967).

12. According to Gerhard Storz, *Goethe-Vigilien* (Stuttgart, 1953), Goethe's novel should not be called a Bildungsroman. The question has recently been discussed by Kurt May, "*Wilhelm Meisters Lehrjahre, ein Bildungsroman?*" *Deutsche Vierteljahrsschrift für Literaturwissenschaft und Geistesgeschichte* 31, no. 1 (1957): 1–37; and by Hans Eichner, "Zur Deutung von *Wilhelm Meisters Lehrjahren*," in *Jahrbuch des Freien Deut- schen Hochstifts 1966* (Tübingen, 1967), pp. 165–196.

13. "Sa manière habituelle d'aller à la chasse du bonheur" (*Vie de*

Henri Brulard, in *Oeuvres complètes de Stendhal,* ed. Edouard Champion, 37 vols. [Paris, 1913–1940], 25:81).

14. Herder was concerned with the education of mankind rather than with that of the individual, as is shown, for instance, in his essay *Auch eine Philosophie der Geschichte zur Bildung der Menschheit* (1774). See also his *Ideen zur Philosophie der Geschichte der Menschheit* (1784–1791).

15. "Ich habe von Jugend auf die Augen meines Geistes mehr nach innen als nach aussen gerichtet, und da ist es sehr natürlich, dass ich *den* Menschen bis auf einen gewissen Grad habe kennen lernen, ohne *die* Menschen im mindesten zu verstehen und zu begreifen" (*Goethe's Werke in sechs Bänden* [Leipzig, 1940], 4:219).

16. There are quite a few studies on the English Bildungsroman: L. Meissner "Der Wandel des englischen Bildungsideal seit der Renaissance," *Archiv für das Studium der neueren Sprachen,* no. 153 (Brunswick and Berlin, 1927); S. Howe, *Wilhelm Meister and his English Kinsmen: Apprentices to Life* (New York, 1930); Konrad Gottbrath, *Der Einfluss von Goethes "Wilhelm Meister" auf die englische Literatur* (Münster, 1934); Hans Wagner, *Der englische Bildungsroman bis in die Zeit des ersten Weltkrieges* (Bern, 1951); G. B. Tennyson, "The Bildungsroman in Nineteenth-Century English Literature," in *Medieval Epic to the "Epic Theater" of Brecht: Essays in Comparative Literature,* ed. Rosario P. Armato and John M. Spalek (Los Angeles, 1968), pp. 135–147. John Hennig's "Englandkunde im *Wilhelm Meister,*" *Goethe* 26 (1964): 199–222, treats a complementary question. For the United States, see Martin L. Kornbluth, "The Reception of *Wilhelm Meister* in America," *Symposium* 13 (1959): 128–134, and Volkmar Sander, "Der deutsche Bildungsroman in Amerika," *Deutsche Rundschau* 87 (1961): 1032–1038.

17. "Pourquoi le roman de la jeune intelligence n'a-t-il pas été écrit?" (*Réflexions sur le roman* [Paris, 1938], p. 13). One year before, Justin O'Brien had published his study *The Novel of Adolescence in France: The Study of a Literary Theme* (New York, 1937).

18. "Pas un méchant homme qui fasse craindre pour les bons . . . rien d'inopiné; point de coup de théâtre" (*Oeuvres complétes,* 5 vols. [Paris, 1961], 2:13. "C'est-à-dire qu'il vous faut des hommes communs et des événements rares? Je crois que j'aimerais mieux le contraire," Ibid.).

19. "Que la trompette du jugement dernier sonne quand elle voudra; je viendrai ce livre à la main me présenter devant le souverain juge. Je dirai hautement: voilà ce que j'ai fait, ce que j'ai pensé, ce que je fus" (Ibid., 1:5).

20. Rousseau's didacticism manifests itself in most of his books. The *Nouvelle Héloïse* contains almost as much instruction as *Emile.* The two works, nevertheless, belong to imaginative literature; the biography of Emile, whom the reader accompanies from birth to marriage, obviously constitutes a plot. At the beginning of *Emile,* Rosseau correctly enough defines the nature of his undertaking by asserting that the public "croira moins lire un traité d'éducation que les rêveries d'un visionnaire sur l'éducation" (Ibid., 4:242).

21. "Natürliche Entwicklung" and "künstliche Schulentwicklung" (*Philosophische Versuche über die menschliche Natur und ihre Entwicklung* 2 vols. [Berlin, 1776–1777]. In turn, Heinrich Pestalozzi expresses himself

as follows: "Durch seine Bildung ist er [der Mensch] ein Resultat des Einflusses, den zufällige Umstände und Verhältnisse auf die Freiheit und Reinheit des Wachstums seiner Kräfte haben. Durch seine Erziehung ist er ein Resultat des Einflusses, den der sittliche Wille des Menschen auf die Freiheit und Reinheit seiner Kräfte hat" ("By his formation man is the result of the influence that accidental circumstances and conditions have on the freedom and righteousness of the growth of his strengths. Through his education he is the result of the influences that the moral will of man has on the freedom and righteousness of his strengths"), ("Rede am zwei-undsiebzigsten Geburtstag," in *Heinrich Pestalozzis lebendiges Werk*, 4 vols., ed. Adolf Haller [Basel, 1946] 3:310).

22. *Emile, Oeuvres complètes*, 4:624–625. To Rousseau printed books are detestable. But since we obviously need some, we would do well to choose them with discrimination. In fact, one alone provokes his enthusiasm: *Robinson Crusoe*, in which the hero's personality develops through experience. Ibid., 4:454–455.

23. "Je ne compte pas non plus l'éducation du monde . . . elle n'est propre qu'à faire des hommes doubles" (Ibid., 4:250). "Quoique entrant dans le monde il [Emile] en ignore absolument les manières . . . Il prend plutôt l'usage du monde précisément parce qu'il en fait peu de cas" (Ibid., 4:667).

24. "Négliger le livre du monde" (Ibid., 4:826).

25. "Le développement interne de nos facultés et de nos organes est l'éducation de la nature; l'usage qu'on nous apprend à faire de ce développement est l'éducation des hommes, et l'acquis de notre propre expérience sur les objets qui nous affectent est l'éducation des choses" (Ibid., 4:247).

26. A systematic comparison of *Emile* and *Wilhelm Meister* should reveal several highly instructive parallels. For example, both works contain a kind of interlude, a pause, with the same structural function, which consists of revealing the inner life, interestingly enough, not of the main heroes but of other characters. Both Rousseau's section "Profession de foi du Vicaire savoyard" and Goethe's diary "Bekenntnisse einer schönen Seele" interrupt the action in order to call to the reader's attention "des états d'âme." And the expression "schöne Seele," i. e. "belle âme," was current in France toward the middle of the eighteenth century. Rousseau uses it twice in the second preface to the *Nouvelle Héloïse* (Ibid., 2:13 and 27). See Hans Schmeer, *Der Begriff der schönen Seele* (Berlin, 1926). Further useful studies are: Max von Waldberg, "Die Entwicklungsge-schichte der *Schönen Seele bei den spanischen Mystikern*," *Literarhisto-rische Forschungen* 49 (1910): 27–41, and Langen, "Der Wortschatz," *Deutsche Wortgeschichte*, ed. Maurer and Stroh, 2:80–81. A comparison between the "Profession" and the "Bekenntnisse" would provide a fine basis for the examination of the secularization process in the pedagogical field touched upon above.

27. See Bernard N. Schilling, "Realism in Nineteenth-Century Fiction: Balzac, Dickens, and the Bildungsroman," in *Proceedings of the Fifth Congress of the International Comparative Literature Association*, ed. N. Banašević (Amsterdam, 1969), pp. 251–259.

28. Léon Degoumois, in *Flaubert à l'école de Goethe* (Geneva, 1925),

writes five pages (45–50) on *Wilhelm Meister* and *L'Education sentimentale;* they sufficiently demonstrate that the subject deserves at least fifty. See Marilyn Smith, *Flaubert, Reader of Goethe: A Study in Literary Relations* (Ph.D. diss., University of Illinois, 1973).

29. For this reason, at the end of the novel, remembrances of things past are the best of the main hero's life. In the last pages, Frédéric and his friend Deslauriers give a summary of their common adventures. "Et ils résumèrent leur vie. Ils l'avaient manquée tous les deux. . . . Et, exhumant leur jeunesse, à chaque phrase, ils se disaient: Te rappelles-tu?" ("And they summoned up their life. For both of them it has been a failure. . . . And in exhuming their youth, they would say with each sentence: You remember?"), (*L'Education sentimentale* (Paris, n.d.), p. 456.

30. *Oeuvres complètes. Henri Brulard*, 1913, 24:91–92.

31. "Je ne pensais jamais aux Beyle qu'avec répugnance" (Ibid., 24:90): a good reason to take a pseudonym. However, why did he choose Stendhal? See note 43.

32. "Mon père reçut mes adieux au Jardin-de-Ville, sous les fenêtres des maisons faisant face à la rue Montorge. Il pleuvait un peu. La seule impression que me firent ses larmes fut de le trouver bien laid" (Ibid., 24:73).

33. "Comme le souvenir d'une abominable indigestion" (Ibid., 24:110). Further on he says: "De 1796 à 1799 je n'ai fait attention qu'à ce qui pouvait me donner les moyens de quitter Grenoble" ("From 1796 to 1799 I only paid attention to what would give me the means to leave Grenoble"), and at another place: "Le seul son des cloches de la cathédrale, même en 1828, quand je suis allé revoir Grenoble, m'a donné une tristesse morne, sèche, sans attendrissement, de cette tristesse voisine de la colère" ("The mere sound of the bells of the cathedral, even in 1828, when I went to see Grenoble again, filled me with a dreary and dry sadness, without any tender regret, a sadness resembling anger.") (Ibid., 245:130 and 50).

34. "Faisant l'effet d'un plat hypocrite" (Ibid., 24:288).

35. "Comme protégé par les prêtres" (Ibid., 25:132).

36. "J'étais fou de Hamlet" (Ibid., 24:13).

37. "Pour que rien ne manquât au pouvoir de Shakespeare sur mon coeur, je crois même que mon père m'en dit du mal" (Ibid., 24:287).

38. "Mépriser sincèrement et souverainement le talent de Voltaire" (Ibid., 24:19). Stendhal never tires of expressing his aversion for the writings of Voltaire. Chapter 32 opens with these words: "J'avais donc un certain beau littéraire dans la tête en 1796 ou 1797, quand je suivis le cours de M. Dubois-Fontanelle; ce beau était fort différent du sien. Le trait le plus marquant de cette différence était mon adoration pour la vérité tragique et simple de Shakespeare, contrastant avec la *puérilité emphatique* de Voltaire" ("In 1796 or 1797, when I attended M. Dubois-Fontanelle's course, I had in my mind a certain ideal of literary beauty; this ideal was quite different from his. The most striking trait of that difference was my adoration for the tragic and simple truth of Shakespeare which contrasts with the emphatic puerility of Voltaire"), (Ibid., 25:23).

39. "Avec adoration, tout en le maudissant comme impie" (Ibid., 24:79).

40. "La lecture de la *Nouvelle Héloïse* et les scrupules de Saint-Preux me formèrent profondément honnête homme. . . . Ainsi, c'est un livre lu en

grande cachette et malgré mes parents qui m'a fait honnête homme"
(Ibid., 24: 211–212).
41. "Les épinards et Saint-Simon ont été mes seuls goûts durables"
(Ibid., 5: 164).
42. By way of an interesting sidelight to this, we quote the following:
"Les auteurs qui me plaisaient alors à la folie furent Cervantès, Don
Quichotte, et l'Arioste (tous les trois traduits) dans des traductions" ("The
authors I was crazy about at that time were Cervantes, *Don Quixote*, and
Ariosto [all three translated] in translations") (Ibid., 24: 288).
43. Stendhal would certainly not have liked this rapprochement, since
the Germanic *génie* was always foreign to him. In chap. 33 (24: 242) of
Henri Brulard, speaking of the Milanese, he writes: "Les autorités alle-
mandes et abhorrées veulent lui faire goûter Schiller, dont la belle âme, si
différente de celle du plat Goethe ["schöne Seele" is Goethe's expression!],
serait bien choquée de voir de tels apôtres à sa gloire" ("The abhorred
German authorities want to give them a taste from Schiller, whose beautiful soul, so different from that of shallow Goethe, would be very shocked
to see such apostles for his fame"). Of all the works by Stendhal that
appeared up to 1830, Goethe preferred *Le Rouge et le noir*, the psychological depth of which he praised highly (*Gespräche mit Eckermann*, Jan. 17,
1831, 2: 705). It is difficult to comprehend why Henri Beyle, who in his
Histoire de la peinture en Italie (1817), takes a rather systematically
opposite stand to that of the famous Winckelmann (for the latter, there
exists "un beau idéal fixe," for Stendhal there are as many beauties as
there are lovers and loves), should have chosen as his *nom de plume* the
name of the little town in Saxony (Stendal or Stendhal) that was Winckelmann's birthplace. Goethe, "le plat Goethe," in his turn, established himself as a pioneer in the art of biography by bringing out his *Winckelmann
und sein Jahrhundert* (Tübingen, 1805) New ed. E. Howald, Bern, 1945.
44. To properly show this development, a certain length is needed.
Thus Kleist's *Michael Kohlhaas* (1810) or Sartre's *L'Enfance d'un chef*
(1939) lack the indispensable amplitude for qualifying as Bildungsromane.
45. "Ein Glück . . . das ich mit nichts in der Welt vertauschen möchte"
(*Wilhelm Meisters Lehrjahre*, in *Goethes Werke in sechs Bänden* [Leipzig,
1940], 4: 527). The problem of the happy denouement in the Bildungsroman has been treated by Gerda Röder, *Glück und glückliches Ende im
deutschen Bildungsroman* (Munich, 1968).
46. In *Werther*, one might recognize an ironic use of the word *Wahl*.
There Wahlheim is the scene in which Werther fulfills his *fatal* destiny.
47. "Es ist gut, dass Sie sich nach und nach mit allem In- und Auslän-
dischen bekannt machen, um zu sehen, wo denn eigentlich eine höhere
Weltbildung, wie sie der Dichter bedarf, zu holen ist" (*Gespräche mit
Eckermann*, Oct. 3, 1828, 1: 262. The same day Goethe says: "[Der Mensch]
bedarf der Klarheit und der Aufheiterung, und es tut ihm not, dass er sich
zu solchen Kunst- und Literaturepochen wende, in denen vorzügliche
Menschen zu vollendeter Bildung gelangten, so dass es ihnen selber wohl
war und sie die Seligkeit ihrer Kultur wieder auf andere auszugiessen
imstande sind" ("Man needs clear ideas and encouragement and should
turn toward those periods of art and literature in which outstanding men
achieved complete *Bildung* so that they, under such conditions, were

happy themselves and in turn could lavish the joyful happiness deriving from their culture on others").

12. The Sonnet in Its European Context

1. The best general histories of the sonnet have been written by Walter Mönch, *Das Sonett: Gestalt und Geschichte* (Heidelberg, 1955), and Efrén Núñez Mata, *Historia y origen del soneto* (Mexico City, 1967). One of the oldest of numerous anthologies of an international character is Capel Lofft's *Laura; or, an Anthology of Sonnets (on the Petrarchan Model) and Elegiac Quatorzains: English, Italian, Spanish, Portuguese, French, and German; Original and Translated . . .*, 5 vols. (London, 1813–1814). A more recent anthology—all sonnets in German or translated into German—is Karl Theodor Busch's *Sonette der Völker: Siebenhundert Sonette aus sieben Jahrhunderten* (Heidelberg, 1954). Examples of classical anthologies within national literatures are those of Giovanni Getto ·and Edoardo Sanguineti, *Il sonetto: Cinquecento sonetti dal duecento al novecento* (Milan, 1957), and Robert M. Bender, *The Sonnet: A Comprehensive Anthology of British and American Sonnets from the Renaissance to the Present* (New York, 1965). For the bibliography of the sonnet, see Mönch, *Das Sonett*, pp. 311–325.

2. *Codice Barberiniano* 45, no. 47, quoted by Everett Ward Olmsted, *The Sonnet in French Literature* (Ithaca, N. Y., 1897), p. 17. The rhyme scheme of Lentino's sonnet (*abab/abab/acd/acd*) did not become classical. One notices that *core* serves twice as rhyme and is used two more times in the sonnet. Some critics think more highly of Lentino's piece for its metaphysical character.

3. *Concrete Poetry: A World View*, ed. and introduction by Mary Ellen Solt (Bloomington and London, 1970), p. 242. Mrs. Solt's comment is to be found in Emmett Williams, ed., *An Anthology of Concrete Poetry* (New York, Villefranche, and Frankfort, 1967), (unpaged). George Darley (1795–1846) wrote a sonnet "To the Moon" under the pseudonym Rogier de Derley, and dated it 1594: he wanted it to be a Renaissance sonnet . . .

4. The average of eight (octave) and six (sestet) is seven, the sacred number, which is the sum of the phenomenal (4) and the noumenal (3); the number seven might have been a kind of symbol for some poets of the High Middle Ages, when mystical numbers played an essential role in all human activities. Dante's *Convivio*, which remained unfinished, was planned in the form of fourteen commented canzoni.

5. See Ernest Langley, "The Extant Repertory of the Early Sicilian Poets," *PMLA* 28 (1913): 454–520; Ernest H. Wilkins, "The Invention of the Sonnet," *Modern Philology* 13 (1915): 463–493; Gianfranco Contini, ed., *Poeti de duecento*, 2 vols. (Milan, 1960).

6. Three hundred seventeen of the three hundred sixty-six compositions found in the first complete edition (1373) of the work are sonnets.

7. See Rocco Montano, *Lo spirito e le lettere: Desegno storico della letteratura italiana*, 4 vols. (Milan, 1970), 1:89ff; C. Cordié, *Rimatori del dolce stil nuovo* (Milan, 1942).

8. This list and those that will follow are intended to name some of

the most famous sonneteers. Hundreds of others are not mentioned. In his anthology *Lirici Marinisti* (Bari, 1910), Benedetto Croce has reproduced 478 sonnets written within a short period by 72 authors.

9. Du Bellay, however, as cited by Emile Littré in his article "Sonnet," in *Dictionnaire de la langue française*, is fully cognizant of the Italian origin of the sonnet: "Etant le sonnet d'italien devenu français, comme je crois, par Mellin de Saint-Gelais." In France the sonnet appears to be a kind of adopted Italian genre.

10. Jacques Hardion, *Nouvelle histoire poétique*, 3 vols. (Paris, 1751), 3:119.

11. "Introduction: Histoire du sonnet," in *Le Livre des sonnets* (1755) (Paris, 1875), pp. vii–xxxvii. This idea goes back at least to the *Art poétique* of Guillaume Colletet (Paris, 1658), pp. 16–26.

12. See Pierre Villey, "Marot et le premier sonnet français," *Revue d'Histoire littéraire de la France* 27 (1920): 538–547; and Joseph Vianey, *Le Pétrarquisme en France au XVe siècle* (Montpellier, 1909). Hugues Vaganay has written a study on *Le Sonnet en Italie et en France au XVIe siècle* (Paris, 1903) giving good historical information.

13. The *Pléiade* influenced not only England, as is well known, but also Holland. The Flemish poet Jan Baptista van der Noot (1539–1596) wrote sonnets inspired by Ronsard and Du Bellay and thus brought the form to the Low Countries, where it was cultivated by Pieter Corneliszoon Hooft (1581–1647) and Joost van den Vondel (1587–1679). Clearly Karel van de Woestijne (1878–1929), Albert Verwey (1865–1937), and Jan van Nijlen (born 1884) were continuing a long tradition. In studying the sonnet in the Netherlands, however, it is important to recall the long presence of Spanish culture in the region.

14. Isolated sonnets are found in the writings of Jean-Baptiste Rousseau, the least obscure of the eighteenth-century French lyric poets (with the exception of André Chénier), in the works of Voltaire, Fontenelle, Lefranc de Pompignan, and Alexis Piron. See Olmsted, *The Sonnet*.

15. See René Etiemble on one sonnet of Rimbaud's: *Le Sonnet des voyelles: De l'audition colorée à la vision érotique* (Paris, 1968).

16. The stanzas of his *Troilus and Criseyde* are of seven lines (ababbcc, rhyme royal). Analogies with sonnet structures have often been noticed. One of the most recent histories of the sonnet in England, though a very succinct one, is Patrick Cruttwell's *The English Sonnet* (London, 1966).

17. It is not possible to mention here the Shakespeare translations that scores of amateurs, poets, and prose writers have published. Stefan George's *Shakespeare Sonette* (Berlin, 1909) is one of the most outstanding. That of Alfred Thomas Barton's brings joy to the heart of a classical scholar: *Guilielmi Shakespeare Carmina* (London, 1913–1923).

18. In his sonnet *Dante al mover* . . . , Carducci presents another list, consisting exclusively of Italian poets: Dante, Petrarch, Tasso, Alfieri, Foscolo, and . . . Carducci: "Io, il sesto" ("I am the sixth"). Among poets of the universe, Dante thought he was number six, after Virgil, Homer, Horace, Ovid, and Lucan (*Divina commedia, Inferno*, Canto 4, lines 85–94).

19. One may compare the first verse of Keats's sonnet *On the Sonnet*, "If by dull rhymes our English must be chained . . .," with the beginning

of Rossetti's *The Sonnet*, "A Sonnet is a moment's monument/Memorial from the Soul's eternity," to understand with which generation enthusiasm for the sonnet is found.

20. He is the author of some 50,000 sonnets. See Merrill Moore, *M: One Thousand Autobiographical Sonnets by Merrill Moore* (New York, 1938), Preface. For a survey on the American sonnet, see Lewis G. Sterner, *The Sonnet in American Literature* (Philadelphia, 1930).

21. See A. Vegue y Goldoni, *Los sonetos "al italico modo" de Don Iñigo López de Mendoza: Estudio crítico y nueva edición de los mismos* (Madrid, 1911); and Rafael Lapesa, *La obra literaria del Marqués de Santillana* (Madrid, 1957).

22. In a historical document to the Duchess of Soma, Boscán explained the reasons for his enthusiasm about the sonnet: "En este modo de invención (si así quiere llamalla) nunca pensé que inventaba ni hacía cosa que hubiese de quedar en el mundo, sino que entré en ello descuidadamente, como en cosa que iba tan poco en hacella que no había para que dexalla de hacella, habiéndola ganado; quando más que vino sobre habla. Porque estando un día en Granada con el Navagero (al qual, por haber sido tan celebrado en nuestros días, he querido aquí nombralle a vuestra señoria), tratando con él en cosa de ingenio y de letras, y especialmente, en las variedades de muchas lenguas, me dixo por qué no brobaba en lengua castellana sonetos y otras artes de trovas usadas por los buenos autores de Italia; y no solamente me lo dixo así livianamente, más aún, me rogó que lo hiciese. Partíme pocos días para mi casa; y con las largueza y soledad del camino, discurriendo por diversas cosas, fui a dar muchas veces en lo que Navagero me había dicho; y así comencé a tentar este género de versos" ("In this means of invention (if one can call it thus), I never thought that anything was invented or done which would remain in the world, except that I enter into it without caution, as in something that takes so little time to do it, that there is no reason not to do it, thus achieving the goal. Being in Granada one day with Navagero (whom I wished to point out to your Excellency, as he has been so celebrated in our time), matters of the creative arts were discussed, and most especially the varieties of the many languages. He inquired as to why I didn't write sonnets in Castillian, why I did not utilize other kinds of forms used by the renowned authors of Italy. He not only spoke vigorously of the subject, but even more, he urged me to attempt it. I left for my home for several days; deliberating over various matters during the length and solitude of the journey, I was inclined to contemplate many times what Navagero had said to me. Thus I began to formulate this standard of verse"), (quoted by Núñez Mata, *Historia y origen*, p. 12).

23. Benedetto Croce, *Intorno al soggiorno di Garcilaso de la Vega in Italia* (Naples, 1894).

24. Lope de Vega's "sonnetomania" assumes a rather harmless form as compared with the apparent "sonnetophrenitis" of Moore (see note 20). A worthwhile study could be undertaken on the usage that Lope de Vega, after Shakespeare, made of the sonnet in his theatrical work. See Antonio Restori, "I sonetti di Lope de Vega," *Archivum Romanicum* 11, no. 14 (1927): 384–391, and Claude E. Anobal, "Lope's Sonnets and Fecundity,"

Hispania 11 (1928): 362–364. See also Joseph G. Fucilla, "Daniello's annotations to Petrarch's *Canzoniere* and Lope de Vega's *El Perro del Hortelano*,' in *Mélanges de littérature comparée et de philologie offerts à Mieczyskaw Brahmer* (Warsaw, 1967), pp. 241–249.

25. According to Jorge de Sena, Camoëns is the author of a minimum of 166 and a maximum of 211 sonnets (*Os sonetos de Camões e o sonêto quinhentista peninsular* [Lisbon, 1969]).

26. For the sonnet in Portuguese, see Agostinho de Campos, *Estudos sôbre o sonêto* (Coimbra, 1936).

27. See Heinrich Welti, *Geschichte des Sonetts in der deutschen Dichtung* (Leipzig, 1884); Gertrud Wilker-Heursch, *Gehalt und Form im deutschen Sonett von Goethe bis Rilke* (Bern, 1952); Mönch, *Das Sonett;* and Jörg Ulrich Fechner, ed., *Das deutsche Sonett: Dichtungen, Gattungspoetik, Dokumente* (Munich, 1969).

28. Cited by Welti, *Geschichte des Sonetts*, p. 241.

29. Twenty-five is also the number of Milton's sonnets, if the one attributed to him (the "dedicatory" poem in a ca. 1630 edition of Shakespeare's plays) is counted. The standard collection of Milton's sonnets includes nineteen regular sonnets in English, four regular sonnets in Italian, and one "sonnetto caudato" or "double sonnet" concluding the series: "On the New Forcers of Conscience under the Long Parliament." See *Milton's Sonnets*, ed. E. A. J. Honigmann (New York, 1966). The final chorus of *Samson Agonistes* is also a sonnet. See below.

30. It is somewhat surprising that Pierre Corneille, in the historical sonnet in which he judges the merits of these two poets, uses the older pattern: *ccd/eed*.

31. C. Cuénot, "Nouvel état présent des études verlainiennes," *L'Information littéraire* 8, no. 4 (1956): 131.

32. The form of these last three pieces is *aabbccddeeffgg;* that of the final chorus of *Agonistes* is *ababcdcdefefef*.

33. "A perfect sonnet is in itself the equal of a long poem" (*Art poétique*, song 2, line 82).

34. English sonnet patterns are also used in French poetry, though a French reader is seldom aware of this fact. One-third of Mallarmé's sonnets are English in type, such as *Eventail, Feuilles d'Album, Chansons bas*. Oddly enough, French criticism has not yet noticed that Baudelaire's *Invitation au voyage* is a series of three sonnets consisting of two pairs of Ronsardian tercets and an English couplet (*aab/ccb/dde/ffe/gg*).

35. Schlegel's rules are illustrated by the sonnet itself. In the first four lines, he describes the characteristics of the quatrains, and in the next four lines those of the tercets. His own tercets, the minor system, is in sharp contrast with the major system. The first three lines explain that the sonnet is not an artificial genre, and the three others praise the true sonneteer. His sonnet reads:

> Zwei Reime heiss ich viermal kehren wieder
> Und stelle sie geteilt in gleiche Reihen,
> Dass hier und dort zwei, eingcfasst von zweien,
> Im Doppelchore schweben auf und nieder.

Dann schlingt des Gleichlauts Kette durch zwei Glieder,
Sich freier wechselnd, jegliches von dreien.
In solcher Ordnung, solcher Zahl gedeihen
Die zartesten und stolzesten der Lieder.

Den werd ich nie mit meinen Zeilen kränzen,
Dem eitle Spielerei mein Wesen dünket,
Und Eigensinn die künstlichen Gesetze.

Doch, wem in mir geheimer Zauber winket
Dem leih ich Hoheit, Füll in engen Grenzen
Und reines Ebenmass der Gegensätze.

36. The movement of Petrarch's sonnets is *decrescendo:* he often states the highest note in the first line; the *crescendo* mode was initiated and practiced by his disciples, Serafino dell'Aquila, for instance, and by the English poets.

37. Composed in 1800 or 1801. In some literatures a respectable number of "sonnets on the sonnet" exists in which the poets have explained their theory of the genre. Authors of such sonnets include A. W. Schlegel (note 35), Regnier-Desmarais, Wordsworth, Keats, and Lope de Vega. For Spanish literature, see Enrique Vazquez de Aldana, *Antologia de Sonetos al Soneto* (Madrid, 1950), and for Portuguese literature, Melo Nóbrega, "Os sonetos do sonêto," *Revista do Livro* 2 (1957) 101–146.

38. For the sonnet cycles in English literature, see Leslie Cecil John, *The Elizabethan Sonnet Sequences: Studies in Conventional Conceits* (New York, 1964); Janet S. Scott, *Les Sonnets élizabéthains* (Paris, 1929); and Brents Stirling, *The Shakespeare Sonnet Order: Poems and Groups* (Berkeley and Los Angeles, 1968). There is also the *corona*, usually consisting of fourteen sonnets interrelated according to certain rules and crowned by a fifteenth; the contemporary Brazilian poet Geir de Campos, for example, wrote in blank verses a classical *Corona de sonetos* (1953).

13. Prolegomenon D

1. *Thematik* and *Thematologie*, and *thématique* and *thématologie* are currently used, *thematics* and *thematology* more reluctantly—since the Anglo-Saxons have a more delicate "linguistic conscience" or slower philological institutions than other peoples. These words appear here as the equivalents of the German and French words. The adjectives *thematic* and *thematical* refer to theme, *motival* to motif, and *thematological* to *thematology*, that is, to the set of elements found in the system of relations between *Rohstoff, Stoff,* and *Motiv.*

2. Usually leitmotiv or *leitmotif* is defined in dictionaries only in the musicological acceptation.

3. See also under *motive:* "2. A theme or dominant feature, as of a literary composition; a motif. 3. Music. The theme or subject; a leading phrase or passage which is reproduced and varied through the course of a composition or a movement."

4. *Current Literary Terms* (New York, 1965), pp. 186 and 291.

5. William Flint Thrall, Addison Hibbard, and C. Hugh Holman, *Handbook to Literature* (New York, 1962), pp. 486 and 294.

6. *A Grammar of Motives and a Rhetoric of Motives* (Los Angeles and Berkeley, 1969).

7. *Aesthetics* (New York, 1958), p. 403.

8. *Types of Thematic Structure: The Nature and Function of Motifs in Gide, Cassius, and Sartre* (Chicago and London, 1967), p. 2. Falk is in complete agreement with Joseph T. Shipley's article "Theme" in his *Dictionary of World Literature* (New York, 1953), which says that the theme is "the general topic, of which the particular story is an illustration" (p. 417). For comparatists, as will be shown in this chapter, this is called, or, rather, should be called, the motif. This example explains the urge for an international terminology. Whenever a topic becomes general, it tends to be abstract, devoid of proper names: these are characteristics of the motif.

9. In *Stoff- und Motivgeschichte* (Berlin, 1966), Elisabeth Frenzel says: "Die wissenschaftliche Diskussion um die Fixierung der Grundbegriffe ist noch immer im Fluss und hat noch nicht zu einer eindeutigen Definition gefürt" ("The scholarly discussion about the fixation of the basic notions is still going on and has not yet led to a clear-cut definition"), (p. 11).

10. Ernst Robert Curtius, *Europäische Literatur und lateinisches Mittelalter*, 4th ed. (Bern, 1963), trans. Willard R. Trask, *European Literature and the Latin Middle Ages* (New York, 1953).

11. *Das sprachliche Kunstwerk*, 10th ed. (Bern, 1964), p. 56.

12. *Stoffe der Weltliteratur: Ein Lexikon dichtungsgeschichlicher Längsschnitte* (Stuttgart, 1962), p. v. While Kurt Bauerhorst (Berlin, 1932) and Franz Anselm Schmitt (Berlin, 1959) each wrote a *Stoff- und Motivgeschichte der deutschen Literatur,* it would be strangely tautological for Frenzel to speak of "Motive der Weltliteratur." The motifs, by their very essence, have universal character.

13. *Sachwörterbuch der Literatur* (Stuttgart, 1955), article on "Motiv."

14. Werner Kohlschmidt and Wolfgang Mohr on "Motiv" in *Reallexikon der deutschen Literaturgeschichte* (Berlin, 1955), p. 427. Von Wilpert on "Motiv" in *Sachwörterbuch explains:* "Strukturelle Einheit als typische, bedeutungsvolle Situation, die *allgemeine* thematische Vorstellungen umfasst (im Gegensatz zum durch konkrete Züge festgelegten und ausgestatteten Stoff, der wiederum mehrere Motive enthalten mag) und Ansatzpunkt eigener Erlebnis- und Erfahrungsgehalte in symbolischer Form werden kann" ("Structural unit as typical and significant situation that includes *general* thematic ideas [as opposed to the Stoff that is defined by and provided with concrete traits and that in turn may contain several Motive] and can in symbolical form come to represent that which the author has experienced and lived through"), (p. 441).

15. This is the sense of the remark we find in the first paragraph of Gottfried Keller's *Romeo und Julia auf dem Dorfe* [A village Romeo and Juliet], in *Gottfried Kellers Werke*, 4 vols. (Leipzig, 1921). Keller states that all the fables on which great works are founded (he means *Urfabeln*, the typical representation or incarnation of basic situations, or, as the Germans would put it, "die Originalverbindung zwischen Stoff und Motiv") are deeply rooted in human life. He adds: "Die Zahl solcher Fabeln ist mässig, aber stets treten sie in neuem Gewande wieder in Erscheinung

und zwingen alsdann die Hand, sie festzuhalten" ("The number of such fables is small, but they constantly reappear in new garments and force the writer's hand to get hold of them"), (3:72).

16. "Hermann Hesse," in *Kritische Essays zur europäischen Literatur* (Bern, 1950), p. 219. Curtius does not use the word Stoff, but Thema; the context, however, shows that he means what we today call Stoff. Curtius adds: "Motiv und Thema sind zweierlei, und die Kritik wird gut tun, sie zu unterscheiden. Das Motiv ist das, was die Fabel (den Mythos der aristotelischen Poetik) in Bewegung setzt und zusammenhält . . . Wer nur Themen hat, kann nicht zum Epos oder Drama-gelangen" ("Motiv and theme are two things, and criticism will be well advised to point out the difference between them. The Motiv is the element that gives impetus and holds together the fable [i.e. the *mythos* in Aristotelian poetics]. He who knows only themes cannot reach the level of the epic or the drama.").

17. *Das sprachliche Kunstwerk*, p. 60; *Sachwörterbuch*, p. 441.

18. *Sachwörterbuch*, p. 441.

19. *Das sprachliche Kunstwerk*, p. 60.

20. In Peter Demetz et al., eds., *The Disciplines of Criticism: Essays in Literary Theory, Interpretations, and History* (New Haven and London, 1968), pp. 125–145.

21. *The Art of "La Celestina"* (Madison, 1956), p. 119.

22. *Un Problème* (Paris, 1965), p. 13.

23. Ibid. In French scholarly tradition Motiv is translated with motif, and Stoff with thème. Trousson does not include the notion of Rohstoff in his system, and sometimes he regards Motive as one might regard Aristotle's "universals." The "idea of happiness, of progress, metaphysical rebellion, avarice" (p. 13) or the "unhappy woman" (pp. 14–15) are nothing, per se, but topics for philosophical or sociological treatises, or Rohstoff for fiction. A specific situation, that is a humanized—though not individualized—idea, not a mere concept, sets a plot in motion.

24. The example of *Madame Bovary* is chosen in reference to the corresponding section in chap. 16.

25. The title of chap. 2 in Victor Brombert's *The Novels of Flaubert: A Study of Themes and Techniques* (Princeton, 1966).

26. Helmuth Petriconi calls it Thema (*Die verführte Unschuld: Bemerkungen über ein literarisches Thema* [Hamburg, 1953]).

27. A book has been written on *The Limping Hero* (by Peter L. Hays [New York, 1971] proving, with a few others of this kind, the usefulness of studies in the second category of motifs. Such a motif is aptly defined in Northrop Frye's Glossary (under *motif*, p. 366) to *Anatomy of Criticism: Four Essays* (Princeton, 1971) as "a symbol in its aspect as a verbal unit in a work of literary art." The German word Motiv and the French motif may also assume this sense. However, with the motifs of the second category, that may be called motifs II, in contrast with the motif that expresses the central idea of a work, the motif I, we are not any longer within the organic thematology system as explained in the present chapter.

28. Many motifs may best be formulated, as in the present case, by leaving open the question of a specific reason, or means, or agency because the opposition between two agents may suggest several possible

agencies. The motif animating historical themes varies according to the knowledge and interpretation of facts. The story of Sir John Oldcastle contains the element "broken friendship"; its central motif, however, is not necessarily comparable with that of Becket. See *The Famous Victories of Henry the Fifth* (1598) by Robert Greene or one of his disciples.

29. A Stoff-type is assimilated with a Motiv-type ordinarily whenever one single and simple action is attached to the hero's memory. Judas or Lucretia are both Stoff-types and Motiv-types. Their historical (thematical) action has become inseparable from its symbolic (motival) interpretation.

30. See Jean Calvet, *Les types universels dans la littérature française*, 2 vols. (Paris, 1963–1964); Charles Nodier, "Les types littéraires," *Romans de Charles Nodier*, new ed. (Paris, 1855), pp. 5–16. The word *type* is as ambivalent as many other literary terms. Studies like those of Irvin Ehrenpreis' *The Types Approach to Literature* (New York, 1945) and M. B. Chrapčenko's "Typologische Literaturforschung und ihre Prinzipien," in *Aktuelle Probleme der vergleichenden Literaturforschung*, ed. Gerhard Ziegengeist (Berlin, 1968), pp. 17–47, are concerned with types *of* works, i. e. literary genres, not with types *in* works, i. e. representative figures. Genology and thematology may still be mingled in a different way, as illustrated by Paul Hernadi, *Beyond Genres* (Ithaca, N. Y., 1972).

31. *Europäische Literatur und lateinisches Mittelalter*, 4th ed. (Bern, 1963), chap. 5, "Topik." By the same author: *Gesammelte Aufsätze zur romanischen Philologie* (Bern, 1960), chaps. "Antike und vergleichende Literaturwissenschaft" and "Antike Pathosformeln in der Literatur des Mittelalters." See Walter Veit "Topostorschung: Ein Forschungsbericht," *Deutsche Vierteljahrsschrift für Literaturwissenschaft und Geistesgeschichte* 37 (1963): 120–163.

32. Helmut Hatzfeld rightly noticed: "If I called the motifs semiformal, I meant that they are not simply *topoi* as to content but have in addition to their frequency a particular stylistic cast. This was . . . the important correction Dámaso Alonso had to make on the theory of Ernst Robert Curtius" ("Comparative Literature as a Necessary Method," in *Disciplines of Criticism*, p. 80).

33. David Evett, " 'Paradice's Only Map': The *Topos* of the *Locus Amoenus* and the Structure of Marvell's 'Upon Appleton House' " *PMLA* 85 (1970): 504–514; Hans Galinsky, *Naturae cursus: Der Weg einer kosmologischen Metapher von der alten in die neue Welt* (Heidelberg, 1968). See below for the use by Virgil, Milton, and Fielding of another topos: the shadow of the mountains as announcing the night.

34. Kayser also points to this confusion in *Das sprachliche Kunstwerk*, pp. 71–72. It seems that the term leitmotiv was first used by the musicologist Hans von Wolzogen, the great admirer of Wagner and editor of the *Bayreuther Blätter*.

35. *Selected Essays 1917–1932* (New York, 1950), pp. 124–125.

36. Often thematological studies are restricted to Stoffgeschichte, while thematology actually is *Stoffkunde*, a word that accurately translates thematology, i.e. the science or knowledge of themes, in contrast with Stoffgeschichte, or the history of themes.

37. "I libri, che si tengono strettamente in quest'ordine di ricerche,

prendono, di necessità, la forma del catalogo o della bibliografia, talvolta
celata alla meglio dall'abilità e dal brio dello scrittore" (*Problemi di estetica*, [Bari, 1910], p. 75).

38. The usefulness of Stoffgeschichte as combined with Stoffkunde
has been most clearly demonstrated by Manfred Beller in an article explaining that thematology, though still usually meaning Stoffgeschichte,
in reality transcends this notion insofar as its true objective is the entire
thematological phenomenon. He points to the necessity to complement
studies in thematics with studies in aesthetics, since Stoff constitutes the
matter only of literature. Beller says: "Thematologie umfasst . . . den
herkömmlichen Gegenstand der 'Stoffgeschichte' und überschreitet ihn
zugleich sowohl durch die extensive Einbeziehung aller Phänomene des
Stofflichen als auch durch die Intensivierung der philologischen Methoden.
'Thema, theme, thème, das Stoffliche' bleibt der Ausgangspunkt der Untersuchung, aber erst wenn die Analyse der Form die Exegese des Gehalts
ergänzt, wird auch dieser Zweig der Literaturwissenschaft den Proteus
Poesie besser fassen können" ("Von der Stoffgeschichte zur Thematologie:
Ein Beitrag zur komparatistischen Methodenlehre," *Arcadia: Zeitschrift
für vergleichende Literaturwissenschaft* 5, no. 1 [1970]: 38. See also these
studies on the theory of thematics: Salvatore Battaglia, *Mitografia del
personaggio* (Milan, 1968); Maud Bodkin, *Architypical Patterns in Poetry:
Psychological Studies of Imagination* (London, 1948); idem, *Studies of
Type Images in Poetry, Religion, and Philosophy* (London, New York,
and Toronto, 1951); Ursula Brumm, *Die religiöse Typologie im amerikanischen Denken: Ihre Bedeutung für die amerikanische Literatur- und Geistesgeschichte* (Leiden, 1963); Joseph Campbell, *The Masks of God: Oriental
Mythology* 2nd ed. (New York, 1968); José Edmundo Clemente, *Los temas
esenciales de la literatura* (Buenos Aires, 1959); Damoso Alonso, "Tradition or Polygenesis?" *Modern Humanities Research Association* 32 (1960):
17–34; Maria Leach, *Dictionary of Folklore*, 2 vols. (New York, 1949–1950);
O. Pöggeler, "Dichtungstheorie und Toposforschung," *Jahrbuch für Aesthetik und allgemeine Kunstwissenschaft* 5 (1960): 89–202; E. Sauer, "Die
Verwertung stoffgeschichtlicher Methoden in der Literaturforschung,"
Euphorion 29 (1928): 222–229; Hans Sperber and Leo Spitzer, *Motiv und
Wort: Studien zur Literatur und Sprachpsychologie* (Bloomington, Ind.,
1918); Stith Thompson, *Motiv-Index of Folk Literature*, 6 vols. (Blooming-
ton, Ind., 1932–1936); Jean-Paul Weber, *Domaines thématiques* (Paris, 1963);
F. Wollman, "Typologichnost v sprovnávaci literárni vede" [Typology in
comparative literature] *Slavia* 36 (1967): 280–290; Mario Praz, *La carne, la
morte e il diavolo nella letteratura romantica* (Florence, 1948), trans.
Angus Davidson, *The Romantic Agony* (Cleveland, 1956).

14.   Thomas à Becket in European Fiction and Drama

1. For a bibliography, including historical, fictional and critical works,
see my *Essais de littérature comparée*, 2 vols. (Fribourg and Urbana, Ill.,
1964–1968), 2: 345–379. Other recent books include Richard Winston's
Thomas Becket (London, 1967). Fictional works on Becket, especially
Eliot's, could also be compared with quite a few mystery plays and
pageants.

2. The treatment of the Becket theme reflects the medieval notion of martyrdom. A martyr's death is not just an accidental death, but implies the idea of a reward for a saintly life; martyrdom, in other words, presupposes saintliness. During the Middle Ages this logic was generally accepted, and the hagiographers, far from establishing the saintliness of the martyrs, devoted themselves to illustrating it with the help of edifying episodes that they had no scruples about inventing. It was not a question of lying. From the perspective of the time, the martyr *must* have accomplished extraordinary acts of virtue; if the memory of them had been lost, the pious biographer had either to find them again or simply to imagine them. This view dominates the interpretation of dramatists, poets, chroniclers, and even historians up to the Reformation.

3. The proof is of an empirical order: Becket never appears as a kind of symbol of the man between church and state. He is a champion of the church in a strictly historical context, and is a type within this context; he never achieves the rank of the archetype, a privilege mostly reserved for imaginary and mythic figures.

4. Dante mentions him in the Canto 13 of the *Inferno*. In Germany the theme has often been treated, especially toward the middle of the nineteenth century (A. Widmann, J. G. Fischer, J. H. von Wessenberg). C. F. Meyer also intended to write about the Vigna Stoff.

5. *Canterbury Tales*, "General Prologue," verse 17.

6. *Thomas: A Novel* (New York, 1965).

7. *Der Heilige* (Leipzig, 1879). I shall give page numbers for *Der Heilige* from the Hans Zeller and Alfred Zäch edition, *Conrad Ferdinand Meyer, Sämtliche Werke; Historisch-kritische Ausgabe*, 14 vols. (Bern, 1958–1964), vol. 13, where the German text may be consulted. *Der Heilige* was first translated into English in 1885 by M. von Wendheim under the title *Thomas à Becket, the Saint*. A translation by M. J. Taber appeared in America in 1887, *The Chancellor's Secret: A Tale of the Twelfth Century* (New Bedford). A third translation was made by Edward Franklin Hauch, *The Saint* (New York, 1930). A first French version, *Le Saint*, translated by Charly Clerc with a preface by Robert d'Harcourt, appeared in Paris in 1929; a second, also *Le Saint*, also in Paris, appeared in a 1949 bilingual edition with the translation by Léon Mis.

8. *Murder in the Cathedral* (London, 1935).

9. *Becket; ou, l'honneur de Dieu* (Paris, 1959). The Catholic interpreter par excellence of our theme, the Irish playwright Aubrey de Vere, entitles his play *Saint Thomas of Canterbury*. The saint venerated by Christendom never did bear the name Becket. Anouilh's play has been translated into English by Lucienne Hill, *Becket; or, the Honor of God* (New York, 1960). My page numbers will refer to the French edition.

10. *Thomas: A Novel*; Henry's quotes, pp. 324 and 325; Becket's, p. 324.

11. The *Encyclopaedia Britannica's* article on Becket thus sums up the situation described by Meyer: "Thomas showed no readiness to negotiate on specific issues; in exile he occupied himself more and more with the general principles governing the relationship of secular to ecclesiastical authority and in his theoretical formulation of the issue he was diverging from his episcopal colleagues," (ed. 1964).

12. Roughly 170,000 words; 50,000 for Meyer.

13. *Thomas: A Novel*, quotations on pp. 17, 398, 415–416, and 417. In *Der Heilige* prophecies and superstitions are utilized for similar ends. The future is revealed to Hans, who had taken holy orders following a murder in his youth—a detail that relates to the problem of ecclesiastical jurisdiction, which will divide Thomas and Henry: "In der Johannisnacht, da ich von Allerheiligen schied, und bevor ich den Sprung über die Mauer tat, habe auch ich hineingestochen zu drei Malen . . . und die Worte getroffen: sagittas, calamo, arcui. Und Virgilius hatte wahr gesprochen: mit Pfeil und Bogen hab' ich all mein Lebtag zu tun gehabt" ("In the night of Saint John's, when I parted from All Saints [name of the monastery] and before I jumped over the wall, I, too, pricked thrice into it [into the roll of Virgil's works] and I hit the words sagittas, calamo, arcui [bolts, arrow, bow]. And Virgil told the truth: I had to deal with arrows and bows during my whole life"), (p. 35).

14. The remark of the London *Sunday Times* (Dec. 5, 1965) is very appropriate: "Apart from the almost sensuous *feel* of the epoch, she [Mrs. Mydans] gives us scores of vivid portraits, from the simple peasantry up through merchants, priests, knights, bishops, to the able and formidable king, Henry II, who gave Becket all the gifts within his power, including martyrdom."

15. *Der Heilige*, p. 145.

16. For the legends arising around Saint Thomas, see Paul A. Brown, *The Development of the Legend of Thomas Becket* (Philadelphia, 1930).

17. *Der Heilige*, p. 127.

18. Ibid., p. 135.

19. Cited by Mydans, *Thomas: A Novel*, p. v.

20. *Der Heilige*, quotations pp. 88 and 87.

21. Ibid., p. 121.

22. Ibid., p. 138.

23. Ibid., quotations on pp. 100, 118, and 33.

24. Ibid., "sein farbloses Antlitz" (p. 29), "ein blasses . . . Antlitz (p. 33), farblos" (p. 37), "bleiches Haupt" (p. 87).

25. "The Essence of Tragedy," *American Playwrights on Drama*, ed. Horst Frenz (New York, 1965), pp. 43–51. The essay was first published in 1939.

26. See Corneille's *Polyeucte* act 5, scene 3:

> PAULINE: Où le conduisez-vous?
> FELIX: A la mort.
> POLYEUCTE: A la gloire.
>   Chère Pauline, adieu; conservez ma mémoire.

See also, Elida M. Szaroda, *Grübler und Rebellen: Studien zum europäischen Märtyrerdrama des 17. Jahrhunderts* (Bern, 1967).

27. Schiller calls *Die Jungfrau von Orleans* "eine romantische Tragödie," the adjective modifying the meaning of the noun.

28. *The Life and Death of Thomas Becket* (London, 1961), p. 27.

29. "T. S. Eliot's *Murder in the Cathedral:* Versuch einer Interpretation," *Die neueren Sprachen* 7 (1958): 319. See also, by the same author, *T. S. Eliot's "Murder in the Cathedral"* (Brunswick, 1964).

30. Schiller's play was written in 1803. In the same year he published

his essay *Über den Gebrauch des Chors in der Tragödie,* an essential source for the study of the chorus.

31. *Hamlet,* act 3, scene 2. The plays of Corneille and of Racine often begin with scenes between confidants who make the spectator aware of the situation, which is one of the functions of the chorus.

32. *Murder,* p. 28.

33. Ibid., p. 11.

34. Ibid., p. 18.

35. Ibid., p. 30.

36. Ibid. The thought expressed here is directly reminiscent of the "und leider auch Theologie" in *Faust I,* line 356.

37. Ibid., p. 17.

38. Ibid., p. 31.

39. Ibid., p. 46.

40. Ibid., pp. 46–47.

41. *Becket,* quotations pp. 120 and 160.

42. *Histoire de la conquête de l'Angleterre par les Normands* 4 vols. (Paris, 1838–1839) 3: 284–285.

43. *Becket,* quotations on pp. 102, 152, 151, and 144.

44. C. H. Haskins, "Henry II as Patron of Literature," *Essays in Medieval History Presented to Thomas Frederick Tout,* ed. A. G. Little and F. M. Powicke (Manchester, 1925); J. Broussard, *Le Gouvernement d'Henri II Plantagenet* (Paris, 1956). Some scholars have advanced plausible reasons for admitting that Marie de France dedicated her *Lais* to Henry II, whom she in fact does not name, but who, it is believed, is recognizable in the expression "noble rei" found in the dedication.

45. *Becket,* quotations on pp. 98 and 172 (the second and third quot.).

46. Ibid., quotations on pp. 39 and 46.

47. What the critic Alfred Cattani said in the *Neue Zürcher Zeitung* (Dec. 10, 1967) with regard to the contemporary drama *Soldaten* by Rolf Hochhuth, applies, *mutatis mutandis,* to *Becket; ou, l'honneur de Dieu.* Cattani's reservations and those we expressed about Anouilh's play are based on the same arguments: a playwright treating historical themes should not at the same time convince his audience of the historicity of the events and cultural facts presented and yet handle these events and facts according to his own fantasy. One may see in this kind of ambiguity the source of many distortions of history. Ambiguities should never be ambiguous; they have to be readily identifiable as ambiguities. Cattani writes:

Hochhuth ist bisher der Kritik an der historischen Treue seines Werkes vor allem mit dem Argument begegnet, als Schriftsteller und Künstler habe er das Recht auf freie Darstellung der Ereignisse und Gestalten. Das ist in diesem Falle nur bedingt richtig. Ein zeitgeschichtlicher Dramatiker hat, wenn er ernst genommen werden will, seine Personen in glaubhafter Form auf die Bühne zu bringen und nicht das einemal Geschehnisse peinlich genau zu datieren und dann die Chronologie wieder wild durcheinanderzuwerfen. Er hat sich mit dem Geschehen ernsthaft und seriös auseinanderzusetzen und nicht nach eigener Erfindung Situationen oder Theaterteufel zu kreieren, um Bühnenwirksamkeit zu erzielen. In dieser Hinsicht war *Die Ermittlung* von Peter Weiss vorbildlich; das Stück liess die schauerliche Wirklichkeit des Auschwitzprozesses tatsachengetreu erstehen. Rolf Hochhuths *Soldaten* hingegen leisten keinen Beitrag an die Klärung der jüngsten Vergangenheit, sondern fördern höchstens eine gefährliche Legendenbildung. Die zwielichtige Methode, je nach Bedarf die Position des Historikers oder des Künstlers zu beziehen, alles verbrämt mit dem Anspruch, im Sinne Schillers das Theater zur *moralischen Anstalt* werden zu lassen, erweckt schwerste Bedenken und Zweifel an den ehrlichen Absichten des Autors. Was Hochhuth auf der Bühne vorstellt, ist ein Zerrbild der britischen politischen und militärischen Führung während des Zweiten Weltkrieges.

48. Shakespeare's anachronisms are in no way comparable with those of Anouilh's. Pope had denounced them, and Johnson, in his 1765 edition of the complete works, remarks that these reproaches have been made "with more zeal than judgement" (Preface). Quite a few studies have been written about factual historical errors or intentional transformations of historical events in Schiller's plays. However, all these plays maintain the specific atmosphere of the epoch.

49. *Becket*, quotations on pp. 42, 157, 79, 29, and 187. The last quotation, on tobacco, reads in French as follows: "Avec sa chique qu'il ne crachera jamais, même pour boire le bouillon." Tobacco is used only in the English translation; the word, however, is quite accurate here since *chique* (a sixteenth-century word) was made only of tobacco.

15. A Mythic Type: William Tell

1. In many heroic legends (the Arthurian cycle offers a few examples) the ruler either challenges his brave followers or he is challenged by them. Tell also has a place in a broader folkloric framework.

2. See among other studies George Webbe Dasent's *Popular Tales from the Norse* (London, n.d.), esp. pp. 11–14) and Johannes Hoops's *Reallexikon der Germanischen Altertumskunde*, 4 vols. (Strasbourg, 1911–1919); 1: 498–499. One of the most extensive studies in sources of the Tell legend is that of Helmut de Boor's "Die nordischen, englischen und deutschen Darstellungen des Apfelschussmotivs," in *Kleine Schriften*, vol. 2, *Germanische und deutsche Heldensagen: Mittelhochdeutsche Metrik* (Berlin, 1966), pp. 117–174.

3. Bern is the medieval German form of Verona, the Italian city.

4. The year of the Swiss Act of Independence (Bundesbrief) is 1291. Tschudi's (1505–1572) *Schweizerchronik* was not published until the eighteenth century (2 vols., 1734–1736).

5. Punker is referred to in *Malleus maleficarum* or *Hexenhammer* [The witches' hammer] 4 vols. (Cologne, 1489), 2:16. The story of Punker belongs rather to the theme of the Free-Shooter, which is characterized by magic elements. Having shot three times at a crucifix, Punker was daily given three arrows by the devil, which would infallibly reach their target. He was forced by a nobleman to shoot a coin off the head of his son, which he promptly did with the devil's help. The best-known treatment of the

Free-Shooter theme belongs to the history of music: Carl Maria von Weber's *Der Freischütz* was first performed in 1821, eight years before Rossini's *William Tell*. In the *Iliad* gods and goddesses guide the darts of their protégés.

6. The ballad is included in Thomas Percy's *Reliques of Ancient English Poetry* (1765).

7. These examples showing that the Tell story is related to international folklore are only some of the best known. Dasent (note 2) says that a saga similar to that of the Tell is also common among "the Turks and Mongolians; and a legend of the wild Samoyeds, who never heard of Tell or saw a book in their lives, relates it, chapter and verse, of one of their famous marksmen" (*Popular Tales*, p. 13).

8. "Es lebt ein Gott, zu strafen und zu rächen" (act 4, scene 3); "Gott hat geholfen" (act 5, scene 2). Emily Dickinson's untitled poem written in 1869 is from *The Poems of Emily Dickinson*, ed. Thomas H. Johnson, 3 vols. (Cambridge, 1955), 2:807.

9. "Des historiens allemands et de Jean de Muller en particulier" (ed. Jean de Pange, 3:291–310). In this chapter Madame de Staël states: "Schiller est à la tête des historiens philosophiques" (p. 295).

10. In the *Gespräche mit Eckermann* we read, under the date May 6, 1827, that Goethe claimed to be the first to entertain the intention of treating the Tell subject, but that in the end he gave it to his friend Schiller.

11.   Und es ruft aus den Tiefen:
                Lieb Knabe, bist mein!
                Ich locke den Schläfer,
                Ich zieh ihn hinein.

12. "Und mit der Axt hab ich ihm's Bad gesegnet" (act 1, scene 1). Murder in the bath: a study on this theme would include more famous personages than the Austrian tax collector, such as Clytemnestra stabbing Agamemnon, and Charlotte Corday assassinating Marat.

13.   Dass er sein bös Gelüste nicht vollbracht,
          Hat Gott und meine gute Axt verhütet (act 1, scene 1).

14. The English translation by Leonard C. Pronko, *Sad Are the Eyes of William Tell*, appeared in *The New Wave Spanish Drama: An Anthology*, ed. George E. Wellwarth (New York, 1970). I will quote from Pronko's translation.

15. See "El Teatro de Alfonso Sastre visto por Alfonso Sastre," *Primer Acto* 5 (1957): 7; and the article by Leonard C. Pronko, "The *Revolutionary Theatre* of Alfonso Sastre," *The Tulane Drama Review* 5 (1960): 2.

16. In 1926, Eugenio d'Ors y Rovira published his *Guillermo Tell, Tragedia política en tres jornadas* (Valencia, 1926). This play, just like Schiller's, preserves the historical framework: "La tragedia se desarrolla en la época feudal, en un grupo de cantones alpinos, que, al comenzar la acción, se encuentran sometidos al Imperio" ("The tragedy takes place in the feudal period, in several alpine cantons, that at the time the action starts happened to be subjects of the Empire"), (p. 12). Schiller's *Wilhelm Tell* was translated into Spanish by Antonio Gil y Zárate (1843). This translation, *Guillermo Tell*, however, reads like an adaptation. In 1933

Alejandro Casona published a narrative "Guillermo Tell" in his collection of legends, *Flos de leyendas* (Madrid).

17. "Dort der Holunderstrauch verbirgt mich ihm" (act 5, scene 3).

18. "Es lebe Tell! der Schütz und der Erretter." The *vox populi* has received some attention in John Van Eerde's essay "The People in Eighteenth-Century Tragedy from *Oedipe* to *Guillaume Tell*," in *Studies on Voltaire and the Eighteenth Century*, ed. Theodore Besterman, 86 vols. to date, vol. 27 (1963), pp. 1703–1713.

19. *Sad Are the Eyes*, scene 7, pp. 318–319.

20. Ibid., scene 6, pp. 315–316.

21. See Rufus W. Mathewson, *The Positive Hero in Russian Literature* (New York, 1958).

22. *Wilhelm Tell*, Act 5, scene 2. In this last act, Schiller indeed touches upon the question of Tell's guilt. But this last part of the play functions in effect as an appendix. Madame de Staël confirms this view: "On supprime au théâtre l'acte accessoire de Jean-le-Parricide, et la toile tombe au moment où la flèche perce le coeur de Gessler" (*De l'Allemagne*, ed. Jean de Pange, 5 vols. [Paris, 1958], 3:19). To interpret Tell's tyrannicide as a murder was quite common in nineteenth-century Germany. See for instance Hermann Kurz (1813–1873), *Die beiden Tubus* [The two telescopes], (Stuttgart, 1948), p. 74, and Louise von François (1817–1893), letter to C. F. Meyer of Oct. 16, 1881 quoted by Anton Bettelheim, *Louise von François und Conrad Ferdinand Meyer* (Berlin and Leipzig, 1920), p. 24.

23. *Der Bauernspiegel oder Lebensgeschichte des Jeremias Gotthelf, von ihm selbst geschrieben: Historische Erzählungen* (Erlenbach-Zurich, 1965), p. 642.

24. See chap. 14, note 2.

25. See A. Aulard, *La Société des Jacobins*, 6 vols. (Paris, 1889–1897), 5:660. The sentence cannot reveal its complete meaning unless we remember that Marat, whose Italian ancestors were called *Mara*, was born at Boudry, near Neuchâtel, Switzerland, where he passed his youth. His father had emigrated from Sardinia to Geneva in 1740, and his mother was a native of Geneva. He was of Swiss nationality, and so in some way a fellow citizen of Tell. The Swiss hero also played a role in American politics: see Harold Jantz, "Wilhelm Tell and the American Revolution," in *A Schiller Symposium* (Austin, Tex., 1960), pp. 65–81. One of the very first accounts of Tell's deeds to be found in France is that of Thevet, *Les vrais portraits et vies des hommes illustres* (Paris, 1584).

26. On the models of Argovia (Aargau) and Thurgovia (Thurgau).

27. See Roger de Figuères, *Les noms révolutionnaires des communes de France, listes par départements et liste générale alphabétique* (Paris, 1901), pp. 15, 29, and 57.

28. Edmund K. Kostka, *Schiller in Russian Literature* (Philadelphia, 1965).

29. Ibid., pp. 189–190.

30. The Tell story has been popular in Italy since Francesco Soave's *Novelle Morali* (1782), a work that has appeared in scores of editions.

31. *Souvenirs d'égotisme*, ed. Pierre Martino (Paris, 1954), p. 147.

32. See the bibliographic notes to my study on "La fortune d'un héros," *Essais de littérature comparée*, vol. 1, *Helvetica* (Fribourg, 1964), pp. 223–

251. The most recent books on Tell are: Max Frisch, *Wilhelm Tell für die Schule* (Frankfort on the Main, 1971) and Lilly Stunzi, *Tell.Werden und Wandern eines Mythos* (Bern, 1972).

33. Obe sie geschehen? Das ist hier nicht zu fragen;
   Die Perle jeder Fabel ist der Sinn.
   Das Mark der Wahrheit ruht hier frisch darin,
   Der reife Kern von allen Völkersagen (*Tellenschüsse* in
      Gottfried Kellers Werke, 4 vols. [Leipzig, 1921], 1:117, lines 1–4).

16. Suicide: Elements of Literary Themes

1. Novalis, *Fragmente*, ed. Ernst Kamnitzer (Dresden, 1929), p. 87.

2. *Le Mythe de Sisyphe* (Paris, 1942), p. 15.

3. The best general but rather dated bibliographies on suicide to consult are those of E. Motta, *Bibliografia del suicidio* (Bellinzona, 1890), and Hans Rost, *Bibliographie des Selbstmordes* (Augsburg, 1927). Rost lists 3,771 studies relating more or less directly to suicide. Some 1,200 titles are also in the bibliography collected by Norman L. Farberow and Edwin S. Schneidman, *The Cry for Help* (New York, Toronto, and London, 1961), pp. 325–388; Farberow and Schneidman, however, adopt a primarily medical and psychoanalytical point of view.

4. *Biathanatos: A Declaration of That Paradox, or Thesis That Self-Homicide Is Not So Naturally Sinn, That It May Never Be Otherwise* (London, 1648; imprimatur, 1644), part 1, dist. 2, sec. 2, art. 5, p. 46. Voluntary death, as may be freely granted, supposes a will. Do animals have a will? That question confronts us with a different problem.

5. The history of the sociological treatment of the suicide problem can be traced in these publications: Adolph Wagner, *Die Gesetzmässigkeit in den scheinbar willkürlichen menschlichen Handlungen* (Hamburg, 1864); Alfred Legoyt, *Le Suicide ancien et moderne; étude historique, morale et statistique* (Paris, 1881). Preceding Legoyt's work was Enrico Morselli's equally well-known book, *Il suicidio: Saggio di statistica morale comparata* (Milan, 1879); both German and English translations of Morselli's study appeared in 1881. Emile Durkheim was the first to formulate precise sociological principles of suicide: see *Le Suicide: Etude de sociologie* (Paris, 1897), most recent edition 1960; first German translation 1912; English, 1951. In 1930 a disciple of Durkheim, Maurice Halbwachs, published *Les Causes du suicide* (Paris), a work that stimulated and aroused Achille-Dalmas to write a study, the thesis of which is made clear in the title: *Psychologie pathologique du suicide* (Paris, 1932). Psychopathology, however, excludes suicide proper: insane persons do not have a free will. Among the more recent sociological and psychological studies on suicide are by Jack D. Douglas, *The Social Meaning of Suicide* (Princeton, 1967); Edwin S. Schneidman, ed., *Essays in Self-Destruction* (New York, 1967); and Gene Lester and David Lester, *The Gamble with Death* (Englewood Cliffs, N.J., 1971). A book related to our topic, psycho-literary in nature, has been written by A. Alvarez: *The Savage God: A Study of Suicide* (New York, 1972). Another recent publication is Jacques Choron's *Suicide* (New York, 1972).

6. *Statistical Abstract*, 1972 ed., pp. 59 and 146. Other statistical data

are available: in 1968 (last figures computed) 15,379 males and 5,993 females committed suicide in the United States. Homicide figures (persons killed) for 1968 are 11,523 and 3,163 respectively.

7. Ihr habt gewählt zum eigenen Verderben,
  Wer mit mir geht, der sei bereit zu sterben. (Schiller, *Wallenstein*, act 3, scene 23).

For the diverse meanings that suicide may assume, see Maurice Van Vyve, "La Notion du suicide," *Revue philosophique de Louvain*, 52 (1954): 593–618. In all countries of the world, theologians and philosophers have accumulated the most subtle *distinguimus*, which possess interest mainly for casuists and dogmatists.

8. *De Civitate Dei*, book 1, chaps. 16 to 26.

9. The list of suicides occurring in the Bible may be found in the article "Suicide," by A. Michel, in Vacant's *Dictionnaire de théologie catholique*, vol. 14, cols. 2739–2749. Michel's article is the best survey from the Catholic point of view. The most considerable work on the morality of suicide is Albert Bayet's *Le Suicide et la morale* (Paris, 1922). See also Sydney Hook, "The Ethics of Suicide," *International Journal of Ethics* 37 1926–1927): 175.

10. See note 4. A reproduction of the first edition was published in New York in 1930.

11. Voltaire alludes to Robeck in *Candide* (*Zadig, Micromegas, Candide* [Geneva, 1944], p. 188) and Rousseau does so in *La Nouvelle Héloïse* (*Oeuvres complètes*, 4 vols. [Paris, 1959–1969], 2:378).

12. *Oeuvres de Louis Racine*, 6 vols. (Paris, 1808), 1:336.

13. *Decline and Fall of the Roman Empire*, 2 vols. (Chicago, London, Toronto, Geneva, 1952), 2:95.

14. *Essais*, "Coutume de l'Ile de Céa, book 3, chap. 2. See also Pierre Charron, *De la sagesse*, book 2, chap. 11.

15. Moses Hadas, ed., *Latin Selections Florilegium Latinum* (New York and Indianapolis, 1962), pp. 189–191.

16. The study of S. E. Sprott, *The English Debate on Suicide from Donne to Hume* (La Salle, Ill., 1961), as the title indicates, goes beyond this period, but is restricted to England. Johannes Hendrick Harder also limits himself to England in his *Observations on Some Tendencies of Sentiment and Ethics in Minor Poetry and Essays in the Eighteenth Century until the Execution of Dr. W. Dodd in 1777* (Amsterdam, 1933) but his study stresses the literary aspect of the suicide problem; the relevant chapter (13, pp. 120–140) is entitled "Despair and Suicide." See also Lester G. Crocker, "The Discussion of Suicide in the Eighteenth Century," *Journal of the History of Ideas* 13, no. 1 (1952): 47–72, and "Suicide in Eighteenth-Century England: The Myth of a Reputation," *The Huntington Library Quarterly* 73, no. 2 (1960): 145–158.

17. *The Philosophical Works of David Hume*, 4 vols. (Boston and Edinburgh, 1854), 4:537.

18. *Oeuvres complètes de Madame la Baronne de Staël*, 3 vols. (Paris and Strasbourg, 1844), 1:191.

19. *Die Welt als Wille und Vorstellung*, in *Sämtliche Werke*, 5 vols. (Stuttgart and Frankfort on the Main, 1960–1965), 1:379–395, 2:590–651.

20. "A burial worthy of an ass or a dog." This theme is alluded to in Matteo Bandello's *Novelle*, 4 vols. (Venice and Lyons, 1554–1573), 2:39th novella; and in Siegfried Wagner's opera *Der Friedensengel*.

21. Roxana, at the end of the book, poisons herself. See also Montesquieu's *L'Esprit des lois*, book 14, chap. 12, and several places in *Les Considérations*, a work to which Goethe refers in *Dichtung und Wahrheit* when he analyzes the question of suicide.

22. *Paralipomena*, in *Sämtliche Werke*, 5:362. The important work showing how legislature and literature dealt with the problem of suicide is that of Louis-Joseph-Cyrille Proal's *Le Crime et le suicide passionnels* (Paris, 1900). See also Glanville Llewelyn Williams, *The Sanctity of Life and the Criminal Law*, 2nd ed. (New York, 1966).

23. Since this thematological study is centered on the literatures of the West, the philosophical and moral implications of suicide elsewhere have not been mentioned. In many nations the problem presents particular aspects—in India, for example, where the Juggernaut crushes its adorers under the wheels of its chariot, and where a widow, on the pyre of her husband, is not unmindful of her duty. Suttee was also a custom on the Island of Bali. In Japan questions of suicide involve hara-kiri and Kamikaze pilots. Such subjects have been treated even in Western literatures. The suttee, for instance, figures as a central element in Lemierre's play *La Veuve du Malabar* (1770), popular in the United States at the end of the eighteenth century in David Humphreys' version, *The Widow of Malabar* (1790).

24. Mallarmé, *Oeuvres poétiques* (Lausanne, 1943), first line of sonnet, p. 130; Borchert, *Draussen vor der Tür* [The man outside], in *Das Gesamtwerk*, cd. B. Meyer-Marwitz (Hamburg, 1959), p. 107.

25. Schiller's line reads: "Der freie Tod nur bricht die Kette des Geschicks" (*Die Braut*, act 4, scene 8).

26. Dino Buzzati gives a striking example in *Il grande ritratto*, where Enriade, speaking to his antagonist Elisa Ismani, makes this statement: "La vita ci riuscirebbe insopportabile, anche nelle condizioni più felici, se ci fosse negata la possibilità di suicidio. Nessuno ci pensa, si capisce. Ma se l'imagina cosa diventerebbe il mondo se un giorno si sapesse che della propria vita nessuno può disporre. Una galera spaventosa. Pazzi, si diventerebbe" ("Life would become insupportable even under the happiest conditions if we were refused the possibility of suicide. Nobody thinks of it, for sure. One may imagine, however, what our world would become if one day one would learn that nobody can dispose of his own life. A dreadful galley. One would become insane"), (4th ed. [Milan, 1965], p. 116).

27. See Donald H. Shively, *The Love Suicide at Amijina* (Cambridge, Mass., 1951). A great variety of studies is available on particular aspects of suicide as treated in literary works, such as James R. McGlathery, "The Suicide Motive in E. T. A. Hoffmann's *Der goldene Topf*," *Monatshefte* 58, no. 2 (1966): 115–123; Marion Monaco, "Racine and the Problem of Suicide," *PMLA* no. 3 (1955): 441–455. F. Eisinger, *Das Problem des Selbstmordes in der Literatur der englischen Renaissance* (Ueberlingen, 1926); Daniel J. Rolfs, *The Theme of Suicide in Italian Literature: From the Middle Ages to the Late Renaissance* (Ph.D. diss., University of California at Berkeley, 1971).

28. *Die Leiden des jungen Werthers* (Leipzig, 1774), trans. Harry Steinhauer, *The Sufferings of Young Werther* (New York, 1962), dual-language ed. Goethe's rev. ed. of 1786 is entitled *Die Leiden des jungen Werther* [not Werthers]. Our quotations refer to *Goethes Werke in sechs Bänden* (Leipzig, 1940), vol. 3. See also Victor Lange's translation (New York, 1958). On the influence of *Werther* upon his contemporaries, see Klaus Scherpe, *Werther und Wertherwirkung: Zum Syndrom bürgerlicher Gesellschaftsordnung im 18. Jahrhundert* (Bad Homburg, Berlin, and Zurich, 1970).

29. See Orie W. Long, "English Translations of Goethe's *Werther*," *Journal of English and German Philology* 14 (1915): 169–203.

30. Other expressions belonging to the same order of ideas include: *Jemanden einschränken* ("to confine somebody"), *eng* ("narrow), *Grenzen* ("borders"), *Käfig* ("cage"), *der Eingekerkerte* ("the prisoner"), *der Gefangene* ("the captive"). See Erna Merker, *Wörterbuch zu Goethes "Werther"* (Berlin, 1958).

31. *Die Leiden*, 3:78. "Vater! den ich nicht kenne! Vater! der sonst meine ganze Seele füllte und nun sein Angesicht von mir gewendet hat! rufe mich zu dir! schweige nicht länger! dein Schweigen wird diese dürstende Seele nicht aufhalten—Und würde ein Mensch, ein Vater zürnen können, dem sein unvermutet rückkehrender Sohn um den Hals fiele und rief: Ich bin wieder da, mein Vater! Zürne nicht, daß ich die Wanderschaft abbreche, die ich nach deinem Willen länger aushalten sollte."

32. Eh, quel crime est-ce donc, devant ce Dieu jaloux,
   De hâter un moment qu'il nous prépare à tous? (*Alzire ou les Américains*, act 5, scene 3).

33. When the servant had brought the pistols loaned to him by Albert and Lotte, he was charged with bringing Werther bread and wine. In Lessing's play, Emilia, at her request, is killed by her father, thus exemplifying in her own way, absolute love.

34. For example, a copy of Lessing's *Emilia Galotti*, which was found on Werther's desk, was in reality found on Jerusalem's. See Victor Lange, "Fact in Fiction," *Comparative Literature Studies* [Special issue on the Art of Narrative] VI (1969): 253–261.

35. Actually, another affair was Goethe's indirect motivation to write *Werther*. After leaving Wetzlar, he sought comfort with charming young Maximiliane La Roche, the daughter of the writer Sophie La Roche. She was to lend to Lotte, in the novel, her love for music and her dark eyes, two striking recurrent images. Charlotte Buff was a blonde with blue eyes. See Thomas Mann, *Lotte in Weimar* (Stockholm, 1940).

36. *Madame Bovary: moeurs de province*, 2 vols. (Paris, 1857), trans. Francis Steemuller, *Madame Bovary: Patterns of Provincial Life* (New York, 1957). Our quotations refer to *Madame Bovary* (Paris, 1961).

37. Barbey d'Aurevilly, *Le roman contemporain* (Paris, 1902), p. 119. See Léon Degoumois, *Flaubert à l'école de Goethe* (Geneva, 1925). There are several studies on persons and events that might have inspired episodes of the novel: Auriant, "Madame Bovary, née Colet," *Mercure de France* (June 1, 1936): 247–281; Gustave Bosquet, "En marge de Madame Bovary;

Delphine Delamare s'est-elle suicidée?" *La Presse médicale* 66 (April 30, 1958): 777–778; G. Dubosc, "La véritable Madame Bovary," *Journal de Rouen*, Nov. 22, 1890. For a bibliography sufficiently exhaustive on the *Madame Bovary* problem, see Claudine Gothot-Mersch's *La genèse de "Madame Bovary"* (Paris, 1966). See, too, the series of essays edited by Raymond Giraud, *Flaubert: A Collection of Essays* (Englewood Cliffs, N. J., 1964); and by Benjamin F. Bart, *Madame Bovary and the Critics: A Collection of Essays* (New York, 1966). Bart's own book, *Flaubert*, was published in 1967 (Syracuse, N. Y.). See also Ednid Starkie's *Flaubert: The Making of a Master* (London, 1967) and Jean-Paul Sartre's *L'Idiot de la famille: Gustave Flaubert de 1821 à 1857*, 2 vols. (Paris, 1971). This work of 2,136 pages comments on the first half of Flaubert's life: "A Literary Enormity" (Harry Levin, *Journal of the History of Ideas*, XXXIII [1972]: 643. The second part (1857–1880) of Sartre's work is expected to be at least of the same size as the first. Combined with the "enormity" it will constitute the perfect literary "monstrosity."

38. Madame Bovary is by no means a female Werther. Another character of Flaubert's, Frédéric Moreau, would to some extent justify a comparison with Goethe's hero (*Education sentimentale* [Paris, n.d.]). Frédéric loves Madame Arnoux, whose behavior and reactions are in many ways reminiscent of Lotte's. Though it is understood that they would never belong to each other (p. 290), Frédéric makes all possible efforts to seduce her. After more than twenty years, however, he gives up his hopes, realizing that platonic love is the best he can enjoy with Madame Arnoux. Some parallels with *Werther* are quite obvious. For example, because of Madame Arnoux' resistance, Frédéric is tempted to commit suicide. Madame Arnoux taking care of her children—like Lotte of her younger brothers and sisters—is a recurring image in Flaubert's novel. Slices of buttered bread recall a famous scene in Lotte's house, and for Frédéric, Lotte's and Madame Arnoux' "tartines" have symbolic taste. They are the only nourishment Lotte could give Werther and Madame Arnoux could give Frédéric; they mean sympathy, charity, spiritual love, all that children may also receive. And Frédéric finally ceased to desire anything else from Madame Arnoux. "Je comprends Werther," he tells her at the end of the novel, "que ne dégoûtent pas les tartines de Charlotte" ("I understand Werther who is not disgusted by Charlotte's tartines"), (p. 451). As one suspects, the French Werther, during the many years of his idealistic liaison with Madame Arnoux, also ate rather substantial meals with some lovely mistresses—and thereby staved off suicide. Instead, "ayant mangé les deux tiers de sa fortune, il vivait en petit bourgeois" the last part of his life. ("after eating up two-thirds of his fortune, he lived the life of a petit bourgeois"), (p. 449).

39. *Madame Bovary*, p. 247.

40. Ibid., two quotations, pp. 295 and 371.

41. Before this opera scene, Scott had been mentioned twice in the novel: book 1, chap. 4; book 2, chap. 2.

42. *Madame Bovary*, p. 269.

43. The evolution of the theme in the different stages of the novel is indicated by Gabrielle Leleu, *"Madame Bovary": Ebauches et fragments*,

2 vols. (Paris, 1936). See also *Madame Bovary: Edition nouvelle précédée des scénarios inédits*, ed. J. Pommier and G. Leleu (Paris, 1949), notably pp. 1–129; and Gothot-Mersch's *La genèse*.

44. Madame de Staël's *Delphine* provides a practical example of such a change. In the first version (1802) of the novel, the heroine commits suicide, in the second (posthumous) the author chooses another conclusion. In *Delphine*, as in *Madame Bovary*, suicide belongs to the theme. A similar example is given in *Anna Karenina*. In his first version, Tolstoy grants Anna a divorce and has her marry Vronsky, while in the second he has her commit suicide.

45. *Oeuvres complètes de Balzac*, ed. Marcel Bouteron and Henri Longnon, 40 vols. (Paris, 1912–1938), 37: 8.

46. *Utopia*, trans. H. V. S. Ogden (New York, 1949), p. 57.

47. *Laws*, book 9.

Bibliography

THIS bibliography is concerned with articles and books on both the theory and the history of comparative literature. It also includes bibliographies, periodicals, proceedings, and collective publications. Works pertaining to the individual topics treated in the illustrative chapters are cited, many of them with bibliographical annotations, in the Notes.

A. Bibliographies

Baldensperger, Fernand, and Werner P. Friederich. *Bibliography of Comparative Literature.* New York, 1960. Supplement: *Yearbook of Comparative and General Literature* (see section B).

Bibliographie générale de littérature comparée. Paris, since 1950. Compiled since 1921 from the annual cumulative bibliographies of the *Revue de Littérature comparée.*

Eppelsheimer, Hanns W., with Köttelwesch, Clemens since 1954. *Bibliographie der deutschen Literaturwissenschaft, 1945–1953* (eight volumes listing publications up to 1968, each volume including a section "Vergleichende Literatur"). Frankfort on the Main, 1957–1969.

Klapp, Otto. *Bibliographie der französischen Literaturwissenschaft, 1956–1958* (seven volumes listing publications up to 1969, each volume including a section "Littérature comparée"). Frankfort on the Main, 1960–1970.

Köttelwesch, Clemens, ed. *Bibliographisches Handbuch der deutschen*

Literaturwissenschaft. 10 vols. Frankfort on the Main, since 1971. Vol.
   3: *Weltliteratur, Vergleichende Literaturgeschichte.*
Modern Language Association of America (annual bibliography since 1921,
   with author index since 1964). New York.

B. *Current Periodicals*

ALTHOUGH most journals devoted to national literatures or
to particular genres have, in recent years, been publishing an increasing
number of articles comparative in nature, these journals along with those
dealing with comparative literature that have ceased publication have
been excluded from the present selection. Only those currently specializing
in comparative literature are listed. Titles in parentheses are those printed
on the back cover.

Arcadia. Zeitschrift für vergleichende Literaturwissenschaft. Berlin and
   New York, since 1966.
*Canadian Review of Comparative Literature/Revue canadienne de littéra-
   ture comparée,* Edmonton, Alberta, Canada, since 1974.
Comparative Literature. Eugene, Ore., since 1949.
Comparative Literature Studies. Urbana, Ill., since 1964.
Filološki Pregled. Belgrade, since 1963.
Helikon: Vilagirodalmi Figyelö. Budapest, since 1954.
Hikaku Bungaku (Journal of Comparative Literature). Tokyo, since 1958
   (annual).
Hikaku Bungaku Kenkyu (Etudes de Littératures Comparées). Tokyo,
   since 1954 (biannual).
Jadavpur Journal of Comparative Literature. Calcutta, since 1961 (annual).
Journal of Aesthetics and Art Criticism. Detroit, since 1941.
Neohelicon. Acta Comparationis Litterarum universarum. Budapest, since
   1973.
Orbis Litterarum. Odense, Denmark, since 1943.
Revue de littérature comparée. Paris, since 1921.
Rivista di letterature moderne e comparate. Florence, since 1948.
*Tamkang Review. A Journal Mainly Devoted to Comparative Studies be-
   tween Chinese and Foreign Literatures.* Taipei, since 1970 (biannual).
Yearbook of Comparative and General Literature. Bloomington, Ind.,
   since 1960.
Zagadnienia Rodajzów Literackich, Les Problèmes des genres littéraires.
   Lódź, since 1958.

C. *Proceedings of Conferences, Festschrifte, and Collective Works*

THIS section is limited to collections that include articles of
a comparative nature by several authors. Excluded are such proceedings,
for example, as those of the Federation for International Languages and
Literatures, which print some papers pertaining to our discipline among a
larger number about national literatures.

Aldridge, A. Owen, ed. *Comparative Literature: Matter and Method.* Urbana, Ill., 1969.

Anisimov, A. Ivan Ivanovich, ed. *Vzaimosvjazi i vzaimodejstvie natsionale 'nykh literatur* (Proceedings of a conference held at the Gorki Institute, 1957). Moscow, 1961.

Banašević, N., ed. *Proceedings of the Fifth Congress of the International Comparative Literature Association* (Belgrade, 1967). Amsterdam, 1969.

Bóka, L., ed. *Acta litteraria Academiae Hungariae* (Conference of comparative literature, Budapest, 1962). Budapest, 1962.

[Brahmer]. *Mélanges de littérature comparée et de philologie offerts à Mieczyslaw Brahmer.* Warsaw, 1967.

[Carré]. *Connaissance de l'étranger: Mélanges offerts à la mémoire de Jean–Marie Carré.* Paris, 1964.

Demetz, Peter; Greene, Thomas; and Nelson, Lowry, Jr., eds. *The Disciplines of Criticism: Essays in Literary Theory, Interpretation, and History* (for René Wellek). New Haven, 1968.

Escarpit, Robert, ed. *Proceedings of the Sixth Congress of the International Comparative Literature Association* (Bordeaux, 1970). The Hague, 1974.

Friederich, Werner P., ed. *Proceedings of the Second Congress of the International Comparative Literature Association* (Chapel Hill, 1958). 2 vols. Chapel Hill, 1959.

[Jakobson]. *To Honor Roman Jakobson: Essays on the Occasion of His Seventieth Birthday.* 3 vols. The Hague, 1967.

Jost, François, ed. *Proceedings of the Fourth Congress of the International Comparative Literature Association* (Fribourg, 1964). 2 vols. The Hague, 1966.

Krauss, Werner, ed. *Probleme der vergleichenden Literaturwissenschaft* (Proceedings of a conference held in Berlin, 1964). Berlin, 1965.

McNeir, Waldo F., ed. *Studies in Comparative Literature.* Baton Rouge, 1962.

Muschg, Walter, and Staiger, Emil, eds. *Weltliteratur: Festgabe für Fritz Strich zum 70. Geburtstag.* Bern, 1962.

Nichols, Stephen G., Jr., and Richard B. Vowles. *Comparatists at Work: Studies in Comparative Literature.* Waltham, Mass., Toronto, and London, 1968.

Pellegrini, Carlo, ed. *Proceedings of the First Congress of the International Comparative Literature Association* (Venice, 1955). Venice and Rome, 1961.

Proceedings of the Conferences and "Colloques" of the Société nationale française de littérature comparée (annual meetings since 1956, except in those years in which an International Comparative Literature Association conference is held).

Reizov, Boris G., ed. *Problemi mezhduna-rodnykh literaturnykh sujazej* (Proceedings of a conference held at the Gorki Institute in 1960). Leningrad, 1962.

Smit, W. A. P., ed. *Proceedings of the Third Congress of the International Comparative Literature Association* (Utrecht, 1961). 2 vols. The Hague, 1962.

Sonderegger, Stefan; Haas, Alois M.; and Burger, Harold, eds. *Typologia litterarium: Festschrift für Max Wehrli*. Zurich, 1969.
Stallknecht, Newton P., and Frenz, Horst. *Comparative Literature: Method and Perspective*. Carbondale, Ill., 1971.
Thorpe, James, ed. *Relations of Literary Studies*. New York, 1967.
Wais, Kurt, and Ernst, Fritz. *Forschungsprobleme der vergleichenden Literaturgeschichte*. 2 vols. Tübingen, 1951–1958.
Ziegengeist, Gerhard, ed. *Aktuelle Probleme der vergleichenden Literaturforschung* (Proceedings of a conference held in Berlin in 1966). Berlin, 1968.

D. *Books*

Books listed here are those on the theory or history of comparative literature or those devoted in large measure to either. Also included are some works from which a theory of comparative literature may directly be derived.

Block, Haskell M. *Nouvelles tendances en littérature comparée*. Paris, 1970.
Brandt Corstius, J. *Introduction to the Comparative Study of Literature*. New York, 1968.
Cioranescu, Alejandro. *Principios de literatura comparada*. La Laguna, 1964.
Deugd, Cornelis de. *De Eenheid van het Comparatisme*. Utrecht, 1962.
Dima, Alexandru. *Principii de literatură comparată*. Bucharest, 1969.
Dima, Alexandru, ed. *Probleme de literatură comparată si şociologie literara*. Bucharest, 1970.
Durišin, D. *Problémy literárnej komparatistiky*. Bratislava, 1967.
Eppelsheimer, Hans W. *Geschichte der Europäischen Weltliteratur*, vol. 1, *Von Homer bis Montaigne*. Frankfort on the Main, 1971.
Etiemble, René. *Comparaison n'est pas raison: La crise de la littérature comparée*. Paris, 1963. Translated by Herbert Weisinger and Georges Joyaux. *The Crisis in Comparative Literature*. East Lansing, 1966.
Farinelli, Arturo. *Aufsätze, Reden und Charakteristiken zur Weltliteratur*. Bonn and Leipzig, 1925.
Friederich, Werner P. *The Challenge of Comparative Literature and Other Addresses*. Edited by William DeSua. Chapel Hill, 1970.
Friederich, Werner P., and Malone, David H. *Outline of Comparative Literature from Dante to O'Neill*. Chapel Hill, 1954.
Frye, Northrop. *Anatomy of Criticism: Four Essays*, 2nd ed. Princeton, 1965.
Gicovate, Bernardo. *Conceptos fundamentales de literatura comparada*. San Juan, 1962.
Gifford, Henry. *Comparative Literature*. London, 1969.
Guillén, Claudio. *Literature as System: Essays Toward the Theory of Literary History*. Princeton, 1971.
Guyard, Marius-François. *La Littérature comparée*. Introduction by Jean–Marie Carré. Paris, 1951.
Hergešić, Ivo. *Poredbena ili komparativna knjizevnost*. Zagreb, 1935.

Hermand, Jost. *Synthetisches Interpretieren: Zur Methode der Literaturwissenschaft.* Munich, 1969.

Hojin, Xano. *Hikaku bungaku* [Comparative literature]. Tokyo, 1956.

Jameson, Raymond de Loy. *A Comparison of Literatures.* London, 1935.

Jeune, Simon. *Littérature générale et littérature comparée: Essais d'orientation.* Paris, 1968.

Jost, François. *Essais de littérature comparée.* 2 vols. Fribourg, 1964, and Fribourg and Urbana, 1968.

Kayser, Wolfgang. *Das sprachliche Kunstwerk: Eine Einführung in die Literaturwissenschaft.* Bern, 1965.

Krauss, Werner. *Grundprobleme der Literaturwissenschaft.* Reinbek by Hamburg, 1968.

Levin, Harry. *Contexts of Criticism.* Cambridge, Mass., 1958.

Levin, Harry. *Refractions: Essays in Comparative Literature.* New York, 1966.

Lovejoye, Arthur O. *The Great Chain of Being: A Study of the History of Ideas.* New York, 1964.

Mayo, Robert S. *Herder and the Beginnings of Comparative Literature.* Chapel Hill, 1969.

Munteano, Basil. *Constantes dialectiques en littérature et en histoire: Recherches, Perspectives.* Paris, 1967.

Neupokoeva, Irina Grigor'evna. *Problemy vzaimodeostvüa sovremennykh literatur; tri ocherka* [Problems of the interrelation of modern literatures: three essays]. Moscow, 1963.

Ota, Saburo. *Hikaku bungaku* [Comparative literature]. Tokyo, 1958.

Pichois, Claude, and Rousseau, André-M. *La littérature comparée.* Paris, 1967.

Podestà, Giuditta. *Letteratura comparata: Saggi.* Genoa, 1966.

Porta, Antonio. *La letteratura comparata nella storia e nella critica.* Milan, 1951.

Posnett, Hutcheson Macaulay. *Comparative Literature.* New York, 1886.

Rüdiger, Horst, ed. *Zur Theorie der Vergleichenden Literaturwissenschaft.* Berlin, 1971.

Silveira, Tasso da. *Literatura comparada.* Rio de Janeiro, 1964.

Sötér, István. *The Dilemma of Literary Science.* Budapest, 1973.

Staiger, Emile. *Grundbegriffe der Poetik.* Zurich, 1951.

Strelka, Joseph. *Vergleichende Literaturkritik. Drei Essays zur Methodologie der Literaturwissenschaft.* Bern and Munich, 1970.

Van Tieghem, Paul. *La littérature comparée.* Paris, 1931.

Wehrli, Max. *Allgemeine Literaturwissenschaft.* Bern, 1969.

Weisstein, Ulrich. *Einführung in die vergleichende Literaturwissenschaft.* Stuttgart, Berlin, Cologne, and Mainz, 1968, trans. William Riggan in collaboration with the author, *Comparative Literature and Literary Theory.* Bloomington (Ind.) and London, 1973.

Wellek, René. *Concepts of Criticism.* New Haven, 1963.

Wellek, René. *Discriminations. Further Concepts of Criticism.* New Haven, 1970.

Wellek, René, and Warren, Austin. *Theory of Literature.* New York, 1962. First ed. 1942.

Wrenn, Charles L. *The Idea of Comparative Literature*. Leeds, 1968.
Zhirmunsky, V. M. *Problemy o sravnitel'noy filologii* [Problems of comparative philology]. Moscow, 1964.

Index

THIS index includes proper names of persons and geographical and ethnic names, as well as the titles of the works quoted in the book. Those geographical names that were frequently repeated (e.g., America, Spain, London, Paris) are omitted from the index. The name of the author is added to the titles of single poems, single articles, and plays, to musical compositions and paintings, as well as to those books that bear identical titles or titles too general as to properly define the work (e.g., *Histoire de la littérature anglaise* [Taine]). Subject entries are omitted, since the main literary concepts we are concerned with are defined or described in the rather short introductory sections or in the prolegomena, and since the illustrative chapters are centered on separate topics, a circumstance that would deprive cross-references of their pertinence.